TEACHING PIANO

VOLUME II

EDITED BY DENES AGAY

ASSOCIATE EDITOR:
Hazel Ghazarian Skaggs

CONTRIBUTING AUTHORS:
Denes Agay
Joseph Banowetz
Louise Cheadle
William Cheadle
John H. Diercks
May L. Etts
Rosetta Goodkind
Maurice Hinson
Stuart Isacoff
Ylda Novik
Sylvia Rabinof
Walter Robert
Hadassah Sahr
Hazel Ghazarian Skaggs
Anita Louise Steele
Judith Lang Zaimont

Yorktown Music Press, Inc.
New York, London, Sydney, Cologne

Editorial Staff for Yorktown Music Press, Inc.:
Jonathan Firstenberg
Janice G. Insolia
Brenda Murphy
Priscilla Newell
Patricia Norcia
Peter Pickow
Susan A. Rothschild
David Sachs

Order No. YK 20261
US International Standard Book Number: 0.8256.8039.5
UK International Standard Book Number: 0.7119.0485.5

Exclusive Distributors:
Music Sales Corporation
257 Park Avenue South, New York, NY 10010 USA
Music Sales Limited
8/9 Frith Street, London W1V 5TZ England
Music Sales Pty. Limited
120 Rothschild Street, Rosebery, Sydney NSW 2018, Australia

Printed in the United States of America by
Vicks Lithograph and Printing Corporation

Contents

VOLUME I

VOLUME II

FOUR

METHODS AND REPERTORY

Piano Methods: An Annotated List with Descriptive Chart

HAZEL GHAZARIAN SKAGGS

There are so many method books on the market that the teacher can find exactly the book or set of books required to fulfill his or her objectives. The choice will depend on the teacher's training, extent of experience, philosophy of education, personality, the time available for preparation, and the student's age, interests, and learning speed.

Also, the teacher may have to consider the cost of the materials used and select the method which in addition to its musical value provides good dollar value.

Methods generally fall into three categories:

(1) Much teacher guidance—useful for the inexperienced teacher (Ex.: Schaum, Thompson)
(2) Less guidance, but fully and progressively structured (Ex.: Steiner, Wagness)
(3) More concentration on repertory than method, for the teacher who wants the freedom to devise a course of study independently, or for use in conjunction with a method. (Ex.: Agay, Waxman.)

It is not uncommon for some teachers to use a combination of methods. For instance, a fingered text such as Aaron's may be combined with the Weybright "devise your own fingering" approach; the Agay book, which is not as tightly structured as most methods, may go well with almost any method when used as a progressive elementary repertory text; the Steiner course may provide additional elementary material for the teacher using the faster-paced books or it may be combined with a chord-approach book, such as Brimhall. Some methods, such as Pace, Clark, and Olson-Bianchi-Blickenstaff, go their own well-structured way and may be difficult to combine.

The choice is an important one. Familiarity with what is available provides a better opportunity to meet not only the teacher's own special needs but also those of the student.

The chart recommends no particular method or approach; it dissects twenty method books in order to give the teacher some insight as to what to look for in the choice of texts. The selection of these twenty methods was somewhat random, but an attempt was made to include representative models of the various teaching methods. (Chart begins on second page following.)

ADDITIONAL METHOD BOOKS

Allison, Irl. *The Irl Allison Piano Library*. Austin, Texas: Irl Allison Publications, 1966. The Irl Allison Library is authored by Dr. Irl Allison, founder and first president of the National Guild of Piano Teachers, and is available from Willis Music Co., 7380 Industrial Road, Florence, Kentucky 41042. Complete listings of compositions in each book may be had by writing to National Guild of Piano Teachers, P.O. Box 1807, Austin, Texas 78767 and asking for the 1980 Annual International Piano Recording Competition pamphlet.

Bartók, Béla, and Sandor Reschofsky. *Piano Method*, revised and edited by Leslie Russel. Budapest: Editio Musica, 1950. This method was originally published in 1913. It is now available through Boosey & Hawkes, Inc. The method (seventy-nine pages) is very much concerned with technical development and includes many exercises, including those for proper hand position, wrist action, and the playing of notes in a chord exactly together. For the serious student, this book is excellent.

Beyer, F. *Elementary Method for the Pianoforte*. New York: Carl Fischer, Inc. This seventy-one page book, with English and German texts, dates back to a time when piano pedagogues were more concerned with developing the fingers and a good rhythmic sense through teacher-pupil ensemble than in providing a course of study that was both educational and entertaining. This is a serious course of study and suitable only for the highly motivated and disciplined student.

De Vito, Albert. *The Albert De Vito Piano Course*, Book 1 (Book 2 is not yet published). New York City: Kenyon Publications, 1968. This has forty pages ending with a two-page quiz, a review of theory. It is a very easy primer book with big notes, and uses the middle C approach. There is verse for most of the music. Left-hand accompaniments are in single notes and finally in fifths.

Girlamo, Florence. *Piano for Pleasure*, Preparatory Book, Book 1, and Book 2. Melville, New York: Belwin-Mills, 1960. By page fifteen the student is playing songs. The middle-C approach is used. There are plenty of finger drills and pencil work. Chords are not introduced until Book 1. In both Books 1 and 2 the student learns to harmonize one-line melodies.

Hirschberg, David. *Piano Course for Juniors*, Preparatory Book and Book 1. Melville, New York: Musicord Publications (Belwin-Mills), 1949. A traditional middle-C approach course with cartoons, illustrations, and verse to make learning fun. It looks like and follows the style of the Musicord Hirshberg Fun books: *Technic is Fun, Theory is Fun, Beethoven is Fun,* etc.

Kohler, Louis. *Practical Method for the Pianoforte*, 4 books. New York: G. Schirmer, 1899, 1913. In English, French, Spanish, this course is for serious students. It includes a great deal of technical work and classical music. The first book ends with all the scales in two octaves.

Levine, Henry. *Henry Levine Piano Course*, Book 1 and Book 2. Boston: The Boston Music Co., 1955. Both books are traditional in concept and presentation, except that Levine appeals to the imagination of the child by introducing "magic" in the learning process. Easy, beginning with the middle C, its pages are attractive and uncluttered. There are some secondo parts for the teacher.

Marwick, Marion and Maryanne Nagy. *Creative Keyboard*, Level I and Level II. Hialeah, Florida: Columbia Publications, 1975. Attractive, with keyboard charts and cartoon guides, helping in the ongoing learning process. Songs, twelve-bar blues, duets, and chords make the course fun while teaching the fundamentals of elementary piano and theory.

Suzuki Piano School. *The Suzuki Method.* Evanston, Illinois: Summy-Birchard Company, 1973. The preface to this sixty-one page book includes three introductions to the Suzuki piano method. The last of these is Constance Starr, *Starting Young Pianists with the Suzuki Method* (*Clavier*, April 1972, revised 1976). Beginning with simple folk tunes, the book advances very rapidly so that by the end of the book the student's repertory includes such pieces as Beethoven's Sonatina in G, Bach Minuets, and Schumann's "The Happy Farmer."

Method books generally do not provide enough material for the student who learns quickly or for the teacher whose weekly assignments are not limited to one or two pages. Below is a list of books that fit well with any method.

REPERTORY

Agay, Denes. *The Joy of First-Year Piano: A Method and Repertory for the Beginning Pianist*. New York: Yorktown Music Press, Inc., 1972. Eighty pages. (See chart for contents.)

Benner, Lora. *Music for Piano Students*. New York: G. Schirmer, 1965. One hundred fifty-five pages. The book consists of six parts: Course Book, Technique, Rhythms and Pieces, Etudes, Compositions, and Duets.

(Continued on page 340.)

	Michael Aaron: *Piano Course* grades I-V, primer available, adult I, II (Belwin Mills, 1945) GRADE I	Denes Agay: *The Joy of First Year Piano*, a method and repertory for the beginning pianist (Yorktown Music Press, Inc., 1972)	James Bastien: *Piano Lessons*, levels I-VI primer available (Kjos West, 1976) LEVEL I	Nathan Bergenfeld: *The Young Beginner, The Very Young Beginner*, also adult beginner (Acorn Basic Lessons, 1977) THE YOUNG BEGINNER
Number of Pages	64	80	48	64
Illustrations	keyboard charts, rhythmic patterns, pictures	hands, keyboard chart	keyboard charts, multicolored prints and pictures	keyboard, photographs of students at piano
Familiar Songs	few	some	some	some
Classical Music	none	few	none	1
Duets	none	some optional teacher duet parts	some with teacher	14 pages may be played solo or duet, and 1 duet
Keyboard Preparation before Reading	2 pages	6 pages	none (but primer available)	none
Note Reading	notes introduced gradually, beginning with middle C (range: C – c^3)	begins with notes neighboring middle C (range: D – c^3)	C Major (5-finger position), followed by F, then G (with I, V7 of each)	introduces G and B lines (r.h.), F and A lines (l.h.); 16 pieces before entire staff appears
Note Drills	yes	none	2 pages	none
With Verse	some	5 songs	about half the music	almost half the music
Note Values	𝅝 𝅗𝅥. 𝅗𝅥 ♩ ♪. 𝅘𝅥𝅯 and rests, ♩. ♪	𝅝 𝅗𝅥. 𝅗𝅥 ♩ ♪ 𝅘𝅥𝅯 and rests. ♩. ♪ ♪.𝅘𝅥𝅯 3 ♪♪♪	𝅝 𝅗𝅥. 𝅗𝅥 ♩ ♪ and rests, ♩. ♪	𝅝 𝅗𝅥. 𝅗𝅥 ♩ ♪ and rests,
Meter	$\frac{2}{4}$ $\frac{3}{4}$ $\frac{4}{4}$ $\frac{6}{8}$	$\frac{2}{4}$ $\frac{3}{4}$ $\frac{4}{4}$ $\frac{5}{4}$ $\frac{6}{8}$	$\frac{2}{4}$ $\frac{3}{4}$ $\frac{4}{4}$	no barlines until p. 16, $\frac{2}{4}$ $\frac{3}{4}$ $\frac{4}{4}$

Rhythm	counts on a few pieces: 1 a 2 a 1 2 3 4 5 6	counting exercises at beginning of book	counting aloud, singing the words	verse on beginning pieces, then verse continues on some pieces
Fingering	every note	sufficient	adequate	adequate
Hands Together	starts on p. 17	starts on 4th piece	2nd piece	35th piece (p. 24)
Technical Studies	trill, double note staccato, finger drills, scales	5-finger patterns	5-finger patterns	none
Scales	all majors in back of book, with tonic triads	majors: C, G, D, A, E	none	none
Key Signatures	majors: C, G, D, A, F, B♭ minors: a, c	majors: C, G, D, A, F, G♭ minors: a, e, some modern tonalities	majors: C, F, G	majors: C, G, D, F minors: a, e, d some modern tonalities
Dynamic Nuances	yes	yes	yes	yes
Phrasing	yes	yes	yes	starts on p. 23
Theory	half and whole steps, intervals, triads of C major scale, tonic, subdominant, dominant of C	basic	I and V7 chords of C, G, F	none
Written Work	some	none	2 pages of note drills	none
Supplementary Materials	French/English and Spanish/English editions, supplementary books include *Technique* (I, II), *Duet Book*, and *Note Reader*	additional "*Joy*" books are *Bach, Baroque, Boogie and Blues, Christmas, Classics, Folk Songs, Jazz* (early and intermediate grades)	*Bastien Piano Library* includes *Theory, Technique, Note Speller, Hanon Studies, Sight Reading, Solo Collections* (for each level)	*Teacher's Guide* available on request

	John Brimhall: *Piano Method*, levels I-V, primer available, adult I, II (Hansen, 1968) BOOK I	Frances Clark and Louise Goss: *The Music Tree*, 4 books; *Time to Begin* (Summy-Birchard, 1973) PART A	Stephen Covello: *The Little Avant-Garde*, books I, II (primer: book I) (Schroeder & Gunther, 1974) THE SECOND BOOK	Ray Green: *Piano Books for Young Pianists*, books A-D (primer: book A) (American Music Edition, 1961) BOOK B
Number of Pages	40	64	72	32
Illustrations	keyboard charts, some pictures	some keyboard charts with notation	few note diagrams with keyboard	ample pictures, music map, progress charts
Familiar Songs	almost entirely folk and popular	none	none	some
Classical Music	few: Czerny, Diabelli	none	none	none
Duets	1 duet	about half with teacher accompaniment	none	none
Keyboard Preparation before Reading	none	none (in *Time to Begin*)	54 pages before reading from bass and treble clefs	2 pages
Note Reading	thumbs on middle C, notes introduced gradually (range: G – e²)	landmarks: F (bass clef), middle C (treble); interval reading from landmarks	line-by-line introduction of staff, full staff on p. 53, almost all notes around middle C	notes neighboring middle C, G and F positions (range: F – d²)
Note Drills	none	yes, in each of 10 units	yes	none
With Verse	8 songs	almost half the music	none	almost all pieces
Note Values	𝅝 𝅗𝅥. 𝅗𝅥 ♩ ♪. and rests	𝅝 𝅗𝅥. 𝅗𝅥 ♩	𝅝 𝅗𝅥 ♩ ♪. and rests	𝅝 𝅗𝅥. 𝅗𝅥 ♩ ♫ and rests
Meter	3/4 4/4	2/4 3/4 4/4 6/4	2/4 3/4 4/4	2/4 3/4 4/4

Rhythm	counting aloud, counts printed on first 12 pieces	counting by note value, then metrical counting	suggests counting on p. 13, count written as 1 & 2 & on p.65	counting suggested on p. 4
Fingering	ample	sparse	sparse	some
Hands Together	9th piece	starts on p. 17	8th piece (p. 20)	9th piece
Technical Studies	5-finger exercises (contrary too), chord studies (C, F, G7, G, D7)	warm-ups for each of 10 units	finger exercises, scale	none
Scales	none for playing	none	C Major (contrary) E minor (r.h.) G Major (l.h.)	none
Key Signatures	majors: C, G	none	none	majors: C, G, F
Dynamic Nuances	*p mp mf f* accent	immediately	yes	not until p. 26
Phrasing	some	starts on p. 7	few	in only 3 pieces
Theory	intervals, chords (C, F, G7, G, D7), chord symbols, half and whole steps, 2 pages fundamentals	intervals	none	none
Written Work	none	at end of each unit	very little	none
Supplementary Materials	*John Brimhall Library* (popular and classic)	levels I-VI: *Piano Literature, Contemporary Piano Literature, Piano Technique, Keyboard Theory*, supplementary music collections including jazz and blues	none	none

	Howard Kasschau: *Piano Course*, levels I-V, primer available (G. Schirmer, 1959)	Mark Nevin: *Piano Course*, levels I-IV, primer (Belwin Mills, 1960) BOOK I	Lynn Freeman Olson, Louise Bianchi, Marvin Blickenstaff: *Music Pathways, Discovery,* IA, IB, IC through V (with record) (Carl Fischer, 1974) BOOK IA	Robert Pace: *Music for Piano*, books I-V (Lee Roberts Music Publications, 1951) BOOK I
Number of Pages	63	64	64	48
Illustrations	photographs of composers, some sketches	few keyboard charts, few pictures	keyboard charts, helpful guides, few pictures	keyboard charts
Familiar Songs	many	some	none	yes
Classical Music	few arrangements	2 simplifications (Beethoven, Haydn), 1 song by Handel	none	2 simplifications
Duets	none	1 duet	some with teacher	2 duets
Keyboard Preparation before Reading	none	none	12 pages	6 pages
Note Reading	EGBDF, FACE, etc. C, G, F positions, major and minor triads	notes neighboring middle C, C position and then other positions (range: C – f^2)	gradual introduction of staff (line-by-line), until grand staff on p. 36 (range: all notes)	notation introduced through grand staff, reading in all keys
Note Drills	1 page at beginning	yes	yes	yes
With Verse	songs with words	some	about 2/3 of book	some
Note Values	𝅝 𝅗𝅥. 𝅗𝅥 ♩ ♪., ♩. ♪	𝅝 𝅗𝅥. 𝅗𝅥 ♩ ♪., ♩. ♪	♩ 𝅗𝅥 𝅗𝅥. 𝄽 𝄼	𝅝 𝅗𝅥. 𝅗𝅥 ♩ ♪. and rests, ♩. ♪
Meter	$\frac{2}{4}$ $\frac{3}{4}$ $\frac{4}{4}$ $\frac{6}{8}$	$\frac{2}{4}$ $\frac{3}{4}$ $\frac{4}{4}$ $\frac{6}{8}$	$\frac{2}{4}$ $\frac{3}{4}$ $\frac{4}{4}$ $\frac{5}{4}$ (meter introduced on p. 45)	$\frac{2}{4}$ $\frac{4}{4}$ $\frac{6}{8}$

Rhythm	counting, metronome	counting (p. 46)	short-long, tah, tah–ah, tah–ah–ah, tapping	clapping hands, tapping foot, saying "quar-ter two-eighths, 1 &"
Fingering	some	some	sparse	adequate
Hands Together	1st piece	4th piece	3rd piece	p. 26
Technical Studies	legato, staccato, phrasing, singing melody with accompaniment	phrasing, legato, staccato, 4 pages of finger exercises	daily finger exercises	legato, staccato, chord study
Scales	10 scales, tetrachord fingering	major: C minor: c	none	none
Key Signatures	majors: C, G, F, C♯, C♭ minors: a, c	majors: C, G, D, B♭ minor: a	none	all major and minor
Dynamic Nuances	starts on p. 34 with brief chart of expressive marks	yes	only ***p*** and ***f***	yes
Phrasing	yes	yes	none	yes
Theory	scales (parallel minors), intervals, chords and inversions	half and whole steps, chords, (C, G, F), tonic, subdominant, dominant, transpositions, cadence	intervals: 2nd, 3rd, 4th, 5th	key signatures, transposition, (all keys), chords (major, minor), cadences (I, V7) harmonization, arrangements
Written Work	none	notes, half and whole steps, rhythm	some	very little
Supplementary Materials	additional materials by Kasschau available, including ensemble pieces and hymns	none	complete course includes *Activity, Performance, Repertoire, Musicianship, Technique, Ensemble, "Something Light"*	*Skills and Drills* coordinated with *Music for Piano*

	Willard A. Palmer and Amanda Vick Lethco: *Creating Music*, books I, II (Alfred Publishers, 1971) **BOOK I**	John W. Schaum: *Piano Course*, levels A-H, primer, adult (Belwin Mills, 1945) **A, THE RED BOOK**	Eric Steiner: *Piano Course*, books I-V, junior approach book, senior approach book (prep. grade) (Belwin Mills, 1960) **BOOK I**	John Thompson: *Modern Course for the Piano*, grades I-V, *Teaching Little Fingers to Play* (prep.) (The Willis Music Co., 1936) **FIRST GRADE BOOK**
Number of Pages	48	48	63	79
Illustrations	keyboard charts, colored pictures, some illustrations	keyboard charts, explanatory charts, preparatory drills, pictures	some keyboard charts, some pictures	keyboard charts with music, sketches
Familiar Songs	mostly	few	some	few
Classical Music	simplification of Beethoven	few simplifications	some	Mozart *Air* (arr.)
Duets	many	none	1 duet with teacher	none
Keyboard Preparation before Reading	none	none	none	none
Note Reading	begins with 1-line staff which can be any note (range: E – f)	both hands in C position (range: C – e)	begins with C position and l.h. intervals of 5th and 6th, then G, F, and D positions	5-finger C position, then G, F, etc.
Note Drills	interval drills	yes	yes	none
With Verse	some	almost entirely	some	many
Note Values	𝅝 𝅗𝅥. 𝅗𝅥 ♩ ♪.	𝅝 𝅗𝅥. 𝅗𝅥 ♩ ♪. ♩. ♪	𝅝 𝅗𝅥 𝅗𝅥 ♩ ♪. and rests	𝅝 𝅗𝅥. 𝅗𝅥 ♩ ♪ 𝅘𝅥𝅯 and syncopation ♩. ♪
Meter	3/4 4/4	2/4 3/4 4/4	2/4 3/4 4/4	2/4 3/4 4/4 6/8

Rhythm	by note values	counting suggested	counting 1 & 2 & 3 4	counting suggested in third piece
Fingering	sparse	ample	plentiful	often every note
Hands Together	starts on p. 37	1st piece (pre-A available	2nd piece (jr. and sr. prep. available)	1st piece (primer available)
Technical Studies	phrasing, legato, finger exercises	phrasing, finger exercises, scale on C	finger exercises	finger drills, phrasing, broken chords, forearm strokes, wrist staccato
Scales	none	C major	majors: C, G, F minor: c	tetrachords (l.h. then r.h.) majors: C, G, D, A, E, B, F
Key Signatures	none	majors: C, G, D, A, F, B♭ minor: d	majors: C, G, F, B♭	majors: C, G, D, A, E, F, B♭, E♭, A♭
Dynamic Nuances	first lesson	yes	starts on p. 20	starts with 5th piece
Phrasing	starts on p. 25	yes, but phrase marks generally omitted	none	short phrases marked
Theory	intervals, transposition	major scales with tetrachords: C, G, D, F half and whole steps	intervals (2nd, 3rd, 4th, 5th, 6th) in C, G, F, half and whole steps, all triads in C, scale pattern	half and whole steps, scale structure, intervals, chords and inversions
Written Work	none	very little	5 pages of note identification	none
Supplementary Materials	*Creating Music, Theory Papers,* 2 books	complete library of supplementary books, including pop course, *John W. Schaum Manual* available	complete library of supplementary books and sheet music, *Piano Teacher's Guide* available free	supplementary books include *The Adult Preparatory Book, Etudes* (grades I-V), varied collections, free illustrated guide available, *"What Shall I Use to Interest My Pupils?"*

	Bernard Wagness: *Piano Course*, books I-V, preparatory (Oliver Ditson Co., 1938) **BOOK I**	John Westmoreland and Marvin Kahn: *Piano Course*, 3 books (Mills Music, Inc., 1969) **BOOK I**	June Weybright: *Belwin Piano Method*, 5 books (Belwin Mills, 1964) **BOOK I**	John M. Williams: *Year by Year*, 5 books, *Tunes for Tiny Tots* (primer) (Theodore Presser Co., 1924) **FIRST YEAR**
Number of Pages	83	80	48	96
Illustrations	keyboard chart with staff notes, sketches	abundance of keyboard charts	keyboard charts, some pictures	keyboard charts (complete range), few small pictures
Familiar Songs	few	many	many	many (including Stephen Foster)
Classical Music	none	simplification of Mozart	none	few classical studies
Duets	rhythmic ensembles, pupil claps while teacher plays	student accompanies voice	11 accompaniments for teacher	none
Keyboard Preparation before Reading	none	6 pages	1 page	none
Note Reading	middle C, introduces positions of 3 Cs (p. 61)	begins with C position, then G and F positions	middle C beginning, directional reading, all notes learned by p. 24 (range: G – f)	middle C, 5 different Cs
Note Drills	54 flash cards	yes	yes	none
With Verse	many	some	many	almost all
Note Values	𝅝 𝅗𝅥. 𝅗𝅥 ♩ ♫ ♩. ♪. 3 (♪♪♪)	abundance of all kinds of rhythmic drills	𝅝 𝅗𝅥 𝅗𝅥 ♩ and rests	𝅝 𝅗𝅥. 𝅗𝅥 ♩ ♪ ♩. ♪ 3 (♪♪♪)
Meter	4/8 2/4 3/4 4/4 6/8	2/4 3/4 4/4 6/8	2/4 3/4 4/4	2/4 3/4 4/4 6/8

Rhythm	counting and clapping, 4 pages of rhythm drills	rhythm-counting drills begin on p. 50: 1 & 2 & etc.	counting aloud (pp. 8-10)	counting aloud from 1st piece, using words to learn rhythm patterns
Fingering	abundant	ample	almost none, guides to plan fingering	plentiful
Hands Together	starts on p. 18	starts on 5th piece	starts on 3rd piece	26th piece
Technical Studies	none	none	2-finger drills	thumb, finger, wrist, all major scales, chords, arpeggios, phrasing
Scales	none	none	none	all majors
Key Signatures	majors: C, D♭, C♯	majors: C, G, D, A, E, F, B♭ minor: a	majors: C, F, G minor: a	majors: C, G, D, F
Dynamic Nuances	none	yes	none	very little (***p***, ***f***, and accent)
Phrasing	on all music except first piece	none	none	on all music
Theory	intervals, scales, transposition, musical forms	solid and broken chords, I and V^7 by rote and then later reading in C, G, D, and F, modulation	half steps	I, IV, V in C, G, D, and F, basic accompaniments
Written Work	none	drills on notes	finger planning	none
Supplementary Materials	an ensemble book provides duet and second piano parts for book I	teacher's edition available for each book	supplementary books by June Weybright available, including *Theory Work Sheets* and *Work Books*	*Older Beginner's Piano Book* for students over 14 years

Freed, Isadore. *First Year Essentials for Young Pianists: An Approach to the Music of the Masters through the Medium of the Folk Song*. New York: Carl Fischer, Inc., 1934. Forty-six pages. Part I consists of folk songs chosen for their musical value; Part II is devoted to études for technical development.

Grove, Roger. *Ready for Reading, Elementary Piano Solos*, Book 1, Book 2, and Book 3, selected and edited by Stecher, Horowitz, and Gordon. Minneapolis: Schmitt Music Center, Inc., 1975. Sixteen pages in each book. Each piece focuses on a single concept. Some have optional accompaniments that may be played by the teacher.

Thomas, Helen Thomson. *First Moments at the Piano*, Part 1 and Part 2. Bryn Mawr, Pennsylvania: Theodore Presser Company, 1967. Twenty-two pages (Part 1), fifteen pages (Part 2). The music is carefully graded so that it may be used as a course book. Some of the music has teacher accompaniments.

Waxman, Donald. *Pageants for Piano: Progressive Pieces for the Early Years of Piano Study*, Introductory Pageant, First Piano Pageant, First Folk Song Pageant, Second Piano Pageant, and Second Folk Song Pageant. New York: Galaxy Music Corp., 1958. Each book is about thirty pages. The Pageant Reader, forty pages, may be used as a supplement to the Pageant books or with any other series of books. The purpose of the Pageant books is to provide the material with which each teacher can more or less use his or her own method.

ELEMENTARY EXERCISES

Bastien, James. *Technic Lessons* (The Bastien Piano Library), Primer Level, Levels 1–4. San Diego, California: Neil A. Kjos, Jr., Publisher, 1976. Twenty-four, thirty-two, thirty-two, forty, forty pages.

Burnam, Edna Mae. *A Dozen a Day: Technical Exercises To Be Done Each Day Before Practicing*, Mini Book, Preparatory Book, Book 1–3. Florence, Kentucky: 1974. Twenty-four, thirty-one pages (Mini and Preparatory Books).

La Magra, Susan. *Creative Keyboard Practice in Progress: Piano Technique and Musicianship*, Levels 1 and 2. Hialeah, Florida: Columbia Publications, 1975. Forty-eight pages each.

Quaile, Elizabeth. *First Book of Technical Studies*. New York: G. Schirmer, 1925. Thirty-five pages. The technical exercises in this book may be used in conjunction with, Angela Diller and Elizabeth Quaile, *The First Solo Book* (G. Schirmer) and are coordinated with that solo book page by page.

Zepp, Arthur. *Let's Learn Major Scales and Chords* (and *Let's Learn Minor Scales and Chords*). Westbury, New York: Pro Art Publications, 1966. Twenty-five, twenty-seven pages.

ÉTUDES

Agay, Denes. *The Technic Treasury*, vols. A, B, C (*The Young Pianist's Library* no. 8-A, B, C) Warner Brothers Publications, 1963. Short, original piano pieces, classic to contemporary, each illustrating a specific aspect of technic. Twenty-four to thirty-two pages each.

Draw, John. *Early Keyboard Technic* in four volumes, containing studies from the masters. Westbury, New York: Pro Art Publications, Inc., 1958. Twenty-five pages each.

Hirschberg, David. *Technic is Fun*, Preparatory Books 1–5. Melville, New York: Musicord Publications (Belwin-Mills), 1948. Forty-eight pages each.

Quaile, Elizabeth. *A Pre-Czerny Book*, volumes 1 and 2. New York: G. Schirmer, 1943. Forty-four pages (forty studies), forty-six pages, thirty-two studies.

Zepp, Arthur, ed. *Developing Technic and Musicianship*. Westbury, New York: Pro Art Publications, Inc., 1971. Twenty-five pages. Selected études with technique aids and suggestions for creative improvisation.

GUIDEBOOKS

Guidebooks for some methods and teaching series, listed below, may be obtained directly from the publishers. Those indicated by an asterisk are available free of charge.

*Agay, Denes. *The Young Pianist's Library Guide*. New York: Warner Brothers Publications. Twenty-four pages.

*Bergenfeld, Nathan. *A Teacher's Guide to the Acorn Basic Lessons in Piano* (A specific guide to *The Very Young Beginner, The Young Beginner, The Older Beginner,* and *The Adult Beginner*). New York: Acorn Music Press (Music Sales Corporation). Twelve pages.

Clark, Frances. *Teaching the Music Tree*, a handbook for teachers. Evanston, Illinois: Summy-Birchard Company, 1973. Twenty-three pages.

——*Library for Piano Students/Source Book*. Evanston, Illinois: Summy-Birchard Company, 1974. Sixty-four pages.

*Glover, David Carr. *Teacher's Guide for David Carr Glover Piano Library*, a complete course of study. Melville, New York: Belwin-Mills. One hundred ninety-two pages.

Olson, Lynn Freeman, Louise Bianchi, and Marvin Blickenstaff. *Introducing Music Pathways: A Guide for Teachers*. New York: Carl Fischer, Inc., 1974. Forty-eight pages.

Palmer, Willard A., and Amanda Vick Lethco. *Creating Music*, Teacher's Manual. New York: Alfred Publishers. Forty-seven pages.

*Schaum, John W. *John W. Schaum Manual*. Melville, New York: Belwin-Mills. Ninety-six pages.

——*Piano Teacher's Guide*. Milwaukee, Wisconsin: Schaum Publications, Inc. Eighty-nine pages.

*Steiner, Eric. *Piano Teacher's Guide* for supplementary books and sheet music to the Eric Steiner Piano Course. Melville, New York: Belwin-Mills. Sixty-four pages.

Westmoreland, John, and Marvin Kahn. *Discovering the Keyboard*,

Teacher's Edition, Westmoreland-Kahn Piano Course, Books 1–3. Melville, New York: Belwin-Mills. Twenty-eight, sixty-four, and twenty-four pages.

*Weybright, June. *June Weybright Piano Manual*. Melville, New York: Belwin-Mills. Seventy-one pages.

The Repertory of Piano Duets: A Graded Annotated List

LOUISE AND WILLIAM CHEADLE

Playing piano ensemble at any level of advancement affords the opportunity for personal and mutual enjoyment and at the same time provides an additional dimension in the development of musicianship. All teachers must recognize the necessity of training piano students not only to listen but to *hear* what they play. Although this can and must be a part of the (solo) piano lesson, one extremely useful way of incorporating such listening training is through piano ensemble at virtually all stages of technical advancement. Too often the student is taught only the mechanics. Mechanics are imporant but subordinate to the essence of piano playing: creating, building musical impressions, learning to communicate with the musical languages.

It is always surprising to note just how many students at a relatively high degree of tactile facility never really hear what they produce at the keyboard. String players, it seems, learn from the first lesson the necessity of hearing, and are often afforded the chance to play in small groups or school orchestras at a relatively early stage. There is no reason why piano students cannot share this experience through piano ensemble. From the start, it becomes evident that such ensemble work requires a basic rhythmic discipline as well as some degree of sensitivity to and understanding of the other player's part.

HISTORICAL OVERVIEW

Although nobody really knows just when and by whom the first duets were written, the two earliest known examples—by Nicholas Carlton and Thomas Tomkins—date from the late sixteenth and early seventeenth centuries. The period's small keyboards would have presented certain limitations to such a medium, but for whatever reason, it appears that no other duets have survived from that era. Dr. Charles Burney claimed in 1777 that his two sets of four sonatas or duets for two performers at one keyboard were the "first that have appeared in print of this kind," and shortly thereafter J.C. Bach, Haydn, and later Clementi and Mozart wrote pieces not only for piano duet but also for two separate keyboards. Along with the earliest extant duets of Carleton and Tompkins is the two-keyboard setting of Giles Farnaby (c. 1560–1600) entitled simply "For Two Virginals," found in the *Fitzwilliam Virginal Book.* It was more than one hundred years later that J.S. Bach wrote his great duo concerto.

With the rapid development of the pianoforte, beginning during the latter part of the eighteenth century and continuing through the nineteenth, came the brilliant performers—C.P.E. Bach, Mozart, then Beethoven and Hummel, later Chopin, Liszt, Anton Rubinstein; and with these virtuosos came the very foundations of the team repertory. Mozart, Schubert, Schumann, and Brahms all wrote duos of the highest quality, comparable to their solo piano works. In our own century Bartók, Hindemith, and Stravinsky, to mention a few, have contributed significantly. Even so, the duo literature has never quite rivalled the solo in terms of quantity, and emerging piano teams have often had to turn to their own and others' arrangements of symphonic and operatic scores. In addition, they often spiced their programs with their own musical compositions. As a result there are huge numbers of arrangements and unpublished works not included in this listing. There is a wealth of material still lying on the shelves of libraries and second-hand bookstores, just waiting to be discovered.

GRADING AND SOURCES

Most of us engaged extensively in teaching will attest to the difficulties of determining the grade level of any given composition. What may be one pianist's bane may be another's strength. In trying to arrive at some logical grading standards for the teacher, we found it necessary to consider many problems beyond those of mere technical difficulty. In duets, for example, such considerations as chordal textures, execution of the notes, configurations, etc. must be weighed along with such ensemble problems as passing over and under of the hands, musical and tonal balance, and relative difficulty of the individual parts. In view of the complexities, we submit that such grading is merely intended as a guideline for the teacher and open to individual adjustments. The following brief examples should be helpful in understanding the grading system used:

Easy—Diabelli: Melodious Pieces on Five Notes
Intermediate—Schubert: *Marche militaire*
Moderately difficult—Ravel: *Mother Goose* Suite
Difficult—Mozart: Sonata in D major for Two Pianos, K. 448
Very difficult—Rachmaninoff: Suite no. 2

Our search through many library shelves, second-hand music bookstores, and countless musical journals—not to mention the generous help of friends and students—has been our collective source for this listing. Although every effort has been made to present as up-to-date a list as possible, we recognize that new works are being published and released regularly, and at the same time others go out of print without advance notice. Many original works never published or no longer available have been omitted for lack of space. We are always on the lookout for new materials and publications, and are grateful to those who may wish to share with us any additional information to keep this list current.

ORIGINAL COMPOSITIONS FOR ONE PIANO, FOUR HANDS

Composer	*Composition*	*Grade*	*Pub.*
Agay, Denes	Dance Toccata	INT	FOX
Alkan, Charles-Henri Valentin	*Bombardo-Carillon* (for organ, but adaptable for piano, four hands)	INT	COS
	Trois Marches, op. 40 (interesting examples of Alkan's unique style; the finale is the least demanding)	MD	COS
Akimenko, Fiodor S.	*Six Pièces ukraniennes*, op. 71	INT	LER
André, Johann Anton	Divertimento in A minor	INT	PET
	Six Sonatinas	INT	SUM
Arensky, Anton	Six Children's Pieces, op. 34	INT	INT
	(well-written, expressive small pieces)	INT	INT
	Twelve Pieces, op. 66	INT	JUR
Arnell, Richard	Sonatina, op. 61	MD	SCT
Auric, Georges	Five Bagatelles	INT	PRS
Babin, Victor	David and Goliath	INT	AUG
Bach, Johann Christian	Three Sonatas	INT	PET
Bach, Johann C. Friedrich	Sonata in A major	INT	PET
Bach, P.D.Q. (see Shickele, Peter)			
Bach, Wilhelm F.	Andante in A minor	INT	GSR
Bacon, Ernst	Battle of Jericho (based on the famous tune; the composer indicates that it may be played either as a duet for	INT	AMC

Composer	Composition	Grade	Pub.
	one piano—four hands or two pianos)		
Badings, Henk	Arkadia (charming suite of ten very short pieces)	INT	SCT
Balakirev, Mili	Suite	MD	LBC
Barber, Samuel	*Souvenirs*, ballet suite, op. 28	VD	GSR
Bardac, Raoul	*Petit Suite*	INT	DUR
Baumer, Cecil	Five Duets for Young Fingers	E	GSR
Beeson, Jack	Round and Round	E	OXF
Beethoven, Ludwig van	*Grosse Fugue*, op. 134	VD	HEN
	Three Marches, op. 45	MD	KAL
	Polonaise in F major	INT	GSR
	Sonata in D major, op. 6	INT	GSR
	Variations in D major	INT	GSR, KAL
	Variations on a Theme of Count Waldstein	INT	KAL
Bennett, Richard Rodney	Capriccio (brilliant twelve-tone piece, literally utilizing all notes on the keyboard with such devices as harmonics, mirror writing, etc.)	VD	UNV
Berens, Hermann	Melodious Exercises, op. 62	E	KAL
Berkeley, Lennox	Sonatina	INT	CHS
Berners, Lord	*Fantasie espagnole*	MD	CHS
	Trois Valses bourgeoises	D	CHS
Beyer, R.	*Une Toute Petite Soirée*	E	LED
Bilbro, Mathilde	By the Sea	E	BMC
Bizet, Georges	*Jeux d'enfants*, op. 22 (charming but somewhat tricky set of twelve pieces)	INT	INT
Boccose, Bio	Tarantella	INT	BER
Bohm, Carl	*Attaque des Ulans*, Grand Military Galop (period piece popular at the turn of the century; heavily martial)	INT	GSR
Borodin, Alexander	Polka; Tarantelle	INT	LEE
Boutry, Roger	*Tabatière à Musique* (very melodic; hands frequently intertwine)	E	SAL
Brahms, Johannes	Hungarian Dances	MD	GSR, PET
	Liebeslieder Waltzes, op. 65	MD	SIM

Composer	*Composition*	*Grade*	*Pub.*
	Variations on a Theme of Schumann, op. 23	D	PET
	Waltzes, op. 39	MD	KAL
Braithwaite, Sam Hartley	Pastorale	INT	AUG
Bruch, Max	Swedish Dances, op. 63	INT	SIM
Bruckner, Anton	Quadrille	INT	HEI
	Three Small Pieces (second and third pieces are slightly more difficult than the first)	E	OXF
Burney, Charles	Sonata	INT	SCT
Busoni, Ferruccio	Finnish Folksongs, op. 27 (unusual, ethnic Busoni)	INT	PET
Caplet, André	*Un Tas de petite choses*	INT	DUR
Carleton, Nicholas	A Verse for Two to Play (one of the two earliest duets; excellent example of choral-style keyboard writing)	INT	SCT
Casella, Alfredo	*Pagine de guerra*	INT	RIC
	Pupazzetti (not too difficult; some passages demand big stretches)	INT	CHS
Chabrier, Emmanuel	*Cortège burlesque*	INT	EMT
	Souvenirs de Munich	INT	EMT
Chopin, Frédéric	Variations on an Air by Moore (recently discovered early work with missing pages [first page secondo, last page primo] very ably reconstructed by Jan Ekier; the primo is considerably more difficult than the secondo)	D	MAR
Clementi, Muzio	Six Sonatas	INT	GSR
	Three Rondos, op. 41	INT	GSR
	Two Duettinos	INT	GSR
Cui, César	Ten Pieces for Five Keys, op. 74	E	LEE
Cundick, Robert	Prelude and Fugue	INT	FIS
Czerny, Karl	Sonatina in G major, op. 50	INT	FOX
Dargomijski, Alexander	Tarantella	E	LBC
Debussy, Claude	Ballade	INT	JOB
	Six Epigraphes antiques	MD	DUR
	Marche écossaise	MD	FRO
	Petit Suite	INT	GSR
Dello Joio, Norman	Family Album (five pieces for children; both primo and secondo parts are easy)	E	MAR

Composer	*Composition*	*Grade*	*Pub.*
	Five Images	INT	MAR
Del Tredici, David	Scherzo (full of polyrhythms)	VD	BOH
Demuth, Norman	Sonatina	INT	MLS
Diabelli, Antonio	Melodious Pieces on Five Notes	E	GSR
	Pleasures of Youth, op. 163	E	GSR
	Rondo militaire	INT	KAL
	Sonatas, op. 32, 33, 37, 38, 73	INT	KAL
	Sonatinas, op. 24, 54, 58, 60	E	KAL
Diercks, John	Suite no. 1	INT	MCA
Donizetti, Gaetano	Four Sonatas	MD	KIR
	Three Pieces	INT	RIC
Durey, Louis	Two Pieces	INT	SAL
Dussek, Johann L.	Three Sonatas, op. 67	INT	ELV
	Sonata in C major, op. 43	INT	MER
	Sonata in B-flat major, op. 74	INT	LBC
Dvořák, Antonin	*Legends*, op. 59	MD	SIM
	Polonaise in E-flat major	MD	PET
	Slavonic Dances, opp. 46 and 72	MD	SIM
Elliott, Robert	*Fantasie sur un motif de sarabande*, op. 3	INT	NOV
Fauré, Gabriel	*Dolly* suite, op. 56 (six pieces; the primo part is generally easier than the secondo)	INT	INT
Felciano, Richard	Gravities (experimental and atonal; very difficult to read; even the arms get to play!)	VD	GSH
Fernandez, Oscar	The Fantastic Horseman (very romantic)	INT	PER
Ferroud, Pierre	Serenade	INT	DUR
	(a blend of popular and neo-classic styles)	INT	DUR
Flothius, Marius	*Valses nobles*, op. 52	INT	DON
Francaix, Jean	*Napoleon* (suite of fourteen titled pieces arranged by the composer from his film score)	MD	TSL
Frid, Géza	*Kermesse à Charleroi*, op. 44a (brilliant showpiece)	MD	SOM
Friml, Rudolph	Twelve Duets (all primo parts in five-finger position)	E	GSR
Fulton, Norman	Dance Miniatures	INT	OXF

Composer	*Composition*	*Grade*	*Pub.*
	(Duets in four sets of two: Minuet and Hornpipe, Tarantella and Rumba, Polonaise and Tango, Waltz and Hungarian Dance)		
Garscia, Janina	Let's Play a Piano Duet vols. 1 and 2 (volume 2 is much easier)	E	BML
Gilbert, Henry P.	Three American Dances (arrangements by the composer of "Uncle Remus," "Delphin," and "Br'er Rabbit," all turn-of-the-century ragtime dances)	INT	BMC
Glinka, Mikhail	*Capriccio sur des thèmes russes*	INT	JUR
Godowski, Leopold	Ancient Dances	E	FIS
	Miniatures (all pieces include either easy or fairly easy secondo or primo parts; these are published separately, though many are difficult to find)	E	FIS
Goolkasian, Diane	Tarantella	E	CAR
Grainger, Percy	Harvest Hymn	INT	GSR
Gretchaninoff, Alexander	On the Green Meadow, op. 99 (ten short descriptive pieces)	E	MCA
Grieg, Edvard	Fantasy, op. 11	MD	AUG
	Four Norwegian Dances, op. 35	INT	PET
	Deux Pièces symphoniques, op. 14	INT	PET
	Valses caprices, op. 37	INT	PET
Griffiths, David	Serenade	E	ELN
Hässler, Johann	Sonata 6 (from Six Easy Sonatas)	INT	SCT
Hauer, Josef Matthias	*Labyrinthischer Tanz "*	MD	UNV
	Zwölftonspiel (rather dissonant, highly contrapuntal)	INT	DOB
Haydn, Franz Josef	*Il Maestro e lo scolare*	INT	GSR
	Partita in F major	INT	GSR
Heiden, Bernhard	Sonata for Four Hands (very well written in the Hindemith style)	D	ASO
Helps, Robert	Saccade	VD	PET
Hessenberg, Kurt	Partita Capricciosa	D	GER
	Sonata in C minor, op. 34 no. 1	D	SCT

Composer	*Composition*	*Grade*	*Pub.*
	Variations on a Children's Tune, op. 34 no. 2	D	SCT
Hiller, Ferdinand	*Operette ohne Text*, op. 106 (romantic pieces with descriptive titles)	INT	AUG
Hindemith, Paul	Sonata for Four Hands	D	SCT
Hofmann, Heinrich	*Danza campestre* (reminiscent of Brahms' Hungarian Dancces)	INT	BER
	Twelve Pieces, op. 46	INT	BER
Hovhaness, Alan	A Child in the Garden, op. 168	INT	PET
Hummel, Johann	Grande Sonata in A-flat major, op. 92	D	PET
	Sonata in E-flat major, op. 51	INT	PET
Husa, Karel	Eight Czech Duets	INT	SCT
Ibert, Jacques	*Histoires* (charming suite in five movements; no. 3 is *Le Petit Ane blanc.*)	INT	LED
Inglebrecht, Désiré-Émile	*Six Pièces enfantines*	INT	LED
Jongen, Joseph	*Jeux d'enfants*, op. 120	INT	CBD
	"Cocass" March, *Petite Berceuse et divertissement*, op. 120	MD	CBD
Juon, Paul	*Tanzrhythmen*, opp. 14, 24, 41	MD	SCL
Kasements, Udo	Squares	D	BMI
Koechlin, Charles	*Quatres Sonatines françaises*	INT	OXF
Kohn, Karl	Recreations	MD	FIS
Kolinski, Mieczyslaw	First Piano Duets	E	GSR
Krieger, Edino	Sonata	INT	PER
Kuhlau, Friedrich	Sonatina in G major	INT	GSR
Kurka, Robert	Dance Suite, op. 29	INT	WTB
Lachner, Franz	Suite, op. 113 (lengthy early romantic piece)	MD	SCT
Lambert, Constance	*Trois Pièces nègres pour les touches blanches*	INT	OXF
La Montaine, John	Sonata, op. 25	D	ELV
Last, Joan	Pantomime Pictures	E	OXF
Low, Joseph	Teacher and Pupil	E	GSR
Lybbert, Donald	Movement	VD	PET
Maykapar, Samuel	First Steps (Easy Duets)	E	LEE
MacDowell, Edward	Lunar Pictures	INT	HAI
	Three Poems, op. 20	INT	GSR
Marx, Karl	Sonatine in E major, op. 48	MD	BRT
Mason, Daniel Gregory	Birthday Waltzes, op. 2	INT	BMC
Masseus, Jan	Zoological Impressions, op. 24	INT	PET

Composer	*Composition*	*Grade*	*Pub.*
Mendelssohn, Felix	Allegro Brilliant, op. 92	VD	GSR
	Andante and Variations	D	GSR
	Six Pieces for Children, op. 72	INT	PAR
Moscheles, Ignaz	Sonata, op. 112	D	CGB
Moss, Lawrence	*Omaggio* (avant-garde piece)	VD	ELV
Moszkowski, Moritz	From Foreign Parts, op. 23	INT	GSR
	Fackeltanz ("Torch Dance")	MD	PET
	Five Waltzes, op. 8	INT	GSR
	Hungarian Dance no. 3, op. 11	INT	GSR
	Spanish Dances, op. 12	INT	GSR
Mozart, Wolfgang	Sonata in B-flat major, K. 240	INT	PET
	Sonata K. 19d	INT	SCT
	Variations in G major, K. 503	INT	KAL
Muczynski, Robert	American Songs (six short pieces based on popular tunes: "When Johnny Comes Marching Home," "Skip to My Lou," etc.)	INT	ASO
Musgrave, Thea	Excursions (eight short pieces depicting automobile driving experiences; a humorous suite, written with teacher and pupil parts)	INT	CHS
Nagan, Tzvi	Seven Pieces (quite dissonant)	INT	IMI
Niemann, Walter	*Kocheler Ländler*, op. 135	INT	PET
Neumann, Walter	*Klavierstücke für Anfänger*	INT	BRE
Niles, John Jacob	American Carols in Easy Arrangements	E	GSR
O'Brien, Eugene	Ambages (difficult piece, with experimental notation)	VD	GSR
Ore, Henry	Three Latvian Folk Songs	INT	CUR
Papineau, Contur Jean	Rondo	INT	PER
Persichetti, Vincent	Concerto for Piano, four hands (written for piano-duet without orchestral accompaniment)	VD	ELV
Philips, Burril	Serenade	MD	SOM
Pierné, Gabriel	*Album pour mes petits amis*	INT	LED
Pleyel, Ignaz	Sonata in G minor	INT	PET
Poser, Hans	Sonata, op. 17	MD	SIK
Poulenc, Francis	Sonata for Piano, four hands	MD	CHS
Pozzoli, Ettore	Ten Little Characteristic Pieces	E	BEL
Rachmaninoff, Serge	Italian Polka	MD	BEL
	Six pieces, op. 11	INT	INT
Ran, Schulamit	Children's Scenes	INT	FIS

Composer	*Composition*	*Grade*	*Pub.*
Raphling, Sam	Sonata	INT	GEN
Ravel, Maurice	*l'Eventail de Jeanne*	MD	CLV
	Mother Goose Suite	MD	DUR
	Rapsodie espagnole	D	DUR
Rawsthorne, Alan	The Creel (a suite)	MD	OXF
Rebikoff, Vladimir	*Petit Suite*	INT	JUR
Reger, Max	Six Burlesques, op. 58	D	SCT
Reinecke, Carl	From the Cradle to the Grave	INT	SCB
	Improvisations on a Gavotte from Orpheus, op. 125	INT	PET
Rochberg, George	Prelude on "Happy Birthday" (although written for one piano, the composer indicates "if there is another piano in the same room, have another pianist play different music at the same time; improvise 'atonally' or play another composer's music"; experimental, reminiscent of Ives)	D	PRS
Rowley, Alec	Six Short Dance Impressions, op. 41	INT	PET
Rubinstein, Anton	*Bal Costume*, op. 103	D	JUR
	Six Characteristic Pieces	INT	GSR
	Sonata for Piano, four hands	VD	LBC
Russell, Robert	Places, op. 9	INT	GEN
Saint-Säens, Camille	Berceuse, op. 105	INT	DUR
	Pas redouble, op. 86	INT	GSR
Satie, Erik	*Aperçus désagreables*	INT	DEM
	En habit de cheval	INT	SAL
	Music for Piano, four hands	MD	ESG
	Trois Morceaux en forme de poire	INT	SAL
	Trois Petites Pieces montées	INT	ASO
Schaffer, Boguslaw	Music for Piano, four hands (avant-garde)	D	SIM
Schickele, Peter (P.D.Q. Bach)	The Civilian Barber (hilariously clever and effective)	MD	ELV
	Toot Suite (written for organ [or calliope, four hands] but can easily be played as a piano duet)	INT	PRS
Schmitt, Florent	*Musique Foraines*, op. 22	D	HAM
	Reflets d'Allemagne	INT	MAT
	Sur les cinq doigts	INT	HEU
Schmitt, Jacques	*Marche pour piano-forte a quatre mains*, op. 17	INT	AOF

Composer	*Composition*	*Grade*	*Pub.*
	Sonata facile, op. 31	INT	AOF
	Variations, op. 30	INT	AOF
Schoenberg, Arnold	Six Pieces for Piano, four hands (early Schoenberg; quite conventionally romantic and very playable)	INT	BMT
Schubert, Franz	Schubert wrote over fifty compositions for piano duet; there are many fine collections available (see Collections)		
Schumann, Georg	*Vier Stücke*, op. 37	INT	SIM
Schumann, Robert	Ball Scenes, op. 109	MD	PET
	Kinderball, op. 130	MD	PET
	Original Compositions	MD	INT
	Pictures from the East, op. 66	MD	GSR
	Twelve Piano Pieces, op. 85	MD	GSR
Schuster, Giori	Mimos I (moderately dissonant)	INT	IMI
Shapero, Harold	Sonata for Piano, four hands	INT	MLS
Shifrin, Seymour	The Modern Temper	D	PET
Sinding, Christian	Norwegian Dance and Melodies	MD	PET
Spiegelman, Joel	Suite, op. 35	VD	MCA
	Morsels (*Kousochki*) (experimental notation; very difficult to decipher)		
Starer, Robert	Fantasia Concertante	D	MCA
	Five Duets for Young Pianists	INT	MCA
Strategien, Herman	Suite	INT	DON
Stravinsky, Igor	Five Easy Pieces	E	GSR
	Petrouchka (1947 version)	VD	BOH
	Three Easy Pieces	E	GSR
Stravinsky, Soulima	The Music Alphabet (two volumes) (the alphabet from A to Z; titles such as "G–Gavotte," "M–Minuet," "E–Étude," etc.)	INT	PET
Tcherepnin, Alexander	Exploring the Piano (pupil parts written sometimes in primo, sometimes in secondo, all in very large notes)	E	PET
Toch, Ernst	Sonata, op. 87	INT	MLS
Tomkins, Thomas	A Fancy for Two to Play (one of the earliest duets; four-part writing adapted to the keyboard)	INT	OXF
Tovey, Donald Francis	Balliol Dances	INT	SCT
Townsend, Douglas	Four Fantasies on American		

Composer	*Composition*	*Grade*	*Pub.*
	Folk Songs	INT	PET
Tchaikovsky, Peter I.	Fifty Russian Folk Songs	INT	INT
Türk, Daniel Gottlob	*Tonstücke für vier Hände*	INT	SCT
Vanhal, Johann Baptist	Six Easy Pieces	E	BRT
Van Slyck, Nicholas	With Twenty Fingers		
	Book 1	E	GEN
	Book 2	INT	
	Book 3	MD	
Van Wyk, Arnold	Three Improvisations on Dutch Folk Songs	MD	BOH
Volkmann, Robert	Three Marches, op. 40	INT	AUG
Wagner, Richard	Polonaise in D major	MD	BRE
Weber, Carl Maria von	Pieces for Piano, four hands, opp. 3, 60	INT	PET
	Six Pieces, op. 10	INT	PET
Weiner, Leo	Suite on Hungarian Folk Dances, op. 18	D	ZEN
Williamson, Malcolm	Travel Diaries (mostly for piano solo, but contains duets in the "Naples" set)	E	CHP
Wolf, Ernst Wilhelm	Sonata in C major	INT	GSR
Woolen, Russell	Sonata for Piano Duo	MD	PAN
Wourinen, Charles	Making Ends Meet	VD	PET

COLLECTIONS OF ORIGINAL PIANO DUETS (One Piano, Four Hands)

Title	*Grade*	*Pub.*
Album for Piano Four Hands vols 1 and 2 Compositions by Gade, Jensen, and others	INT	GSR
Classical Album Twelve compositions by Haydn, Mozart, Beethoven, Clementi, Kuhlau, and Weber	INT	GSR
Duets of Early American Music Edited by Anne McClenny and Maurice Hinson	INT	BEL
Easy Original Piano Duets (vol. 23, *Music for Millions*) Edited by Poldi Zeitlin and David Goldberger; includes fifty pieces	E-INT	CON
Eighteen Original Piano Duets Compositions by Bizet, Dvořák, Fauré, and others	E-D	GSR
Eleven Piano Duets by the Masters Edited by Poldi Zeitlin and David Goldberger; works by Haydn, Mozart, Beethoven, Schumann, Grieg, and others	INT	GSR

	Grade	Pub.
Festivities for Four Hands (or Two People) Edited by Joseph Rollino and Paul Sheftel; original pieces for elementary-grade students	E	FIS
Forty-four Original Piano Duets Haydn to Stravinsky; edited by Walter Eckard	E-INT	PRS
Four Hands at the Keyboard Twelve little pieces	E	FIS
Original 18th-Century Piano Duets Collected and edited by Alfred Mirovitch; works by Colizzi, Giordani, Weber	INT-MD	WIT
Sonaten für Liebhaber Bach, Hässler, Haydn, and others	INT	SCT
Style and Interpretation, vols. 5 and 6 Edited by Howard Ferguson vol. 5: Tomkins, Haydn, J.S. Bach, Clementi, Mozart, Beethoven, Weber vol. 6: Schubert, Schumann, Brahms, Bizet, Dvořák, Debussy	INT-MD	OXF
Teacher and Student Edited by Ernest Lubin; forty-seven duets by Haydn, Reinecke, Cui, Tchaikovsky, Stravinsky, and others	E-INT	AMS

ORIGINAL COMPOSITIONS FOR TWO PIANOS, FOUR HANDS

Composer	*Composition*	*Grade*	*Pub.*
Arensky, Anton	Suite no. 1, op. 15 (Romanze, Waltz [very well known], and Polonaise)	D	GSR
	Suite no. 2, op. 23 ("Silhouettes") (five movements; subtle sketches in familiar compositional styles such as canon, waltz, etc.)	D	PET
	Suite no. 4, op. 62 in D-flat major (Prelude, Romanze, *Le Rêve*, Finale; may be very difficult to find)	D	JUR
	Suite no. 5, op. 65 in Canon Form (eight short charming canons, well within a good student's ability)	INT	GSR
Ashton, Algernon	Suite, op. 50	D	HEI

Composer	*Composition*	*Grade*	*Pub.*
	(five movements: Praeludium, Pastorale, Scherzo, March Triomphale, and Finale; rather long)		
Aubert, Louis	Suite, op. 6 (written for Paris Exposition of 1900; influences of Debussy and Ravel)	MD	DUR
Auric, Georges	*Double Jeux*	MD	SAL
	Partita (three movements)	D	ESG
Babin, Victor	Six Études for Two Pianos (no. 4 is his version of Rimsky-Korsakov's "Flight of the Bumblebee")	D	UNV
	Three March Rhythms	D	BOH
Bach, Carl Philipp Emanuel	Four Little Duets for Two Pianos	INT	GSR
Bach, Johann Christian	Sonata in G major	INT	INT
Bach, Johann Sebastian	Two Fugues from *The Art of Fugue*	D	PET
Bach, Wilhelm Friedemann	Sonata in F major	MD	INT
Bacon, Ernst	The Battle of Jericho (based on the famous tune; the composer indicates that it may be played on one or two pianos)	INT	AMC
	The Burr Frolic	INT	ASO
Bacon, Ernst and Otto Luening	Coal Scuttle Blues	D	ASO
Badings, Henk	*Balletto grottesco*	MD	UNV
Baervoets, Raymond	*Scherzo pour deux pianos*	INT	CBD
Balogh, Ernö	Peasant Dance	D	JFIS
Bartók, Béla	Rhapsody, op. 1 (originally for orchestra, arranged by the composer)	D	BOH
	Seven Pieces from *Mikrokosmos* (selections from Book 4 and 5, arranged by the composer)	D	BOH
	Sonata for Two Pianos and Percussion	VD	BOH
	Suite for Two Pianos, op. 46 (originally written as an orchestral suite, rewritten in 1941 for two pianos)	VD	BOH

Composer	*Composition*	*Grade*	*Pub.*
Bate, Stanley	Three Pieces for Two Pianos (Prelude, Pastorale, Rondo)	MD	AMP
Bax, Arnold	Hardanger	INT	MUR
	Moy Mell	INT	MUR
	Poisoned Fountain	INT	MUR
	Sonata for Two Pianos	MD	MUR
Beach, Mrs. H.H.A.	Suite for Two Pianos	MD	CHU
	Variations on Balkan Themes	MD	APS
Beck, Arthur	Sonata for Two Pianos	INT	ASO
Beecher, Carl	The Jester	MD	DIT
Benjamin, Arthur	From San Domingo (conventional writing; uses knuckles on the piano wood for rhythmic effects)	INT	BOH
	Jamaicalypso	MD	BOH
	Jamaican Rumba	MD	BOH
	Two Jamaican Street Songs ("Cookie" and "Mattie Rag")	MD	BOH
Berger, Arthur	Three Pieces	MD	
Berger, Jean	Caribbean Cruise	MD	BRO
Berkeley, Lennox	Nocturne	D	CHS
	Polka	MD	CHS
Bloch, Ernest	*Evocations* (symphonic suite for orchestra, transcribed by the composer)	D	GSR
Boulez, Pierre	"Structures" for Two Pianos (exceedingly difficult twelve-tone piece)	VD	UNV
Boutry, Roger	*Trasne pour deux pianos*	D	SAL
Bowen, York	Suite, op. 111 (Prelude, Rigadoon, Intermezzo, and Tarantella; each published separately)	INT	OXF
Bowles, Paul	Sonata for Two Pianos	D	GSR
Bozza, Eugene	Sonata for Two Pianos	VD	LED
Braggiotti, Mario	Variations on "Yankee Doodle" (in the styles of Bach, Beethoven, Chopin, Debussy, and Gershwin)	D	GSR
Brahms, Johannes	Sonata in F minor, op. 34b (alternate version of the Piano Quintet, op. 34a)	VD	INT
	Variations on a Theme of Haydn, op. 56b	VD	GSR

Composer	*Composition*	*Grade*	*Pub.*
	Waltzes, op. 39 (arranged by the composer)	MD	GSR
Branson, David	By a Water Mill	E	ELN
Britten, Benjamin	Introduction and Rondo alla Burlesca, op. 23 no. 1	D	BOH
	Mazurka Elegiaca, op. 23 no. 2	D	BOH
Bruch, Max	Fantasie in D minor	D	BOH
Burleigh, Cecil	Mountain Pictures Suite, op. 42	INT	GSR
Bush, Geoffrey	An Oxford Scherzo	INT	AUG
Busoni, Ferruccio	*Fantasia contrapuntistica* (very long, very interesting postromantic piece)	D	BRE
Carmichael, John	Tourbillon (valse brilliante)	MD	AUG
Casadesus, Robert	*Dances mediterranéennes*	D	FIS
	Six Pièces pour deux pianos (Algerienne, Russe, Sicilienne, Française, Espagnole, Anglaise)	D	DUR
Cazden, Norman	Stony Hollow, op. 47a	INT	SPT
Chabrier, Emmanuel	*España Rhapsody* (transcribed by the composer)	MD	BEL
	Trois Valses romantiques	MD	INT
Chaminade, Cecile	Andante, op. 59	MD	GSR
	Scherzettino	MD	GSR
Chanler, Theodore	The Second Joyful Mystery	MD	ASO
Chasins, Abram	Period Suite	MD	CHP
	Rush Hour in Hong Kong	D	FIS
Chopin, Frédéric	Rondo in C major, op. 73 (the only known two-piano piece; Chopin's beautiful, brilliant work)	D	GSR
Clementi, Muzio	Two Sonatas in B-flat major, opp. 12, 46	INT	GSR
Copland, Aaron	*Danzon cubano*	MD	BOH
	Danzon de jalisco (commissioned by the Festival of Two Worlds in Spoleto, first written for chamber orchestra; arranged by the composer for two pianos in 1963)	MD	BOH
Cordero, Roque	Duo	MD	PER
Corigliano, John	Kaleidoscope	D	GSR
Cowell, Henry	Celtic Set (composer's arrangement of a set of solo pieces, written in very traditional style; three	INT	GSR

Composer	*Composition*	*Grade*	*Pub.*
	movements: Reel, Caoine, and Hornpipe)		
Debussy, Claude	*En blanc et noir* (large, magnificent piece in three movements, written during World War I; the second movement, with its bugle calls, drums, and Luther chorale, strongly depicts the tragedy of war)	D	DUR
	Lindaraja	MD	JOB
	Fêtes (Arranged by Ravel from *Nocturnes*)	D	ELV
	Nuages (Arranged by Ravel from *Nocturnes*)	D	FRO
Dello Joio, Norman	Aria and Toccata	MD	FIS
Diamond, David	Concerto for Two Solo Pianos	D	SOM
Dougherty, Celius	Music from Seas and Ships	MD	GSR
Dunford, Nancy	Fanfare and March	INT	FIS
Dussek, Johann L.	Sonata in F major, op. 26	MD	SCT
Duvernoy, Jean Baptiste	*Feu roulant*, op. 256	MD	MAR
Elkus, Albert	On a Merry Folk Tune	MD	JFIS
Enesco, Georges	Variations, op. 5	D	BOH
Faith, Richard	Concerto for Two Pianos (written for two solo pianos; there are no octaves in primo)	MD	SHW
Farnaby, Giles	For Two Virginals (from the *Fitzwilliam Virginal Book*; the earliest known piece for two keyboards)	INT	OXF
Federer, Ralph	Fantasy in C-sharp minor	VD	PRS
Ferguson, Howard	Partita (large work in four movements, written in a style reminiscent of Brahms)	D	BOH
Ficher, Jacobo	Three Hebrew Dances (Wedding Dance, Mystic Dance, Hora)	MD	SOM
Françaix, Jean	*Huit Dances exotiques* (eight dances: Pambiche, Baiao, Nube gris, Merengue, Mambo, Samba lente, Malambeando, Rock 'n' Roll)	MD	SCT
Freed, Isadore	Carnival	MD	PRE
Frid, Géza	Prelude and Fugue, op. 23	MD	SOM
Friedman, Ignace	Suite, op. 70	D	HAN

Composer	*Composition*	*Grade*	*Pub.*
	(Tema con Variazioni, Choral, and Finale; may be difficult to find)		
Fuleihan, Anis	Toccata	D	SOM
Fulton, Norman	Air for Two Pianos (one of a set of three pieces written for two pianos)	MD	OXF
Gershwin, George	"I Got Rhythm" Variations (transcribed by the composer)	MD	NWM
Glière, Reinhold	Six Pieces, op. 41 (Prelude, Valse triste, Chanson, Basso ostinato, Air de Ballet, Mazurka)	MD	INT
Godowsky, Leopold	*Alt Wien* (although not technically difficult to play, the key signature of six flats may make it difficult for some students to learn)	MD	GSR
Goldman, Richard	*Le Bobino,* Burlesque in Three Scenes (Overture, Entr'acte, Le Jazz Cold)	MD	SOM
Gould, Morton	Pavane (arranged by the composer from Symphonette no. 2)	INT	BEL
	Rumbolero	MD	FIS
Grainger, Percy	Country Gardens (primo has no big chords and is much easier than secondo)	INT-MD	GSR
	Spoon River (primo fairly easy, with no stretches over a seventh; secondo fairly hard, with no stretches over an octave)	INT-MD	GSR
Gretchaninoff, Alexander	*Deux Morceaux* (*Poème* and *Cortège*)	MD	RMP
Grieg, Edvard	Romanze with Variations, op. 51	MD	PET
Gruen, Rudolph	Humoresque	MD	ASO
	Scherzo, op. 4a	MD	ASO
Grunn, Homer	*Humoresque nègre*	MD	GSR
Guion, David	The Harmonica Player	D	GSR
Gurlitt, Cornelius	Eight Melodious Pieces, op. 174	INT	GSR
	Rondo in D, op. 175 no. 1	INT	GSR
	Rondo in E Flat, op. 175 no. 2	INT	GSR
	Rondo in E minor, op. 175 no. 3	INT	GSR
	(All of the above Gurlitt pieces		

Composer	*Composition*	*Grade*	*Pub.*
	are excellent teaching pieces.)		
Haieff, Alexei	Sonata for Two Pianos	D	CHP
Harris, Edward	Croon-A Southland Idyll	MD	JFIS
Haubiel, Charles	Miniatures for Two Pianos (A Mystery, Madonna, Gayety, Shadows, Snowflakes, and Festival.)	INT	CPR
	Suite Passecaille (Allemande, Menuet, Sarabande, and Gavotte. All published separately.)	D	CPR
Heiller, Anton	Toccata	D	UNV
Hemmer, Eugene	Introduction and Dance	INT	AME
Henselt, Adolph von	Romance in B minor, op. 10	MD	BOH
Hill, Edward Burlingame	Jazz Studies for Two Pianos (four pieces)	MD	GSR
Hindemith, Paul	Sonata for Two Pianos	D	SCT
Hovhaness, Alan	*Vijag*, op. 37	MD	PET
Howe, Mary	Three Spanish Folk Tunes (Habañera de Cinna, Peteñera Spanish Folk Dance)	MD	BMC
Hummel, Johann Nepomuk	Introduction and Rondo	MD	BOH
Infante, Manuel	*Danses andalouses* (Ritmo, Sentimiento, Gracia [El Vito])	D	SAL/LC
	Musiques d'Espagne (Ferruca, Montagnarde, Tirana, Seguidille)	MD	SAL
Ives, Charles	Three Quarter-tone Pieces	D	PET
Jacobson, Maurice	Ballade	MD	ELN
Jadassohn, Salomon	Chaconne for Two Pianos, op. 82 (may be difficult to find)	MD	KIS
Juon, Paul	Sonata for Two Pianos	D	SCL
Kadosa, Paul	Sonata for Two Pianos, op. 37	D	ZEN
Kaun, Hugo	Suite (*Im alten Styl*) (four movements: Praeludium, Passacaglia, Gavotte, and Gigue)	D	HEI
Kelterborn, Rudolf	Sonata for Two Pianos	MD	BRT
Kettering, Eunice Lea	Rigadoon	INT	GSR
Khatchaturian, Aram	Three Pieces (Ostinato, Romance, Fantastic Waltz)	MD	KAL
Kirschner, Theodor	Waltzes, op. 86	MD	PET
Klein, John	Three Dances (Jig-Waltz, Stoop Dance, Whirl)	MD	ASO

Composer	*Composition*	*Grade*	*Pub.*
Kountz, Richard	The Sleigh (originally for voice and piano; transcribed by the composer)	MD	GSR
Krěnek, Ernst	*Basler Massarbeit* (written in the twelve-tone technique)	D	BRT
Labor, Joseph	Phantasie on an Original Theme, op. 1	D	UNV
Lees, Benjamin	Sonata for Two Pianos	MD	BOH
Levitzki, Mischa	*Valse tzigane*	MD	FLM
Liszt, Franz	*Concerto pathetique* in E minor (for two solo pianos without orchestral accompaniment)	VD	GSR
	Symphonic Poems, 1–12 (originally written for orchestra, arranged by the composer for two pianos; 1: *Ce qu'on entend sur la montagne*; 2: *Tasso*; 3: *Les Préludes*; 4: *Orpheus*; 5: *Prometheus*; 6: *Mazeppa*; 7: *Festklange*; 8: *Heroïde funebre*; 9: *Hungaria*; 10: *Hamlet*; 11: *Hunnenschlacht*; 12: *Les Idéals*)	VD	BRE
Longo, Alessandro	*Sei Divertimenti facili* (Six Pieces: *Variazioni sul tema, Tempo de gavotta, Piccola Suite, Studio in forma de valzen, Idillio, Tema con variazioni*; all published separately)	INT	RIC
Leuning, Otto and Ernst Bacon	Coal Scuttle Blues	D	ASO
Lutoslawski, Witold	Variations on a Theme of Paganini	VD	PWM
Mattheson, Johann	Sonata for Two Pianos G minor	INT	HEI
Martinu, Bohuslav	La Fantasie	D	ESG
McKay, George Frederic	Dancing in a Dream	INT	DEL
McPhee, Colin	Balinese Ceremonial Music (vol. 1: *Pemoengkah*; vol. 2: *Gambangan*; vol. 3: *Taboeh Teloe*)	D	GSR
Merlet, Michel	Music for Two Pianos (Prelude, Andante, Scherzo)	D	LED
Messiaen, Olivier	*Visions de l'amen*	VD	DUR
Milhaud, Darius	*Kentuckiana* (Divertissement		

Composer	*Composition*	*Grade*	*Pub.*
	on twenty Kentucky Airs) (not difficult technically, but many large stretches in both parts)	MD	ELV
	Le Bal martiniquais (two-movement suite; Chanson créole and Beguine)	MD	LEE
	Scaramouche (three-movement suite: Vif, Moderé, Brazilera)	MD	ELV
	Six Dances in Three Movements (1: Tarantelle-Bourrée; 2: Sarabande-Pavane; 3: Rumba-Gigue)	D	ESG
Moscheles, Ignaz	*Hommage à Handel*, op. 92	MD	AUG
Mozart, Wolfgang Amadeus	Fugue in C minor, K. 426	D	GSR
	Sonata in D major, K. 448	D	GSR
Newman, Frank	A Frolic (based on the traditional English tune "Lincolnshire Poacher")	MD	AUG
Niles, John Jacob	The Story of the Bee (arrangement of the American folksong "Do Take Care of the Bee, Boys")	INT	GSR
Ohana, Maurice	*Soron-ngo*	VD	SAL
Paganucci, A.	*Valse debonnaire*	INT	GSR
Palmer, Robert	Sonata for Two Pianos	D	PER
Palmgren, Selim	*Maskenball* (four pieces: *Der Improvisator, Die Tanzerin, Der Schwarze Domino, Humoristisches*; each published separately)	D	SCL
Pasquini, Bernardo	Sonata in D minor	MD	NOV
	Sonata in E minor	MD	BER
Persichetti, Vincent	Sonata for Two Pianos, op. 13	D	LEE
Peters, J.V.	Prelude and Chorale	INT	OXF
Petyrek, Felix	Six Concert Etudes	D	UNV
	Toccata and Fugue in the Mixolydian Style	MD	UNV
Philipp, Isadore	*Feux-Follets*, op. 24 no. 3	MD	GSR
Pierre-Petit	*Le Diable à deux*	MD	ESG
Pinto, Octavio	*Scenas infantis*	INT	GSR
Pirani, Eugenio	Gavotte, op. 36	INT	FIS
Pisk, Paul	My Pretty Little Pink: A Merry Fugue on a Southern		

Composer	Composition	Grade	Pub.
	Folk Song	MD	LEE
Platt, Richard	Pastorale	INT	DIT
	Prelude	INT	DIT
Portnoff, Mischa	Brief Flirtation	INT	JFIS
	March of the Imps	INT	JFIS
	Playful Leaves	INT	JFIS
	Sentimental Parting	INT	JFIS
Poulenc, Francis	*Elégie*	D	ESG
	l'Embarquement pour Cythère	MD	ESG
	Sonata for Two Pianos	D	ESG
Rachmaninoff, Sergei	Fantasy, op. 5 (Suite no. 1) (Barcarolle, A Night for Love, Tears, Russian Easter)	VD	INT
	Suite no. 2, op. 17 (Introduction, Valse, Romanze, Tarantella)	VD	INT
	Symphonic Dances, op. 45 (written concurrently with the orchestral version)	VD	FOL
Raphling, Sam	Bagatelle Cubana	E	FOX
	Square Dance	INT	MUS
Ravel, Maurice	"Frontispiece" for two pianos, five hands	MD	SAL
	Rhapsodie espagnole	MD	DUR
	Sites auriculaires (*Habanera; Entre cloches*)	MD	SAL
	La Valse (transcribed by the composer)	D	DUR
Reger, Max	Variations and Fugue on a Theme of Beethoven, op. 86	D	BOK
	Introduction, Passacaglia and Fugue, op. 96	D	BOK
Riegger, Wallingford	The Cry	MD	PER
	Evocation	MD	PER
	New Dance	MD	PER
	Scherzo, op. 13a	MD	PER
	Variations, op. 54a	MD	ASO
Rieti, Vittorio	Chess Serenade (five pieces: Prelude, Gavotte, Serenade, Valse, Clown March)	MD	ASO
	Second Avenue Waltz	MD	ASO
	Suite champêtre	MD	ASO
	Three Vaudeville Marches	INT	GEN
	Valse fugitive	INT	GEN
Rochberg, George	Prelude on "Happy Birthday" (although written for one piano,	D	PRS

Composer	*Composition*	*Grade*	*Pub.*
	the composer indicates "if there is another piano in the same room, have another pianist play different music at the same time; improvise 'atonally' or play another composer's music"; very experimental; reminiscent of Ives)		
Rorem, Ned	Sicilienne	MD	SOM
Rosenbloom, Sydney	Variations and Fugue on an Original Theme, op. 16	MD	AUG
Rowley, Alec	Prelude and Toccata	MD	CHS
Rubinstein, Beryl	Suite for Two Pianos (Prelude, Canzonetta, Jig, Masks)	D	GSR
Saar, Louis Victor	Gavotte-Intermezzo, op. 75 no. 2	MD	FIS
Saint-Saëns, Camille	Caprice, op. 96	D	DUR
	Danse macabre, op. 40 (transcribed by the composer)	D	DUR
	Le Rouet d'Omphale (transcribed by the composer)	D	DUR
	Scherzo, op. 87	D	INT
	Variations on a Theme of Beethoven	MD	GSR
	Introduction and Rondo Capriccioso, op. 28 (transcribed by Debussy)	MD	INT
Schmitt, Florent	Three Rhapsodies, op. 53	MD	DUR
Schulz, Edwin	Rondino in F major, op. 162 no. 1	INT	GSR
Schumann, Georg	Variations and Fugue on a Theme of Beethoven	D	SIM
Schumann, Robert	Andante and Variations, op. 46	MD	GSR
	Six Études in Canon Form, op. 56 (six of Schumann's pieces originally written for the "pedal piano" beautifully transcribed by Debussy for two pianos)	MD	INT
Schütt, Edouard	Impromptu Rococo, op. 58 no. 2	MD	ASO
Schytte, Ludwig	*Festmarch*, op. 115 no. 2	MD	KIS
Scott, Cyril	Theme and Variations	D	ELN
Scriabin, Alexander	Fantasy for Two Pianos	D	MTP
Simmons, Homer	Scherzino for Two Pianos	MD	JFIS
Sinding, Christian	Andante (from Duets for Two Pianos, op. 41)	D	AUG
	Deciso ma non troppo (from Duets for Two Pianos, op. 41; a glissando-lover's	D	AUG

Composer	*Composition*	*Grade*	*Pub.*
	delight; pages and pages of it, plus rolled chords)		
	Variations in E-flat minor, op. 2	D	HAN
Sitsky, Larry	Concerto for Two Solo Pianos	VD	BOH
Smith, Julia	American Dance Suite	MD	PRS
	(four pieces: "One Morning in May"; "Lost My Partner"; "Negro Lullaby"; "Chicken Reel")		
Soler, Antonio	Six Concertos for Two Keyboards	MD	UME
	(published separately; among the earliest sets of pieces for two keyboards)		
Spinks, Charles	Variations on a Greek Folk Song	VD	HEI
Starer, Robert	The Fringes of a Ball	D	PRS
Stone, Gregory	*Burlesque tzigane*	D	MAR
	Boogie Woogie Étude	MD	CHP
Stravinsky, Igor	Capriccio	VD	BOH
	(arranged by the composer)		
	Concerto for Two Solo Pianos	VD	SCT
	Sonata for Two Pianos	MD	ASO
	Scherzo à la Russe	D	ASO
	(transcribed by the composer)		
Tailleferre, Germaine	*Jeux de plain air*	MD	DUR
	Valses	MD	LEM
	(*Valse lente* and *Valse brillante*)		
Talma, Louise	Four-Handed Fun	MD	FIS
Tansman, Alexandre	*Fantasie sur les valses de Johann Strauss*	MD	ESG
	Sonatine transatlantique	MD	LED
	(three pieces: Fox-Trot; Spiritual and Blues; Charleston)		
Tcherepnin, Alexander	Rondo, op. 87a	MD	PET
Thomson, Virgil	Synthetic Waltzes	INT	ELV
Tippett, Michael	Fantasia on a Theme by Handel	MD	ASO
Triggs, Harold	*Danza braziliana*	MD	FIS
	Valse	MD	GSR
Trimble, Joan	Buttermilk Point (Reel)	INT	BOH
	The Garten Mother's Lullaby		
	The Heather Glen	MD	BOH
	(set of pieces from Herbert Hughes' collection of Irish Country Songs)		

Composer	Composition	Grade	Pub.
	The Green Bough	MD	BOH
Van Dyke, May	Barcarolle	MD	ASO
Vaughan Williams, Ralph	Introduction and Fugue	D	OXF
Viozzi, Giulio	Tempo de Samba	MD	BER
Walker, Ernest	Waltz Suite, op. 60		
	West African Fantasy, op. 53	MD	OXF
Weinberger, Jaromir	Polka and Fugue from *Schwanda*	MD	ASO
Wiener, Jean	Cadences (Jazz; Java; Tango Argentin; Final [*Paso Doble*])	MD	SAL
	Variations on a Hungarian Folk Song	MD	EMU
Williamson, Malcolm	Sonata for Two Pianos	VD	WEI
Wilm, Nicolai von	Variations, op. 64	MD	LEU
Wolff, Christian	Duo for Pianists 1 and 2	D	PET
Zabrack, Harold	Sonata for Two Pianos (a brilliant three-movement twelve-tone piece written in a very romantic style)	VD	KEN

COMPOSITIONS FOR TWO PIANOS AND ORCHESTRA

Composer	Composition	Pub.
Bach, C.P.E.	Concerto in E-flat major for Two Pianos and Orchestra	EUL
Bach, Johann Sebastian	Concerto in C minor for Two Pianos and Orchestra	KAL
	Concerto in C major for Two Pianos and Orchestra	PET
Britten, Benjamin	Scottish Ballad for Two Pianos and Orchestra	BOH
Martinu, Bohuslav	Concerto for Two Pianos and Orchestra	ASO
Mendelssohn, Felix	Concerto in A-flat major for Two Pianos and Orchestra	VDV
	Concerto in E major for Two Pianos and Orchestra	VDV
Mozart, Wolfgang Amadeus	Concerto in E-flat major for Two Pianos and Orchestra, K. 365	INT
Poulenc, Francis	Concerto in D minor for Two Pianos and Orchestra	SAL
Saint-Saëns, Camille	Carnival of the Animals	DUR
Vaughan Williams, Ralph	Concerto for Two Pianos and Orchestra	OXF

PUBLISHERS

Code	Publisher
AMC	American Music Center
AME	American Music Editions
AMS	AMSCO
APS	A.P. Schmidt
AOF	André-Offenbach
ASO	Associated
AUG	Augener (Galaxy)
BAR	M. Baron and Co.
BEL	Belwin-Mills
BER	Berben
BMC	Boston Music Company
BMI	BMI
BMT	Belmont
BOH	Boosey and Hawkes
BOK	Bote and Bock
BRE	Breitkopf & Härtel
BRM	British Museum
BRO	Broude
BRT	Barenreiter
CAR	Carousel
CBD	CBDM
CGB	Czech-Ger-GB
CHP	Chappell
CHS	Chester
CHU	John Church (Theodore Presser)
CLV	*Clavier* Magazine (October 1975)
COL	Columbia University Library
CON	Consolidated Music Publishers
COS	Costallat & Cie (Southern)
CPR	Composers Press
CUR	Curwen Associates (Schirmer)
DEL	Delkas Publishing
DEM	Demets
DIT	Oliver Ditson (Theodore Presser)
DOB	Doblinger
DON	Donemus
DUR	Durand
MTP	Music Treasure Publications
MUR	Murdoch
ELN	Elkin
ELV	Elkan-Vogel (Theodore Presser)
EMT	Edition Musicales Translatic
EMU	Editio Musica Budapest
ESG	Max Eschig
EUL	Eulenberg
FIS	Carl Fischer
FLM	Harold Flammer
FOL	Charles Foley
FOX	Sam Fox
FRO	Fromont
GEN	General Music
GER	Gerig HG
GSR	G. Schirmer
HAI	Hainauer
HAM	Hamelle
HAN	Hansen
HEI	Heinrichshofen
HEN	Henle
HEU	Heugel
IMI	Israel Music Institute
INT	International
JFIS	J. Fischer Bros.
JOB	Jean Jobert
JUR	Jurgenson
KAL	Kalmus
KEN	Kenyon Press
KIR	E. C. Kirby
KIS	Kistner
LBC	Library of Congress
LED	Alphonse Leduc
LEE	Leeds (MCA)
LEM	Henry Lemoine
LER	Rouart Lerolle
LEU	Leuckart
MAR	E. B. Marks
MAT	Mathot, Paris
MAU	Maurer
MCA	MCA
MER	Mercury
MLS	Mills
SCB	Schuberth & Company
SCL	Schlesinger
SCT	Schott

MUS	Editions Musicus
NOV	Novello
NWM	New World Music
OET	J. Oetri
OXF	Oxford University Press
PAN	Pan American
PAR	Paragon
PER	Peer International
PET	C. F. Peters
PRS	Theodore Presser
PWM	Polskie Wydawnictwo Muczcne
RIC	Ricordi
RSP	Russian State Publishing House
SAL	Salabert
SHW	Shawnee
SIK	Sikorski
SIM	Simrock
SOM	Southern
SPT	Spratt Music (Conn)
SUM	Summy-Birchard
TSL	Transatlantiques
UME	Union Musical Espagne
UNV	Universal
VDV	Veb Deutscher Verlag
WEI	Weinberger
WIT	Witmark & Sons (Warner Bros.)
WOL	W. Wollenweber
WTB	Weintraub
ZEN	Zenemükiadò (Editio Musica), Budapest

Addresses or affiliations of the above listed publishers may be obtained from one of the three performing rights societies listed on page 663.

Sonatinas and Sonatas: A Graded Annotated List

JOHN H. DIERCKS

Composers have used the term *sonata* for almost four centuries to describe works in various media, employing diverse forms and textures. As applied to the keyboard, *sonata* appears with increasing frequency after 1700. In the second half of the eighteenth century, a certain formal procedure crystallized in compositions so designated.

If the sonatas of J.C. Bach, Haydn, Clementi, Mozart, Beethoven, and their contemporaries demonstrate no overall conformity of pattern, in sum they established a classic procedural norm. Further, in writing such works, these composers and their successors through our own time entrusted some of their most considered and complex—and their noblest—thoughts to the medium of the piano sonata.

Sonatina usually indicates a piece of rather modest dimension, often technically easier and interpretively more accessible. While some consider sonatinas primarily a somewhat parenthetic preparation for embarking on the sonata literature, this outlook would seem a mistake. After surveying the riches of the genre, both teacher and player should feel satisfaction in programming the best of these works for their scope of expression as well as high intrinsic worth.

The prime factor in distinguishing sonatinas and sonatas is the designation chosen by the composer. The publisher's title may also be relevant, or, as in the case of Haydn, later determinations by music scholars. Because of these considerations, a few works may be found in an unexpected category. Selected piano ensemble music has also been included to represent this pleasurable medium. The Mozart Viennese sonatinas, later transcriptions of woodwind pieces, also appear. Inevitably, worthy compositions might not be shown.

The six sonatinas of Clementi's op. 36 set a standard few can surpass. They have dominated the style for two centuries, except for those pieces which have brought an especially individual, often national flavor to the form. Many fine contemporary examples exist. They are readily available for examination and effective use, and only a sampling need be given here. The Jon George collection is singled out as a particularly successful updating of earlier models.

This survey is organized by level of difficulty as determined by the most difficult sections of a work. Style and interpretive demands have also been taken into consideration. Clementi's op. 36 no. 1 (Level One) and Beethoven's op. 27 no. 2 (Level Ten) establish the outer limits for this listing.

These levels do not represent any given time span of study-performance, but suggest an approximate order in which works might be undertaken. The musical inclinations of those involved could well establish a different ordering; love for a composition or style can readily modify any type of *Gradus ad Parnassum* sequence.

When appropriate, details have been appended relative to the work's style, keyboard orientation, and length. The number following each entry provides a source of the music; it refers to the publishers and collections listed in Appendix I. Realistically it must be added that publishers, distributors, and titles change constantly. The reader must rely on individual research and a knowledgeable supplier to most easily locate desired compositions. Second-hand sources can often prove valuable. Some items go out of print; others will reappear.

For purposes of precise identification (where title, opus number, and/or key may not suffice), the following thematic catalogs have served as reference.

Bach, C.P.E.	Wotquenne (W)
Bach, J.S.	Schmieder (S)
Beethoven	Kinsky (K)
Clementi	Tyson (T)
Haydn	Hoboken (H)
Mozart	Köchel (K)
Scarlatti	Kirkpatrick (K) with Longo (L) equivalents
Schubert	Deutsch (D)

MAB-Artia has collected the charming Benda sonatinas. It provides the source for this numbering, as does the Eschig edition of thirty-two Cimarosa sonatas. The liberal representation of these composers stems from the possibility of grouping their rather brief essays into larger, contrasting program units.

SONATINAS

Note: Numbers in parentheses refer to standard sources of the works which follow; these are found on p.385. (See also "Recommended Editions of Standard Keyboard Literature," p. 437)

Level One

Classic

André: C major, 2 mvts. (1-vol. 1)
Attwood: G major (2)
Clementi: op. 36 no. 1, C major (3,4-vol. 2)
Czerny: op. 792 no. 8, C major, 3 mvts. (5-vol. 1)
Diabelli: op. 24 no. 1, C major, four hands (6)
Duncombe: C major, 3 mvts. (2)
Haslinger: C major, 2 mvts. (7, 8-vol. 1)
Latour: no. 1, C major (3, 7)
no. 2, G major (9-2A)
Türk: Little Sonata, F major (9-2B)

Romantic

Bertini: C major (5-vol. 1)
Biehl: op. 57 no. 1, C major, 2 mvts. (1-vol. 1, 9-2A)
Gurlitt: op. 76 no. 2, G major (11-67)
Köhler: op. 300, G major, 3 mvts. (1-vol. 1)
Reinecke: op. 136 no. 1, C major, 4 mvts. (11-67, 10)
op. 136 no. 2, G major, 3 mvts. (10)
Schmitt: G major (9-2A)
op. 207 no. 2, A major, 3 mvts. (11-67, 8-vol. 1)
op. 208 no. 1, A minor, 2 mvts. (3)
Spindler: op. 157 no. 1, C major (3, 4-vol. 1)
op. 157 no. 4, C major, 2 mvts. (4-vol. 3, 10)

Twentieth Century

Agay: no. 1, C major (9-2A)
George: nos. 1–6, C major, D minor, G major, F major and A major, A minor, D major and E major, 3 mvts. (12)
Green: March Sonatina, A major (13)
Johnson: op. 49 no. 1, G major, 3 mvts. (14)
op. 49 no. 2, D major, 3 mvts. (14)
Kadosa: C major, Allegro. (15)
Persichetti: no. 4, op. 63, C, 3 mvts. (16)
no. 5, op. 64, C, 2 mvts. (16)
no. 6, op. 65, C (16)
Sorokin: op. 5 no. 1, G major (3, 17)
op. 5 no. 3, A minor (17)

Level Two

Baroque

Handel: B-flat major (9-2B, 18)

Classic

André: G major (5-vol. 2)
Beethoven: F major (3, 4-vol. 2, 8-vol. 1)
G major (3, 4-vol. 1, 8, 11-27)

Benda: no. 3, A minor, Allegro (3, 19)
no. 10, F major, Allegretto (19)
no. 16, G minor, Allegro (19)
no. 17, D major, Presto (19)
no. 24, G major, Menuet (19)
no. 34, D major, Presto (11-67, 19)
Clementi: op. 36 no. 2, G major (20, 21)
Diabelli: op. 24 no. 2, G major, four hands (6)
op. 151 no. 1, G major (9-2B, 22)
op. 168 no. 2, G major (3,22)
Hook: D major, 3 mvts. (9-2B, 2)
G major, 2 mvts. (2)
Kuhlau: op. 55 no. 1, C major, 2 mvts. (3, 4-vol. 3, 8-vol. 1)
Pleyel: D major, 2 mvts. (7)
Türk: G major (23)

Romantic

Elgar: G major, 2 mvts. (24)
Gurlitt: op. 76 no. 5, A minor, 3 mvts. (1-vol. 1, 3)
Lichner: opp. 4, 49, 66, all 3 mvts. (A few ascend to Level Three; C major, F major, and G major prevail) (25)
Reinecke: op. 36 no. 2, G major, 3 mvts. (5-vol. 1)
op. 136 no. 4, A minor (1)
Schmitt: C major, 2 mvts. (9-2B)

Twentieth Century

Agay: Sonatina Toccata, C major (11-67)
Sonatina in Classic Style, D major, 3 mvts. (3)
Arányi: Sonatina for Children, C major, 3 mvts. (26)
Hajdú: F major, 2 mvts. (26)
Járdányi: F major, 2 mvts. (26)
Kabalevsky: A minor (3, 9-2B, 4-vol. 3)
Kadosa: B-flat (26)
C major, 3 mvts. (27)
Sorokin: D major, (9-2B)

Level Three

Baroque

Bach, C.P.E.: Six New Sonatinas no. 2, W. 63, E major (28, 29)
Six New Sonatinas no. 4, W. 63, B-flat major (9-2C)
Six New Sonatinas no. 6, W. 63, D minor (29)

Classic

Benda: no. 1, D major, Rondeau: Andante, $\frac{2}{4}$ (19)
no. 2, F major, Andantino, $\frac{3}{4}$ (no octaves) (19)
no. 6, D minor, Allegretto, $\frac{2}{4}$ (9-2C, 19)
no. 8, D major, Allegro assai, $\frac{3}{8}$ (19)
no. 9, F major, Andante quasi allegretto, $\frac{4}{4}$; followed by a variant, Tempo de Minuetto, $\frac{3}{4}$ (19)

no. 11, C major, Menuet, $\frac{3}{4}$ (19)
no. 14, A major, Allegro con spirito, $\frac{2}{4}$ (19)

Clementi: op. 36 no. 3, C major (4-vol. 3, 20, 21)
op. 36 no. 5, G major, (20, 21, 8-vol. 1)

Diabelli: op. 168, nos. 1, 3–6 (22)
op. 163, nos. 1–6, four hands, "The Pleasures of Youth" (though based "on five notes," the primo part requires individual articulation and characterization as well as sensitivity to ensemble; the secondo demands in addition more keyboard flexibility, hence it implies greater difficulty than Level Three) (49)

Kuhlau: op. 55 no. 2, G major (31)

Sander: G major, 3 mvts. (32)

Schilling: B-flat major, 2 mvts. (32)

Türk: F major, 3 mvts. (32)

Romantic

Lichner: op. 49 no. 2, G major, 3 mvts. (25)

Reinecke: op. 47 no. 1, C major, 3 mvts. (33)

Schytte: op. 76 no. 4, F major (5-vol. 5)

Weber: op. 3 no. 1, C major, four hands (lower part about Level Five) (34, 35)

Twentieth Century

Agay: Folk Tune Sonatina (9-2C)

Koch: no. 1, F major, 3 mvts. (36)

Reiman: Circus Sonatina (3)

Sorokin: op. 5 no. 3, A minor (11-67)

Stravinsky, S.: no. 1, 3 mvts. (37)
no. 2, 2 mvts. (37)
no. 3, Fantasia piccola (unbarred right-hand solo), Marcia, Epilogue (left-hand solo) (37)
no. 4, Fanfare, Plainchant, Bourrée d'Auvergne (38)

Székely: A minor, 3 mvts. (26)

Level Four

Baroque

Handel: A minor, Allegretto, $\frac{3}{4}$ (4-vol. 4)
D minor, Allegro, $\frac{12}{8}$ (39)

Classic

Benda: no. 21, F major, Allegretto moderato, $\frac{2}{4}$ (19)
no. 26, C major, Andantino quasi un poco allegretto, $\frac{2}{4}$ (19)
no. 28, C major, Tempo di Minuetto, $\frac{3}{4}$ (19)
no. 32, A major, Rondeau: Andante con moto, quasi mezzo allegretto, $\frac{2}{4}$ (rather Mozartean) (19)

Clementi: op. 36 no. 4, F major (23, 20, 21)
op. 37 and op. 38 are popularly published as a group of three sonatinas each; they would generally fall here or in Level Five (20, 21)

Diabelli: op. 151 no. 4, C major (22)
op. 168 no. 7, A minor (22)
Wolf, G.F.: D major, 3 mvts. (9-2C)

Romantic

Glazunov: A minor, Andantino, $\frac{3}{4}$ (the extensions required in the left hand, despite possible facilitation, make this attractive piece more difficult than it first appears) (3)
Gurlitt: op. 54 no. 4, D major, 3 mvts. (10)

Twentieth Century

Dahl: Sonatina alla marcia (each two-page movement may be played separately and is available separately) (40)
Alla marcia moderato, E-flat major, $\frac{2}{4}$
Alla marcia funebre, C minor, $\frac{4}{4}$
Alla marcia allegro, E-flat major, $\frac{6}{8}$
Decsenyi: G major, 3 mvts. (26)
Hajdu: D major (based on Hungarian folktunes), 3 mvts. (26)
Hovhaness: op. 120, 3 mvts. (60)
Sárai: D major, 3 mvts. (26)
Stravinsky, S.: no. 5, Quodlibet, Badinage, Rondino (38)
Szervánszky: D major, four hands (41)
Szokolay: E minor, 3 mvts. (26)

Level Five

Baroque

Bach, C.P.E.: Six New Sonatinas no. 3, W. 63, D major (28)

Classic

Beethoven: WoO 51, C major, 1 mvt., Allegro, $\frac{4}{4}$ (42)
Benda: no. 4, C major, Mezzo allegro con variazioni, $\frac{4}{4}$ (19)
Clementi: op. 36 no. 6, D major (20, 21)
Diabelli: op. 151 no. 3, F major (22)
Dussek: op. 20 no. 1, G major, 2 mvts. (9-2C, 43, 44)
Kuhlau: op. 20 no. 1, C major (31)
op. 20 no. 2, G major (31)
op. 55 no. 4, F major (31)
op. 55 no. 5, D major (31)
op. 88 no. 1, C major (10, 43)
op. 88 no. 2, G major (43, 8-vol. 1)
op. 88 no. 3, A minor (43)
Mozart: Six Viennese Sonatinas, C major, A major, D major, B-flat major, F major, and C major (45, 46) (numerous editorial differences exist between the two sources, but in total they would seem of equal value)

Romantic

Handrock: "Spring" Sonatina, F major (9-2C)

Twentieth Century

Agay: no. 3, 3 mvts. (Level Six at a fast tempo) (47)
Kurka: Sonatina for Young Persons, op. 40 (48)

Satie: *Sonatina bureaucratique*, A major, 3 mvts. (based on the Clementi op. 36 no. 1) (61)
Stravinsky, S.: no. 6, 3 mvts. (on themes of Machaut) (38)

Level Six

Classic
Beethoven: WoO 47 no. 1, E-flat major, 3 mvts. (42)
Benda: no. 13, C minor, Allegro non troppo, $\frac{6}{8}$ (19)
Kuhlau: op. 20 no. 3, F major (31)
op. 55 no. 3, C major, 2 mvts. (9-2C, 8-vol. 1, 31)

Twentieth Century
Calabro: Young People's Sonatina, 3 mvts. (62)
Khatchaturian: C major, 3 mvts. (49, 50)
Templeton: Sonatina Ballade, 1 mvt. (not for small hands) (51)

Level Seven

Classic
Beethoven: WoO 47 no. 2, F minor, 3 mvts. (42)
Kuhlau: op. 55 no. 6, C major, 2 mvts. (31)
op. 59 no. 1, A major, 2 mvts. (31)

Romantic
Kirchner: op. 70 no. 1, C major, 3 mvts. (8-vol. 1)
op. 70 no. 3, C major, 3 mvts. (8-vol. 2)

Twentieth Century
Agay: Sonatina Hungarica, 3 mvts. (requires stylistic identification and flair) (52)
Kabalevsky: op. 13 no. 1, C major (53, 49, 50)
op. 13 no. 2, G major (49)

Level Eight

Classic
Beethoven: WoO 47 no. 3, D major, 3 mvts. (42)

Romantic
Goetz: op. 8 no. 1, F major (54)
op. 8 no. 2, E-flat major (54)

Twentieth Century
Bartók: D major, 3 mvts. (55)
Gretchaninoff: no. 1, G (56)
no. 2, F (8-vol. 2, 56)
Kadosa: op. 11b, 2 mvts. (brief, intense) (55)

Level Nine

Twentieth Century
Busoni: no. 3, *ad usum infantis* (57)
no. 5, Sonatina brevis (after Bach) (57)

Level Ten

Twentieth Century

Busoni: no. 4, *in Diem Nativitatis Christi* (57)
Casella: Sonatina *in tre tempi* (the reach of a tenth is requisite) (51)
Guarnieri: no. 3, F major, 3 mvts. (in the treble clef) (58)
Okumura: no. 5, 3 mvts. (59)
Ravel: F-sharp, 3 mvts. (53, 49, 50)

SONATAS

Level One

The compiler recognizes that sonatas at Level One exist; however, sonatinas of fine quality might better serve at this stage of development.

Level Two

Baroque

Scarlatti: K. 32 (L. 423), D minor, Allegretto, $\frac{3}{8}$ (1)
K. 34 (L.S. 7), D minor, Larghetto, $\frac{3}{4}$ (1)
K. 73b (L. 217), C major, Allegro, $\frac{3}{8}$ (1)
K. 73c (L. 217), C minor, Allegro, $\frac{3}{8}$ (1)
K. 80 G major, "Minuet," Allegro, $\frac{3}{8}$ (1)
K. 431 (L. 83), G major, Allegro, $\frac{3}{4}$ (1, 2-37)

Classic

Cimarosa: no. 19, B-flat major, Allegro, $\frac{6}{8}$ (3-vol. 2)
no. 23, A minor, Largo, $\frac{6}{8}$ (3-vol. 3)

Twentieth Century

Thomson: no. 3, C, 4 mvts. (requires an octave span) (4)

Level Three

Baroque

Arne: no. 5, B-flat major, 2 mvts. (5)
no. 6, G minor, 2 mvts. (5)
Handel: C major (6)
Scarlatti: K. 415 (L. 11), D major, "Pastorale," Allegro, $\frac{12}{8}$ (1)

Classic

Cimarosa: no. 11, B-flat major, Allegro, $\frac{3}{8}$ (3-vol. 2)
no. 14, G major, Allegro, $\frac{3}{8}$ (3-vol. 2)
Haydn: H.16/7, C major, 3 mvts. (7-2C, 8-vol. 4, 9-vol. 1a, 10)
H. 16/8, G major, 4 mvts. (9-vol. 1a, 10, 11-vol. 1)
H. 16/9, F major, 3 mvts. (9-vol. 1a, 10)
Newman: op. 1 no. 1, C major, 3 mvts. (13)

Romantic

Glazunov: "Easy" Sonata, G major (some facilitation necessary for smaller hands; strong ending) (14)

Level Four

Baroque

Bach, C.P.E.: W. 62, G major, 3 mvts. (2-67)

Handel: A major, Vivo, $\frac{4}{4}$ (15)
Scarlatti: K. 284 (L. 90), G major, Allegro, $\frac{3}{8}$ (2-47)
K. 322 (L. 483), A major, Allegro, $\frac{3}{2}$ (16)
Soler: C major, Andantino, $\frac{2}{4}$ (15)

Classic

Beethoven: op. 49 no. 1, G minor (11-vol. 2)
op. 49 no. 2, G major (17, 8-vol. 4, 11-vol. 1)
Cimarosa: no. 13, B-flat major, Andantino, $\frac{3}{4}$ (3-vol. 2)
no. 17, B-flat major, Allegro alla francese, $\frac{2}{2}$ (2-67, 3-vol. 2)
Clementi: T. op. 14, three sonatas for four hands, C major, F major, and E-flat major (18)
Haydn: H. 16/2, B-flat major, 3 mvts. (9-vol. 1a)
H. 16/10, C major, 3 mvts. (9-vol. 1a, 10, 11-vol. 2)
H. 16/12, A major, 3 mvts. (9-vol. 1a)
H. 16/G1, G major, 3 mvts. (9-vol. 1a)
H. 17/D1, D major, 3 mvts. (9-vol. 1a)

Romantic

Schumann: op. 118 no. 1, "To Julia," G major, 4 mvts. (19)

Level Five

Baroque

Kirnberger: G major, Moderato assai, $\frac{2}{4}$ (11-vol. 2, 30)
Platti: C major, 4 mvts. (20)
Scarlatti: K. 309 (L. 454), C major, Allegro, $\frac{2}{2}$ (21, 22-vol. 2)
K. 430 (L. 463), D major, Non presto, ma a tempo di ballo, $\frac{3}{8}$ (21)
K. 446 (L. 433), "Pastorale," F major, Allegrissimo, $\frac{12}{8}$ (21)
K. 544 (L. 497), B-flat major, Cantabile, $\frac{3}{4}$ (21)

Classic

Bach, J.C.: op. 5 no. 1, B-flat major, 2 mvts. (2-67, 24)
Cimarosa: no. 4, B-flat major, Allegro, $\frac{4}{4}$ (3-vol. 1)
no. 8, C major, Allegro, $\frac{4}{4}$ (3-vol. 1)
no. 10, B-flat major, Maestoso, $\frac{4}{4}$ (3-vol. 1)
no. 15, G major, Allegro, $\frac{3}{8}$ (3-vol. 2)
no. 18, D major, Allegro, $\frac{2}{2}$ (3-vol. 2)
no. 20, B-flat minor and major, Andantino, $\frac{4}{4}$; Allegro assai, $\frac{6}{8}$ (3-vol. 2)
no. 22, D minor, Andante, $\frac{2}{2}$ (3-vol. 3)
no. 26, G minor, Largo (to the eighth note), $\frac{4}{4}$ (3-vol. 3)
no. 29, C minor, Larghetto, $\frac{4}{4}$ (3-vol. 3)
no. 31, G major, Allegro, $\frac{4}{4}$ (3-vol. 3)
Clementi: T. op. 10 no. 2, D major, 2 mvts. (25-vol. 8)
T. op. 3, three sonatas for four hands, C major, E-flat major, and G major (18)
T. oeuvre 1, no. 6, Duo Sonata in B-flat major, 2 mvts. (26)
Haydn: H. 16/6, G major, 4 mvts. (9-vol. 1a)
H. 16/24, D major, 3 mvts. (9-vol. 2)
Moller: D major, Allegro, $\frac{3}{4}$ (13)

Mozart: K. 358, B-flat major, four hands, 3 mvts. (27)
K. 381, D major, four hands, 3 mvts. (27)
K. 545, C major, (17, 8-vol. 4)
Wolf, E.W.: E major, 3 mvts. (2-67)

Twentieth Century

Thomson: no. 2, 3 mvts. (28)
no. 4. (4)

Level Six

Baroque

Bach, C.P.E.: W. 48, Six "Prussian" Sonatas, no. 1, F major, 3 mvts. (29)
Paradies: no. 6, A major, 2 mvts. (second movement able to stand alone) (45)
Scarlatti: K. 9 (L. 413), D minor, Allegro, $\substack{6\\8}$ (21)
K. 380 (L. 23), E major, Andantino, $\substack{3\\4}$ (2-67)
Soler: no. 84, D major, Allegro, $\substack{3\\8}$ (30)

Classic

Beethoven: op. 6, D major, four hands, 2 mvts. (31)
Cimarosa: no. 21, F major, Allegro, $\substack{4\\4}$ (3-vol. 3)
no. 28, B-flat major, "Perfide," Vivacissimo, $\substack{2\\2}$ (3-vol. 3)
Clementi: T. op. 10 no. 3, B-flat major, 3 mvts. (25-vol. 8)
T. op. 12 no. 5, Duo Sonata, B-flat major, 3 mvts. (26)
T. op. 13 no. 4, B-flat major, 3 mvts. (25-vol. 10)
T. op. 25 no. 2, G major, 2 mvts. (25-vol. 2)
Hassler: Six Easy Sonatas, no. 5, F major, 3 mvts. (17)
Haydn: H. 16/21, C major, 3 mvts. (the first movement is particularly beautiful and comfortable for smaller hands) (9-vol. 2)
H. 16/23, F major, 3 mvts. (2-67, 9-vol. 2)
H. 16/35, C major, 3 mvts. (9-vol. 2, many others)

Romantic

Grieg: Second-piano part to Mozart's Sonata K. 545, 3 mvts. (large hand, as well as sensitivity, requisite to bring off this curious stylistic marriage) (33)

Twentieth Century

Miaskovsky: op. 83, D minor, 3 mvts. (34)

Level Seven

Baroque

Kuhnau: Biblical Sonata no. 5, Gideon, the Deliverer of Israel, 7 mvts. (35) (others in this series of six sonatas are available complete from Broude or separately from Peters)
Scarlatti: K. 3 (L. 378), A minor, Presto, $\substack{2\\2}$ (for great tempo and style, a higher level) (21)
K. 11 (L. 352), C minor, Allegro, $\substack{4\\4}$ (21)
K. 159 (L. 104), C major, Allegro, $\substack{6\\8}$ (21, 2-47)
K. 381 (L. 225), E major, Allegro, $\substack{3\\8}$ (36-vol. 8)
K. 471 (L. 82), G major, Minuet, $\substack{3\\4}$ (22-vol. 2)

K. 477 (L. 290), G major, Allegrissimo, $\frac{6}{8}$ (22-vol. 2)
K. 531 (L. 430), E major, Allegro, $\frac{6}{8}$ (22-vol. 2)

Classic

Bach, J.C.: op. 17 no. 5, A major, 2 mvts. (23-vol. 1)
op. 18 no. 6, F major, four hands, 2 mvts. (37)
Cimarosa: no. 1, C minor, Allegro giusto, $\frac{4}{4}$ (3-vol. 1)
no. 30, D major, Allegro, $\frac{4}{4}$ (3-vol. 3)
Clementi: T. op. 10 no. 1, A major, 3 mvts. (25-vol. 8)
T. op. 11, E-flat major, 3 mvts. (25-vol. 6)
Haydn: H. 16/32, B minor, 3 mvts. (9-vol. 2)
H. 16/34, E minor, 3 mvts. (9-vol. 3)
H. 16/37, D major, 3 mvts. (17, 9-vol. 2)
H. 16/51, D major, 2 mvts. (9-vol. 3)
Holder: E-flat major, 3 mvts. (24)
Mozart: K. 312, G minor, 1 mvt. (2-47)
Pleyel: op. 7 no. 1, B-flat major, 3 mvts. (24)

Romantic

Schumann: op. 118 no. 2, "To Eliza," D major, 4 mvts. (19)

Twentieth Century

Poulenc: Sonata for four hands, 3 mvts. (38)

Level Eight

Baroque

Scarlatti: K. 14 (L. 387), G major, Presto, $\frac{12}{8}$ (21)
K. 26 (L. 368), D major, Presto, $\frac{3}{8}$ (21)
K. 274 (L. 297), F major, Andante, $\frac{2}{2}$ (36-vol. 6)
K. 374 (L. 76), G minor, Presto e fugato, $\frac{2}{2}$ (36-vol. 8)
K. 395 (L. 65), E major, Allegro, $\frac{3}{8}$ (22-vol. 2)
K. 403 (L. 470), E major, Allegro, $\frac{6}{8}$ (22-vol. 2)
K. 420 (L S. 2), C major, Allegro, $\frac{2}{2}$ (22-vol. 2)

Classic

Bach, J.C.: op. 5 no. 2, D major, 3 mvts. (23-vol. 1)
op. 17 no. 2, C minor, 3 mvts. (23-vol. 1)
Beethoven: op. 14 no. 1, E major, 3 mvts. (17)
op. 79, G major, 3 mvts.
Buée: no. 2, A minor, 3 mvts. (24)
Clementi: T. op. 6 no. 2, E-flat major, 2 mvts. (25-vol. 3)
T. op. 8 no. 1, G minor, 3 mvts. (25-vol. 1)
T. op. 23 no 1, E-flat major, 2 mvts. (25-vol. 1)
T. op. 25 no. 3, B-flat major, 2 mvts. (25-vol. 2)
T. op. 25 no. 6, D major, 3 mvts. (2-67, 32-vol. 1) (listed as "op. 26 no. 3")
T. op. 33 no. 1, A major, 2 mvts. (32-vol. 1) (listed as "op. 36 no. 1")
T. op. 34 no. 1, C major, 3 mvts. (32-vol. 1)
T. op. 37 no. 3, D major, 3 mvts. (25-vol. 9)
Haydn: H. 16/29, F major, 3 mvts. (9-vol. 2)

Mozart: K. 282, E-flat major, 3 mvts.
K. 283, G major, 3 mvts. (2-67)
de Nebra: op. 1 no. 4, G minor, 2 mvts. (24)
Reinagle: no. 1, D major, 2 mvts. (13)
Turini: no. 6, D-flat major, 3 mvts. (39)

Romantic

Schumann: op. 118, no. 3, "To Mary," C major, 4 mvts. (19)

Twentieth Century

Hovhaness: op. 145, 3 mvts. (40)

Level Nine

Baroque

Bach, C.P.E.: W. 63, F minor, (41)
Scarlatti: K. 14 (L. 387), G major, Presto, $\frac{12}{8}$ (21)
K. 175 (L. 429), A minor, Allegro, $\frac{2}{4}$ (36-vol. 4)
K. 276 (L.S. 20), F major, Allegro, $\frac{3}{8}$ (36-vol. 6)
K. 513 (L.S. 3), G major, "Pastorale," Moderato, Molto allegro, Presto, $\frac{12}{8}$ (22-vol. 2)
K. 544 (L. 497), B-flat major, Cantabile, $\frac{3}{4}$ (22-vol. 2)

Classic

Bach, J.C.: op. 17 no. 6, B-flat major, 3 mvts. (23-vol. 2)
Beethoven: op. 2 no. 1, F-minor, 4 mvts.
Clementi: T. op. 9 no. 1, B-flat major, 3 mvts. (25-vol. 6)
T. op. 13 no 6, F minor, 3 mvts. (25-vol. 10, 42)
T. op. 20, C major, 3 mvts. (25-vol. 6)
T. op. 24 no. 1, F major, 3 mvts. (25-vol. 8)
T. op. 24 no. 2, B-flat major, 3 mvts. (25-vol. 6, 32-vol. 2)
T. op. 37 no. 2, G major, 3 mvts. (25-vol. 9)
T. WO 3, F major, 2 mvts. (25-vol. 3)
Haydn: H. 16/50, C major, 3 mvts. (9-vol. 3)
Mozart: K. 547a, F major, 3 mvts.
K. 570, B-flat major, 3 mvts. (17)

Romantic

Schubert: op. 164 (D. 537), A minor, 3 mvts. (43-vol. 2)

Twentieth Century

Kabalevsky: no. 3, F major, 3 mvts. (2-67, 44)
Stravinsky: Sonata for Two Pianos, 3 mvts. (45)

Level Ten

Baroque

Bach, C.P.E.: W. 49, "Württemberg" Sonata no. 1, A minor, 3 mvts. (46)
W. 55, A major, 3 mvts. (47)
Scarlatti: K. 13, (L. 486), G major, Presto, $\frac{2}{4}$
K. 96, (L. 465), D major, Allegro, $\frac{3}{8}$ (21)
K. 113, (L. 345), A major, Allegrissimo, $\frac{2}{2}$ (21)

Classic

Bach, J.C.: op. 5 no. 6, C minor, 3 mvts. (23-vol. 2)

op. 17 no. 3, E-flat major, 2 mvts. (23-vol. 2)

Beethoven: op. 7, E-flat major, 4 mvts. (the Largo, elegant and elevated, could well stand by itself)
op. 10 no. 1, C minor, 3 mvts. (2-67)
op. 13, C minor, 3 mvts. (17)
op. 14 no. 2, G major, 3 mvts.
op. 26, A-flat major, 4 mvts.
op. 27 no. 2, C-sharp minor, 3 mvts.

Clementi: T. op. 37 no. 1, C major, 3 mvts. (25-vol. 9)
T. op. 41 no. 1, E-flat major, 3 mvts. (25-vol. 6)

Haydn: H. 16/49, E-flat major, 3 mvts. (9-vol. 3)
H. 16/52, E-flat major, 3 mvts. (9-vol. 3)

Mozart: K. 279, C major, 3 mvts.
K. 280, F major, 3 mvts. (17)
K. 281, B-flat major, 3 mvts.
K. 284, D major, 3 mvts.
K. 310, A minor, 3 mvts.
K. 311, D major, 3 mvts.
K. 330, C major, 3 mvts.
K. 331, A major, 3 mvts.
K. 332, F major, 3 mvts.
K. 333, B-flat major, 3 mvts.
K. 547, C minor, 3 mvts.

Romantic

Grieg: op. 7, E minor, 4 mvts. (2-67, 48)

Schubert: op. 120 (D. 664), A major, 3 mvts. (2-67, 43-vol. 1)
op. 122 (D. 568), E-flat major, 4 mvts. (43-vol. 1)
op. 147 (D. 575), B major, 4 mvts. (43-vol. 1)

Scriabin: Sonata-Fantaisie, G-sharp minor (1886) (49)

Twentieth Century

Hovhaness: op. 12, Sonata Ricercare, 3 mvts. (50)
op. 175, "Lake of Van" Sonata, 3 mvts. (50)
op. 176, "Madras" Sonata, 3 mvts. (50)
op. 192, "Bardo" Sonata, 3 mvts. (50)

Ives: *Concord* Sonata, "The Alcotts" mvt. (51)

Prokofiev: no. 2, D minor (comfortable for players who reach just an octave) (52)

The organization of the foregoing pieces into levels has attempted to ameliorate (but not ignore) a certain pressure, felt particularly with the sonatas of Mozart and Beethoven, to perform all music with complete "stylistic authenticity," often adding greatly to its difficulty. Great joy and a feeling of communication may come to the player aware of but not unduly subservient to this concept. Also, other fine classic composers should not be constrained to lurk in the masters' shadows. Increasingly good performance editions reveal the riches of sonata production in this period.

Further, a study of contemporary performance practices should encourage a sensible excerpting of "easier" movements from longer works, as with the song movements of Beethoven's op. 13 and op. 27 no. 2—and even the opening of the op. 101. This would seem eminently feasible, at times rescuing music of great beauty (as in op. 7) from a problematic whole.

Although most levels reflect the uppermost limit of a work, many sonatas exist which may prove as accessible as Beethoven's "Moonlight." Some demand yet more maturity, but possibly less facility and stamina; others may require a different stylistic orientation, or a special state of mind and emotion. Examples from the standard repertory include the following. (Some of the greatest creations in the literature by Beethoven, Schubert, Schumann, Chopin, Liszt, Scriabin, Prokofiev, and more contemporary composers go still beyond the technical limits of this listing.)

Beethoven: op. 2 no. 2, A major
op. 2 no. 3, C major
op. 10 no. 2, F major
op. 10 no. 3, D major
op. 22, B-flat major
op. 27 no. 1, E-flat major
op. 28, D major
op. 31 no. 1, G major
op. 31 no. 2, D minor
op. 31 no. 3, E-flat major
op. 78, F-sharp major
op. 90, E minor (a large hand facilitates first movement)
Clementi: T. op. 7 no. 3, G minor (25-vol. 1)
T. op. 33 no. 2 ("op. 36 no. 2")
T. op. 40 no. 1 (32-vol. 2)
Dello Joio: no. 3 (Carl Fischer)
Elwell: 3 mvts. (Oxford University Press)
Ginastera: 4 mvts. (Boosey & Hawkes)
Hindemith: no. 2 (Schott)
MacDowell: no. 3, D minor (Kalmus)
Mozart: K. 309, C major
K. 457, C minor
K. 533/494, F major
K. 576, D major (Broder—Theodore Presser)
Prokofiev: nos. 1 (Kalmus) and 3 (Kalmus and Agay 2-67)
Scarlatti: Many in the two volumes edited by Ralph Kirkpatrick (G. Schirmer)
Scriabin: no. 2, G-sharp minor, 2 mvts. (International)
Shapero: Three Sonatas (G. Schirmer)
Stravinsky: Sonata (Boosey & Hawkes)

The literature for piano and orchestra requires not only keyboard facility, but also the soloist's capability for informed, sensitive ensemble performance. As a concerted effort, it demands very high competence of all players. From this standpoint, the following works (in varying degrees, and not graded by level) might be considered relatively accessible.

Concertos

Bach, J.C.: op. 13 no. 2, D major
op. 13 no. 4, B-flat major
Bach, J.S.: no. 1, S. 1052, D minor
no. 5, S. 1056, F minor
S. 1060, C minor, two pianos
S. 1061, C major, two pianos
Beethoven: op. 19 no. 2, B-flat major
Bloch: Concerto grosso no. 1 (piano and strings)
Gershwin: Rhapsody in Blue
Haydn: H. 18/11, D major
Kabalevsky: op. 50 no. 3, D major, "Youth"
Mendelssohn: op. 25 no. 1, G minor
op. 40 no. 2, D minor
Mozart: K. 466, no. 20, D minor
K. 488, no. 23, A major
Prokofiev: op. 10 no. 1, D-flat major
Saint-Saëns: Carnival of the Animals, two pianos
Shostakovich: op. 35 no. 1
op. 102 no. 2

APPENDIX 1: SOURCES FOR SONATINAS

(Note: Abbreviations of publishers-distributors are explained at the end of the chapter.)

(1) Zeitlin, Poldi and David Goldberger. *The Sonatina Book,* four volumes. CMP.
(2) Rowley, Alec. *Early English Sonatinas*. Boosey
(3) Agay, Denes. *The Joy of Sonatinas*. YMP.
(4) Bastien, James and Jane. *Piano Literature*, four volumes. General Words and Music Co.
(5) Podolsky, Leo. *Select Sonatinas*, five volumes. BM.
(6) SL of MC # 187.
(7) Palmer, Willard. *The First Sonatina Book*. Alfred.
(8) Frey, Martin, ed. *Das neue Sonatinen Buch*, two volumes, Schott, nos. 2511 and 2512.
(9) Agay, Denes. *Sonatinas*, three volumes (*The Young Pianist's Library*, nos. 2/A-B-C). Warner.
(10) SL of MC # 1594.
(11) Agay, Denes. *Classics to Moderns*, five volumes, *Music for Millions* nos. 17-27-37-47-67-77. CMP.
(12) *Six Sonatinas*. Alfred.
(13) American Music Edition.
(14) Puget Music Publications.
(15) EMB (separately).

(16) EV, through TP. (4-6 in 1 vol.).
(17) *The Library of a Young Piano-Player* (from 2nd to 5th class of the Children's Music School), Moscow #1428.
(18) Lucktenburg, George. *Handel.* Alfred.
(19) MAB-Artia.
(20) Kalmus. op. 36: #3300; opp. 36, 37, 38: #3301. From BM.
(21) SL of MC. #811 for op. 36; #40 for opp. 36–38.
(22) SL of MC #266.
(23) Agay, Denes. *The Classical Period* (*Anthology of Piano Music*, vol. 2). YMP.
(24) Keith Prowse & Co., London, distributed by Sam Fox.
(25) SL of MC. #989, "Nine Sonatinas."
(26) EMB #3594.
(27) EMB #1280.
(28) Agay, Denes. *The Joy of Baroque*. YMP.
(29) Clark, Frances. *Piano Literature*, vol. 5a-6a. Summy-Birchard.
(30) Kalmus #3398. From BM.
(31) SL of MC #52.
(32) Kreutz, Alfred, ed. *Clavier-Sonatinen für Liebhaber und ungeubte Spieler*. Schott #3765.
(33) SL of MC #1595. "Selected Sonatinas."
(34) Lyke, James. *Ensemble Music for Group Piano*, 2nd rev. ed. Stipes Publishing Co., Champaign, Ill.
(35) UE #10. *Complete Works for Piano Four-hands*.
(36) Seesaw, through GS.
(37) Peters 6590A.
(38) Peters 6590B.
(39) Agay, Denes. *The Baroque Period* (*Anthology of Piano Music*, vol. 1). YMP.
(40) *Contemporary Piano Music by Distinguished Composers*, through TP.
(41) EMB #9641.
(42) Kalmus #3199. Sonatinas, complete. Through BM.
(43) Kalmus #3417. Sonatinas, op. 20. Through BM.
(44) SL of MC #41. Six Sonatinas, op. 20.
(45) Heritage Music Publications (Mercury); Felix Guenther, ed.
(46) SL of MC #1797; Joseph Prostakoff, ed.
(47) Sam Fox.
(48) Weintraub.
(49) Kalmus, by title.
(50) GS, by title.
(51) Ricordi, possibly available only second-hand.
(52) MCA, through BM.
(53) Agay, Denes. *The Twentieth Century* (*Anthology of Piano Music*, vol. 4). YMP.
(54) Music Treasure Publications, P.O. Box 127, Highbridge Station, Bronx, N.Y. 10452.
(55) Boosey.

(56) Schott.
(57) Br & H.
(58) AMP.
(59) Kawai Gakufu.
(60) Peters.
(61) Salabert.
(62) EV, through TP.
(63) SL of MC #1596.

APPENDIX 2: SOURCES FOR SONATAS

(Note: Abbreviations of publishers-distributors are explained at the end of this chapter.)

(1) Alfred. *Scarlatti.*
(2) Agay, Denes. *Classics to Moderns*, five volumes, *Music for Millions* nos. 17-27-37-47-67. CMP.
(3) Eschig. Cimarosa Sonatas, in three volumes.
(4) Mercury.
(5) Augener. Pauer, ed.
(6) Clark, Frances. *Piano Literature*, vol. 5a-6a. Summy-Birchard.
(7) Agay, Denes. Sonatinas, three volumes (*The Young Pianist's Library*, nos. 2/A-B-C.)
(8) Bastien, James and Jane. *Piano Literature*, four volumes. General Words and Music Co.
(9) Landon, Christa. Haydn Sonatas, three volumes. VUE.
(10) Palmer, Willard. *Haydn*. Alfred.
(11) Frey, Martin, ed. *Das neue Sonatinen Buch*, two volumes. Schott, nos. 2511 and 2512.
(12) For Haydn sonatas, see also the Martienssen edition of 43 works. CFP.
(13) McClenny, Anne and Maurice Hinson. *Collection of Early American Keyboard Music*. Willis.
(14) Zeitlin, Poldi and David Goldberger. *Russian Music*, vol. 4. MCA.
(15) Agay, Denes. *The Joy of Baroque*. YMP.
(16) Ferguson, Howard. *Style and Interpretation*, vol. 2. Oxford.
(17) Agay, Denes. *The Classical Period* (*Anthology of Piano Music*, vol. 2). YMP.
(18) SL of MC #1796.
(19) GS.
(20) 12 Sonatas. Br&H.
(21) 60 Sonatas. Kalmus.
(22) SL of MC #1774 and #1775.
(23) 10 Sonatas, in two volumes. CFP.
(24) Smart, James. *Keyboard Sonatas of the 18th Century*. GS.
(25) *Collected Works of Muzio Clementi*, 13 volumes (Br&H); reprinted in five volumes. (Da Capo)–1. vols. 1 and 2; 2. vols. 3 and 4; 3. vols. 5, 6, and 7; 4. vols. 8, 9, and 10; 5. vols. 11, 12, and 13.
(26) SL of MC #1532.

(27) CFP, Kalmus.
(28) American Music Center, New York.
(29) Kalmus, by title.
(30) Agay, Denes. *The Baroque Period* (*Anthology of Piano Music*, vol. 1). YMP.
(31) Int, CFP.
(32) 12 Sonatas, SL of MC #385 and 386.
(33) SL of MC #1440.
(34) #23018 of USSR (Schirmer).
(35) Alfred, Margery Halford, ed.
(36) Heugel, 11 volumes, Kenneth Gilbert, ed.
(37) CFP #4516.
(38) Chester.
(39) *Les Maitres du clavecin*, Kohler-Litolff, ed.
(40) CFP.
(41) *Sechs Sonatinen*. Schott #2354.
(42) EBM, three volumes, Mirovitch, ed.
(43) Sonatas, in two volumes. Kalmus.
(44) Separately by Kalmus, MCA, CFP, GS.
(45) AMP.
(46) Kalmus, vol. 1.
(47) Br&H #4401.
(48) Br&H.
(49) Music Treasure Publications, P.O. Box 127, Highbridge Station, Bronx, N.Y. 10452.
(50) CFP, by title.
(51) Agay, Denes. *The Twentieth Century* (*Anthology of Piano Music*, vol. 4). YMP.
(52) Kalmus (separately).

ABBREVIATIONS

AMP	Associated Music Publishers
BM	Belwin-Mills
Br&H	Breitkopf & Härtel
CMP	Consolidated Music Publishers
EMB	Editio Musica Budapest
EV	Elkan-Vogel, through TP
GS	G. Schirmer
MAB	Musica Antiqua Bohemica
SL of MC	Schirmer's Library of Musical Classics
TP	Theodore Presser
UE	Universal Edition
VUE	Vienna Urtext Edition
YMP	Yorktown Music Press

Twentieth-Century Music for the Developing Pianist: A Graded Annotated List

JUDITH LANG ZAIMONT

In exploring the literature of our time, even the most eager and sympathetic pianist or teacher may become bewildered by the wide array of publications available. Two main factors contribute to the confusion: an abundance of clearly-differentiated styles are used interchangeably by many composers; and publishers of both "educational" and "concert" music tend to think of their individual markets as distinct and mutually exclusive, thus creating problems for anyone whose interest in current serious music is quite general in nature.

Added to these, of course, is the reality of our position in time: for us, the "verdict" regarding most of the music written within the last sixty or so years is still pending. Until the sieve of history filters out the masterworks, many of us may find it difficult to form conclusive opinions about the relative merits of any single composition, particularly in terms of its suitability as a piece for long-term study.

Thus from the standpoint of the individual pianist or teacher who may not have the advantage of generous amounts of money and time with which to conduct a personal search for worthy representative works, the lack of sustained, general guidance is sorely felt.

Columns of new music reviews in *The Piano Quarterly, Clavier,* and other periodicals are useful in clearing away some of the confusion. Similarly, graded lists of suggested repertory issued by national, state, or local music organizations are distinctly helpful. With a view toward providing a more comprehensive guide of the same type, the author has compiled a basic library of twentieth-century piano music, using a format which permits the inclusion of descriptive notes for every title listed.

CRITERIA FOR INCLUSION

The list contains music originally written for the piano. It is restricted for reasons of manageability to works for one performer at one piano, excluding concertos and other works with featured piano soloist, as well as works for more than one player at one or more instruments. (A graded listing of original four-hand piano music [for one and two pianos] appears on pages 343-67. Also, an annotated list compiled by Cameron McGraw was published in the Fall 1975 issue of *The Piano Quarterly*; it includes many dates of composition, thus making it easy to locate works from this century.)

Several criteria were used in evaluating music for inclusion:

(1) That the music be of significant artistic merit.

(2) That it be modern in spirit, and relatively contemporary in language.(For this reason, works by composers—no matter how fine—whose roots and sympathies stem from nineteenth-century styles were regretfully excluded. Thus, Rachmaninoff's music does not appear. In addition, concert paraphrases or mood pieces based on sophisticated popular idioms, such as the many "modern" compositions published from the 1930s through the 1950s, have also been excluded.) A further stipulation is that the music sound "comfortable" in its chosen stylistic language. Several compositions surveyed appeared to strive for modernity at all costs; the composers consciously decided to trade the naturalness of expression which would have been theirs in an older style for the supposedly greater audience appeal of a more advanced idiom. Music which seemed "artificial" in this sense was not included.

(3) That the piece be either "pianistic" in a traditional sense or useful as a means of introducing a particular aspect of idiomatic twentieth-century technique.

(4) That the music be readily available for purchase or rental. It need not be published; several circulating libraries, including the Fleisher Collection and the American Composers Alliance Library, maintain extensive catalogs of unpublished music.

The list does include a very few pieces, of considerable merit, which are technically out of print; one hopes for their reissue if sufficient interest in them is forthcoming.

Dates of compositions are indicated only where they are of more than routine statistical interest; criterion no. 2, above makes them otherwise unnecessary.

SOURCES

All the music on the list—with three minor exceptions, as noted—was played through by the author. Between four and five times as much music was reviewed as was finally selected.

Music selected for review was drawn from various sources: publisher catalogues; the New York State Music Teachers Association's *Syllabus for Piano* (a committee project of admirable scope issued in 1973); the National Federation of Music Clubs "Junior Festivals" *Bulletins* for 1975–1976 and 1977–1978; the NYSSMA *Manual* section of graded repertory for piano (1975); the selected list of noneducational *Twentieth-Century Piano Music by American Composers* compiled by Judith Greenberg Finell (October 1973); and new music reviews from the last ten years of *Clavier* and *The Piano Quarterly*. In addition, the author canvassed the entire collections of published piano music at both the American Music Center Library and the music library of Queens College, CUNY.

Both educational and concert music are included, with no distinction drawn between them. The music is listed in order of increasing difficulty, graded as follows:

Primary (where available)
Lower through Upper Elementary (two sections)
Lower through Upper Intermediate (three sections)
Lower through Upper Advanced (three sections)

Although all the music is of considerable artistic merit, the author found certain pieces to be of even higher caliber and distinguishes these by the notation "recommended." A very few are noted as "highly recommended," and a handful are "very highly recommended."

(For someone just starting a library of new music, a selection from the two latter categories is suggested. Indeed, an adequate skeletal library could be assembled with just three titles: Bartók's *Mikrokosmos*, volumes 1 through 6; *Contemporary Music and the Pianist: A Guidebook of Resources and Materials*, compiled by Alice Canaday; and volume 4 of *An Anthology of Piano Music*, "The Twentieth Century," compiled by Denes Agay.)

The list is broken down into three sublists containing four categories of music. Single Pieces and Composer Collections are treated as separate categories within each grade level, then collated grade by grade to form the *first* sublist. Anthologies (which often contain music of several degrees of difficulty) are treated as a *second* sublist. (The best anthologies make very sound investments: an able editor's informed taste is as good a quality control as one can hope to find. In addition, the pieces contained are certainly "cheaper by the dozen.") The *third* contains music written for pedagogical purposes which is nevertheless of esthetic value; much of the latter is issued in multivolume sets.

For those readers interested in investigating a single composer's output or music in a specific style, the following comments may be helpful.

Certain publishing houses, such as Theodore Presser, devote a large proportion of their catalog to new music, whereas others do not. Obtaining catalogs from contemporary-music specialists is the first step, to be followed by requests for specific works. Most houses are more than willing to mail out single copies of requested works "on approval" for a thirty-day trial period. The music is then either paid for and retained, or returned in good condition.

This is a boon to the interested pianist or teacher, since reviewing a work at one's leisure—and at the instrument—is very different from leafing through it in the busy environment of a music store. Figurations which appear formidable at a glance may later prove to lie well within the hands; also, much newly devised notation needs to be deciphered in surroundings of maximum tranquility.

What can we look forward to in future publications? Publishers no less than other business people are subject to economic pressures which may exert significant influence on the choice of music they issue, particularly with respect to preferred stylistic language and genre. Compositions in conservative idioms and small forms (such as suite movements) stand a better chance of being published because their potential appeal is to a wider audience; even a work in an abstract or difficult idiom will fare better if cast in a small form or a sectionalized one, such as theme and variations. Thus, we can anticipate a dearth of sonatas and other large-scale pieces in favor of short, multimovement ones.

Even the copyright—the "composer's comfort"—exerts its particular limiting influence. Older music jostles the new in clamoring for a performer's attention. Much of the older music is by now in the public domain, and therefore available for reissue by any interested publishing house. The result is that multiple editions of these older works are in plentiful supply, which in turn further stimulates public interest in the music. By contrast, the copyright limits a covered work to issue by a single house, usually in one edition (until, or unless, the rights are assigned elsewhere). In a sense, then, the copyright has become an exclusionary as well as an exclusive right.

Safeguarding one's rights as creator while striving for maximum exposure poses a dilemma for the composer. Even Stravinsky—well aware of the explicit advantage in concurrent multiple editions—wasn't above revising one of his works, in the public domain, respelling a few pitches enharmonically, or discreetly altering a few rhythms, in order to qualify for another copyright through claiming "substantial" alterations.

We'll have to wait and see how the new copyright law succeeds in coping with this situation. According to the new law, which came into effect in 1978, the term of copyright is extended to the composer's lifetime plus an additional 50 years, and is nonrenewable. Whatever the outcome, it will bear directly on the array of new music available to the prospective performer. (See the chapter "The New Copyright Law: A Primer for Music Teachers," p. 659.)

COMPOSERS

It is essential that we consider the nature of a twentieth-century composer's career, and the manner in which it differs from that of an older master.

The term *musical period*, when used to discuss the output of creators from former centuries, is understood to refer to a particular stage in their artistic development. Their careers, in toto, may be seen as straight-line progressions toward absolute command over the materials of their chosen stylistic language. We can further distinguish the overall direction of certain composers' careers, in a general way, as progress from an initial expansiveness in utterance toward increasing succinctness (as with Brahms and Debussy), or just the reverse (as with Milhaud). In our time, by contrast, we use the term to designate that portion of a composer's career devoted to writing in one stylistic language, before moving on to the next. Thus we talk of Stravinsky's late shift to twelve-tone writing, George Rochberg's late-'60s move toward neoromanticism, or Schoenberg's late return to tonality as definitely specific periods within their careers.

This is relevant to the list's content because the piano is not the most expressive vehicle for every twentieth-century style, and a given composer may turn to the instrument during only one of several periods. (John Cage's precisely timed *4'33"* of silence, while a dead end of a sort in the annals of keyboard repertory, illustrates the instrument's versatility and usefulness for music cast in even the most alien idiom).

For the arts of Debussy and Ravel, at least, the piano proved a perfect vehicle. Debussy's pianistic style stems from the romanticism of Chopin; his music for the instrument spans his entire career, progressing from early works which are quite conventional in their textures, rhythms, balanced phrases, and predictable sequences, toward refined, motivic, almost epigrammatic statements. Ravel's output, by contrast, is more of a piece, emerging virtually full-blown in *Jeux d'eau*; even the very early *Sérénade grotesque* is a close cousin to the *Alborada del gracioso*, differing from the later work only in relative sophistication of detail, rather than esthetic. Ravel's heritage is the music of Liszt, with its dazzling figurations and finished surfaces, tempered by a classical feeling for carefully-balanced forms. Virtually all the piano music of both men is worthy of study, and most is included below.

A last word about style. Because today's composer may choose to use several discrete languages within his or her career, it becomes important for the knowledgeable performer to distinguish between an individual's creative "fingerprints" (such as Stravinsky's feeling for rhythm, Hindemith's long-breathed pastoral melodies, or Prokofiev's abrupt cadential key shifts) and the more general usages which actually define the style as a whole. As in other times, it is the presence of just such individual "fingerprints" which alerts us to the work of a potential master creator. No matter what musical language is spoken, it's the individual's accent that makes the speaker unique.

COMPOSER COLLECTIONS

Lower Elementary

Robert Starer:
Twelve Pieces for Ten Fingers (Sam Fox)
The pieces introduce whole-tone writing (no. 7), clusters (no. 8), uneven and changing meters (no. 9), and the idea of no fixed tonic (no. 11). No. 10 concerns itself with various successions of parallel diatonic sixths and their particular effect of erasing any sense of being seated in a specific key.

Ruth Schonthal:
Miniscules (Carl Fischer)
A series of ten tiny tone poems, many through-composed, which are distinguished by the prevalance of plastic, well-shaped phrases that do not, however, impede each piece's momentum. Especially notable are the bitonal "Bugles from Afar," "Bells on the Top of the Hill," and "Sunset." Recommended.

Joan Last:
Black and White: Eight Tunes for Young Pianists (Oxford University Press)
Valuable, nontonal set, especially useful to expand the ear. Textures are clear and rhythms define rather than run counter to the meters. (Also to be commended is the composer's determination not to "hedge" by giving in and cadencing in a key, which would detract markedly from the effectiveness of a direct encounter with pure, nontonal writing.) Notable individual selections are no. 6, "Echoing Horns," and no. 7, "A Sad Picture." Example in *The Piano Quarterly* Spring 1975.

Leo Kraft:
Easy Animal Pieces (Boston Music Co.)
A valuable set of half-page pieces stressing rhythmic independence of the hands and employing many newer compositional techniques, including bitonality, clusters, nonsymmetric phrases, and nondefinitive (tonally amorphous) cadences. Recommended.

Halsey Stevens:
Music for Ann (Helios Music)
Genial, five-piece set of two-page pieces, in two voices for the most part. The writing is tonal-modal, in some cases pandiatonic, using various traditional textural arrangements. The music unfolds in a rhythmically spacious manner.

Béla Bartók (Denes Agay, ed.):
Forty-three Little Pieces and Studies for Piano (Theodore Presser)
Fine collection of tonal and modal music for the beginner. Especially valuable as it stresses independence of each hand from the very beginning. (Lower elementary through lower intermediate.)

Soulima Stravinsky:
Piano Music for Children (C.F. Peters)
Books 1 and 2. An exceedingly valuable set of thirty short pieces for hands in proximate position. Although all have definite tonic pitches, in tonal, modal, or pandiatonic contexts, free use is made of chromatic tones outside the key, and some occasionally cadence elsewhere than on the tonic sonority. Where used, rhythmic ostinatos are treated in the manner of the composer's father; chromatic clashes and some bitonal writing also recall the elder Stravinsky. Limitation: the hands usually operate in concord, ending phrases and sections together, rather than proceeding with maximum rhythmic independence. (Lower elementary through lower intermediate.) Book 1 is highly recommended.

Elie Siegmeister:
American Kaleidoscope (Summy-Birchard)
Sets 1 and 2. A total of nineteen short pieces in roughly ascending order of difficulty, several of which have been anthologized. Many use "national" rhythms, but the best seem to fall within the international neoclassic style so familiar from the easier piano pieces of the Russians. Notable selections from Set 1 are "Street Games," "Blues," and "Fairy Tales"; from Set 2, "The Chase" and "Marching." (Lower elementary through lower intermediate.)

INDIVIDUAL PIECES

Upper Elementary

Jean Eichelberger Ivey:
"Sleepy Time" & "Water Wheel" (Lee Roberts Music Publications, Inc.)
Two charming one-page, black-key pentatonic pieces. In slow $\frac{5}{4}$, "Sleepy Time" features an ostinato bass (with E-flat tonic) and a floating, chordal right-hand part with G-flat tonic. "Water Wheel," in $\frac{7}{8}$, reverses the texture with an ostinato in the right and single-line melody in the left. Both use a signature of five flats. Published as a unit.

Ramon Zupko:
March (Lee Roberts/Schirmer)
Clean, clear piece featuring polytonal writing, stressing rhythmic and harmonic independence of the hands. Dynamic contrasts are important and serve as form-building elements; the piece is really through-composed, although there are intimations of ABA form. Crisp, unexpected accents often interrupted the marching. In effect, an easier, more sharply defined distant cousin of Siegmeister's "Festive March." (See p. 408) Example in *The Piano Quarterly* Winter 1967–1968.

George Frederick McKay:
My Wish for Your Happiness (J. Fischer [Belwin-Mills])
Lyrical two-page piece in $\frac{3}{4}$, ostensibly in E minor with a terminal cadence in A major. Uses several phrases of odd lengths, one relatively mild cross-relation, and some quartal harmonies. Lovely.

Pal Kadosa:
Sonatina in B-flat (Editio Musica, Budapest [Boosey & Hawkes])
One-movement, three-page piece which wanders far afield chromatically and yet remains ultimately triadically based. Technically it proceeds mostly in five-finger positions and is clean in rhythms and textures. In $\frac{2}{4}$, marked *Poco allegro*, with no key signature.

Henry Cowell:
Sway Dance (Merion Music [Theodore Presser])
Gentle, lovely two-page piece in the Mixolydian mode on C, with a mid-section in the Aeolian. Major seconds add extra weight to a ruminative, back-and-forth main motive in the right hand, and the midsection makes a good exercise in a legato ostinato for the left. No fingering.

Halsey Stevens:
Jumping Colts (Helios [Mark Foster])
Clear, clean, fresh piece in $\frac{6}{8}$ throughout its four pages; in D minor/major with some unexpected tonicizations and added chromatic alterations. Technically it exploits registral shifts, using cross-hands when necessary; phrase lengths are plastic and sensitively shaped, and the piece as a whole is rhythmically charming. No fingering. Example in *The Piano Quarterly* Spring 1968.

Alan Hovhaness:
Mystic Flute, op. 22 (C.F. Peters)
Exotic, evocative three-page piece, using a symmetric scale on D which contains two augmented seconds: D—E-flat—F-sharp—G/A—B-flat—C-sharp—D. The piece proceeds in $\frac{7}{8}$ throughout (divided ♪♪♪ ♪♪ ♪♪), and features some cross-hands writing. Less dilatory than usual for music by this composer. No fingering.

Ihor Bilohrud:
Night Shadows (Summy-Birchard)
Lovely, waltzing serial piece with just the merest hint of D minor as a hidden tonic. Row manipulations are explained in a preface. A haunting, finely made two-page piece. Recommended, particularly at this level.

COMPOSER COLLECTIONS

Upper Elementary

Dmitri Shostakovich:
Six Children's Pieces (MCA)
Fine set of mostly two-voice, one- or two-page pieces, using modest chromaticism. Emphasis is given to exploring upper and lower registers; harmonic refreshment is provided through temporarily tonicizing, or actually modulating, down or up a chromatic half step from the original key. Contains the well-known, lovely, "Happy" and "Sad" Fairy Tales.

Ross Lee Finney:
Thirty-two Piano Games (C.F. Peters)
An excellent set; develops keyboard technique and emancipates the ear at the same time. Pieces range in length from two lines to several pages; several selections use a single note (often middle C) as a locus for symmetrical explorations above and below, but not in the traditional sense of a tonic. Registral extremes are often explored, and the new techniques introduced include proportionate notation, clusters, free improvisation, and aleatory elements within a notated context; all these are introduced naturally, with no intimation of their use as anything but genuine means of expression. Example in *The Piano Quarterly* Spring 1970. Recommended. (Upper elementary through midintermediate)

Arpad Balazs:
Fourteen Easy Pieces for Piano (Boosey & Hawkes)
Superb set of beautifully crafted pieces, each one or two pages long, in an admirably fingered and edited edition. The music is tonal, with free use of all chromatic pitches, and each selection is fully differentiated from the others in matters of tempo, texture, and technique. Rhythmic independence of the hands is stressed, and phrases balance one another according to the composer's original, and very satisfying, sense of proportion. Each piece is titled in Hungarian and English, along these lines: "Dance in Front of a Mirror," "Trudging," "Game," "Playing at Soldiers." One piece, "Intermezzo," is left open-ended, to fade away at will. The composer's interest in and involvement with this music is evident on every page. Highly recommended.

Katrina Knerr:
Year Thing (C.F. Peters)
Fine set of sixteen short pieces, four per season of the year. Many twentieth-century techniques are used, always in a natural manner rather than as devices, pinpointed for use in a single selection only to be dropped in the next. Among the techniques are naturally evolving, nondevelopmental forms, often left unrounded; free-breathing phrases, often nonsymmetric; highlighted registral contrasts; parallel sonorities—fourths, thirds, as well as triads; polytonality; multimetric writing. Recommended. (Somewhat similar in scope, aims, and content is a fine collection of thirty-one very short pieces titled *Sound/World*, by Stanley Applebaum, published by Schroeder and Gunther.)

Denes Agay:
Seven Piano Pieces (G. Schirmer)
A collection of diversified, short, two-, three-, or four-page tonal pieces remarkable for their clear textures. Reminiscences of Hungarian-style folk melody and impressionist harmonies color the music in an unobtrusive fashion. Notable selections: "The Shepherd's Night Song," featuring nondiatonic harmonies; "Frolic," a delightful, deftly made piece with its leading motive a phrase of three measures; and the lovely "Dancing Leaves," featuring white-key sonorities built in fourths.

Béla Bartók (Willard A. Palmer, ed.):
Pieces for Children (Alfred Publishing Company)
Beautifully edited collection of forty-two pieces drawn from various sources, containing much of the music in the smaller collections issued by the same publisher found elsewhere on this list. Many of the pieces in this volume consist of two or more reprises of identical melodic material, each setting given a fresh cast by being harmonized in a differing key while the melody remains at the original pitch. The pieces are all one or two pages long; the writing is rhythmically plastic and stresses independence of the hands. Over all, this is a well-chosen collection. Highly recommended. (Upper elementary through upper intermediate)

Norman Dello Joio:
Suite for the Young (E.B. Marks)
Ten short, well-made pieces; quite tonal and presented in a framework of traditional rhythms and symmetric phrases.

Dmitri Kabalevsky:
Favorite Kabalevsky: Thirty Piano Pieces for Young People (Alfred)
Well-produced volume, completely fingered, containing the entire op. 27. The music—very tonal, with a certain chromatic quirkiness at times—includes the well-known A-minor Toccatina; the one-movement Sonatina in A minor; and "A Short Story" (E-flat major). Selections are arranged in approximate order of difficulty. (Limitation: the left-hand writing is noticeably less advanced than that for the right hand, and rhythmically dependent on the right as well. This grows out of a bias toward conventional homophonic textures and is self-limiting if not counterracted at an early stage.) Recommended. Another handsomely produced volume, *Kabalevsky: Twenty-five of his Easiest Piano Selections*, is available from the same publisher. It contains very conventional pieces from op. 39, and the op. 27 Toccatina. Op. 39 and op. 27, in a two-book edition, are also available from Leeds Music Corporation in volumes edited by Alfred Mirovitch. A student who has enjoyed these two collections and is ready to advance to the intermediate level might also wish to investigate the A-minor Theme and Variations op. 40 no. 2, published by Leeds.)

Béla Bartók:
Twenty-four of His Easiest Piano Pieces and Selected Children's Pieces (Willard A. Palmer, ed.): (Alfred)
Two beautiful editions of some of Bartók's more traditional, though hardly conventional, easiest pieces. This volume contains thirteen short pieces, many of which are also included in the other book. Both sets use individual short (one- to three-page) pieces drawn from the composer's Ten Easy Pieces (1908); For Children, vols. 1 and 2; and The First Term at the Piano (1913), all written while Bartók was a professor of piano at the conservatory in Budapest. The music is tonal or modal, cast in symmetric phrases, and quite charming. Recommended.

Vincent Persichetti:
Little Piano Book (Elkan-Vogel)
Well-known, valuable set of short pieces using the devices of displaced harmony and pandiatonic writing to expand tonality. A fine example of particularly American neoclassicism. No fingerings.

INDIVIDUAL PIECES

Lower Intermediate

John La Montaine:
Sparklers (Summy-Birchard)
Lively perpetuum mobile in $\frac{6}{8}$, with an occasional $\frac{3}{8}$, in A major. Alternating-hand arpeggios exploit the piquant flavor of major-third pitted against minor—a favorite "spicing" device of this composer.

Henry Cowell:
Bounce Dance (Theodore Presser)
A cousin to the "Sway Dance," in B-flat major and regular $\frac{3}{4}$ throughout. Diatonic clusters of three notes each are featured.

Vincent Persichetti:
Variations for an Album (Theodore Presser)
Engaging small set of variations that is both rhythmically plastic and tonally fresh. A theme, in $\frac{5}{4}$, A minor, is followed by five variations, each two or three lines long and meant to be repeated.

Erik Satie:
Gymnopédie no. 1 (E.B. Marks)
Languid, enchanting short piece in the Lydian mode on G, with two form-defining cadences to the minor dominant. This very well known work is the first of three similarly conceived pieces, all in $\frac{3}{4}$ time with arching melodies spun out over a gently syncopated accompaniment.

Halsey Stevens:
Lyric Piece (Merion Music [Theodore Presser])
Two-page Andante con moto in D major-minor; $\frac{3}{4}$ time. A sensitive study in parallel thirds (sixths), also concerned with shifting accents, expressed in phrases which arch easily over the bar line, and highlighting the appoggiatura (an unprepared upper-neighbor note which falls on the beat and is of short duration). Recommended.

William L. Gillock:
Mirage (Summy-Birchard)
Three-page introduction to the whole-tone scale. Lovely, idiomatic to the instrument, and never condescending in any way to a pianist of modest technique. The piece is in $\frac{4}{4}$ throughout, and is based on interlocking, arpeggiated figurations distributed equally to both hands.

Karol Rathaus:
Crosstalk (Carl Fischer)
A fresh example of polytonal writing, using all white keys for the right hand while the left is assigned the key signature of F minor. Each hand

stoutly maintains its own tonal centers—many tonics are hinted at in the course of the piece—and both converge at the close for a definite cadence in F. Two pages; charming.

George Perle:
Interrupted Story (Theodore Presser)
A two-page, well-crafted piece which builds its form gradually from motivic nuggets. As the title suggests, a lyrical, often-repeated fragment (punctuated by mildly dissonating octaves) is forcefully interrupted by unrelated material several times in the course of the piece.

Edward Diementi:
Regina Coeli (Theodore Presser)
Interesting two-page piece based on the juxtaposition, not of two differing keys, but of two clashing tonal planes, each consonant in itself. The piece cadences tonally at the close, and is cast in AB form with a chordal section followed by one in a more lyric vein.

Wallingford Riegger:
Petite Étude, op. 62 (Merion Music [Theodore Presser])
A surprisingly lineal descentant of Debussy's "The Snow is Dancing" and "Jimbo's Lullaby" (from the *Children's Corner* Suite) as well as "Beauty and the Beast" (from Ravel's *Mother* Goose Suite). The piece pits black keys against white in a straightforward and unclichéd manner, using some three-note clusters, and remains rhythmically pungent throughout its three-page course. The final C-major chord is quite appropriate.

COMPOSER COLLECTIONS

Lower Intermediate

Zsolt Durko:
Dwarfs and Giants (Editio Musica, Budapest [Boosey & Hawkes])
Eight well-crafted pieces emphasizing palm and forearm clusters. The writing is multimetric, does not venture outward to registral extremes, and is tonal at times. Especially notable is the lovely "Winter's Tale."

Elie Siegmeister:
The Children's Day (Leeds)
Six genial one- and two-page pieces; the often-anthologized "On a Golden Afternoon" is from this set.

Norman Cazden:
Music for Study (Arrow Music Press [Boosey & Hawkes])
Eight morsels, mostly for two voices. Tonal centers are hinted at and cadences are always triads.

Ruth Shaw Wylie:
Five Easy Pieces for Piano, op. 4 (Camera Music Publisher [E.C. Schirmer])
Nicely flowing music, much of it based on rhythmically independent

scale patterns in each hand. Notable selections: a free-spirited "Dance for a Sunny Morning" in F major; an A-minor "Prayer"; and the delightful $\frac{6}{8}$ "Dance for Saturday," full of unexpected tonal shifts (always at a distance of a major third).

Aram Khachaturian:
Adventures of Ivan (MCA)
Eight short pieces, many of which have been frequently anthologized. Especially notable is no. 2, "Ivan Can't Go Out Today."

Ruth Schonthal:
Pot-Pourri: Ten Piano Pieces in a (Mostly) Festive Mood (Carl Fischer)
Despite the subtitle, this collection offers both introspective and buoyant selections, and will be most effective in performance if played with scrupulous attention to the indicated pedaling as well as a delicate touch and tasteful rubato. Atmospheric, sensitive music, notable for the plasticity of its phrasing.

Ulysses Kay:
Ten Short Essays (MCA)
Tonal music with triadic harmonies; however, several of the terminal cadences are to chords other than the tonic.

Alan Hovhaness:
Twelve Armenian Folk Songs, op. 43 (C.F. Peters)
Short, modal pieces, consciously repetitive in a rather pleasant manner; a selection of three or four of these should be ample. The music represents a departure from the composer's usual exotic style and is quite idiomatic for the instrument. Of special interest are nos. 3 and 11. (An interesting approach would be to introduce these pieces at the same time as Bach's *Anna Magdalena Bach Notebook*, as there is a notable resemblance between the two collections in scope and intent.) For the more adventurous pianist, Hovhaness's "Hymn to a Celestial Musician" op. 111 no. 3 is well worth examining; it uses a soft plectrum to pluck the strings, in addition to a two-voiced refrain played on the keyboard. (Upper intermediate.)

Donald Waxman:
First Recital Pageant (Galaxy)
Second Recital Pageant: A Natural History (Galaxy)
Two fine sets of concert pieces, stressing rhythmic freshness and a variety of asymmetric phrase structures. The writing is tonal/modal with some nontraditional chromatic interpolations and an occasional nontriadic terminal cadence. The first book is the finer of the two.

David Diamond:
Album for the Young (Elkan Vogel)
Although this set of ten short pieces (one page or less) contains some music of lesser quality, the best selections are indeed excellent. The writing is tonal and rhythmically plastic in a natural, most appealing manner. Parallel fifths, quartal harmonies, and triads with added notes

abound in a style not unlike that of Milhaud's The Household Muse. Notable selections: "Waltz," "Happy-Go-Lucky," "A Gambol," "Christmastide," "Spring Song," and "The Day's End."

Béla Bartók:
Ten Easy Pieces (Boosey & Hawkes; Alfred)
Impeccable collection of ten of the master's least tonal, least traditional, easier pieces. Among those included are "Dedication," spare, haunting, dissonant; "Peasant's Song," a single line cast in the Dorian mode on C-sharp; "Slow Struggle"; the chromatically wandering, impressionist "Dawn"; the whole-tone "Etude"; as well as the familiar "Evening in the Country" and "Bear Dance." All the music is of a very high order. Very highly recommended.

Béla Bartók:
For Children (Boosey & Hawkes)
vol. 1: (forty pieces) based on Hungarian folk tunes
vol. 2: (thirty-nine pieces) based on Slovakian folk tunes (1945 rev. ed.)
These are among the most important works of twentieth-century piano literature, which became models of modern folk-song adaptations. The original 1908 edition contained eighty-five pieces and is available from Schirmer or Alfred (ed. Palmer). The grading in each volume is between Lower Elementary and Upper Intermediate. Very highly recommended.

Sergei Prokofiev (Willard A. Palmer, ed.):
Music for Children, op. 65 (Alfred)
Superior music, in the composer's most mellow and melodic vein. Most of the twelve pieces in this collection are favorites and often have been anthologized. Particularly notable are "Morning," in bright C major; the ambling, $\frac{3}{4}$ "Promenade"; "Fairy Tale," in a subdued A minor; the forthright, chromatically colorful "March"; and the spacious, beautiful F-major "Evening." A fine edition, completely fingered, with occasional pedal markings. Highly recommended. (Lower through upper intermediate.)

Arthur Greene:
Seven Wild Mushrooms and a Waltz (Galaxy)
Absolutely delightful set of eight pieces for prepared piano. Meticulous directions are provided for preparing the instrument by inserting rubber erasers and metal wood-screws at designated places on the strings. The altered, eerie timbres of the prepared pitches contrast in a carefully planned manner with the unaltered remainder of the keyboard. Four of the pieces are bitonal, and the whole set is quite fascinating. Especially fine are "The Three Blind Mice Rollin' Along Toccata," "Scale Study 1," and "Dies Irae circa 1974." Highly recommended.

Heitor Villa-Lobos:
The Piano Music of Heitor Villa-Lobos (rev. ed.) (Consolidated Music Publishers Inc. [Music Sales Corporation])
A large cross-section of the piano music of the Brazilian impressionist-romantic. The easiest pieces are three albums of the *Guia Pratico*; also

included are three pieces from *Prole do Bebê* no. 1, among them the well-known "O Polichinelo," which pits black keys against white. The plates for this collection were drawn from various sources and the degree of legibility consequently varies considerably. (Lower intermediate through very advanced.)

Roy Harris:
Little Suite (G. Schirmer)
Four lyric pieces, each descriptive to some extent. "Bells," written out on three staves, uses parallel quartal and freely triadic harmonies, plus low sonorities held with the sostenuto pedal, to paint its picture. Both "Sad News" and "Children at Play" are in $\frac{7}{8}$, with the bar alternately divided into groupings of three + four or four + three. "Slumber," the last piece, is quiet and sonorous. The music is always idiomatic for the instrument. (Lower through upper intermediate.) Recommended.

INDIVIDUAL PIECES

Mid-Intermediate

Howard Hanson:
Clog Dance (Carl Fischer)
Clear, clean piece in $\frac{6}{8}$ throughout, using much whole-tone writing although ostensibly in C minor, with a constant Phrygian cadence characterizing the main melodic material. Ominous, shifting parallel fifths provide a restless, eerie accompaniment. The whole piece is interesting and involving for the player. (Some of the octave writing in the middle section could conceivably be trimmed to single notes, making the work suitable for lower intermediate level.) No fingering. Recommended.

Henry Cowell:
Amiable Conversation (Second Encore to "Dynamic Motion") (Breitkopf & Härtel)
Shows this composer in his element: forearm clusters to the fore. The right hand (white keys) is pitted against the left (black), with no reconciliation. Delightful, straightforward.

Claude Debussy:
Rêverie (Durand)
Lovely, languid piece in $\frac{4}{4}$. With a key signature of one flat it moves through several keys, touching down in each briefly before finally cadencing in F major. The two midsections are slightly square, rhythmically, though the piece as a whole is charming.

Dmitri Kabalevsky (Isidor Philipp, ed.)
Sonatina in C major, op. 13 no. 1 (International Music Company)
Perfectly proportioned, elegant, self-assured work; a minor masterpiece by one of the most felicitous writers for the piano. The music is truly inspired and is distinguished by a suppleness of phrasing and freedom from dogmatic rhythms that delight both listener and player. (Such is not the case with op. 13 no. 2, unfortunately; it is rhythmically inhibited and academically made throughout.) The C-major Sonatina opens

with a sonata-allegro movement in C-major; continues with a lyric andantino in the relative minor, featuring some cross hands; and closes with a delicate tarantella-toccata in $\frac{9}{8}$ which alights periodically both in A minor and C major before closing clearly in the home key. (Students able to manage the Sonatina might also be interested in exploring the composer's Four Little Pieces, op. 14, especially "A Brisk Game" and "In the Gymnasium.") Highly recommended.

Anton Webern:
Kinderstück (Carl Fischer)
Delicate arching contours are traced across the keyboard throughout this elegant, five-line twelve-tone piece. Pitches are exchanged from one hand to the other quickly, and much cross-hands writing is featured. Rhythms are of the nonpulsed, fragmented variety, and the dynamics vary from ***mp*** to ***pp***. In $\frac{3}{4}$ throughout. Recommended.

Robert Palmer:
Evening Music (Theodore Presser)
A very beautiful three-page piece in compound meters. That it is written in the Mixolydian mode on A is not as important as the fact that a variety of tonally fresh nuances greet the ear at every turn. Two outer sections in gentle, pastoral rhythms with Hindemithian melodic curves frame a contrasting section featuring several striking chordal sequences, in $\frac{9}{8}$ (divided ♫ ♫♪ ♫ ♫). Outstanding at this level. Highly recommended.

COMPOSER COLLECTIONS

Mid-Intermediate

Norman Dello Joio:
Lyric Pieces for the Young (E.B. Marks)
Six genial pieces, loosely rather than compactly fashioned, each in a single tempo and meter. Harmonic and melodic materials are quite traditional. No fingering.

Miriam Gideon:
Three-Cornered Pieces (American Composers Alliance–ACE Edition)
Attractive set of six short waltz-like pieces, each based on two or three simple motives. Interesting rhythmic shifts are the outstanding feature; harmonically, the writing is largely modal/tonal, with many quartal sonorities. Thin textures are the rule, and the hands are often widely separated. Moderate tempos predominate.

Ross Lee Finney:
Twenty-four Inventions (new edition, 1971) (C.F. Peters)
Very fine set of pieces using every modern technique, involving precise notation (no aleatory or approximate notation). Multimetric writing is the exception rather than the rule here. According to the composer, each piece is a game or puzzle; in "deciphering" them, the descriptive titles will be of help. Example in *The Piano Quarterly*, Fall 1971. Recommended. (Intermediate through upper intermediate.)

Mickey Cohen:
The First Book of Isms (Clark & Cruikshank [Berandol Music Ltd.])

Six short one-page pieces, each varied in touch and texture, and quite dissonant. Registral extremes are explored in a series of static "sound events" which follow one another according to the composer's sense of proportion and design. No time signatures are indicated, but pedalings are precisely given. Much of the sound is drawn directly from the strings by plucking and strumming, as well as by exciting them to sound through sympathetic vibration. Performance instructions are sparse. Recommended. (Intermediate through upper intermediate.)

Witold Lutoslawski:
Bucolics for Piano (Polskie Wyndownictwo Muzyczne)

An engaging set of small pastoral pieces by a master composer. Fresh forms are crafted for each in response to the requirements of the basic melodic material; the working out is contrapuntal. (Limitation: tonal terminal cadences often appear inappropriate in light of what has gone before.) Recommended.

Maurice Ravel:
Prelude (Durand)

Twenty-seven superbly stylish measures that could serve as the kernel for an additional *"Valse sentimentale."* In $\frac{3}{4}$ throughout, with a sensitive terminal cadence in A minor which is delightfully unanticipated. Recommended.

Barbara Pentland:
Space Studies (Waterloo)

In the Canaday anthology. If the rest of the pieces are as interesting as this one, the set is excellent indeed.

Witold Lutoslawski:
Folk Melodies for Piano (Polskie Wyndownictwo Muzyczne)

Clean, neat, harmonically spicy settings of twelve authentic folk melodies. Rhythms and harmonies are crisp, often using irregularly balanced phrase groups. Most are one page in length, and all have tonal terminal cadences, which sometimes anchor the entire piece in an unexpected key. Explanatory notes are in Polish and English; titles in Polish only. A fine edition, scrupulously fingered and pedaled. Recommended.

Igor Stravinsky:
The Five Fingers (Kalmus)

Eight pieces in pandiatonic style, typical of the composer's neoclassicism. The hands move with extreme independence, yet all the music is in five-finger positions. Phrases often end abruptly, and close attention must be paid to tricky rhythmic ostinatos and the indicated dynamic contrasts. Highly recommended.

Ernest Toch:
Echoes from a Small Town (Associated Music Publishers)
Truly excellent set of fourteen very pianistic miniatures. Tonal centers are avoided for the most part, except at terminal cadences. The composer's sureness in shaping melodic curves, and his creativity in discovering fresh rhythmic frameworks, fully distinguish each small gem of a piece from the others. Very highly recommended. (Intermediate through upper intermediate.)

Denes Agay:
Mosaics: Six Piano Pieces on Hebrew Folk Themes (MCA)
Inventive, richly textured, diversified concert pieces. All have tonal terminal cadences, although not always the expected ones. A mini-grouping of three from among the entire set is suggested: no. 3, a clean, neat *Vivo* in $\frac{2}{4}$; no. 4, a lovely, Hungarian-flavored, harmonically surprising *Lento espressivo*; and no. 5, a toccata-like multimetric *Animato*. Recommended. (Intermediate through lower advanced.)

Robert Starer:
Sketches in Color, Book 1 (MCA)
Seven short pieces, each an exposition of a single twentieth-century device, cast in traditional keyboard technique. Included are examples of polytonality; "catchy" syncopations; black key versus white; a twelve-tone essay using quartal harmonies, clusters, and sonorities built in sevenths; and a piece in $\frac{7}{8}$. Each piece carries a color name for a title. The composer has also written a second, more ambitious and technically difficult—although less successful—volume of the same name. (Intermediate through upper intermediate.)

Béla Bartók:
Twenty-four of His Most Popular Piano Pieces (Alfred)
This well-edited collection of slightly more advanced pieces contains the entire Sonatina (1915) and Rhapsody (1904) as well as excerpts from Ten Easy Pieces, For Children (vols. 1 and 2), Fourteen Bagatelles, op. 6, Seven Sketches, op. 9, and The First Term at the Piano. Each selection is preceded by a pertinent explanatory note. Highly recommended. (Intermediate through lower advanced.)

Claude Debussy:
Coin des enfants (Children's Corner Suite) (Durand)
Very popular six-movement suite written for the composer's daughter. "Jimbo's Lullaby" uses a pentatonic melody; both "Serenade for the Doll" and "The Snow is Dancing" present delicate, pointillistic surfaces; and "Golliwogg's Cake Walk" features catchy syncopations, resembling the composer's easier *"Le Petit Nègre"* in atmosphere and musical materials. (Mid through upper intermediate.)

INDIVIDUAL PIECES

Upper Intermediate

Hugo Weisgall:
Sine Nomine ("Graven Images" no. 3) (Theodore Presser)

Lovely, free-flowing nontonal piece. The hands remain at the center of the keyboard in a relatively stable position. In $\frac{4}{4}$ throughout and rhythmically plastic; the piece's total effect is of something unusual and beautiful, suspended in time and place. Example in *The Piano Quarterly* Fall 1968. Recommended. (The composer's more formidable "Two Improvisations" ["Graven Images" no. 6] is also available from T. Presser.)

Earl George:
Lento (Oxford University Press)
A two-page musing, cast loosely in E minor with occasional, unexpected piquant harmonic shifts. In $\frac{3}{4}$ throughout; requires a large hand spread. No fingering.

Paul Creston:
Prelude and Dance (G. Schirmer)
A single movement in two parts; an introductory section, reminiscent of the opening of Rachmaninoff's C-sharp minor Prelude, but not as difficult; and a delightful dance, full of rhythmic shifts and unexpected accents, which might almost be Debussy's "third Arabesque"—with a twist. Note: the tonic for the dance is definitely B minor; at the final cadence, deemphasize the left-hand descent to G-flat and bring out the last first-inversion B-minor triad.

Béla Bartók:
"Bear Dance" (from Ten Easy Pieces) (Boosey & Hawkes)
Popular one-texture piece in which stabbing chords punctuate streams of repeated eighth notes. Direct and exciting music. D is the tonic by an effort of will, since most of the piece is ambiguous as to key, using whole-tone writing and free chromaticism to create a feeling of unease. Basically in $\frac{2}{2}$, allegro vivace.

Francis Poulenc:
Valse-improvisation sur le nom de Bach (Salabert)
Tongue-in-cheek waltz featuring every one of Poulenc's witty compositional "fingerprints." A music-hall atmosphere prevails, but there is room for everything from cadences in "wrong" keys to phrases either overly spun-out or abruptly truncated, as well as unexpected shifts of accent and register. In short, the quintessential Poulenc.

Claude Debussy:
La plus que lente (Durand)
A haunting, hesitating waltz in G-flat (really G-flat minor). Marked *Molto rubato con morbidezza*. Highly recommended.

Aaron Copland:
The Cat and the Mouse (Boosey & Hawkes)
(*Scherzo humoristique*)
Well-known impressionist picture of the two creatures and their adversary relationship. A very pianistic concert piece, featuring many figurations for interlocking hands. Structurally, the work leans to wholetone writing and pentatonic black key vs. white; all the musical gestures are clear and quite direct. Highly recommended.

Elie Siegmeister:
Festive March (Sam Fox)
Bright, cheerful four-page concert piece in moderate $\frac{4}{4}$, in the Lydian mode on A. Brilliant trumpet fanfares are conjured up via polytonal clashes, as each hand goes its own way in parallel triads. An advanced left-hand technique calls for a span large enough to manage three-note sonorities spread over the distance of a tenth.

COMPOSER COLLECTIONS

Upper Intermediate

Ann Southam:
Four Bagatelles (Clark & Cruikshank [Berandol Music Ltd.])
Well-crafted short pieces featuring quartal harmonies and mild dissonance. A large stretch is required for both hands. No fingering.

Claude Debussy:
Deux Arabesques (Durand)
The composer in two favorite guises: dreamer and Puckish dancer. The first Arabesque, in E major, uses ABA form, drifting through a haze of triplet eighth notes. The second, in G major, contains several interior lyric sections which contrast with the main "scherzando" motif. Available separately. Recommended.

Erik Satie (Joseph Prostakoff, ed.):
Trois Gnossiennes (G. Schirmer)
Cousins to the *Gymnopédies* in texture and mood, though these are in a gentle (unbarred) $\frac{4}{4}$. In modal cast and mellow character they relate to the Cowell "Sway Dance," although much more sophisticated. For those interested in investigating more music by this French eccentric, Associated Music has collected the piano music, much of it quite easy, from the years 1912–1914 (ten sets of three pieces each). Most of it resembles a "piano story," with narrative and descriptive comments freely sprinkled across the page (as in Ives).

Ernst Bloch:
Poems of the Sea (G. Schirmer)
Three movements: "Waves," in pulsing triplets; "Chanty," a reflective song; and "At Sea," a perpetuum mobile.

Netty Simons:
Night Sounds for Piano (Merion Music Company [Theodore Presser])
Four short nontonal pieces that are serially constructed, though not dodecaphonic. Rhythms remain traditional, reinforcing the indicated metrical pattern, and each movement is in one meter throughout: "Evening Haze," lovely, atmospheric; "Thinking of Past Things," a kind of "filtered" waltz; "Stars on the Pond," a lovely stasis in $\frac{2}{2}$, using several two-note fragments extracted from the series as repeated mottoes; and "The Rain Beats on the Rain," in $\frac{4}{4}$. Recommended. Example in *The Piano Quarterly* Winter 1976.

Leo Kraft:
Partita (General [Boston Music Company])
Four movements in clean, lean neoclassic style; pandiatonic. The last is an excellent toccata. Example in *The Piano Quarterly* Fall 1969.

Benjamin Lees:
Kaleidoscope (Boosey & Hawkes)
Fine, mostly one-page pieces which are really études; each concentrates on a single texture and technical problem. The writing is tonal with some free chromaticism. Nos. 9 and 10 are of lesser quality than the others. No fingering.

Paul Hindemith:
Kleine Klaviermusik, no. 4 (B. Schott)
(Recommended by Canaday: "Twelve pieces based on five-finger patterns, but involving the eight half tones of the interval of the fifth. They demand fine coordination and concentration.")

Alberto Ginastera:
Twelve American Preludes (Carl Fischer)
(vols. 1 and 2)
Powerful, rhythmically pungent, lively short pieces; fresh and invigorating. The music is essentially tonal but freely chromatic; clusters, polytonal, and modal writing abound. No fingering. Vol. 2 is more rambling and, as a result, less effective; vol. 1 is recommended.

Theodore Chanler:
Three Short Pieces (Arrow [Boosey & Hawkes])
Modest, attractive music. No. 1 is an andante chorale, slowly syncopated; no. 2, a three-voice andante con moto in C-sharp minor, $\frac{5}{8}$; no. 3 is a kind of "skipping tune," freely chromatic around in D-flat tonic, marked *Allegramente.*

William Schuman:
Three Piano Moods: (1) Lyrical, (2) Pensive, (3) Dynamic (Merion Music [Theodore Presser])
A set of miniatures, freely chromatic with ostensible tonal underpinnings. Linear and rhythmic ideas dominate harmonic considerations, for the most part; textures are lean and clean. No. 2 is quite lovely; no. 3 sounds just like an obstinate student repeatedly balking at a tricky rhythmic figure. Issued separately.

Claude Debussy:
Preludes, Books 1 and 2 (Durand)
All are available as separate publications. The best-known are *Voiles* ("Sails"), a prime example of whole-tone writing at its most appropriate; *La Fille aux cheveux de lin* ("The Girl with the Flaxen Hair"), a pastoral miniature in G-flat; and *La Cathédrale engloutie* ("The Sunken Cathedral"), all from Book 1; and *Bruyères* ("Heather"), a companion to *La Fille aux cheveux de lin* in A-flat; and *Feux d'artifice* ("Fireworks") from Book 2. (Upper intermediate through mid-advanced.)

Otto Luening:
Two Inventions (Mercury Music)
Two studies—one in constant sixteenths, the other variations on a ground bass. The first is more interesting, featuring cross-hands writing while it explores the registral resources of the instrument; in pandiatonic C. The second is in A modal—minor/major.

Nicolas Slonimsky:
Studies in Black and White (New Music Quarterly [Theodore Presser])
Ten small one- or two-page studies, contrasting black keys against white (left against right). Ten are too many, and all the toccata-like ones may be omitted. The author recommends a "minisuite" of four: "Jazzelette"; "A Penny for Your Thoughts"; "Anatomy of Melancholy," a gem of beauty; and "Typographical Errors." Recommended. (Upper intermediate through lower advanced.)

Arnold Schoenberg:
Six Little Piano Pieces op. 19 (Universal Edition)
Six lovely, powerful, brooding expressionistic miniatures; completely atonal. A lower intermediate student could easily cope with the more reflective nos. 2, 3, and 6, although a large hand span (ninths for both hands) is expected in the latter. Recommended.

Robert Muczynski:
Diversions, op. 23 (G. Schirmer)
Nine well-constructed pieces between one and three pages long, reminiscent of Toch's type of neat, artistically concise writing. Particularly fine are no. 6, a lento (very chromatic though clearing away to a final cadence in B minor); the rhythmically fresh no. 7; and no. 8 in $\frac{5}{8}$. Readers interested in other examples of the composer's work may wish to look over Muczynski's Six Preludes, op. 6, also G. Schirmer. Of this set, the author recommends two: no. 2, a lovely Shostakovich-like lento; and no. 6, a compact three-page toccata in B-flat, excellent preparation for the Prokofiev op. 11.

Darius Milhaud:
The Household Muse (*La Muse menagère*) (Elkan-Vogel)
Suite of fifteen mostly one-page sketches of domestic scenes. Genial music, very well conceived; it is tonal with many shifts of tonic, and the final cadences are usually in the "expected" key. Each piece is in a single meter; a selection of the finest might include no. 1, "My Own"; no. 2, "The Awakening"; no. 3, "Household Cares"; no. 5, "Cooking"; no. 8, "Music Together"; no. 9, "The Son Who Paints"; no. 10, "The Cat"; no. 11, "Fortune-telling"; no. 14, "Reading at Night"; and no. 15, "Gratitude to the Muse," which features quartal harmony, polytonality, plastic $\frac{6}{8}$ rhythms which arch over the bar, and clusters (very like the second movement of *Scaramouche*.) No fingering. Recommended. (Upper intermediate through lower advanced.)

Luigi Dallapiccola:
Quaderno Musicale de Annalibera (S.A. Edizioni
(Annalibera's Musical Notebook) [Suvini Zerboni])
Eleven compact serial pieces of a brooding intensity and lyricism. The composer has consciously wrought this set as a modern counterpart to Bach's *Notebook for Anna Magdalena Bach*: the first piece, *Simbolo* ("Symbol"), features Bach's own name motive (B-flat–A–C–B-natural) as its motto. In a bow to Bach's "Goldberg" Variations, Dallapiccola's set intersperses canons at various intervals with pieces in freer formats. The music is atmospheric and dramatic, by turns. The composer's *Variations for Orchestra* is an instrumental reworking of this set. (Really upper intermediate through lower advanced, although two excerpts—*Linee* and *Colori* ("Lines" and "Colors")—could be handled by a lower intermediate performer.) Recommended.

Dmitri Shostakovich:
Twenty-four Preludes, op. 34 (MCA)
Diverse set, occasionally showing the composer's ingenuity and flair. Several are worthy of note: no. 4, an E-minor fugue; no. 14, a powerful E-flat minor funereal fanfare; and the lyric no. 10 in C-sharp minor. The set also includes two "wrong-note" polkas and a gently sarcastic, Chopinesque waltz (no. 17). (Upper intermediate through lower advanced.)

Alexander Tcherepnin:
Expressions, op. 81 (Leeds)
Ten short pieces, varied in tempos, textures, and moods. Stravinsky's neoclassic spirit (as in *L'Histoire du soldat*) hovers easily over much of this set. (Upper intermediate through lower advanced.)

Kent Kennan:
Three Preludes (G. Schirmer)
Nos. 1 and 2 are recommended. Full of attractive sounds, the music combines Hindemithian progressions with several impressionist sonorities in an appealing mix. No. 2 is a slow, four-phrase chorale, rich in texture and noble in effect. (Upper intermediate through lower advanced.)

Seymour Bernstein:
Birds, Book 1 (Schroeder and Guenther)
Eight short impressionistic solos, one and two pages in length. A venerable tradition of avian "pictures" for the keyboard exists: the works of the eighteenth-century French harpsichord masters Couperin, Daquin, and Rameau; Mussorgsky's "Battle of the Chicks in Their Shells" from *Pictures at an Exhibition*; Saint-Saëns's "Birds," "The Swan," and "The Cuckoos in the Woods" from *Carnival of the Animals*; Granados's *Goyescas*; and much of Messiaen's music, just to name a few. The Bernstein set is a commendable addition to this specialized literature. His pieces work best when they comment on the bird's function (as in "The Vulture," where the *Dies Irae* is used in a clever manner) rather than merely depicting their activities in sound. Example in *The Piano Quarterly* Winter 1976. Recommended.

Morton Feldman:
Last Pieces (C.F. Peters)
Four soft pieces; nos. 1 and 3 are slow, nos. 2 and 4 are fast. All durations are free (no bar lines), permitting the performer's mood at the moment of playing to become an important factor in the performance.

Claude Debussy (Joseph Prostakoff, ed.):
Selected Works for the Piano (G. Schirmer)
Wonderful collection of the master's best-known piano music from his first period, 1888–1905. Contains the two Arabesques, Reverie, Mazurka, *Tarantelle styrienne*, Sarabande (from *Pour le Piano*), *Clair de lune* and Passepied (from *Suite bergamasque*), *Soirée dans Granade; Jardins sous la pluie; Masques; l'Isle joyeuse, Reflets dans l'eau.* Highly recommended.

Alexander Scriabin:
Preludes, op. 11 nos. 1–21, op. 67 nos. 1, 2 (Dover)
Op. 11 begins in a highly inflected, extrachromatic Chopinesque world and goes beyond it into the realm of the exquisite. Most of these are one or two pages long, mere beginnings in some cases. The pieces from op. 67 are two two-page, nontonal, unresolved veils of chromatic mist. No. 1 undulates uneasily in $\frac{5}{8}$; no. 2 flutters briefly in presto $\frac{4}{8}$, never alighting. (Also of interest are Scriabin's twenty-one Mazurkas in three sets, op. 3, op. 9, and op. 40. All are tonal with very decorated surfaces, chromatically intricate, and are generally more elaborate than are the Preludes.)

Wallingford Riegger:
Four Tone-Pictures op. 14 (C.F. Peters)
Four dandy, contrasting one- and two-page pieces, atonal but not serial. Distinguished by their forthrightness of expression and pulsed rhythms. Much use of ostinatos and multimetrics; always very pianistic. "Wishful Thinking" is an atonal bow to Chopin's "Berceuse"; and the vigorous, effective "Grotesque" features palm-slapped clusters, black key vs. white, and cadences in E-flat major. Highly recommended. (Upper intermediate through lower advanced.)

INDIVIDUAL PIECES

Lower Advanced

Aram Khachaturian (Nadia Reisenberg, ed.):
Toccata (Leeds)
Popular pianistic showpiece. Registral extremes are explored (particularly the treble); the main motive features rapidly repeated single notes. The piece is built in five sections of unequal length: Introduction (allegro marcatissimo); the A section (vivace con brio), a contrasting slower section using an oriental-colored melody and several sophisticated cross-rhythms (andante espressivo); a return to the A section (tempo primo); and a brief codetta. The key signature is six flats in regular order; the author finds that the piece makes most sense when considered to be in

the Phrygian mode on B-flat, rather than in the B-flat minor implied by the reinforced terminal cadence. Highly recommended.

Chou Wen-chung:
The Willows Are New (C.F. Peters)
An atmospheric piece which transfers certain idioms and sounds of Chinese long-zither (*ch'in*) technique to the keyboard. There are almost constant meter changes and a kind of stepping *rubato* quite characteristic of oriental chant. The piece is not as difficult as it looks, although minor ninths are called for in both hands. The performance directions should be thoroughly studied.

Henry Cowell:
The Banshee (W.A. Quincke)
A menacing wailing is produced by depressing the damper pedal, then plucking and stroking the strings. A striking, well-known work.

Norman Dello Joio:
Prelude to a Young Musician (G. Schirmer)
Genial, ambling meditation in ABA form, in E major–C-sharp minor. Phrases flow freely; a large hand span is needed.

Elie Siegmeister:
Toccata on Flight Rhythms (E.B. Marks)
Lively, well-built touch-piece in the Mixolydian mode on D, based on the rhythm: $\frac{8}{8}$, with occasional alternations with straight $\frac{4}{4}$. Recommended.

Ernst Toch:
The Juggler, op. 30 no. 3 (Schott [Belwin-Mills])
Display piece that sounds as if it might be another *Pictures at an Exhibition*. In $\frac{2}{4}$ throughout, this perpetuum mobile features forthright rhythms and explores registral extremes. Harmonically it alternates between sections in C major and whole-tone writing.

William Mathias:
Toccata alla Danza (Oxford University Press)
Good recital piece that lies well under the hand (despite two major tenths for the left). Although cast in D major-minor, it employs much quartal harmony; rhythmic verve and crystal-clear textures, in the manner of American neoclassicism, help to make this a brilliant vehicle. Example in *The Piano Quarterly* Winter 1972.

Anton Webern:
Klavierstück op. post. (Universal Edition [Theodore Presser])
Twelve-tone piece.

Doris Hays:
Sunday Nights (Quinska Publications)
Evocative, well-constructed mood picture in one movement. Rhythms are fluid and bar lines are used for sectional divisions only. Among contemporary techniques employed are sympathetic vibration, forearm clusters, and damping selected strings with the fingers. An inventive, original treatment. Recommended.

Charles Griffes:
The Lake at Evening, op. 5 no. 1 (G. Schirmer)
The first of *Three Tone-Pictures*, this three-page piece makes a fine introduction to Griffes's style. It is well-seated in A major (in $\frac{3}{4}$) with harmonic shifts reminiscent of late Wagner or early Scriabin, rather than the impressionists. Extensive use of pedal tones keeps the work tonally anchored.

Ruth Crawford Seeger:
Piano Study in Mixed Accents (New Music Quarterly [Theodore Presser])
A distant descendant of the presto finale of Chopin's B-flat minor Sonata, this is a chromatically sinuous, nontonal, very pianistic study in running sixteenths. Each hand plays the same notes an octave apart. The piece proceeds by degrees from the depths of the keyboard to top C and then back down again, in three pages. It is fully fingered and not overlong.

Béla Bartók:
Allegro Barbaro (Boosey & Hawkes)
Healthy, direct piece in $\frac{2}{4}$, well-seated in F-sharp minor, with a modal cast, although carrying no key signature. Rather easier than it looks, the piece is straight-forward in its appeal, as it contains many sequences and proceeds in an orderly fashion with well-marked sectional divisions. Plenty of room has been left—by means of repeating a sonority for several measures—in which to negotiate structurally important long-range crescendos and diminuendos. Recommended.

Benjamin Lees:
Fantasia (Boosey & Hawkes)
Driving rhythms, strong, thrusting contours and restless chromatic motion characterize this concert piece. Clean, well-made, virtuosic writing. A bit long.

Aaron Copland:
Night Thoughts (Homage to Ives) (Boosey & Hawkes)
A variety of dissonant bell and gong sounds are conjured in the course of this four-page piece. It may be viewed as a study in sonorities, featuring several combinations of accented and unaccented attacks in consort with various damper pedal effects. Tempo and meter shifts abound, though overall structural unity is preserved.

Paul Hindemith:
Sonata no. 2 (Schott)
One of the finest examples of Hindemith's style, the sonata contains three neatly proportioned, tightly crafted movements. The first is in sonata-allegro form in G major with no key signature; the second—lively, waltzlike—dances through many keys before touching down in E major; the last is a lively rondo, just a touch long-winded, which is bracketed by a "prelude" and coda of a pastoral character. Highly recommended.

George Antheil:
Sonata no. 2 ("The Airplane") (New Music Quarterly [Theodore Presser])

Two-movement work full of constant eighth notes and overlapping ostinatos (one per hand) which stubbornly refuse to reconcile. The first movement is more motoric; the second, more reflective. The two are tied together, ending in the same reiterated E octaves. Machine music at its most effective.

Dmitri Kabalevsky:
Sonata no. 3 (Kalmus)

A three-movement work which is surely one of this composer's happiest inspirations: neat, "songful" music, very well made, idiomatic, and direct in its appeal. In F major. Tackling this sonata is good preparation for the more difficult Prokofiev Sonata no. 7. Recommended.

Maurice Ravel:
Sonatine (F-sharp minor) (Durand)

An admirable balance between classical forms and sensuous, subjective harmonic materials distinguishes these three movements. The first sits a bit squarely on the beats; the second is a masterful, chromatically inflected Menuet; and the third, a delicious, fluttering flight of fancy. Recommended.

COMPOSER COLLECTIONS

Lower Advanced

Gerhard Wuensch:
Twelve Glimpses into Twentieth-Century Idioms (Leeds [Belwin-Mills])

Fits its title description perfectly. Each one-, two- or three-page piece is devoted to a specific technique and is preceded by a clear explanation of that technique as well as several preparatory exercises to acclimate the fingers and ears. Techniques explored: newly invented scales; whole-tone writing; quartal and other harmonies based on fifths, minor sixths, minor seconds, and major sevenths; bitonality; disjunct lines; "beatless counting"; rhythms which counteract the meter; clusters; improvisational notational symbols; and sympathetic vibrations to sound silently depressed keys (nothing for the strings alone). As unpedantic as a collection of this sort can be. Recommended.

Attila Bozay:
Bagatelles, op. 4 (Editio Musica, Budapest [Boosey & Hawkes])

Three pieces, the second with no bar lines or indicated meter. Atmospheric, nontonal music; pianistic and easier than it appears at first glance.

Erik Satie:
Danses gothiques (Salabert)

A precursor of things to come, and typical of Satie's music in its mesmerizing capacity. A cathedral-like atmosphere is evoked through wandering parallel chords which stop and start, and occasionally cadence in one key or another. Not truly tonal. Nine "preludes" of differing lengths are cut at random from the material just described. The phrases are nonprogressive, generating a mood of massive stagnation. Worth investigating.

Béla Bartók:
Fourteen Bagatelles, op. 6 (Boosey & Hawkes)
Generally superior set of direct, nondiscursive pieces, each beautifully realized and pegged to a readily recognizable motivic kernel; forms vary. No. 6 is perhaps the best known. Recommended. (Upper intermediate through lower advanced.)

George Gershwin:
Three Preludes for Piano (Harms, Inc. [Warner])
An American classic; a perfect period piece. The two outer preludes (in B-flat major and E-flat minor), both marked *Allegro ben ritmato e deciso*, capture the hustle and bustle of syncopated "city music" of the '20s and '30s in settings that continue to seem fresh and exciting. Wide leaps are exploited, and the piano is definitely considered an instrument "with hammers." The second prelude (Andante con moto e poco rubato, in $\frac{4}{4}$ C-sharp minor) is an easy-going gem in three sections, featuring a left-hand ostinato which requires a black-to-white-key tenth. Highly recommended.

Claude Debussy:
Suite bergamasque (G. Schirmer)
Although the two outer movements are long-winded, the delicate, eerie Menuet is captivating, even if it can't decide whether it's in the Dorian mode or a minor. And there's always *Clair de lune*.

Leonard Bernstein:
Four Anniversaries (G. Schirmer)
Always pianistic, these four charming birthday preludes are a delight; no. 1 is especially appealing. The pieces are basically well-seated in a key, but employ chromaticism freely around the tonic. Nos. 3 and 4 require more independence of the hands than do the first two.

Seymour Bernstein:
Birds, Book 2 (Schroeder and Guenther)
A second book of impressionistic bird pictures. Good fun, rather like an old-fashioned piano story; the portraits are all literal renderings—almost caricatures—in tones. All are meticulously notated (nothing left to "chance") and not overlong. The idiom is overtly, almost defiantly, dissonant, in a pointedly programmatic context.

Claude Debussy:
Pour le piano (Elkan-Vogel [Presser]; G. Schirmer)
Three movements; the Prelude is particularly remarkable as it prefigures *Jardins sous la pluie* in concept and technique; it uses whole-tone writing to contrast with sections in A minor and C major.

Henry Cowell:
Piano Music by Henry Cowell (Associated Music Publishers)
Here are nine of Cowell's most characteristic, bristly, original works. Forearm clusters abound, as do polytonal writing, polyrhythms, newly devised notations for odd-length notes (for example, 4/5 notes, 8/11 notes, etc.), sympathetic vibration of silently depressed pitches, and all manner of touches on the strings. The collection includes "The Banshee," "Aeolian Harp," and "Tiger." Recommended. (Lower advanced through upper advanced.)

Blythe Owen:
Serially Serious (Daira Kalnajs Langens, Benton Harbor, Michigan)
Three delightful pieces using clear rhythms, varied textures; well thought-out music that is never overextended. A fine, nonformidable introduction to the serial usage of pitch, naturally integrated with traditional employment of other musical elements. Published in a limited edition. Recommended.

Ernst Křenek:
Twelve Short Piano Pieces, op. 83 (G. Schirmer)
Very well made, severely beautiful music; twelve-tone technique. Descriptive titles help to crystallize each as a tiny tone poem in the performer's view. The technical plan for each piece is given in the preface. Recommended.

Wolfgang Wijdeveld:
Escapades (Donemus)
Four movements of real textural and rhythmic interest. The music is fundamentally tonal, but the composer's chromatic imagination is quite individual. Especially fine and sensitive is the Adagio, no. 4.

Dmitri Shostakovich:
Five Preludes (MCA).
Mature writing; tasteful, balanced, highly crafted, individualistic forms. Rhetoric and wayward harmonies are kept to a minimum. By far the most notable is no. 4, in D-flat major.

Judith Lang Zaimont:
Annual Album: Twelve Prelude-Studies for the Developing Pianist (Alfred)
Highly chromatic, basically tonal "portraits" of the months. Each piece addresses itself to a distinct technical problem and is differentiated musically from the others in texture, tempo, dynamic plan, and mood. Among the compositional techniques explored are multimetric writing, polytonality, polyrhythms, clusters, and nonbarred music. Registral extremes are explored, and finger dexterity and independence of the hands are stressed. Three of the preludes are not definitively tonal and have open-ended terminal cadences.

Sergei Prokofiev:
Visions fugitives (PWM Edition [Belwin-Mills])
Well-known collection of twenty miniatures written between 1915–1917. Many feature ostinato figures in one hand while the other wanders semiautonomously, occasionally returning to coordinate a phrase ending. (The notes for this edition are in Polish and French. The editor has correlated two preexisting editions and refingered all the rough spots.)

Ben Weber: (New Music Quarterly
Five Bagatelles [Theodore Presser])
Each is distinguished through its texture. The music is not completely atonal, and a single texture is used throughout each bagatelle. No. 2 is recommended.

Samuel Barber:
Excursions (G. Schirmer)
Four very tonal pieces, straight-forward in gesture; all are too long for their basic ideas but well worth investigating. The set is exactly as described in a prefatory note: " 'Excursions' in small classical forms into regional American idioms." The most intriguing are no. 3, which abounds in cross-rhythms, and no. 4, an all-treble quasi-cakewalk.

Sergei Prokofiev:
Episodes, op. 12 (ten pieces) and (MCA)
Devilish Inspiration, op. 4 no. 4
Despite the disparity in the opus numbers, these pieces all share the vitality, exuberance, and abandon of youth. (They were written between 1906 and 1910.) Of interest in op. 12 are the Capriccio (no. 5); a rather beautiful Legend (no. 6); and the well-known C-major Prelude (no.7), originally written for harp. Also notable is the Scherzo (no. 10), despite the fact that the material is developed in a rather mechanical fashion. Op. 4 no. 4 is a favorite of the author. (Lower through upper advanced.)

Béla Bartók:
Three Burlesques, op. 8C (Editio Musica, Budapest)
Three remarkable whole-tone pieces, each economical in form and texture. While undoubtedly the work of Bartók (the savagery and cut of the melodic profiles, and rhythmic security and plasticity in shaping phrases are unmistakable), each Burlesque owes something to the music of another recent creator: no. 1 (a neat, linear beauty) emits strong overtones of Scriabin, especially in its polyrhythms; no. 2 is more the Debussy of the Prelude in alternating thirds (Book 2, no. 11); no. 3 is derived from the polytonal *Petrouchka* clash. They are lots of fun to play—the hands often overlap and cross—and deserve to be better known. Recommended.

Béla Bartók:
Improvisations on Hungarian Peasant Songs, op. 20 (Boosey & Hawkes)
Eight settings of Hungarian tunes (really concert paraphrases), each very different in texture, motive, and mood. Of particular interest are nos. 1, 2, 4, and 5.

Dennis Riley:
Five Little Movements (C.F. Peters)
Loosely strung-together group of tiny, two-line pieces, consistently dissonant. The work is quite representative of post-'50s writing, and calls for abrupt shifts of register, frequent hand crosses, and rhythms of the fragmented-pulse type. The sonorities are delicate, and the work is pianistic at all times; hand stretches never exceed the major seventh. Less formidable than it appears.

Dmitri Kabalevsky:
Twenty-four Preludes op. 38 (MCA)
A range of moods and a variety of technical and compositional approaches are found within this group. The music is most intriguing when the composer strays from his usual straight-forward expressions and strives for something a bit less obvious. Particularly noteworthy are nos. 10, 12, 14, 17, 20, and 24.

Virgil Thomson:
Ten Études (Carl Fischer)
Three of these are of interest beyond the merely technical: "Tenor Lead (Madrigal)," which hides a pleasant surprise in an inner voice; "Double Glissando (Waltz)," a dashing, glittery showpiece; and "Ragtime Bass," straight-forward, kissin' cousin to Gottschalk's "Banjo." (Lower through upper mid-advanced.)

Zoltán Kodály (Denes Agay, ed.):
Nine Piano Pieces, op. 3 and "Valsette" (MCA)
Fine set of miniature poems in tones, basically through-composed. "Valsette" plays several rhythmic tricks (heavy on the hemiolas) and may also be found in the editor's *Anthology*, vol. IV.

Alexander Scriabin (Murray Baylor, ed.):
Selected Works for the Piano (Alfred)
This beautifully finished edition contains a sampling of the composer's works arranged chronologically from op. 2 through op. 74. The thirty pieces include études and preludes (excerpts from almost all the sets of each); individual occasional pieces; the Mazurka, op. 40 no. 1; and the complete Fourth Sonata. The volume contains an introductory biographical article, an essay on the nature of the music, a valuable guide to idiomatic performance, and photographs. All the music is completely fingered and pedaled. Very highly recommended. (Lower advanced through upper advanced.)

Roy Harris:
American Ballads for Piano (Carl Fischer)
Concert paraphrases of five well-known tunes. The writing is distinguished by free-shifting accents, almost constant polytonality, unexpected harmonizations, and great verve, exuberance, and assurance of workmanship. Perhaps the most effective are "The Streets of Laredo," "Black is the Color of My True Love's Hair," and "The Bird" (these also are available separately). Recommended.

Peter Mennin:
Five Piano Pieces (Carl Fischer)
Among the very finest American neoclassic music, this group features crystal-clear textures, elegant forms, and is exceedingly well-built. A secure sense of formal balances permits each gesture just the right amount of time in which to make its point. The music is freely chromatic around pronounced tonal centers; predominantly linear in texture, and polytonal when chordal; rhythmically vital; multimetric; and cadences to a tonic sonority (not necessarily the one implied by the opening phrases). Thought should be given to fingering, which must be done before beginning study of the work. Highly recommended. (Lower advanced through mid-advanced.)

Charles Ives:
"Three Protests" or "Varied Air and Variations" (New Music Quarterly [Theodore Presser])
Good, short pieces typical of the composer's idiosyncratic style of chromatic wandering. The theme uses all twelve tones. The first "Protest" is in two-voice mirror counterpoint, closing on clusters; the second, a dissonant chromatic chorale in E minor, adds a coda of C-major chords, marked "Applause"; the third uses the right-hand material of the first with left-hand imitations in a free canon at the fifth.

INDIVIDUAL PIECES

Mid-Advanced

Claude Debussy:
Reflets dans l'eau (Durand)
The perfect complement in sound to Monet's paintings (from *Images*, Book 1). Highly recommended.

Anton Webern:
Variations, op. 27 (Universal Edition)
A three-movement abstract set. From the practical standpoint the piece is an excellent study in agile cross-hands and note-exchange systems. It is not rhythmically difficult, keeping a single meter throughout the course of each movement. It covers a five-octave range almost constantly, and takes on a glassy beauty in performance. Clef changes abound for both hands.

Maurice Ravel:
Valses nobles et sentimentales (Durand)
Seven suave, carefully made miniature waltzes linked together, plus an epilogue. Exquisite. Recommended.

Louise Talma:
Alleluia in the Form of a Toccata (Carl Fischer)
A neoclassic work of great purity. Crystal-clear textures, constantly shifting accents and virtuosic writing in general, particularly with regard to registral shifts, mark this perpetuum mobile as a tour de force. Although a D tonic is implied throughout, the final cadence is in B-flat major. At thirteen pages, it requires great care in gauging dynamic shadings to preserve involvement on the parts of both performer and audience throughout its entirety. (For another fine example of this composer's preserial style, see the second movement of the Sonata no. 1, a haunting larghetto.)

Walter Piston:
Passacaglia (Mercury)
Well-built, sternly beautiful work in $\frac{5}{8}$ virtually throughout. In just four pages the composer erects a commanding tonal structure, ranging harmonically far afield, by means of free use of all chromatic pitches, although the putative tonic is B. (Available individually or in Agay's *Anthology*, vol. IV.) Recommended.

Charles Griffes:
The Night Winds, op. 5 no. 3 (G. Schirmer)
The third of *Three Tone-Pictures*, this is highly descriptive, using constant ***pp*** hand-over-hand arpeggios in an impressionist manner. In $\frac{4}{4}$ throughout, the piece is a study in whole-tone writing anchored to E-flat, with the key signature of E-flat minor.

Sergei Prokofiev:
Toccata, op. 11 (Kalmus)
Well-known monolith in D minor. Relentless sixteenths and cascades of slippery chromatic scalewise clusters add excitement to a work definitely meant for an instrument with hammers. Care should be given to emphasizing all implied contrasts of "light" and "dark," as indicated by dynamic markings.

Charles Ives:
Three-page Sonata (Mercury)
So-called because it is three pages long in manuscript; most of the writing within this single movement is polyrhythmic. It divides into eight sections: A (practically unbarred Allegro); B (Andante); C (Adagio); D (Allegro—"March Time"); E (Più mosso); D; E; D (Coda using the last three lines of the "March").

Sergei Prokofiev:
Sonata no. 9, op. 103 (Leeds)
That this work is dedicated to pianist Sviatoslav Richter implies much about its stress on lyricism. Each of the four movements is streamlined,

reflective, but never dull in character, and well-differentiated in texture and mood from the others. More line-conscious than any other of the composer's sonatas, the Ninth is an inward-looking work of occasional great beauty; the first movement is particularly fine. Each movement concludes with a reference to the material of the next, stressing the overall unity of conception.

Claude Debussy:
L'Isle joyeuse (Durand)
An extended, atmospheric evocation of Watteau's "Island of Pleasure" in the Lydian mode on A.

William Sydeman:
Variations for Piano (Leeds)
Six variations follow the theme in this well-constructed, nontonal concert piece which employs textural, tempo, and registral differentiations for good effect. It is quite pianistic and involving; only the last *toccata*-like variation seems a bit overextended.

Toru Takemitsu:
Far Away (Salabert)
A rhythmically complex mood piece, music of great delicacy and effectiveness. Specific sonic structures are erected slowly, note by note, and proceed to shift and gradually merge to others. This nontonal work requires extreme care in pedaling to achieve its effects; all three pedals are called for. (The rhythmic notation is so precise as to appear fussy to a degree beyond that of average human discrimination.)

COMPOSER COLLECTIONS

Mid-Advanced

Roger Sessions:
From My Diary (E.B. Marks)
Fine set of four contrasting nontonal pieces, although tonal centers do insinuate themselves into the consciousness during the course of each movement. For instance, no. 3, larghissimo e misterioso, is really in D-sharp minor, and would not prove too difficult for an adventurous upper-intermediate student.

Francis Poulenc:
Nocturnes (Heugel)
Possibly the finest nonvocal music by this composer, these are for a mature hand span and sophisticated musical sensibility. Proportions and forms have been refined by a masterly hand; harmonic and rhythmic daring abounds (for example, his idiosyncratic brand of *non sequitur* cadence, and abrupt interruption of an otherwise flowing line); no banalities here. Especially fine are nos. 1, 3, 5, and 6. Very fresh-sounding music that is a joy to play. Highly recommended.

Claude Debussy:
Estampes (Durand)

Three of the master's most descriptive pieces. *Pagodes*, in B major, is full of Gamelan effects, and employs a pentatonic black-key melody in G-sharp minor. *Soirée dans Grenade* evokes a Spanish night through the intermittent use of a Habañera rhythm. *Jardins sous la pluie*, an arpeggiated pointillist picture of "gardens in the rain," features much whole-tone writing, and quotes two French songs, *Nous n'irons plus au bois* and *Do do, l'enfant do*. Each available separately. Recommended.

Arnold Schoenberg:
Three Piano Pieces, op. 11 (Universal Edition)
One of the first works in Schoenberg's mature nontonal but nonserial idiom. Motivic considerations dictate the extent to which the form of each piece will be permitted to flower. No. 1 is particularly fine.

Claude Debussy:
Images, Book 2 (Durand)
Three extraordinary pieces, less direct than the three in Book 1 but more surely, more perfectly made. The second piece from this set, *Et la lune descend sur le temple qui fut,* is an inward-looking meditation (using clusters and floating quartal harmonies) that is one of Debussy's most perfect creations. Highly recommended.

Alexander Scriabin:
Works for Piano, Selections Book 3– (Peters)
Preludes, Poems and Other Pieces
Contains op. 11 and op. 67.

Maurice Ravel:
Tombeau de Couperin (Durand)
The composer's last music for piano alone, dedicated to his friends killed in World War I. The writing is less exuberant, more detached, than his earlier music, and he turned to stricter forms from the past: Prelude in the form of a Courante; Fugue; Forlane; Rigaudon; another of his suave Menuets; and the final blazing Toccata, really a tour de force for interlocking hands. Highly recommended.

Lou Harrison:
Sarabande and Prelude for Grand Piano (New Music Quarterly [Theodore Presser])

The Sarabande is a one-page, stately rhythmed, well-made piece in two-part form, using what seems to be free atonality for its body, with several polytonal cadences; it closes on C minor–D major. The delightful four-page Prelude is dedicated to Henry Cowell. It uses no bar lines but is cleverly put together from strongly-pulsed eighth-note sections periodically interrupted by slower, clustered "recitatives," some of which employ strummed clusters and plucked single tones to good effect. Recommended.

Robert Helps:
Quartet for Piano (C.F. Peters)
Four pieces, each nontonal, highly chromatic and multimetric, well-made and pianistic throughout. Of special merit is no. 3, a lyric intermezzo, which could be managed by a pianist of lower advanced technique.

Frank Martin:
Eight Preludes for Piano (Universal Edition)
A set of superbly realized concert pieces by the Swiss master too little known in America. Among the most effective individual Preludes are the towering no. 2 in B minor; the austere but lovely no. 3; and the chromatic, fluttering no. 5. The shades of Chopin and Debussy hover distantly over the set, which is highly chromatic, very often absolutely nontonal, and exceedingly pianistic throughout. Highly recommended.

INDIVIDUAL PIECES

Upper Advanced

Alban Berg:
Sonata, op. 1 (Universal Edition)
Densely chromatic, beautiful one-movement work in loose sonata-allegro form. Ostensibly in B minor, this is restless, emotional, lyrical, striking, and pianistic music in a post-post-Wagnerian idiom. Highly recommended.

Maurice Ravel:
Jeux d'eau (G. Schirmer)
A remarkable evocation of splashing fountains, waterfalls, and streams. Ravel, who was twenty-six when he composed the piece, wrote that it is "the original of all the novelties in pianism which people have noted in my work." Though cast loosely in sonata-allegro form, it is distinguished chiefly by highly figurated surfaces, overall suavity of expression, and a deft combination of whole-tone writing with traditional major and minor tonalities. A stunning piece. Highly recommended.

Sergei Prokofiev:
Sonata no. 7, op. 83 (International Music Company)
Perhaps the composer's finest music for the instrument. Though begun in the same year as Sonatas no. 6 and no. 8, this is a different, superior work. All three movements are imbued with a sense of sureness and economy of expression: the music is linear in a lean but sensuous fashion, and chromaticism is functional rather than diversionary, as is so often the case in his earlier works. A tempered, nostalgic sentimentality colors the second movement, and the finale is a compact, well-proportioned *perpetuo moto* in constant $\frac{7}{8}$. Highly recommended.

Ned Rorem:
Toccata (C.F. Peters)
Exciting showpiece in B minor. Features many tricky registral shifts and introduces sections of quasi-lyricism for contrast at several intermediate points. In $\frac{8}{8}$ throughout, always divided . Recommended.

Ernst Křenek:
George Washington Variations (Southern Music Company)
A set of six variations on "Washington's Grand March" in the style of a nineteenth-century concert paraphrase. These virtuosic, delightful, Ivesian paraphrases are a welcome surprise: texturally elaborate, traditional in scheme, and ranging tonally far afield.

Lowndes Maury:
Wind-Sweep (Theodore Presser)
An eerie, fluttery piece with many phrases of unusual length, and much rhythmic interest. In B minor, with spicy dissonances; the writing is virtuosic, primarily for the right hand, and constantly agitated. In $\frac{3}{8}$, molto vivace throughout.

Vivian Fine:
Concerto for Piano, Strings, and Percussion (one performer) (Catamount Facsimile Edition, Box 245, Shaftsbury, Vermont 05262)
A demanding, dramatic work for a single performer who plays the tympani, flexatone, cymbal, triangle, piano keyboard, and piano strings—all while stationed conventionally at the keyboard. Varieties of clusters; various (and novel) ways of playing on the strings; the use of both explicitly detailed and imprecise notations, by turns; and emphasis on extreme registral and timbral effects characterize the work. The Concerto is really an intricate soundpiece in one movement which has been assembled rather than built. As one might expect in a collage piece, several direct quotations are featured—most prominently the first eight measures of Bach's Two-part Invention in C major, played completely on the strings.

Samuel Barber:
Sonata (G. Schirmer)
Virtuosic blockbuster on a huge scale. A lyric sensibility governs all four movements, though rhythmic interest and grandiose gestures abound. The last movement, a fitting climax, is a mighty fugue in E-flat minor with a clear-cut, syncopated subject. An admirable work with which to demonstrate one's prowess. Highly recommended.

Donald Martino:
Piano Fantasy (Ione Press, Inc. [G. Schirmer])
An expressive serial piece that builds up its delicate lines from pinpoints of sound, each a tiny rhythmic fragment of a quarter note. Although the lines are quite disjunct and the piece as a whole is rhythmically formidable, it has been well thought-out from the performer's standpoint: most gestures lie well within the hands, and stretches of a ninth seem to be the technical limit.

COMPOSER COLLECTIONS

Upper Advanced

Charles Griffes:
Roman Sketches, op 7 (G. Schirmer)
Four tone poems in Griffes' personal impressionist idiom: "The White Peacock," "Nightfall," "The Fountain of the Acqua Paola," "Clouds." Parallelisms (triads and clusters) abound, as do pentatonic melodic fragments on the black keys. The writing is vituosic, imagistic (a black-key glissando for the left hand in "Nightfall"), and features many languid cross-rhythms. All are available separately. "Nightfall," a brooding piece in G-sharp minor reminiscent of Scriabin and Ravel (*Vallée des cloches*) should be better known.

Noël Lee:
Quatres Études (Series 1) (Gerard Villaudot [Theodore Presser])
Four exceedingly showy nontonal studies which use the entire keyboard routinely. The music is always idiomatic for the instrument. Especially notable are no. 2, a lovely sound study using plucked strings and sympathetic vibration; and no. 3, *"Aux sons aigus"* (*vivacissimo*), a touch-piece spraying single notes all over the keyboard pointillistically; it uses no bar lines.

Grazyna Bacewicz:
Ten Studies (PWM Edition, Polskie Wydawnictwo Muzyczne)
Vivid, highly pianistic writing in a harmonically pungent, often polytonal idiom. Dramatic gestures abound in an often linear context, producing sensations of great centrifugal force. Among the most outstanding are no. 4, built as a single line of overlapping, shifting arpeggiated triads; no. 6, which explodes outward by leaps in both hands; and no. 8, a contemporary companion piece to Chopin's op. 10 no. 3. Highly recommended. (Bacewicz' music is strong and notable, and should be better known in this country; her Second Sonata is equally worth discovering.)

Maurice Ravel:
Miroirs (G. Schirmer)
Five superb pictures-in-tones which coexist uneasily as a set. Elusive *Noctuelles* ("Night Moths"); haunting *Oiseaux tristes* ("Sad Birds"); *Une Barque sur l'océan* ("A Boat on the Billowing Sea"); the stinging, crackling *Alborada del gracioso*; and *La Vallée des cloches*, a valley filled with the indistinct, overlapped echoes of church bells at evening. Each piece is available separately. Highly recommended.

Maurice Ravel Masterpieces: Album
of Selected Piano Compositions (E. B. Marks)
Contains *Jeux d'eau, Pavane pour une infant défunte*, and all five movements from *Miroirs* (though not in order).

Maurice Ravel:
Gaspard de la nuit (Durand)
The summit of Ravel's pianistic virtuosity. *Ondine, Le Gibet,* and *Scarbo.* Available separately. Recommended.

George Crumb:
Makrokosmos, vol. 1: Twelve Fantasy-Pieces after the Zodiac for Amplified Piano (C.F. Peters)
A set of impressionist mood and tone pictures which ingeniously explore the expanded timbral resources of an amplified, partially prepared instrument. The performer often plays on the strings—using fingertips, metal plectrum, thimble-capped fingers, etc.—and is occasionally required to moan or chant aloud. The more ethereal effects are easily distinguished by virtue of the electrical amplification. Clouded, mysterious, precious music, not meant for a self-conscious performer. (David Burge, for whom the work was written, has recorded a splendid performance on Nonesuch Records, H-71293.)

Alexander Scriabin:
Ten Sonatas (Leeds [MCA])
The evolution of this mystic master's personal style can be easily traced in these ten Sonatas: no. 1, op. 6 (1893) to no. 10, op. 70 (1912–13) 207 pages. In recent years, the two-movement no. 4, op. 30 (1903); no. 5, op. 53 (1907), a single, galvanic, open-ended sonata-allegro; and the one-movement no. 7, op. 64 (1911–1912) have been appearing on concert programs with increasing frequency. They are presented here in an excellent edition. Essential for devotees of Scriabin's work. (Mid-advanced through very advanced.)

ANTHOLOGIES

Five-Finger Music (Summy-Birchard)
Primary through lower elementary. A single volume which contains a set of pieces each by four composers. By far the best is John La Montaine's "Copycats," fourteen tiny pieces which stress independence of the hands throughout; many of them are canonic, thus permitting each hand to cadence separately. Syncopations are introduced, as is both modal writing and the tritone (treated as a natural musical component rather than as a "frightening" or "devilish" sonority). "Copycats" is highly recommended.

Frances Clark, ed.:
Contemporary Piano Literature, Book 1 (Summy-Birchard)
Lower through elementary. Well-produced set of six books, graded from elementary through lower advanced, containing contemporary music of a decidedly conservative nature. The music in Book 1 is by Tcherepnin, Bartók, Kabalevsky, Tansman, and Kraehenbuehl. Tcherepnin's contributions are the most notable here, but the Kraehenbuehl piece, in $\frac{5}{4}$ with shifting accents, is also quite interesting.

Cleveland Composer's Guild:
Piano Music for the Young, Books 1 and 2 (Galaxy)
Book 1–elementary through lower intermediate; Book 2–lower through upper intermediate. A fine set, comprising two books of short pieces. From the start, stress is laid on developing independence of the hands while the ear is opened by means of quartal and quintal harmonies. All registers of the keyboard are explored and traditional tonality is often set aside. A piece for duet is included (Book 1), as well as a set of four pieces for prepared piano (Book 2). Textures are quite clean. Book 1 is somewhat more focused and concise in its music than Book 2, which contains some pieces which wander excessively. Often, too, a tonal final cadence is appended when the body of the piece doesn't warrant it.

Denes Agay, ed.:
Modern Miniatures (Yorktown Music Press)
Upper elementary. Elegant, well-made, one-page tonal (or tonal-modal) pieces, most of which are in moderate or lively tempos. Composers represented are Kabalevsky, Satie, Kalmanoff, Kurka, Khachaturian, Salutrinskaya, Agay, Iordansky, Bartók, and E. Gnessina.

Frances Goldstein et al, eds.:
Contemporary Collection for Piano Students (Summy-Birchard)
Collection of thirty-seven pieces by twenty-two composers geared to the older pianist of elementary level, arranged in order of increasing difficulty. The level of sophistication rapidly increases in the second half of the book as the pieces begin to expand beyond the conventional tonal-modal writing found in the first half. Among the most interesting inclusions are "Game" and "Swinging" by Blythe Owen; Lynn Freeman Olson's impressionist "Half-Asleep"; "The Mirror" by William Pottebaum; two crisp, delicious pieces by Dennis Riley, a whole-tone "Scherzo" and the multimetric "Rain"; the open-ended, whole-tone "Magic Circle" by Jean Eichelberger Ivey; and Robert Lombardo's "Lyric Piece." This collection also contains the haunting twelve-tone "Night Shadows" by Ihor Bilohrud, cited elsewhere on this list as a single publication. Recommended.

Frances Clark, ed.:
Contemporary Piano Literature, Book 2 (Summy-Birchard)
Upper elementary. Includes music by Kabalevsky, Tansman, Tcherepnin, Bartók, and Shostakovich. Notable are Siegmeister's "Street Games" and Tcherepnin's "To and Fro."

Mark Nevin, ed.:
Modern Masters (Belwin-Mills)
Upper elementary through lower intermediate. An excellent collection (at this level) of tonal music by several masterly twentieth-century composers. Every piece has considerable artistic merit as well as a distinct technical point to make. The volume consists of one- and two-page pieces by Bartók, Kabalevsky, Gretchaninoff, Prokofiev, Khachaturian, Shostakovich, and Debussy. The latter's *Le Petit Nègre* and Kabalevsky's "Sad Story" and Scherzo are notable inclusions. A fine sampling of music in a particular vein. Highly recommended.

Denes Agay, ed.:
The Joy of Modern Piano Pieces (Yorktown Music Press)
Elementary through mid-intermediate. Fine collection of fifty-three moderately short pieces by forty composers. Notable individual selections include the Debussy "Album Leaf" (1916); a pretty "Evening Song" by Khachaturian; "The Bear" by Shostakovich, full of unexpected registral shifts and octave displacements; Siegmeister's jaunty "Street Game"; "Barcarolette" by Agay; a brilliant Bagatelle in E minor by Tcherepnin; and Nicholas Flagello's chromatically spiced and compact March. Also represented are Prokofiev, Kabalevsky, Leo Kraft, Robert Starer, Satie, Bartók, and others. Recommended.

The Young Pianist's Anthology of Modern Music (Associated Music Publishers)
Upper elementary through upper intermediate. Forty-two pieces by twenty-three composers. A good sampling of the simpler music of our century, much slanted toward tonal writing with mild dissonances. Among the most interesting inclusions are nos. 1 and 5 of Bernstein's "Five Anniversaries"; "A Boat Slowly Sails" op. 83 no. 6 by Krenek; George List's "Blue Gray Fog"; the entire "Little Suite" by Roy Harris; S. Strohbach's "The Roly-Poly" from the suite The Toy-Chest; "Witch Dance" by Carlos Surinach; Cowell's well-known "Aeolian Harp"; and the entire "Three-Score Set" by William Schuman. This volume also includes music by Bartók, Creston, Hovhaness, Kabalevsky, Muczynski, Tansman, Satie, and others. Recommended.

Das Neue Klavierbuch, Book 1 (of two) (Schott [Belwin-Mills])
Lower intermediate. Music by European composers, including Hindemith, Stravinsky, Bartók, Badings, Martinu, Honegger, Lutoslawski, Milhaud, Poulenc, Tcherepnin, and others. The music is all more or less conservative and just a touch academic. The most notable inclusions in Book 1 are Bartók's "Allegro ironico" from For Children; a marvelously catchy, tricky "Toccatina" by Matyas Seiber (in quartal harmony); and a Hindemith March from *Wir bauen eine Stadt*. Book 1 is particularly recommended.

Frances Clark, ed.:
Contemporary Piano Literature, Book 3 and 4 (Summy-Birchard)
Lower intermediate. Contains music by Bartók, Tcherepnin, Kabalevsky, Douglas Moore, Shostakovich, Cyril Scott, Gretchaninoff, Ross Lee Finney, Stravinsky, and Prokofiev. Notable inclusions are Bartók's "Jeering Song"; Tcherepnin's "Merry-go-round"; the "Toccatina" and the one-movement A-minor Sonatina by Kabalevsky; Finney's "There and Back"; and three pieces from "Five Fingers" by Stravinsky.

Denes Agay, ed.:
The World of Modern Piano Music (MCA)
Lower through mid-intermediate. Tonal miniatures by composers from various countries, including several pieces not readily found in other collections. Among the contents are two very interesting pieces by Boris Kremenliev; Shostakovich's "Happy" and "Sad" Fairy Tales; Prokofiev's "Evening" from Music for Children; Siegmeister's "On a Gold-

en Afternoon"; five selections by Bartók; and the editor's Two Bagatelles. Highly recommended.

American Composers of Today (E.B. Marks)
Lower through upper intermediate. The volume contains twenty-three pieces by twenty-two composers plus a biographical sketch of each creator. Music by Babbitt, Cazden, Cowell, Dello Joio, Gideon, Harrison, Helps, Hovhaness, Sessions, Slonimsky, and Ben Weber, among others. Especially fine is Gideon's "Walk," a one-page study in genial, shifting meters in which major and minor thirds serve as contrasting building blocks ("Walk" is available only in this anthology).

Isadore Freed, ed.:
American Music by Distinguished Composers (Theodore Presser)
Lower through upper intermediate. A collection of ten short, mostly two-page pieces. Several selections which appear on this list elsewhere as single publications are included here: Henry Cowell's "Sway Dance," the *Petite Étude* of Wallingford Riegger, and Douglas Moore's Prelude. The rest of the music is negligible, with the exception of the following: "Perky Pete" by Leo Kraft; Wagenaar's "The Flickering Candle"; and "Dance for a Holiday" by Moore.

Saminsky and Freed, eds.:
Masters of Our Day (Carl Fischer)
Lower through upper intermediate. A collection of small-scale tonal pieces by mostly American composers. Among the best are "The Bell" by Howard Hanson; Douglas Moore's "Careful Etta" (a minuet with a Prokofiev-style modulation); *Touches blanches* and *Touches noires* by Milhaud; and Copland's "Young Pioneers" (certain of these are also available as individual pieces from the same publisher). Recommended.

Frances Clark, ed.:
Contemporary Piano Literature, Books 5 and 6 (Summy-Birchard)
Upper intermediate. Music by Tcherepnin, Finney, Kabalevsky, Bartók, and Prokofiev. A notable inclusion is the complete Sonatina in C major, op. 13 no. 1 of Kabalevsky.

Das Neue Klavierbuch, Book 2 (Schott [Belwin-Mills])
Upper intermediate. (See Book 1, p. 429).

Martin Canin, ed.:
French Piano Music of the Early Twentieth Century (Salabert)
Lower intermediate through lower advanced. Music of five French composers, most of it written in the '20s and '30s. Sentimentality is generally avoided—an accolade to the compiler. The music is tasteful, tonal, civilized but not superficial. The best contributions are Charles Koechlin's *Dix Petites Pièces faciles*, which uses bar lines only to indicate sectional divisions and not, in the traditional way, to define a meter (lower intermediate); and the *Quatres Romances sans paroles* by Milhaud, which are well-made, lovely one-page miniatures (upper intermediate). A glossary of all the French terms is included at the beginning of the volume. None of the music is fingered.

Denes Agay, ed.:
An Anthology of Piano Music, vol. 4: "The Twentieth Century" (Yorktown Music Press)
Lower through upper advanced. Extensive, excellent collection illustrating many twentieth-century styles; includes music by forty-two composers. Fingering and pedaling directions are generally indicated. Among the inclusions are nine Bartók pieces, among them the "Bear Dance"; Casella's polytonal, magical music-box "Carillon"; the Cowell "Sway Dance"; four early Debussy pieces; "The Alcotts" movement from Charles Ives' "Concord" Sonata; Kabalevsky's C-major Sonatina op. 13 no. 1; two pieces from "Bucolics" by Lutoslawski; Frank Martin's Prelude no. 2 from Eight Preludes; the Piston Passacaglia; six mature pieces by Prokofiev; two of the Six Little Piano Pieces, op. 19 by Schoenberg; four pieces by Scriabin; three by Shostakovich; three excerpts from Stravinsky's "Five Fingers"; and Webern's *Klavierstück*, op. post. In all, eighty pieces. The volume also contains biographical sketches of each composer and a glossary. An important collection; very highly recommended.

Piano Performance: Modern Pieces for the Young Artist in Recital (AMSCO)
Lower through upper advanced. Well-edited, meticulously fingered collection of nineteen concert pieces; most of them established "classics" from the first part of the twentieth century. Among the best known are Bartok's "Bear Dance"; both Debussy Arabesques; the Khachaturian Toccata; Prelude in C major op. 12 no. 7 by Prokofiev; Rachmaninoff's G-sharp minor Prelude, op. 32 no. 12; the *Pavane pour une infante défunte* and *Vallée des cloches* by Ravel; Satie's three *Gymnopédies*; and the Polka from the *Golden Age* ballet of Shostakovich. All the music is tonal and the collection includes several "finds": Kabalevsky's Prelude and Fugue, op. 61 no. 6 in F major; Scriabin's "Album Leaf" op. 45 no. 1; and an early, romantically styled Stravinsky Étude in E minor, op. 7 no. 3. Highly recommended.

Joseph Prostakoff, ed.:
New Music for the Piano (Lawson-Gould [G. Schirmer])
Advanced through very advanced. A collection of one piece each by twenty-four American composers. There is much rhetoric in this music, which ranges through a wide variety of styles, including a fair number of neoclassical and serial works. The format and clarity of notation are admirable; care has been taken in the production of the volume. (Recorded by Robert Helps on RCA Victor LM-7042.)

CONTEMPORARY PEDAGOGICAL STUDIES

Alice Canaday, ed.:
Contemporary Music and the Pianist: A Guidebook of Resources and Materials (Alfred)
Extremely valuable, carefully researched volume containing a sampling of contemporary pieces presented in a graded format. Also includes a

detailed, illustrated introductory section discussing every technique germane to the piano music of our time (with the single exception of prepared piano), and an extensive, annotated list of suggested repertory. Very highly recommended.

Béla Bartók:
Mikrokosmos, Books 1–6 (Boosey & Hawkes)
Independence of the hands is stressed throughout, and the player's ear is gradually drawn beyond the major-minor system into the contemporary world of bitonal or modal writing; artificial scales; quartal and quintal harmonies; clusters. Conventional phrases give way immediately to asymmetrical arrangements; irregular rhythms and multimetric writing abound. Textures are polyphonic and homophonic by turns, and elements of folk music from several continents are introduced. A monumental work.

Books 1 and 2: elementary
Book 3: lower intermediate
Book 4: upper intermediate
Book 5 and 6: lower advanced

Very highly recommended.

Barbara Pentland:
Music of Now, Books 1–3 (Waterloo)
Recommended by Canaday: "A real attempt to deal with a pedagogy of contemporary music at the elementary level. It bypasses the major-minor harmonic system and scales as such, dealing instead with interval relations and inversions. It emphasizes half-step relations, canonic writing, clusters, and early reading of chromatics."

Donald Waxman:
Pageants for Piano, Books 1–5 (Galaxy)
Together, these form a method "for the early years." Independence of the hands is stressed almost from the beginning; the entire keyboard is used, not just a limited range, and asymmetrical phrases are featured. The music is tonal, often modal, and cast in clear, varied textures, using a single meter per piece. Rhythmic interest and vitality, extended consequent phrases, and well-considered accompaniment patterns are to be found on every page. Often, terminal cadences are purposefully altered away from the tonic, even when not strictly necessary.

Samuel Adler:
Gradus, Books 1 and 2 (Oxford University Press)
Twenty short exercises per volume, each "utilizing a technique of composition which has become a common practice in the last half century." An admirable attempt to present a diversity of compositional devices within a graded format, it includes sample of modal writing, bitonality, mirror writing, irregular rhythms, asymmetric phrases, expanded notation, and aleatory procedures. Each exercise is discussed in detail in the

prefatory notes. Book 1, upper elementary through mid-intermediate; Book 2, upper intermediate through lower advanced. Pedantic considerations often intrude uncomfortably, however. (The pieces were tested in piano classes in the preparatory department at the Eastman School of Music). Example in *The Piano Quarterly* Winter 1972.

Yoram Paporisz:
Discoveries at the Piano, Books 1–4 (Alexander Broude, Inc.)
An admirable, progressive set of 143 short pieces touching almost all contemporary bases (including modal, bitonal, and serial writing, free atonality, irregular rhythms, and multimetric schemes, plus examples of separate barring for each hand, clusters, indefinite pitch notation, and extra-piano sonorities), though tending to emphasize serialism in the later volumes. Textures are usually spare; the music emphasizes contrapuntal rather than homophonic arrangements. The level of difficulty increases rapidly: Books 3 and 4 would coordinate well with Books 3 and 4 of Waxman's *Études*. A valuable alternative to Adler's *Gradus*, and useful companion to *Mikrokosmos*. Titles and notes in English and German. Upper elementary through lower advanced. Recommended.

Ross Lee Finney:
Thirty-two Piano Games (C.F. Peters)
Upper elementary through mid-intermediate. Described in Composer Collections, p. 397.

Ross Lee Finney:
Twenty-four Inventions (C.F. Peters)
Intermediate through upper intermediate. Described in Composer Collections, p. 404.

Wallingford Riegger:
New and Old (Boosey & Hawkes)
Though didactic in intent, these twelve pieces make good musical sense. An introductory note is provided for each piece, discussing its technical point in detail. Among the techniques illustrated are "augmented triad," "the tritone," "shifted rhythm," "tone clusters," "polytonality," and "fourths and fifths." Of particular interest is no. 3, "The Twelve Tones," which manages to establish a tonal center (F-sharp) despite the rigorous nature of its compositional matrix. Upper intermediate through lower advanced.

Marguerite Miller, ed.:
Mosaics: Thirty-two Piano Pieces for Learning Musicianship; Musicianship Series, Book 1 (Sonos Music Resources)
An anthology of new compositional practices, including aleatory, modal, twelve-tone, cluster, and timbre writing, plus examples of newer notations: graphic, proportional, indeterminate pitch. Familiarity with extra-keyboard sound sources is stressed. Written to help the performer create and perform, as well as understand, the new music. Commen-

taries are provided for each piece; these contain not only information about the piece's construction, but questions to be answered by the player, and suggestions for listening or looking at more advanced music built along the same lines. Space is allotted for students to experiment with creating pieces in new notational symbols as well as on the staff. A complete index by subject, as well as the usual table of contents, encourages skipping around to suit the interests of the moment. Composers included are Ross Lee Finney, Vincent Persichetti, Paul Creston, Merrill Bradshaw, Paul Cooper, John Fitch, and Eliot Newsome. Highly recommended. From upper elementary onward. (A valuable adjunct to *Mosaics* is a collection of eight pieces by Tom Long, entitled *Alea: Music by Chance*, published by Canyon Press. At least one new abstract notation symbol is introduced in each piece, and the explanations provided by the composer and their employment in the music itself render them all easy to comprehend and comfortable to use.)

Donald Waxman:
Fifty Études for Piano, Books 1–4 (Galaxy)
Admirable, progressive series exploring areas of traditional and contemporary keyboard techniques. Finger dexterity as well as independent and equal development of the hands are stressed. Each piece (two to four pages) takes an extended look at the targeted technique, using an individual style remarkable for its rhythmic freshness and vitality. The music is basically tonal with free chromaticism, and distinguished by unexpected accents, syncopations, and asymmetric phrasing. No undue fuss is made over the contemporary devices when they are introduced: clusters, quartal and quintal sonorities, plucking, strumming or stroking the strings, etc. Books 1 and 2, intermediate through upper intermediate; Books 3 and 4, upper intermediate through lower advanced. Each étude has both technical and descriptive titles. Highly recommended.

GUIDEBOOKS

Robert Starer:
Rhythmic Training (MCA)
Explores the rhythmic problems inherent in contemporary music, with a stress on pulsed rhythms expressed in irregularly accented streams of eighth notes, rather than fragmented ones formed from tiny splinterings of quarter notes. Many examples are provided of intricate rhythms, polyrhythms, and irregular meters. Graded in increasing order of difficulty, from lower intermediate. Highly recommended.

Gardner Read:
Music Notation: A Manual of Modern Practice (2nd ed.) (Allyn and Bacon)
Definitive treatment of standard contemporary notational practices. In addition to detailed discussion of all the symbols in current use (broken down by category of relevant musical element or instrument), the volume includes a brief history of the development of notation as well as

an alphabetized index of notation symbols. Suggestions are offered as to which of several newly devised symbols for the newest new-music effects will prove most suitable from the interpreter's standpoint. Standard reference work. Very highly recommended.

Kurt Stone:
"New Notation for New Music" (*Music Educators Journal*,
parts 1 and 2 October and November 1976)
In 1974, an International Conference on New Musical Notation was held at the University of Ghent, Belgium, for the purpose of reaching an agreement on the best symbols for expressing new-music devices and effects, selecting from among the many already devised by individual composers. Dr. Stone, director of the Index of New Musical Notation in the New York Public Library, Lincoln Center, here describes the results of that conference while discussing each agreed-upon new symbol in detail. In addition, he pursues several points relevant to the whole question of devising notations to fit the techniques of our time, and stresses three criteria by which to judge proposed symbols: "clarity, practicability, and necessity from the performer's point of view." An excellent, concise, detailed presentation. (Dr. Stone is presently preparing a considerably more comprehensive, detailed book on this subject for W.W. Norton; until that volume appears, these articles are essential.) Very highly recommended.

(The author gratefully acknowledges the help of numerous editors, publishers, and composers in providing materials for review; special thanks go to Karen Famera, chief librarian, and the staff of the American Music Center, and to Dr. Barbara Greener and the staff of the music library at Queens College, CUNY.)

Recommended Editions of Standard Keyboard Literature

JOHN H. DIERCKS

At least four considerations enter into recommending editions of works in the standard repertory. Three may be stated briefly: cost, availability, and format (quality of print and paper, layout of the music on the page, overall clarity). Of prime importance, however, is the level of authenticity achieved by the publication—that is, its faithfulness to the composer's intent.

While one can assume that this intent transfers almost automatically from manuscript to print for contemporary writers, everyone recognizes certain difficulties in establishing a definitive version of older music. Problems center on illegibility of the composer's autograph; faulty proofreading of the printed copy; changes imposed by a publisher or later editor; and revisions—usually minor, but sometimes major—undertaken by the composer.

In view of these difficulties, music scholars have attempted reconstructions of composers' works by studying all original manuscripts available, early composer-approved editions, and other relevant materials. Selective compilation results in a *critical edition*, which customarily notes all significant variants from this printed "definitive" version. Often costly, this type of publication may be found in libraries, where it serves as an indispensable reference for all.

Somewhat different is an *Urtext* ("from the source") edition; while it may derive from the composer's manuscript, it may also be a reprinting of one of the first editions or of an early attempt at a critical edition. The label *Urtext* does not inevitably ensure authenticity, although it points well in that direction.

For the purposes of this list, emphasis is placed on the *practical editions*, which result from an editor's careful assessment of the scholars' work; then his or her judicious use of any necessary standard markings (for tempo, dynamics, articulation, pedal) and fingerings to produce a stylistically convincing interpretation of the music by teacher and player. A preface or distinctive type face can account for all additions to the original text. The editor will often include personal insights regarding appropriate performance practice in the preface or as footnotes.

What follows represents an endeavor to recommend objectively the best editions of complete works as well as some individual pieces. In some cases where "authenticity" proves difficult to determine, various practical sources are given.

For those composers, mostly contemporary, who have written substantially for the instrument but who have a number of publishers, a relatively comprehensive listing appears in *The Pianist's Resource Guide: Piano Music in Print and Literature on the Pianistic Art* by Joseph Rezits and Gerald Deatsman (Pallma Music Corp./Neil A. Kjos Jr., 1978).

In addition, Maurice Hinson's *Guide to the Pianist's Repertoire* (Indiana University Press 1973) proves of inestimable value for those wishing to explore further the vast riches of the keyboard literature. (Please refer to the list of abbreviations at the end of this section for coding of publishers and, when applicable, their current distributor.)

Albéniz, Isaac (1860–1909)
  Album of Masterpieces. EBM.
  España op. 165. K, CFP.
  Iberia (four vols.). K, Int, EBM.
d'Albert, Eugene (1864–1932)
  Suite in D minor. Bote & Bock.
Alkan, Charles-Henri Valentin (1813–1888)
  The Piano Music of Alkan. GS (Lewenthal). A fine selection enhanced by elegant editorial commentary.
Bach, Carl Philipp Emanuel (1714–1788)
  "Prussian" Sonatas (six) W. 48; "Württemberg" Sonatas (six) W. 49 (both in two vols.). K, Nagel (Steglich).
  Klavier Sonaten und freie Fantasien, nebst einigen Rondos für Kenner und Liebhaber. Br&H (Krebs); also K (two vols.).
  Achtzehn Probestücke. Schott (Doflein).
  Six Sonatas. Galaxy (Friedheim, P.).
  Vier leichte Sonaten W. 65. Nagel (Vrieslander).
  Sonatas and Pieces. CFP (Hermann).
  Twenty-four Short Pieces. K, Nagel (Vrieslander). Contains the C-minor *Solfeggietto* and Six New Sonatinas.
Bach, Johann Christian (1735–1782)
  Ten Sonatas. CFP (Landshoff).
    Vol. 1: op. 5 nos. 2 and 5; op. 17 nos. 2, 4, 5.
    Vol. 2: op. 5 nos. 3, 4, 6; op. 17 nos. 3, 6.

Bach, Johann Sebastian (1685–1750)

The monumental *Bach Gesellschaft*, a critical edition from the nineteenth century, remains the principal resource for study of his music. The keyboard works, volumes 3, 13, 14, 36, and 45, have been available in reduced size in Lea Pocket Scores. They may be obtained in full-size format from J.W. Edwards (Ann Arbor, Michigan). The Kalmus publications were well-edited by Bischoff years ago.

Little Notebook for Anna Magdalena Bach. K.

Little Notebook for Wilhelm Friedemann Bach. K.

Short Preludes and Fugues. Henle, K.

Two-part Inventions. Alfred (Palmer), Henle, GWM (Banowetz).

*Two- and Three-part Inventions. Bär #5150 is an excellent, clear text; otherwise, CFP (Landshoff), Alfred, K.

The Well-Tempered Clavier, vols. 1 and 2. Henle #256 and 258, CFP (Kroll), K.

**Six French Suites. Henle, CFP, K.

**Six English Suites. Henle, CFP, K.

**Six Partitas. Henle, CFP, K.

Seven Toccatas. Henle, CFP, K.

**Goldberg Variations. GS (Kirkpatrick). A distinguished edition.

Fantasia in C minor. Henle, K.

Capriccio on the Departure of a Beloved Brother. Henle, CFP, K.

Italian Concerto. Henle, K.

Chromatic Fantasy and Fugue in D minor. CFP #9006.

Bach, Wilhelm Friedemann (1710–1784)

Nine Sonatas (complete; three vols.). K, Nagel.

Barber, Samuel (1910–   )

GS.

Bartók, Béla (1881–1945)

Boosey publishes all; K, most of the early works. A good GS collection contains the Sonatina. A number of the shorter works appear in varying composer-authorized forms, so that the writings of Bartók specialists should be consulted.

Beethoven, Ludwig van (1770–1827)

Thirty-two Sonatas. Henle, K, GS (Urtext edition), Dover 23134-8 and 23135-6 (Schenker). The von Bülow (GS) and Schnabel (Simon & Schuster) editions can provide some valuable fingerings as well as interpretive insights. Most of the sonatas are available separately from Henle, K, and Schott.

Six Sonatinas. K, CFP.

Variations (complete). Henle, CFP. Selected variations: Henle, K.

Short Works (Bagatelles, Rondos, etc.). VUE, Henle.

Duets. Int, CFP.

*Dover reprint (21982-8) of the B.G. edition and original autograph manuscript.

**In a Dover reprint (22360-4) of the B.G. edition.

Benda, Georg (1722–1795)
Sixteen Sonatas. MAB, vol. 24.
Thirty-four Sonatinas. MAB, vol. 37.
Bloch, Ernest (1880–1959)
GS the principal publisher.
Brahms, Johannes (1833–1897)
Complete Works. GS (Mandyczewski) (three vols.), K (Sauer) (three vols.), CFP (Sauer) (two vols.).
Complete Sonatas and Variations. Dover 22650-6.
Complete Shorter Works. Dover 22651-4. Both Mandyczewski.
Individual opus nos. CFP (Sauer), Henle (Georgii). Late lyric pieces: K.
Waltzes, op. 39 and Hungarian Dances. Int, Henle.
Complete Works for Four Hands. Dover 23271-9 (Mandyczewski).
Variations on a Theme of Haydn, for duo piano. GS, CFP, Int.
Busoni, Ferruccio (1866–1924)
Most available through Br&H.
Cage, John (1912–).
Available through CFP.
Casella, Alfredo (1883–1947).
Eleven *Pièces enfantines*. UE.
Sonatina. Ricordi.
Chabrier, Emmanuel (1841–1894)
Pièces pittoresques. Int.
Chopin, Frédéric (1810–1849)
The complete solo works are best found in the "Polish" edition of the Chopin Institute, distributed by EBM. Individual groups of pieces (by genre) are available at not-at-all prohibitive cost. Another set has been prepared recently by VUE. The older editions by GS include interesting prefatory material as well as some very skillful fingerings by the master teacher-performers who edited them. For the reprints by K, the "Liszt" edition is preferred.
Cimarosa, Domenico (1749–1801)
Thirty-two Sonatas. Eschig (three vols.: 1–10, 11–20, 21–32).
Clementi, Muzio (1752–1832)
The Da Capo reprinting of an early nineteenth-century edition by Br&H, a library item, though not considered totally "authentic," remains the richest source, containing sixty sonatas from an output which might number more than eighty. Small, critically edited publications appear increasingly; individual works are included in larger general anthologies.
Sonatas (four vols.). CFP (Ruthardt). The editing fails to inspire confidence.
Clementi–Rediscovered Masterworks. EBM (Mirovitch). Vol. 1: Short pieces. Vol. 2: Two Sonatas and a Rondo. Vol. 3: Three Sonatas.
Sonatinas op. 36. Alfred (Palmer).
Seven Sonatas, duet. K, GS.
Two Sonatas, duo. GS, CFP.

Copland, Aaron (1900–   )
Boosey & Hawkes.
Couperin, François (1668–1733)
Pièces de clavecin (4 vols.). Heugel (Gilbert). An older edition worthy of respect: Augener (Brahms-Chrysander).
L'Art de toucher le clavecin. Br&H.
Cowell, Henry (1897–1965)
Piano Works. AMP.
Debussy, Claude (1862–1918)
All available from Durand, now in a format of standard size. K has reprinted separately many works through 1905. Dover publishes a collection of the music from 1888–1905 (22771-5); another fine collection of early works is SL of MC #1813.
Dello Joio, Norman (1913–   )
GS, CF, EBM.
Diabelli, Anton (1781–1858)
Sonatinas, op. 20. CFP, K, GS.
Dohnányi, Ernst von (1877–1960)
Album of Dohnanyi Masterpieces. EBM.
Dussek, Johann L. (1760–1812)
Twenty-nine Sonatas. MAB, vols. 46, 53, 59, 63.
Six Sonatinas op. 20. CFP, K, GS.
Dvořák, Antonin (1841–1904)
Artia has Collected Works, as well as some individually.
Thirteen Poetic Tone Pictures op. 85. GS, Simrock.
Twenty-four Selected Piano Pieces. CFP.
Falla, Manuel De (1876–1946)
Pièces espagnoles. Durand.
Fauré, Gabriel (1845–1924)
Most of the genre pieces are published in partial or complete sets by Int. and K. The complete catalog is divided between Hamelle and Heugel.
Theme and Variations op. 73. Int, K.
Dolly Suite, op. 56, duet. Int.
Field, John (1782–1837)
Eighteen Nocturnes. CFP, GS (Liszt).
Finney, Ross Lee (1906–   )
CFP for later works.
Franck, César (1822–1890)
Selected Piano Compositions published by Dover (23269-7) includes the two largest works.
Eighteen Short Pieces. CFP.
Forty-six Short Pieces for the Piano. TP (Agay).
Gershwin, George (1898–1937)
Warner Brothers.
Ginastera, Alberto (1916–   )
Twelve American Preludes. CF.
Sonata. Boosey.

Gottschalk, Louis Moreau (1829–1869)
Arno Press collection contains one hundred twelve works in five volumes.
Piano Music of Louis M. Gottschalk. TP (Behrend).
Granados, Enrique (1867–1916)
Twelve Spanish Dances, four books. K, EBM, GS, Int.
Goyescas. Int.
Gretchaninoff, Alexander (1864–1956)
Schott publishes many works, including the Sonata and two Sonatinas. Groups of shorter pieces are issued by EBM and Int. Single items have been widely anthologized.
"Glass Beads" op. 12. K, MCA (Agay).
Grieg, Edvard (1843–1907)
Complete Piano Works (three vols.). CFP.
Lyric Pieces (complete; thirteen vols.). CFP.
Sonata, op. 7. Br&H.
Griffes, Charles Tomlinson (1884–1920)
Almost all by GS.
Handel, George Frideric (1685–1759)
Keyboard Works (three vols.), Bär., in an unusually clear edition; (five vols.) CFP (Serauky).
Sixteen Suites. K, reprint of Durand.
Haydn, Joseph (1732–1809)
Complete Sonatas. VUE (Christa Landon) currently definitive, superceding CFP (Martienssen). See Hinson, pp. 309–11, for Landon numberings and their equivalent in the Hoboken catalog.
Variations in F minor. Henle (Georgii).
Heller, Stephen (1813–1888)
Most of the standard works published by GS, CFP.
Hindemith, Paul (1895–1963)
Schott.
Honegger, Arthur (1892–1955)
Primarily by Salabert and Eschig.
Hovhaness, Alan (1911–)
Almost entirely by CFP; occasional AMP, Peer.
Ibert, Jacques (1890–1962)
Histoires (including *Le Petit Âne blanc*). Leduc.
Ives, Charles (1874–1954)
Sonata no. 1. Peer.
Sonata no. 2. Arrow.
Three-Page Sonata. Mercury.
Kabalevsky, Dmitri (1904–)
Most of his keyboard music has been published in varying amounts by MCA, K, Int, CFP with "authenticity" difficult to establish. Under a new agreement with the Soviet Union, GS/AMP plans to release editions of the older generation as well as newer composers.
Khatchaturian, Aram (1903–1978)
As with Kabalevsky: MCA, K, CFP, GS/AMP.

Kodály, Zoltán (1882–1967)
Twenty-four Little Canons on the Black Keys. Boosey.
Nine Piano Pieces, op. 3. MCA (Agay).
Seven Piano Pieces, op. 11. UE.
Liszt, Franz (1811–1886)
Gregg Press has reprinted the Collected Works in a slightly reduced, somewhat crowded-looking format. The new Bärenreiter-EMB series aims at highest scholarship, yet its occasional interpretive comments seem unevenly valid. Both sets are an essential reference. For a performing edition of the complete works: CFP (Sauer) (twelve vols.). Otherwise, most of the major publishers, especially CFP, issue the standard pieces in very usable versions. The GS edition of the twelve Transcendental Études retains value for the fingerings and supplementary exercises provided by Paul Gallico. GS publishes the *Consolations* and *Liebestraume* together. Its edition of the *Années de Pelerinage*, Book Two, includes translations of the Petrarch sonnets.
MacDowell, Edward (1861–1908)
More and more major publishers have begun to reprint or reedit the lyric pieces. Presently a number of sets are available from K and GS. K supplies both groups of études and the four sonatas.
Martinu, Bohuslav (1890–1908)
Études and Polkas. Boosey.
Other works by Leduc, Artia, Eschig, Schott.
Medtner, Nicholai (1880–1951)
Album of Selected Pieces. Int.
CFP lists shorter works.
Mendelssohn, Felix (1809–1847)
Complete Works. Dover 23136-4 and 23184–4, K (three vols.), CFP (five vols.).
Songs Without Words. K, CFP.
Rondo Capriccioso op. 14. CFP, GS.
Variations sérieuses. CFP, GS, K.
Messiaen, Olivier (1908–   )
Durand; more recently UE (*Canteyodjaya*) and Leduc.
Milhaud, Darius (1892–1974)
Saudades do Brasil (two vols.). Eschig.
For other works, check Hinson.
Moszkowski, Moritz (1854–1925)
Album of Selected Piano Compositions. EBM.
CFP, GS, and Leduc publish a variety of works.
Mozart, Wolfgang Amadeus (1756–1791)
Sonatas, complete. The Broder version from TP (one vol.) approaches an ideal. High ranking should be given the Henle (Lampe) version (two vols.). K has an Urtext of twenty (two vols.). Schott publishes fourteen separately.
Variations. Henle.
Selected Works. CFP, K.
Duets. CFP, Henle, K.

Mussorgsky, Modest (1839–1881)
  Pictures at an Exhibition. Int., Schott, CFP.
Persichetti, Vincent (1915–   )
  Elkan-Vogel.
Poulenc, Francis (1899–1963)
  Works published by Chester, Heugel, Salabert, Durand.
  Movements perpêtuels. Chester.
  Huit nocturnes. Heugel.
Prokofiev, Sergei (1891–1953)
  Sonatas (complete). Leeds (Freundlich), MCA (Sandor), Int, K.
  Sonatas (separately). K, MCA, Int.
  Shorter works available from K, MCA, GS, CFP, Boosey, Int.
Purcell, Henry (c. 1659–1695)
  Six Suites. Vol. 7 in the Purcell Society Practical Edition, Novello.
Rachmaninoff, Sergei (1873–1943)
  For the important individual pieces (such as the two Sonatas), one looks first to Int. For the others (sets) Int, EBM, K, and MCA serve equally. Other collections of early works have appeared recently.
Rameau, Jean Philippe (1683–1764)
  Pièces de clavecin. Bär (Jacobi).
  The above without the treatise "On the technique of the fingers on the harpsichord": Durand (ed. Saint-Saens).
Ravel, Maurice (1875–1937)
  Almost all from Durand.
  Works in print by 1905 can be obtained individually and as collections from EBM, K, GS.
  A la manière pieces. Salabert ("Borodin" especially nice).
Reger, Max (1873–1916)
  Besides the Complete Works, his stupendous output appears in Bote & Bock, UE, CFP, Br&H, and anthologized collections. Isolated works, such as some from *Aus meinem Tagebuch*, deserve more frequent, loving performance.
Rossini, Gioacchino (1792–1868)
  A variety of genial pieces, selected, published by CFP, K, and others.
Saint-Saëns, Camille (1835–1921)
  Durand for most of the solo works.
  Carnival of the Animals. Durand (TP).
Satie, Erik (1866–1925)
  Mostly published by Eschig and Salabert; also anthologized.
  The Piano Music of Erik Satie. AMP.
  Sports et divertissements. Salabert.
  Sonatine bureaucratique. Salabert.
Scarlatti, Domenico (1685–1757)
  By present-day standards, the Longo listing and edition no longer serve for Scarlatti's significant output of almost six hundred sonatas.
  The Ralph Kirkpatrick listing represents an ideal source.
  Best ongoing complete source: Heugel (Gilbert, K.).
  Sixty Sonatas. GS (Kirkpatrick) (two vols.).

Sixty Sonatas. Kal. One of the better other editions.

Schoenberg, Arnold (1874–1951)

Almost all available from UE: otherwise Wilhelm Hansen for op. 23. See Complete Works, in progress; also the Busoni "interpretation" of op. 11 no. 2 in UE. Belmont has begun to issue those (earlier) works whose copyrights have reverted to the composer's heirs.

Schubert, Franz (1797–1828)

Sonatas (complete). Dover 22647-6; Henle, Br&H (Sauer), K. Opp. 90, 94, 142. Dover 22648-4; Henle CFP, K.

Dances. Henle, CFP, K.

Duets. CFP, Int, K (five vols.), Henle (three vols.).

Schumann, Robert (1810–1856)

Complete Works. Henle, CFP (Sauer), K (Clara Schumann).

Dover reprints the latter version–and many feel it to be less-than-authentic–of her husband's "major compositions" as 21459-1 and 21461-3.

Most firms have published the important individual items separately. Alfred (Palmer) has issued both Scenes from Childhood, op. 15 and Album for the Young, op. 68.

Scott, Cyril (1879–1970)

"Impressions from Kipling's *Jungle Book*"; "Poems"; "Indian Suite." Schott.

Collection of Eight Selected Works. GS.

Scriabin, Alexander (1872–1915)

Sonatas (complete). MCA, Int.

Sonatas nos. 2, 3, 4, 5, 9, 10 from Int.

Complete Preludes and Études. Dover 22919-X.

Selected Piano Works. CFP.

Vol. 1: Etudes opp. 8, 42, 65.

Vol. 2: Shorter Works opp. 11, 27, 32, 47, 56, 72, 73, 74.

Vol. 3: Shorter Works opp. 13, 16, 38, 45, 46, 48, 49, 51, 52, 57, 58, 59, 61, 63, 67, 69, 71.

Fantasy, op. 28; Tragic Poem, op. 34; Satanic Poem, op. 36; Int, K.

Youthful and Early Works. MTP. (Garvelmann).

Shostakovich, Dmitri (1906–1975)

Selected Works. Int, K.

All music available separately from MCA; much from K, CFP.

Smetana, Bedřich (1824–1884)

Bohemian Dances. K, CFP.

Selected Pieces. CFP.

Stravinsky, Igor (1882–1971)

Most available from Boosey.

The Five Fingers. K.

Stravinsky, Soulima (1910–   )

CFP.

Szymanowski, Karol (1882–1937)

UE.

Tansman, Alexandre (1897–   )

Primarily Eschig; then UE, MCA.

Tchaikovsky, Peter Ilyich (1840–1893)
Selected Works (three vols.). CFP.
Album for the Young, op. 39. K, EBM, CFP, GS.
Seventeen Selected Pieces. GS.

Tcherepnin, Alexander (1899–1977)
Bagatelles, op. 5. GS (edited and revised by the composer); otherwise Int.
A great variety for other works: EBM, CFP, Boosey, Eschig, etc.

Telemann, Georg Philipp (1681–1767)
Twelve Fantasies. CFP.
Thirty-six Fantasies. Bär.

Toch, Ernst (1887–1964)
Early works by Schott; then AMP, MCA, BM.

Turina, Joaquin (1882–1949)
Mostly Salabert.
Album de Viaje. Int.
Selected Masterpieces. EBM.

Türk, Daniel Gottlob (1750–1813)
Forty-nine Pieces for Small Hands. K.
Sixty Easy Pieces. CFP.

Villa-Lobos, Heitor (1887–1959)
Mostly Eschig.
Selected Works. CMP.
Prole do Bébé, Suite 1, EBM, K, Eschig.

Weber, Carl Maria von (1786–1826)
Complete Works (three vols.). CFP.
Invitation to the Dance. CFP, GS, CF.
Duets (complete). CFP.

ABBREVIATIONS

AMP	Associated Music Publishers
Bar	Bärenreiter
BM	Belwin-Mills
Boosey	Boosey & Hawkes
Br&H	Breitkopf & Härtel
CF	Carl Fischer
CFP	C.F. Peters
CMP	Consolidated Music Publishers
EBM	E.B. Marks
EMB	Editio Musica Budapest
GS	G. Schirmer
GWM	General Words and Music
Int	International Music Corporation
K (al)	Kalmus, through BM
MAB	Musica Antiqua Bohemica
MTP	Music Treasure Publications, P.O. Box 127, Highbridge Station, Bronx, N.Y. 10452
Peer	Peer International Corporation
TP	Theodore Presser
SL of MC	Schirmer's Library of Musical Classics (GS)
UE	Universal Edition
VUE	Vienna Urtext Edition, through TP

Piano Literature Based on American Folk Songs

MAURICE HINSON

Folk music is the musical repertory and tradition of communities, as distinguished from art music, which is the artistic expression of musically trained individuals.

American folk tunes date back mainly to the time of our country's founding, the latter part of the eighteenth century. Many of our tunes came from other countries, as did our ancestors. The tune "Yankee Doodle," for instance, came from England, but it was completely taken into our own culture and made "American." Many of our most popular folk songs are of traceable authorship, such as "Dixie," by Dan Emmett, and the numerous "folksongs" of Stephen C. Foster.

There are two separate types of folk songs in the U.S.: the melodies of Native Americans (see Farwell's "American Indian Melodies," listed below) and the more recent folk songs of the white settlers and the Afro-Americans. In the last few decades interest in our cultural heritage has caused many American composers to incorporate folk tunes into their piano music.

The following list, far from complete, includes some of the most interesting solo piano works based on American folk tunes. They have been graded in the following terms: Easy, Int. (Intermediate), M.D. (Moderately Difficult).

Author	*Title*	*Publisher*	*Grade*
Denes Agay	Folk Tune Sonatina	Warner Bros. (in *Sonatinas—The Young Pianist's Library, vol. 2-C*)	Int.
Anonymous	Early American Music "Columbus," "Ladies' Choice" ("Buffalo Gal, Won't You Come Out Tonight?")	Belwin-Mills	Easy to Int.
Anonymous	"Yankee Doodle" arranged with Variations	Willis (in *A Collection of Early American Keyboard Music*)	Int.
Ernst Bacon	Byways (Contains "A Kansas Cowboy"; "Br'er Rabbit"; "Goober Peas"; "My Evaline"; "Noli-chucky River"; "Pil-grim Hymn"; "Put-nam's Hill"; "The Gimcrack"; "The Hebrew Children.")	G. Schirmer	Int.
Blind Tom (Thomas Greene Bethune)	Battle of Manassas (based on "The Girl I Left Behind Me"; "Dixie"; "Yankee Doodle"; *"La Mar-seillaise"*; "Star-Spangled Banner.")	Hinshaw (in *Piano Music in Nineteenth-Century America,* vol. 1)	M.D.
Fred Coulter	Variations for Agnes (based on "Twinkle, Twinkle, Little Star.")	Hinshaw	M.D.
Paul Bowles	Folk Preludes (con-tains "Cape Ann"; "Ching a Ring Chaw"; "Oh! Potatoes, They Grow Small Over There"; "Kentucky Moonshiner"; "Ole Tare River"; "Peter Gray"; "Whar Did You Cum From?")	Mercury	Int.
Allen Brings	Variations on an American Folk Tune	American Music Center	M.D.

Author	*Title*	*Publisher*	*Grade*
Benjamin Carr	Federal Overture (based on "Yankee Doodle"; "Oh! Dear, What Can the Matter Be," and six other contemporary popular tunes.)	Musical Americana	M.D.
Michael G. Cunningham	American Folksongs	Seesaw	Int.
Arthur Farwell	American Indian Melodies (twelve pieces based on Native American folk materials.)	Hinshaw	Int.
	"Sourwood Mountain"	G. Schirmer (in *Fifty-one Piano Pieces from the Modern Repertoire*)	M.D.
Ross Lee Finney	Medley (contains "Red River Valley"; "Dinah Won't You Blow Your Horn?"	Hinshaw (in *12 x 11*)	Int.
Louis M. Gottschalk	The Banjo (inspired by "The Camptown Races.")	T. Presser (in *Piano Music of Louis M. Gottschalk*)	M.D.
Roy Harris	American Ballads ("Black is the Color of My True Love's Hair"; "Cod Liver Ile"; "Streets of Laredo"; "The Bird"; "Wayfaring Stranger.")	Carl Fischer	M.D.
Herbert Haufrecht	Toccata on Familiar Tunes	Schroeder & Gunther	M.D.
James Hewitt	Mark My Alford (based on "Twinkle, Twinkle, Little Star.")	Willis (in *A Collection of Early American Keyboard Music*)	M.D.
W. Iucho	The Arkansas Traveller: A Western Refrain with Easy Variations.	Galaxy (in *The American Book*)	Int.
Arthur Jannery	Pensive Pentad—Virginia '76 op. 48 (based on English, Irish, or Scottish folk	Ms. available from composer: c/o Music Dept.,Westfield State College, Westfield, MA	Int. to M.D.

Author	Title	Publisher	Grade
	tunes from Botetourt County, Virginia: "Lord Thomas and Fair Eleanor"; "Come All You Fair and Tender Ladies"; "The Tree in the Wood"; "Jack Went A-Sailing"; "Brennan on the Moor.")	01085	
Nelson Keyes	Three Love Songs ("Gently Johnny My Gingalo"; "Shenandoah"; "Lolly Too Dum.")	Hinshaw (in *12 x 11*)	Int.
Douglas Moore	"Fiddlin' Joe"	Carl Fischer	Easy
	"Grievin' Annie"	Carl Fischer	Easy
Preston Ware Orem	American Indian Rhapsody (on ten Native American folk themes collected and recorded by Thurlow Lieurance.)	T. Presser	M.D.
Vincent Persichetti	Appalachian Christmas (carols for piano, four hands.)	Elkan-Vogel	Int.
Paul A. Pisk	Dance from the Rio Grande Valley	T. Presser	Int.
Sam Raphling	Folk Song Piano Recital (forty solo pieces based on American folk tunes.)	Consolidated	Int. to M.D.
Peter Schickele	Three Folk Settings ("Henry Martin"; "Turtle Dove"; "Old Joe Clark.")	Elkan-Vogel	Int.
Elie Siegmeister	Folk-Ways U.S.A. in three volumes) A progressive series of American songs, scenes, and sketches.	T. Presser	Easy-Int.
Julia Smith	American Dance Suite, for two pianos, four hands ("One Morning in May"; "Lost My Partner";	T. Presser	Int. to M.D.

Author	Title	Publisher	Grade
	"Negro Lullaby" ["All the Pretty Little Horses"]; "Chicken Reel.")		
Donald Waxman	Folk Song Pageants (two volumes) Mostly American tunes in simple, attractive settings.	Galaxy	Easy

PUBLISHERS' ADDRESSES

American Music Center, 145 West 58th Street, New York, N.Y. 10019
Belwin-Mills, Melville, N.Y. 11746
Consolidated Music Publishers, 33 West 60th Street, New York, N.Y. 10023
Elkan-Vogel, Presser Place, Bryn Mawr, PA 19010
Carl Fischer, 56-62 Cooper Sq., New York, N.Y. 10003
Galaxy Music Corp., 2121 Broadway, New York, N.Y. 10023
Hinshaw Music, Inc., P. O. Box 470, Chapel Hill, N.C. 27514
Mercury Music Corp., 170 West 60th Street, New York, N.Y. 10023
Musical Americana, c/o Harry Dichter, Apt. 808, Brighton Towers, Atlantic City, N.J. 08401
G. Schirmer, 866 Third Avenue, New York, N.Y. 10022
Schroeder & Gunther, 866 Third Avenue, New York, N.Y. 10022
Seesaw Music, 1966 Broadway, New York, N.Y. 10023
Theodore Presser Co., Presser Place, Bryn Mawr, PA 19010
Willis Music Co., 7380 Industrial Road, Florence, KY 41042
Warner Bros. Music, 75 Rockefeller Plaza, New York, N.Y. 10019

FIVE

SURVEY OF STYLES AND IDIOMS

Styles in Composition and Performance

DENES AGAY

Numerous definitions exist that try to pin down the essence of style in music. While this elusive concept can be explained, to a degree, by objective facts and data, the ultimate insight into its nature can come only through a thorough understanding of, and instinctive identification with, the music at hand. For an actor to play Hamlet convincingly it is necessary not only for him to be familiar with Shakespeare's language and with Elizabethan theater, but, in fact, to *become* Hamlet on the stage. Similarly, a pianist performing Mozart must assume a Mozartean stance, with all the mental, emotional, and physical preparations and preconditions such an attitude implies.

For the purposes of this essay—to furnish the piano teacher with a pedagogically feasible and practical starting point—we define *style* here as the collective characteristic traits of musical works in reference to a certain period or a certain composer. In this sense we may speak of baroque or romantic style, Mozart or Chopin style, and so on. The term *style* can also be applied to a manner of rendition which adheres to musicologically proven performance practices of an era, such as a stylistic Bach, Mendelssohn, or Bartók performance.

In the literature of keyboard works we usually distinguish four major periods and corresponding styles: *baroque* (from about 1600 to 1750), *classical* (about 1750 to 1820), *romantic* (from about 1820 to 1900), and *contemporary* (the twentieth century). It should be noted immediately that the division of music history into these four periods is rather tentative and flexible, entailing a great deal of chronological and idiomatic overlapping. The works of Bach's sons, for instance, may be catalogued as either late baroque or early classical. Sibelius, Rachmaninoff, and Richard Strauss are twentieth century writers with unmistakably romantic traits. Also, within the four large eras and often transcending their boundaries, there are many stylistic subdivisions, according to regional traits (German, French, Italian baroque, for instance), individual creative characteristics (late Beethoven, Chopin, Satie, Ives, etc.), or compositional techniques (polyphony, modality, impressionism, etc.).

The piano student's stylistic education is a long and continuous process. It should begin as early as possible, certainly as soon as the simplest little pieces of the masters become negotiable. A little two-voice baroque minuet or a simple German dance by Haydn can well illustrate polyphony and homophony, respectively. They can also furnish attractive examples of elementary two- and three-part song forms. Brief biographies of the composers help to put them and their works into an historical and stylistic perspective, or at least into a chronological time-frame even the very young can understand. (For instance: Mozart lived 200 years ago, was a contemporary of Washington, Jefferson, and Franklin; he began to compose and give recitals at the age of five; he played on pianos which were smaller and lighter in weight and tone than today's; his compositions usually consist of melody in the right hand and accompaniment in the left; he wrote not only piano pieces, but also symphonies, chamber music, operas, etc.) Characteristic features of various forms, textures, and compositional techniques, as well as conventions in the performance practices of various eras, should be pointed out to the student gradually, parallel with the growing capacity to play, understand, and enjoy a progressively planned curriculum from all segments of keyboard literature.

The following four sections present synopses of each period's most important style elements, to serve as a guide and checklist for imparting this information to the student.

THE BAROQUE PERIOD (An Amazing Age of Limitless Variety)

The first flowering of keyboard literature occurred during the baroque period. The astonishingly varied creative output of this era is in many respects the fertile soil from which the forms, tonal organizations, and modes of expression of subsequent periods grew. The pedagogic implications of this fact are extremely important. A piano student's musical growth and technical training are unimaginable without considerable reliance on the music of this era.

The Instruments

Baroque keyboard works were not written for the piano, but for a variety of other instruments: the harpsichord, clavichord, virginal, and organ. Every opportunity should be seized by the teacher to demonstrate these instruments (especially the first two) to the student; a description of them, including their characteristic sonorities, can be found on pages 485-87. Acquainting the student with the harpsichord and clavichord should by no means, however, implant the idea that it is wrong or unstylistic to perform baroque works on the modern piano. This pedantic notion, which had many adherents during the past few rigidly authenticity-conscious decades, is fortunately giving way to a less stilted and less narrow view. To adopt a reasonable and proper approach to this problem, one should keep in mind that baroque composers were not particularly instrument-conscious in the modern sense. Bach, especially, did not conceive a work for one specific instrument exclusively (a trait, incidentally, which was largely shared by Mozart). Consider Bach's many transcriptions from one instrument to another, or the almost complete lack of stated preference whether a piece should be performed on the harpsichord or clavichord.

The piano, properly handled, is a most appropriate vehicle for the realization of baroque ideas. Obviously its full sonorities and expressive capabilities do not have to be, and should not be, unleashed when playing this music, but neither do they have to be constrained to the point of merely imitating the baroque instruments. The best advice is "to preserve in a piano performance all the esthetic qualities of the harpsichord that we can: brilliance, sudden dramatic changes of dynamic level and color, above all its clarity. But beyond this there is no need to perpetuate its limitations, particularly its inability to shade or to produce a prolongued crescendo. (These disadvantages irked Couperin, and to assume that Bach was less musically sensitive is ridiculous.)"* The clavichord, of course, was capable of shadings within its modest range of dynamics and can serve as an inspiration, but not as a model, for today's pianists when performing eighteenth century works of gentle and subtle character.

Forms and Textures

The texture of baroque music is predominantly polyphonic and rich in imitative counterpoint. The most frequently occurring forms are the fugue, fantasy, toccata, suite (of dances), variations (chaconne, passacaglia, ground) and numerous other smaller forms such as inventions, preludes, and cappriccios (brief descriptions of these forms may be found on page 183-87).

To introduce the student to the baroque world, it is best to start with little dance pieces in slow or moderate tempo, such as the minuet, gavotte, polonaise, or sarabande, with simple two-voice textures and minimal ornamentation. The source of such pieces should not be restricted to the few well-known selections culled from Bach's *Little Notebook for Anna Magdalena Bach*, as is too often the case. Baroque masters, including some of the lesser-known ones, created many small keyboard works which are utterly melodic, simple in structure, easier than the Bach Inventions, and as such are ideally suitable preparatory

*Louis L. Crowder "The Baroque Period" (introductory article to *An Anthology of Piano Music*, Denes Agay, ed. Yorktown Music Press).

studies for polyphonic play and a delightful introduction to baroque keyboard music in general. A common mistake is to confront the student with Bach's Two-part Inventions too early. These unique little masterpieces, which demand secure technical control and quite mature musical understanding, belong in every serious student's repertory, but should be assigned only at the proper time, after adequate preparation. A progressive repertory of charming and still largely neglected preparatory materials can well be assembled from folios listed at the end of this chapter (p. 462).

Harmonic concepts in prebaroque periods, especially during the Renaissance, were predominantly based on the church modes (Dorian, Phrygian, Lydian, and Mixolydian). Baroque masters developed the major and minor scales and through them a rich harmonic vocabulary which was to dominate compositional styles for at least a century and a half. The theoretical principles of this harmonic system were so clearly defined and organized (by Rameau and others) that a bass part alone, with certain appropriate figures above or beneath it, was sufficient notation from which to reconstruct and play a complete four-voice harmonic texture. This stenographic manner of keyboard notation, a continuous figured bass running throughout the composition, called *thorough bass* or *basso continuo*, was so widely used during the baroque that the era is often referred to as the "thoroughbass period." From the figured bass the player was able not only to fill in the correct harmonies in an improvisatory manner, but also to execute patterns of accompaniment which fit the composition's mood and character. This ability, rather rare today, gives evidence of the baroque performer's secure musicianship and also explains the wide interpretative leeways and freedoms enjoyed.

Performance Practices

Baroque masters did not notate their works in complete detail. Even when committing to paper all notes to be played, they left many aspects of execution, including tempo, dynamics, and phrasing, to the performer's discretion. This wide choice of options available to the seventeenth- and eighteenth-century performer is one of the essential facts to keep in mind when playing a baroque *Urtext*. It is especially important today, when the search for and insistence on stylistic authenticity in editions and performance practices has often been exaggerated to the point of obsessive rigidity, putting inhibiting pressures on teachers and performers alike. All objective data and historical facts confirm that a stifling of interpretative freedom and initiative is in sharp contrast to baroque principles and to the composer's original intent.

Before applying this privilege (and responsibility) of choices, today's performer must, of course, become familiar with the basic stylistic conventions of the period. This, however, is not such an awesome task as some overzealous purists would make it appear. One does not need a degree in musicology to grasp the more important fundamental principles of baroque performance and thereby relax and enjoy the great variety, depth, and vigor of this music. As a first step the following essential guidelines should be kept in mind:

Tempo: Generally steady, with a pronounced metric pulse. Excessive speeds should be avoided. Retards in concluding measures can be taken for granted. (See also "Tempo," p. 29).

Dynamics: The range is between ***p*** and ***f***; extreme contrasts (***pp*** – ***ff***) are unidiomatic. As a rule a dynamic level should be maintained for at least a phrase or phrase-section (terrace dynamics), although slight shadings (*cresc., dim.*) within these form units are also feasible, if applied occasionally and with moderation.

Touch and Articulation: Legato, non legato, and *staccato* are all acceptable if applied knowingly within a consistent articulation scheme. Observe, for instance, the various possibilities of articulating the following excerpt:

Froberger: Canzon

Any of the following three articulation patterns is possible, if applied consistently to *all* appearances of the theme:

A. An even non legato, as notated above.

B. All eighth notes staccato, sixteenth notes slurred:

C. A somewhat refined variant of version B:

Pedal: Should be used very sparingly, mostly in "short touches," or not at all.

Ornaments: Familiarity with the proper execution of basic symbols is essential. Equally important is the realization that all tables of ornamentation, even the most authoritative ones, are only guidelines, and the final shaping of an embellishment properly belongs in the performer's domain. This means that certain liberties can be taken, which, if done with taste and moderation, will not violate baroque performance practices. Ornaments should always be performed lightly, gracefully, in a quasi-improvisatory manner; never should they sound heavy or clumsy. It is preferable to alter, simplify, or omit a certain ornament than to let it become a hurdle in the path of an otherwise smooth and pleasing performance. (See "Ornamentation," p. 123).

Expression: This is the lifeblood of musical interpretation and it applies to baroque music as well as to music of any other period. The student should learn early that a steady tempo and polyphonic textures are not incompatible with expressiveness. Romantic sentimentality is, of course, out of the question, but noble eloquence, deep feeling, and even passion are not. It can be very helpful and inspiring for the student to hear the teacher play a few simple selections illustrating the rich emotional content and vitality of baroque music. It should be conveyed to the pupil at the earliest possible stage that these works are not cold museum pieces, not dusty examples of a great but archaic art, but *living* music, as valid, inspiring, and diverting today as they were two to three centuries ago.

RECOMMENDED READING

Bodky, Erwin. *The Interpretation of Bach's Keyboard Works.* Cambridge: Harvard University Press, 1960.

Bukofzer, Manfred. *Music in the Baroque Era.* New York: W.W. Norton, 1947.

Dart, Thurston. *The Interpretation of Music.* New York: Harper & Row, 1963.

Dolmetsch, Arnold. *The Interpretation of the Music of the Seventeenth and Eighteenth Centuries.* London: Oxford University Press, 1915. (More recent paperback reprints are available in the U.S.)

Donnington, Robert. *A Performer's Guide to Baroque Music.* New York: Scribner's, 1973.

RECOMMENDED COLLECTIONS

The following list of pertinent collections can provide an ample source of appealing and, in many cases, rather rarely encountered introductory materials on the easy-to-intermediate levels:

"The Baroque Period." *An Anthology of Piano Music,* vol. I (Agay, ed.). Yorktown.
The Joy of Baroque (Agay). Yorktown.
Introduction to the Study of Bach, vol. I (Mirovitch). Schirmer.
Early Keyboard Music, vol. 2 (Ferguson). Oxford.
German Masters of the Seventeenth and Eighteenth Centuries. Kalmus.
Airs and Dances, vol. 2 (Dorolle). Boosey & Hawkes.
Anson Introduces Handel, Book 1. Willis.
First Scarlatti (Kreutzer). Boston.
Telemann: *Three Dozen Klavier Fantasias* (Seiffert). Bärenreiter.
Telemann: *Little Klavier Book* (Irmer). Schott.
Purcell: *Pieces for Klavier or Harpsichord* (Hilleman). Schott.
C.P.E. Bach: *Piano Pieces* (Luithlen-Kraus). Universal.

THE CLASSICAL PERIOD (Golden Age of the Sonata)

Within the relatively short span of hardly more than half a century (approximately between 1760 and 1820) a magnificent literature of music was produced which in simplicity, serenity, and perfect balance of form and content has remained unsurpassed. The period is also noteworthy on numerous other accounts. It is the time when the pianoforte replaced the harpsichord as the most popular keyboard instrument, an event which had far-reaching implications on successive compositional styles, sonorities, techniques of interpretation, and pedagogy. Also, this is the age of the first solo recitals, the first traveling virtuosos, the appearance of the first piano methods and teaching publications by Türk, Dussek, Hummel, and others. Most important, this is the era in which the sonata, that supreme configuration of musical architecture, was perfected by the three great protagonists of the era: Haydn, Mozart, and Beethoven.

What is the importance of the sonata in musical education? During the past two centuries an overwhelming portion of great music was written in this form, which includes not only solo sonatas, but also string quartets, trios, and symphonies, all of which are sonatas conceived for various instrumental combinations. Familiarity with this form is thus essential for all students and practitioners of music.

Of course, the study of forms should not start with the sonata, but with the component form elements: motive, phrase, sentence, and the small song forms (binary, ternary). Music of the classical period is ideally suited for all phases of form analysis, because of its compact clarity, symmetry, and uncluttered texture. On the earliest grade levels, the charming German dances, minuets, contredanses, and ecossaises of the masters, which illustrate with textbook clarity all constructional features, can be used for this purpose, preparatory to the study of sonatas.

The Sonata

The word *sonata* comes from the Italian *sonare* "to sound." Originally, during the sixteenth and seventeenth centuries it meant merely a *sound piece*, a musical thought sounded on one or more instruments. It was first applied to a keyboard solo by Kuhnau (1696). As developed and crystallized by the classical masters, the sonata, as a musical form, is the first section of a work usually consisting of three or four movements. This form, often referred to as *sonata-allegro* form or *first-movement* form, is essentially a simple ABA patterned structure (exposition–development–recapitulation) which the mind grasps easily and which, at the same time, is sturdy and elastic enough to be the repository of an infinite variety of musical inventions and manipulations. This form concept has acquired tremendous significance in the organization of musical thoughts ever since.

To create an extended work, the baroque composer had to depend on stringing together small sections of various tempos, rhythmic characters, and textures as in the dance suites, partitas, toccatas, and fantasies. The sonata form enabled composers of subsequent periods to convey ideas of larger dimensions within a thematically constructed unified scheme. The typical sonata form comprises the following elements:

EXPOSITION				DEVELOPMENT	RECAPITULATION				CODA
First Theme or Theme Group	Transition	Second Theme or Theme Group	Closing Theme (optional)	Expands or manipulates Themes or Theme fragments of the Exposition	First Theme or Theme Group	Transition	Second Theme or Theme Group	Closing Theme	Concluding section of varying lengths
KEY: Tonic	Modulatory	Dominant or Related Key		Various Keys	Tonic				Tonic

The *sonatina* "little sonata" is usually shorter and easier to perform than the sonata, and does not always contain all components of the sonata form. The closing theme of the exposition is often missing and instead of a development section there is just a brief modulatory transition leading to the recapitulation. Sonatinas were and are often written for instructional purposes. They are marked by simplicity and clarity of design and, in most cases, make rather moderate demands on technical facility. For these reasons they are excellent preparatory materials for the exploration of the sonata literature.

It should be noted that many excellent sonatas and sonatinas written before the end of the eighteenth century represent this form in a transitional stage, not fully developed in its classical sense. Many of these charming and useful works by Benda, Hassler, Cimarosa, and others, are constructed in two- or three-part song forms. To view the sonata form in its fully developed stage, but still within the early-to-intermediate levels of difficulty, the Clementi Sonatinas (opus 36) and the easiest Mozart and Beethoven Sonatas are recommended. The middle section of a three-movement sonata or sonatina is usually a melodic *andante* or *adagio*, constructed in an extended song form. Another movement, preceding or following the slow section, is usually a *minuet* or *scherzo*, both dance forms.

The sonata's last movement is, in most cases, a *rondo*. This form is of French origin, often employed by the *clavecinists* (Couperin, Rameau, and others). It has an ABACA pattern, where A represents the main theme, and B and C the episodes (couplets). A more developed classical rondo pattern is ABACABA. Here the sections are not set apart but follow in a smooth, uninterrupted sequence with the proper transitional materials between the themes. In some cases the middle episode (C) is replaced by a development section, which brings the construction quite close to the sonata form. Examine the last movements of Haydn's Sonata in D major Hob. XVI:37 (pattern ABACA) and Mozart's Sonata in C major K. 545 (pattern ABACA coda where episode C is a development section). The rondo movements of most Clementi and Kuhlau sonatinas are also ideal subjects for analyses.

Performance Practices

From about the middle of the eighteenth century composers began to notate their works in ever-increasing detail; indications of tempo, dynamics, and articulation appear with some measure of regularity. However, by no means are all particulars spelled out consistently, and so the performer is still quite often left to his or her own resources. Of course, the leeway is not as wide and the options not as numerous as in performing baroque music, but still, whatever choices are made and decisions arrived at must be based on sound musical and stylistic judgment. Toward that end the following guidelines are helpful.

Tempo: Within a section, the pace is generally uniform and steady, but without the constant, firm, and unyielding metric pulse underlying much baroque music. In the classics the natural accents of the bar are not pronounced, only hinted at; the forward momentum is airier and lighter, propelled and shaped by the component form elements (motives, phrases). Given tempo marks should be adhered to, but in some instances, slightly adjusted toward moderation at both tempo extremes; not extremely slow and not excessively fast should be the motto. A presto indication by Clementi, for instance, can safely be taken at an allegro pace. Also tempo modifications (rit., accel., a tempo) are not always marked and should be employed at the player's discretion. Just before the entrance of the second theme in a sonata, for instance, it is often natural and desirable to relax the pace slightly. Mood contrasts in a set of variations also may frequently call for minor adjustments of tempo. A delicate rubato, of the kind where the melody sings out with a certain freedom against the strictly maintained pulse of the accompaniment (*melodic rubato*), is also at the player's option.

Touches and Articulation: In the absence of other indications, the "normal" keyboard touch is *non legato* at least until Beethoven's middle period, when, probably under the influence of Clementi, the "legato as a rule" trend became predominant.

Legato slurs, *staccato*, and *tenuto* signs appear with increased frequency in the music of the classics, but cannot at all times be accepted at their face value, because of frequent inconsistencies and certain idiomatic notation habits which differ from modern usage. For instance, the three staccato marks of Haydn and Mozart—the stroke I , the wedge ▼ , and the dot • —had nearly identical meanings as far as we can judge today. Certainly, the wedge was not yet the mark of a sharp staccato (*staccatissimo*) which it became during the early nineteenth century, when the dot came to be the normal staccato sign. Whatever marginal differences there may be between the true meanings of these signs as the classics used them will have to be decided by the performer on the basis of musical clues, such as tempos, articulation patterns, and dynamic contexts. Within an adagio movement, for instance, staccato should not be as short and crisp as it can be in a fast tempo. Note values will also influence the character and sharpness of a particular staccato. Obviously, the dots over the quarter notes in the following example call for a shorter sound than the ones over the half notes.

Beethoven: Sonata no. 8, op. 13
("Pathetique")

The placing of slurs is also quite strange and ambiguous in the classical literature. Only rarely does a slur cover a complete two- or four-measure phrase; rather it is drawn from bar line to bar line, as in the following excerpt:

Mozart: Sonata, K. 570

The above notation notwithstanding, a bar-to-bar articulation would be misplaced here; the phrase should be performed as if indicated by a single unbroken slur extending from the first note to the downbeat of measure four. This, indeed, is the manner in which Mozart notated the theme in several subsequent repetitions.

When slurs connecting small note groups are meant to denote a certain touch, stress, or articulation within the phrase, the indications are usually valid and should be strictly observed:

Haydn: Sonata, Hob. XVI:37

Ornamentation: In this era ornamentation is not as rich as during the baroque. Many compound ornaments disappeared or became simplified; composers increasingly wrote out trills, appoggiaturas, and turns in full notation. Certain ambiguities, however, remain and must be resolved in performance. The trill, for instance, still starts on the upper auxiliary note, in theory at least, but there are many exceptions; each case must be decided on the basis of its technical and expressive context. By the time of Schubert, trills generally began on the main note. A specific symbol often used by Haydn should also be clarified here. The sign ⸗ should be performed as a turn ∾ and not as a mordent 𝆝.

Expression–Pedal: Behind a disarmingly simple facade, the music of classicism offers a wealth of variety, vitality, and subtle emotions. This should be expressed through sensitive, graceful articulation, within a framework of steady but not rigid tempo. The dynamic range should not be excessive and the contrasts not overdramatic.

The use of pedal is at the performer's discretion, as Haydn and Mozart did not indicate it and Beethoven did so only erratically. To preserve the clarity of melodic lines and harmonic sequences, pedaling should be judicious and restrained at all times.

RECOMMENDED READING

Badura-Skoda, Eva and Paul. *Interpreting Mozart on the Keyboard*. New York: St. Martin's press, 1957.

Ferguson, Howard. *Keyboard Interpretation from the Fourteenth to the Nineteenth Century*. New York and London: Oxford University Press, 1975.

Newman, William. *Performance Practices in Beethoven's Piano Sonatas: An Introduction*. New York: W.W. Norton, 1971.

Rosen, Charles. *The Classical Style: Haydn, Mozart and Beethoven.* New York: Viking Press, 1971.

Rothschild, Fritz. *Musical Performance in the Times of Mozart and Beethoven.* Fair Lawn, N.J.: Oxford University Press, 1961.

THE ROMANTIC PERIOD (Century of the Piano)

Of all the musical styles and periods, romanticism is the one to become the principal source of our everyday musical diet. The bulk of concert repertories and study materials was written in the nineteenth century, and even popular music, in its best manifestations, is nourished by the melodic and harmonic ingredients of the romantic idiom. In contrast to the universality, serenity, and restraint of the classical era, the esthetic ideals of romancism extol the artistic freedom of the individual and the unrestrained expression of personal feelings. To convey these ideals, new forms, sonorities, and compositional techniques were created. The sonata, a uniquely apt vehicle for classical expression, could not by itself, suffice. A host of other smaller musical structures, mostly lyric character pieces, were conceived: *impromptus, moments musicaux, songs without words, nocturnes, intermezzi.* The modern piano, emerging in the early 1800s, provided the new sonorities and inspired composers to create an unprecedented wealth of piano music of every kind and for every degree of advancement. Although the baroque and classical eras both contributed enormously to the literature of keyboard music, by far the largest windfall came from romanticism during the nineteenth, the "century of the piano."

There is of course a great variety in style, form, intensity, and quality of expression within the romantic school itself, from the still classically oriented Schubert and Mendelssohn, through the strongly innovative expression of Schumann, Chopin, Liszt and Brahms, to the late-romantic, ethnically flavored and often preimpressionistic tendencies of Grieg, Fauré, Albéniz, Rachmaninoff, and others.

In spite of these widely variegated traits, however, certain stylistic characteristics emerge as generally valid and may be noted as helpful guidelines in the understanding, playing, and teaching of this vast repertory.

Performance Practices

Although romantic composers notated their works in great detail, their scores are by no means complete and free from ambiguities. This is due largely to the built-in imperfections of the Western notation system, which, among other things, cannot satisfactorily convey the subtle tempo fluctuations and dynamic nuances inherent in the sophisticated textures of much romantic music. In addition, the notation habits of numerous nineteenth century masters are quite idiosyncratic, requiring awareness and familiarity on the performer's part. Thus the performance of romantic music calls not only for an emotional involvement—as is, unfortunately, so often the case—but also for an intellectual stance to channel and guide these emotions within esthetically and stylistically proper conduits toward a pleasing and tasteful interpretation. The suggestions that follow are meant to promote familiarity with the main earmarks of romantic style.

Tempo: Markings in one form or another are always supplied by nineteenth century composers. Often they are quite precise, coupled with mood descriptions and metronome indications. In spite of this, one of the most difficult tasks confronting the performer of truly romantic music is the right choice of tempo, including its fluctuations. The key here is the proper and effective use of *rubato*, with all its possibilities for interpretative enhancement and all its pitfalls for tasteless exaggerations. By tempo fluctuation is meant not only *melodic rubato* in which, in Chopin's words, "the singing hand may deviate, the accompaniment must keep time," but also the *structural rubato*, in which both melody and accompaniment divert from the rigid tempo.

Thalberg, the great nineteenth-century piano virtuoso, on hearing some Chopin works performed by the master himself, wondered how such music could be committed to paper in a manner that could give a faithful indication of the many subtle tempo deviations and dynamic shadings. It is true that such nuances can only be approximated through notation, in spite of all the composer's painstaking efforts. Chopin, in his Nocturne in C-sharp minor (op. 27 no. 1) for instance, gives the following indications, in quick succession, of his intended tempo fluctuations in bars 49 to 70: sostenuto – rit. – agitato – poco a poco cresc. ed accel. – ritenuto – con anima – ten. – stretto – ten. Within a brief span of twenty-one measures there are nine instructions affecting tempo to a greater or lesser degree. This assiduously detailed notational effort is very helpful, but even its most faithful observance will result only in a cold, mechanistic, insensitive performance if the player lacks empathetic emotional involvement and firm esthetic control. This is the very essence of good romantic playing—that instinctive give-and-take in the melodic flow, rubato.

Metronome: Metronome marks appear with increased frequency in nineteenth-century music. They should always be carefully noted, but never blindly trusted. There are several reasons for this. The marks of some masters, Beethoven and Schumann included, are often incorrect and misleading to begin with and need careful examination and testing before acceptance. (After Schumann's death, his widow, Clara, altered many of his metronome marks in his editions.) A metronome mark judged reasonable can be useful in determining the basic tempo within a movement or section; but always keep in mind that certain deviations are natural and inevitable.

Textures: The romantic piano literature is almost entirely homophonic (melody and accompaniment). Momentary instances of contrapuntal writing do occur, mainly as a device to add harmonic and rhythmic color and piquancy to the forward momentum of melodic flow.

Schubert: Allegretto

Grieg: "Longing for Home," op. 57 no. 6

The characteristic texture of romantic music is a single melodic line supported by chords or other subordinate parts. In many instances this is a three-tier texture: melody, bass, and inner voices. The performer's primary task is to recognize and properly balance these three components, usually according to the familiar hierarchy of sound: the melody line predominates, closely coordinated in volume with the bass part, and both are supported, more discreetly, by the inner voices and figurations. The melody may appear, in any of the three tiers, and always receives dynamic priority. The following are typical romantic voice textures:

Single melody line in treble with solid or broken chord accompaniment:

Chopin: Nocturne, op. 55 no. 1

Top-line melody in the upper notes of harmonic intervals:

Mendelssohn: "Venetian Boat Song," op. 19 no. 6

Melody in top notes of chord sequences:

Schumann: "Important Event," op. 15 no. 6

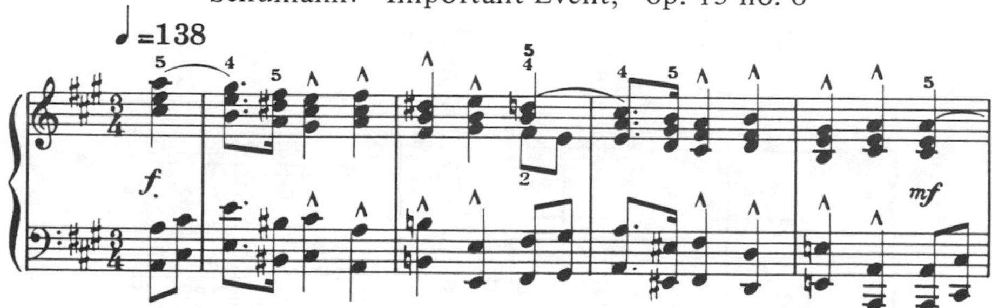

Melody in middle voice:

Brahms: Intermezzo, op. 117 no. 1

Melody in bass:

Chopin: Prelude, op. 28 no. 6

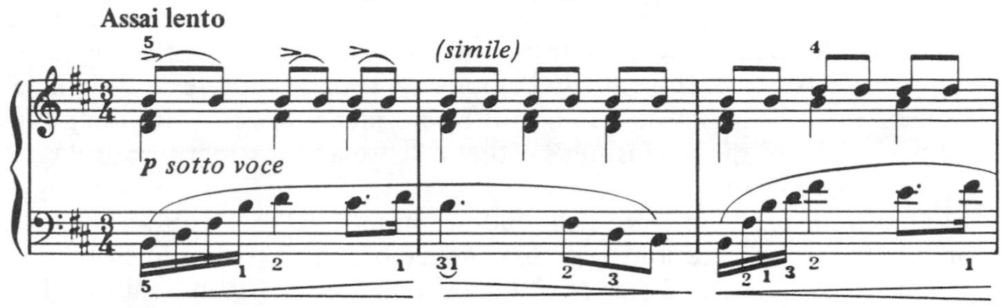

Dynamics: With the increase in the weight and power of the nineteenth-century piano, and with the many marked improvements in its player mechanism, composers had a wider dynamic scope at their disposal than ever before. Schubert, Mendelssohn, and Schumann stay pretty much within the ***pp***-to-***ff*** range, but Liszt, Brahms, and occasionally even Chopin indicate a ***ppp*** or ***fff***. But more important than absolute dynamic values is a judicious and sensitive apportioning of sound levels among the components of a given texture (melody, bass, middle voices).

Accents: There is a profusion of accent marks in the notation of romantic music; it is important that their meaning, including their relative intensity, should be clearly understood. The idiomatic and occasionally obscure usage of marks by some of the masters also needs clarification. Schumann's often-used sign , for instance, is obsolete and can safely be considered the equivalent of today's most often-used symbol, . On occasion both Schubert and Schumann also use the ***f*** sign as an accent.

Schumann: Novelette, op. 99 no. 9

The ***f*** sign in the third measure is the culmination of a crescendo sequence and as such is a dynamic mark; the two ***f*** signs at the end are accent marks.

It should be remembered (and this is often overlooked by even experienced players) that an accent mark over a note does not necessarily prescribe loudness, except in those cases where the emphasis is indicated with letter-like signs involving the ***f*** mark (***sf***, ***sff***, ***fp***, ***sfp***, or simple ***f***); the other graphic symbols (> ∧ –) should be read within the prevailing dynamic level and can, within the context of a soft sequence, indicate only a delicate emphasis. (Schumann: "The Prophet Bird," op. 82 no. 7, first measure.)

Phrasing and Articulation: Sensitive, well-articulated melody playing is the single most important factor in the performance of the romantic repertory. Nineteenth-century composers usually notate the delineation of melody in ample detail, but by no means always with unambiguous clarity, so the performer's esthetic sense and instincts are still vital elements of interpretation.

The main problem is still the indeterminate usage of slurs. The long ones usually indicate a general prevalence of legato. (Chopin's Etude in F minor, op. 25 no. 2 has one slur over the first fifty measures.) The shorter ones, in addition to serving as legato signs, also outline form elements of various lengths and, in contrast to classical usage, freely cross bar lines in a structurally more realistic manner. The form segments encompassed by these slurs may be a phrase or half phrase (Schumann: Melody, op. 68 no. 1) or, as is more often the case, smaller subdivisions denoting details of articulation (Schumann: "First Loss," op. 68 no. 16).

Phrases, by virtue of their structural role in musical architecture, are usually repeated to form larger units, and the repetition often differs from the first presentation of the phrase. One of the many charms of Chopin's music is the skill and inventiveness with which he alters such recurring themes. Sometimes the changes are minimal, such as the addition of a single grace note (as in bar 4 of his Nocturne, op. 55 no. 1), or they can involve more substantial melodic and rhythmic alterations, as in measures 3 and 4 of the following example from the same work:

Chopin: Nocturne, op. 55 no. 1

Even when the notation does not indicate any variation in the repetition of phrases, the performer of romantic piano music has a clear option to provide subtle changes in the repeated section. Contemporary accounts of the performances of nineteenth-century virtuosos, including Chopin and Liszt, amply substantiate the stylistic propriety of this interpretative freedom. It goes without saying that such changes may not ever tamper with the work's basic melodic, harmonic, and rhythmic elements as notated by the composer. They may, however, involve delicate new dynamic shadings, slight tempo modifications, various metric accents, and pedal colorations.

Technique: In the romantic era the technique of piano playing reached a plateau of virtuosity which has not been surpassed since. The twentieth century, with all its innovations in sounds, textures, and colors, could add but little to the romantic arsenal of pianistic capabilities. These skills encompass the gamut of playing patterns: rapid passages of scales and figures, arpeggios, double notes, octaves, chords, wide stretches and leaps, all manners of touches from molto legato to staccatissimo, and, last but by no means least, a secure, sensitive handling of the sustaining pedal.

It is obvious from the foregoing that light and nimble finger action, which had been the mainstay of classical keyboard technique, did not by itself suffice in performing the romantic repertory, and the involvement of the larger muscles of hands, arms, and shoulders became necessary. Even the most elementary aspect of romantic playing—the production of a fine singing tone—necessitates the application of varying degrees of arm weight.

Pedaling: The sustaining pedal is an indispensable tool of romantic interpretation, and there is hardly a piece in the nineteenth-century repertory which could dispense with it. Anton Rubinstein called the pedal "the soul of the piano," and Czerny thought it as useful as if it were a "third hand," enabling the bass notes to vibrate while the two hands are engaged in playing the melody and accompaniment. The pedal, when properly used, actually does much more than sustain certain sounds; it also increases carrying power, enhances a singing tone, generates dynamic shadings, and makes possible the rendition of sophisticated textures, such as voice leading in inner parts, countermelodies, and a multitude of other nuances.

The masters' pedal notation is not always reliable and should not be followed blindly. The differences in the mechanisms and sonorities between nineteenth-century and modern pianos account for this. The prevalent, rather indefinite older notation method (*ped.* . . .*), which did not always pinpoint where the pedal should be depressed and released, is another causative factor. When in doubt about the appropriateness of a given pedal mark, the player must decide on the basis of other evidence. As a rule, pedaling is guided by harmonic changes, but a variety of other factors may also have to be considered, including aspects of articulation, dynamic priorities, and technical conveniences.

Modern pedal marks in the form of brackets └──┘ └──∧──┘ are more precise as to attack and release, but even these cannot indicate fine nuances such as "half pedal," "short touches," by which the damper mechanism is lifted only partially or is manipulated in various other ways to allow some but not full vibration of the strings. These are important coloring devices of romantic interpretation and are left entirely to the performer's discretion. (See "Pedaling Technique," p. 91)

Ornaments: In the nineteenth-century repertory, ornamental symbols are fewer and the notation of embellishments more explicit than in the literature of previous eras. Often the ornaments are written out in full (Chopin: Polonaise, op. 26 no. 1, bars 39, 42, 43, etc.). The correct execution of trills still requires discernment. As a rule they begin on the main note, except in Chopin's works, where, in the absence of contrary indications, they should start on the upper auxiliary. Beginnings and termination of trills are usually written out (Chopin: Nocturne, op. 55 no. 1, bar 30). If the notation is not explicit, all alternatives, including whether the first note of an ornamental group should be played on the beat or begin before it, should be decided by the performer on the basis of musical context and technical convenience.

RECOMMENDED READING

Abraham, Gerald. *Chopin's Musical Style*. Fair Lawn, N.J.: Oxford University Press, 1960.

Einstein, Alfred. *Music in the Romantic Era*. New York: W.W. Norton, 1947.

Klaus, Kenneth B. *The Romantic Period in Music*. Boston: Allyn and Bacon, 1970.

Ferguson, Howard. *Keyboard Interpretation from the Fourteenth to the Nineteenth Century*. New York and London: Oxford University Press, 1975.

Longyear, Rey M. *Nineteenth-Century Romanticism in Music*. Englewood Cliffs, N.J.: Prentice-Hall, 1969.

THE TWENTIETH CENTURY (A Dazzling Musical Kaleidoscope)

The music of our time, a time of search, turmoil, experimentation, and discovery, is a faithful reflection of the profound changes in twentieth-century society. It does not have the relative unanimity of ideals and purpose that other periods exhibit. It is kaleidoscopic, often puzzling, and, at times, unsure of its direction. It is, however, richly imaginative and, in point of diversity at least, unparalleled since the baroque. The many significant trends of twentieth-century compositional styles—impressionism, neoclassicism, expressionism, polytonality, atonality, serialism—and combinations and variations of these styles, often spiced with jazz and folk elements, offer a profuse variety of musical fare. And if after more than a half-century Schoenberg and Bartók still perplex or affront anyone, that person may find composers writing in traditional idioms not far removed from more familiar sounds.

Because of this great variety of musical expression from conservative to avant-garde, today's listener is often confused, indeed bewildered, for lack of a secure, comfortable esthetic vantage point so readily available when listening to or playing music of earlier periods. This confronts the piano teacher with certain problems and tasks which are quite unique, and must be dealt with in an intelligent, empathetic, and constructive manner.

Why the Esthetic Insecurity

When teaching or playing the music of the eighteenth and nineteenth centuries, one has at one's disposal a carefully charted hierarchy of values, which reveals the excellence, mediocrity, or inferiority, the importance or irrelevance, of nearly all specific works and forms of musical expression. We do not have to form opinions and judgments on our own initiative. We know, because of the imprimatur of critical consensus, that Bach is greater than Telemann, Beethoven greater than

Clementi, and Stephen Heller inferior to Chopin. Although one can and does have individual preferences and may indulge in a degree of non-conformity, the main guidelines are given and by and large adhered to. No such assistance and directives are available to the listener of modern music. On hearing a new work we must employ our own esthetic yardsticks,and arrive at our own judgements. Although certain solid and durable values seem to have already crystallized (Debussy and Ravel, for instance) other trends, after having been extant for several decades (serialism, for example) are still on probation as to their viable future.

The insecure, erratic critical stance toward new works in general is due mainly to the fact that twentieth-century music, however fascinating in its numerous manifestations, is in a constant flux and as yet has been unable to evolve a solid and dependable set of artistic tenets which could serve as generally applicable critical standards. Consequently, the frame of reference in listening to modern music is still largely derived from eighteenth- and nineteenth-century sounds and patterns. This, of course, is anachronistic and unrealistic, and can be remedied only by enlarging and enriching the artistic premises by adding new concepts and devices to the old ones and accepting them as feasible, but not necessarily preferable, tools of the creative process.

A modern composition should not be spurned because of the listener's *a priori* aversion toward its mode of expression (atonality, for instance); it should be judged solely on whether or not, or to what extent it can convey a musical experience of esthetic validity and emotional import, regardless of its idiomatic label.

Guidelines for the Teacher

"There is no excellent beauty that hath not some strangeness in the proportion," said Francis Bacon, and the statement is as pertinent today as it was nearly four centuries ago. The piano teacher's task is to acquaint the student with this "strangeness," to analyze it, explain it, strip from it the aura of oddity and make it a familiar phenomenon in the glossary of musical concepts at the earliest possible stage. Children, who are known to be able to learn a foreign language within a few months, do not, as a rule, resist confrontations with novelty; being unencumbered by rigid preconceptions they readily accept and absorb new ideas and concepts. The older, more mature student may require a more cautious, systematic approach when exploring the frontiers of modern music.

In this writer's experience atonality is the most challenging hurdle in the path of such explorations. The traditional pull of gravity toward a secure tonal base, the yearning for a tonal habitat, is sometimes so strong that it may require a conscious effort and patient direction on the part of the teacher to remove the encumbrances. In such cases one should proceed gradually from the more traditional and only slightly innovative styles to the more daring, radically new ones.

As a first step it might be helpful to point out that the centuries-old reign of major and minor tonalities has never been absolute. To attain a special mood or effect, some romantic masters have allowed themselves the freedom to forego a concluding tonic cadence in favor of a different harmonic function (Schumann: "Child Falling Asleep," op. 15 no. 12; Chopin: Mazurka, op. 17 no. 4, etc.). More importantly, melodic and harmonic formations based on the church modes had been employed with increased frequency during the nineteenth century to give works a certain archaic or ethnic flavor (Mussorgsky, Grieg, and others). In impressionism and folk-oriented modern idioms, the role of modality is even more basic and becomes one of the most important stylistic earmarks. The ancient pentatonic scale is also the source of many modern works.

Impressionism, still within tonal boundaries, revolutionized the old rules of harmony with a fascinating array of new devices: whole-tone chords, chord clusters, novel harmonic sequences. Also maintaining strong ties with tonality, although often sharply dissonant, is *pandiatonicism*, which utilizes tones of a single key or mode (usually the white keys of the piano) but without any harmonic implications; each tone is independent and not a "degree" of a scale. Stravinsky was the initiator and most successful exponent of this idiom. *Bitonality* uses two keys simultaneously. In piano music the division is usually between the two hands. After having examined and savoured the foregoing idioms, all of which maintain links of varying degrees with tonality, the student should be better prepared and in a more receptive frame of mind to meet other, more radical styles.

Atonality is a compositional technique in which a definite tonality, or key center, is lacking; the twelve tones within the octave are independent, unrelated units, not components of any scale. The letter names of these tones (C, C-sharp, D, D-sharp, etc.) do not furnish an adequate nomenclature for these autonomous pitches, because the names imply a derivative relationship between C and C-sharp, D and D-sharp, etc., where, within the scheme of atonality, none exists. The lack of the accustomed key center does not necessarily mean that the listener is left adrift in an uncharted sea of sound. Other aural landmarks of pitch and rhythm are usually present to serve as guideposts of orientation and as a framework of musical construction. Furthermore, many modern works, although not tonal in the traditional sense, maintain certain tenuous ties with key centers. For instance, in Bartók's "Bear Dance" from *Ten Easy Pieces* the repeated Ds serve as a quasi-tonic foundation supporting a whole-tone construction. In Schoenberg's entirely atonal Little Piano Piece op. 19 no. 2, the oft-repeated harmonic interval G–B is the magnetic device around which all other elements coalesce.

Farthest removed from conventional tonality are pieces built on a *tone row* or *series*, a predetermined order of the twelve tones manipulated in various fashions (retrograde, inversion, transposition, etc.). But even with this technique certain rhythmic, melodic, or intervallic configurations invariably stand out, propelling a forward momentum and giving the piece an explicit constructional profile.

The leading composers of our century, while breaking new grounds, may bypass or abandon the aural and constructional premises of the past, but they do not eradicate them; rather, they transform them within the context of their aims and musical ideology. Whether or not we, the audience, can understand, adopt, and ultimately enjoy their language depends not only on the esthetic value and durability of their ideas, but also on our, the audience's attitudes. Certainly, the assimilation of modern sounds and forms requires a degree of active participation on the listener's part; perhaps hardly more than a measure of interest and alertness. The piano teacher, of all people, can especially ill afford the "luxury" of submerging exclusively in the comfortable sounds of the past. Today's youngster cannot be brought up, musically speaking, on teaching materials written solely a hundred or two hundred years ago; exposure to the music of our time is indispensable. Hence the importance of familiarity with the various contemporary idioms and the ways to convey their essential traits to the student.

Technique: The emergence and flowering of modern music, with its dazzling repertory of new sounds and its revolutionary compositional systems and procedures, is largely due to the creative exploits of the pianist composer at the keyboard. Many of the great innovators—Debussy, Ravel, Stravinsky, Bartók, to mention a few—were also pianists of high caliber. Consequently, it is no wonder that all aspects of technique, all pianistic problems extant for the past three centuries, are profusely represented in the keyboard literature of our time. Because of the diversity of idioms, no generalization can be made as to the performance of twentieth-century piano music; the details of technical execution must depend on the stylistic orientation of each work.

Impressionism demands a pliable tempo, a supple forward motion. The resulting subtle rubato is guided by pictorial considerations rather than emotional impulses (as in Chopin). A sensitive, refined touch and a most sophisticated pedal technique (including half pedal, fractional pedaling, etc.) are the brushes with which the pianist can reproduce the shapes and hues on the canvas of musical impressionism. The dynamic range is full, but never harsh or brittle, with some moderation toward the high decibels. Gradations of sound (cresc., dim., accents, etc.) involve the most delicate tolerances ever employed in the performance of music.

The neoclassicism and pandiatonicism of Stravinsky, Hindemith, and others, require the generally steady tempo of eighteenth-century music, with no rubato, or only the sparsest hint of it. Clearly drawn lines, projected with a secure, right-on-target technique and a well-controlled, variegated touch are called for here. Bartók, Prokofiev, and their school, too, need an "objective" approach to interpretation. The earmarks are well-maintained, even tempos; occasional rubatos in slow sections, in the manner of ethnic inflections, a touch which can be fiercely percussive or gently caressing; and the full dynamic range of the modern piano.

Becoming familiar with the trends of twentieth-century music is a task that the piano teacher cannot shirk. This is a process of self-education which if pursued diligently, with an open and inquisitive mind, can have its rewards every step of the way for teacher and student alike. (See "Twentieth-century Music: An Analysis and Appreciation" pagc 489 and its bibliography.)

RECOMMENDED READING

Larue, Jan. *Guidelines for Style Analysis.* New York: Norton, Nov. 1971

Moore, Douglas. *A Guide to Musical Styles: From Madrigal to Modern Music.* New York: Norton, Jan. 1963

The Search for Authenticity (The Lost Art of Thoroughbass Playing)

DENES AGAY

The search for authenticity in editions and performance practices, a dominant and all pervasive trait in the musical life of our time, came about as a healthy and most welcome reaction to the editorial excesses of the nineteenth century. Editors of the romantic period so thoroughly and abundantly marked, annotated, analyzed, and dissected the works of baroque and classical masters–they so overburdened the originally clear, uncluttered note picture with slurs, brackets, and a profusion of expression marks–that the composer's original conception, in essence the music itself, was nearly obliterated, and sunk under the weight of editorial overlay. Eliminating the excessive markings and getting back to the original texts (*Urtexts*) as notated by the masters themselves was like clearing a path in a jungle, or like opening a window and letting fresh air into a musty, overstuffed Victorian parlor. As a result of this trend, today's teachers, students, and performers have at their disposal a very wide choice of dependable texts in all areas of keyboard literature.

Unfortunately, this noble crusade has been somewhat marred of late by an excess of zeal and dogmatic pedantry, which, unwittingly perhaps, tends to turn the quest for reliable editions into a doctrinaire compulsion. (Recently I heard this malaise aptly diagnosed as "Urtextitis.") Without elaborating on the various hair-splitting aspects of this trend, suffice it to say that it is one thing to search for authenticity,

---

Portions of this section are reprinted from *Clavier*, November 1975. By permission of the Instrumentalist Company.

and quite another to let it become a rigid cult, with the Urtext as the gospel, with every particle of the note picture an object of devout veneration and any manifestation of interpretive freedom an act of heresy. All this is not only terribly inhibiting for the student, teacher, and performer, but also in direct contradiction to the baroque practice of allowing the player a considerable degree of interpretative freedom.

The baroque masters' manuscripts are rather sparing, in that they present only the notes, with hardly any other marks of interpretation. It was left to the performer to select the proper tempo, dynamics, and phrasing, and to bring to life the skeletal text with warmth and imagination. The performer was not only allowed to do so, but indeed, expected to do so; this was his or her privilege and responsibility. We should hasten to add that, from all we know, performers were quite up to the task. The goal of music education during the eighteenth century was not only technical prowess, but thorough musicianship through knowledge of harmony, counterpoint, and improvisation, including the ability to fill in at sight the missing voices when a work was notated only by the melody and a figured (or sometimes unfigured) bass (*basso continuo, thoroughbass*), a very common practice during the seventeenth and eighteenth centuries.

Present-day music education does not equip the player with all these skills, and this is why the absolute insistence on textural authenticity is somewhat unreasonable from a pedagogical point of view. We proclaim the sanctity of Urtexts and pressure everyone to abide by them from the earliest grades on, but we largely fail to give the student even a fraction of the interpretative know-how the baroque performer had.

What is needed is a simple preparatory course dealing with such topics as the baroque conventions of tempo, dynamics, touch, and articulation; a description of the mechanics and the sound of the keyboard instruments the pieces were written for; the composer's notation habits, which quite often differ from modern rules and usage; and the rudiments of thoroughbass playing, or at least an awareness that a great deal of baroque music was notated in a stenographic manner which the player was expected to supplement. Many selections in Bach's *Little Notebook for Anna Magdalena Bach* and Leopold Mozart's *Notebook for Wolfgang* were meant to teach this skill and are ideally suited for that purpose even today.

WHEN AND HOW TO FILL IN VOICES

It should not be assumed that *basso continuo*—the method of improvising keyboard accompaniment from the bass notes only—was employed solely in pieces where the top line was meant to be played by a melody instrument (flute, violin, recorder, etc.) or voice. A good deal of solo keyboard music, especially during the first two-thirds of the eighteenth century, was also notated in this manner and was meant to be performed with tastefully interpolated voices, even where figures indicating harmonic functions were missing.

As many simple two-voice compositions of this type are used in early-grade piano instruction, one wonders why this notation method and the proper execution of works written this way does not generate more interest, or why, indeed, it is largely ignored. Several possible reasons come to mind. The believers in "Urtexts only on all grade levels" may be concerned that any addition of notes by the performer may establish a dangerous precedent and undermine the credo of absolute adherence to the venerated texts. Others may refrain from filling in voices because they lack the proper guidelines and simply do not know whether, in a specific case, this procedure is proper or not. Most important, today's student is not oriented and trained thoroughly enough to be able to do it. In any case, a step in the right direction is to recognize the fact that the addition of mid-voices in a certain type of two-voice baroque keyboard music is proper and stylistically correct.

What type of keyboard music is this? First, it should be remembered that these are pieces written mostly for the harpsichord or clavichord. Works written originally for the piano rarely qualify. Also excluded are all works of a contrapuntal and polyphonic nature, especially where the two voices are engaged in an imitative motivic play, as in the Bach Inventions and Partitas; neither do the Scarlatti Sonatas, the Handel Suites or the works of the French clavecinists belong in this category. On the other hand, many small dance pieces and fantasias by writers of the middle and late baroque (Handel, Telemann) and especially by the exponents of the so-called gallant style may well be amplified and enhanced by additional voices, especially when performed on the instruments they were written for, the harpsichord and clavichord. Not only would this inflict no stylistic damage, but, on the contrary, would conform to the composer's intention. To avoid any doubts and confusion, the characteristics of such a piece should be well understood and clearly remembered. All of the following traits must be present: a two-voice texture consisting of a distinct top-line melody, supported by a typical bass line in which each note implies a definite harmonic function. The two voices are usually at least an octave—more often even further—apart, without any thematic relationship or motivic interaction; the role of the bass is only to serve as harmonic underpinning for the treble.

In the following excerpts the large notes represent the composer's original notation; the small notes furnish an example of the many ways the textures may be amplified.

Telemann: Minuet

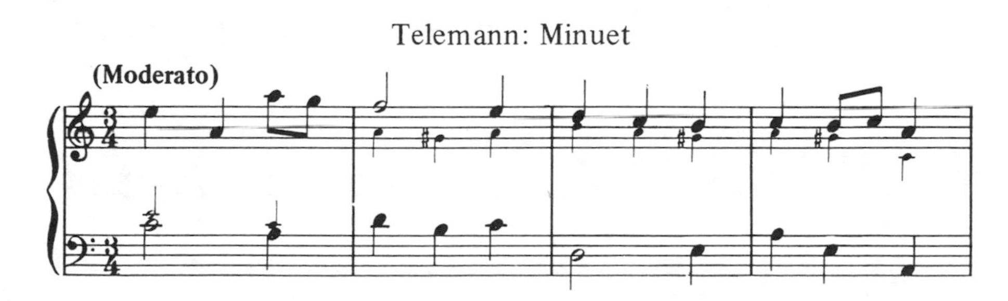

3
3
Telemann: Fantasia
Vivace
tr
Handel: Bourrée
(Allegretto)
Handel: Minuet
(Andantino)
p
mf
p

After all this has been said, it should also be emphasized that this article does not mean to encourage an indiscriminate practice of voice additions, even in those pieces where careful analysis would indicate it to be stylistically correct and musically feasible. There are several reasons for this. A two-voice texture may sound rather thin and dry on the eighteenth-century instrument for which it was written; the modern piano, however, with its superior built-in resonance, sustaining power, and expressive capability, will in many cases deliver a rounded and satisfying sound without additional tones. More importantly, thoroughbass playing is a skill which requires specialized training; the added inner voices have to be not only harmonically correct, but applied with secure knowledge and fine instinct to be consonant with the composition's style and mood. Only those capable of doing this should be tempted to enrich the texture between the treble and the bass line. As to the printed version of such bass realizations, the desirable method is to have the additional notes printed in small type, so that the performer has the option to play or not play the voice additions, or—if capable of so doing—to change them to suit individual taste.

Amplifying such two-voice textures should always be done with taste and restraint. Heavy chords, or thick layers of added notes at each harmony change, are out of place. In most cases a few interpolated sustained notes and some harmonically illuminating inner voices here and there are sufficient to give the piece a fuller sound and a more interesting profile, without impairing its simple, often fragile character.

To repeat: the notation of a great deal of simple eighteenth-century keyboard music implies some amplification on the performer's part. Whether or not today, on the modern piano, one should or should not add voices, and if so, how one should go about it, is best left to well-informed individual judgments and convictions. The search for authenticity should always be a quest for more complete esthetic fulfillment, and not an ever-narrowing road to dogmatic restrictiveness.

Not long ago, at a concert and subsequent symposium on early music, I witnessed two experts become embroiled in a shouting match and nearly come to blows over the question of whether all baroque trills should start on the upper auxiliary note. It was quite a scene—absurd and thought-provoking—all in the name of authenticity. There is clearly a great pedagogic need for more well-balanced information, more constructive dialogue, less pedantic hair-splitting, and less academic rivalry. Most important, the student should be taught gradually and systematically, from the earliest stages of study, the elements of style, the various fashions in composition and performance, and the changing attitudes toward the music of the past; he or she can then approach the urtexts fully equipped, relaxed, and able to enjoy the baroque music the way it was meant to be: with a degree of freedom, guided by the taste one develops through knowledge.

RECOMMENDED READING

Keller, Hermann (Carl Parrish, tr.). *Thoroughbass Method*. New York: W.W. Norton, 1972.

See also "Styles in Composition and Performance," p.457.

Keller, Hermann (Carl Parrish, tr.). *Thoroughbass Method*. New York: W.W. Nor-

Baroque Keyboard Instruments

DENES AGAY

The *harpsichord* is the principal stringed instrument of the baroque period. Most of the keyboard works of Bach, Handel, Couperin, Rameau, Scarlatti, and scores of other masters of the seventeenth and eighteenth centuries—including the early works of Haydn and Mozart—were written for this instrument. Although today these works are performed mostly on the modern piano, it is of utmost importance that the player become familiar with the harpsichord's tone production and sound. Not, to be sure, in an attempt to imitate it, but rather to be guided by its esthetic qualities: the crispness of sound, the clarity in reproducing polyphonic textures, the dramatic possibilities in sudden dynamic changes, all of which are essential traits of stylistic baroque interpretation.

In appearance the harpsichord resembles a slender grand piano with a compass of at least five octaves. Strings are stretched from front to back, at right angles to the keyboard. It often has two manuals, each activating a separate set of strings tuned an octave apart. The basic difference between the piano and the harpsichord is in the manner of tone production. On the piano, strings are *struck* by felt hammers; on the harpsichord, strings are *plucked* by quills or leather plectra, producing a somewhat clipped, quite brilliant pizzicato-like sound. Since the harpsichord has no sustaining pedal, gradations of dynamics (crescendo-decrescendo) are not possible and the player has little direct control over the quality and volume of sound, except through mechanical means. This involves the manipulations of various stops and registers, similar to those of the organ, through which sets of strings may be coupled or disengaged, or some other special effects attained. An accomplished player can, however, expand the expressive potential of this fascinating instrument through nuances of touch and attack, and through a sensitive application of agogic accents.

During the past two or three decades, thorough explorations of baroque music literature and performance practices have also brought about a renewed interest in the harpsichord on the part of composers, performers, and teachers.

The *clavichord* is one of the most ancient of keyboard instruments. Its origins go back to the thirteenth century and it reached the height of its popularity during the baroque era. In appearance it is a rectangular, often quite ornate, wooden box, about two-by-four feet, either placed on a table or standing on legs. Its compass is from three-and-a-half to five octaves. The strings, metal or gut, are stretched horizontally, parallel to the keyboard. When a key is depressed, it activates a metal wedge, called a *tangent*, which strikes the string from below, producing a pleasing mellow sound. Tone quality, including dynamics, can be controlled to some extent by the player's manner of touch. An especially characteristic vibrato effect can be obtained by keeping the key depressed with a rocking motion of the finger (*Bebung*).

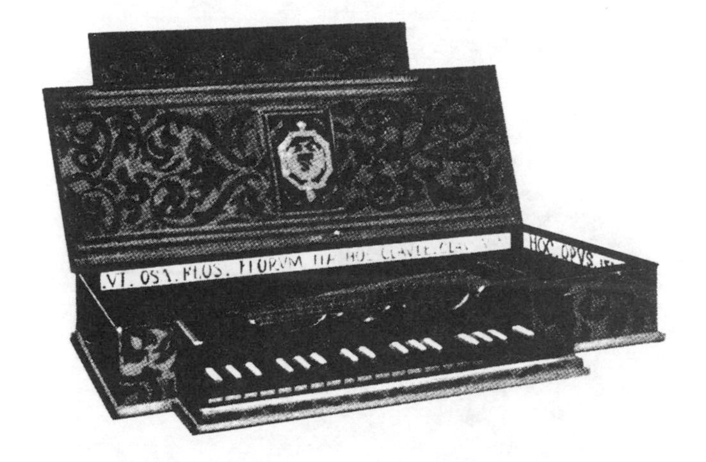

Because of its lack of volume and limited dynamic range (from ***pp*** to ***mf***), the clavichord is rarely used in a concert hall, or as an ensemble instrument. Its delicate, expressive sound makes it ideally suited for performance in an intimate atmosphere, such as a private home.

Music written expressly for the clavichord is rather rare, but there is no doubt that a large body of baroque and rococo keyboard music was, by preference, performed on this subtle, expressive instrument. It remained popular until the end of the eighteenth century.

The *virginal*, a small keyboard instrument of the harpsichord family, was very popular in sixteenth- and seventeenth-century England and the Netherlands. It has an oblong-shaped case, usually set upon a table, with a single keyboard encompassing about four octaves. The strings run parallel to the keyboard. Contrary to popular belief, the instrument was not named after Queen Elizabeth I ("the virgin queen"), who was an expert player on it. The term was in use well before her time, and probably originates from the Latin *virga*, meaning a little stick, or jack, which is part of all harpsichord-type mechanisms.

Music written for this instrument by the English masters William Byrd (1543–1623), John Bull (1563–1628), and Orlando Gibbons (1583–1625) embodies a rich and idiomatic keyboard style of composition, which had great influence on the harpsichord literature of the high baroque.

The *spinet* is a small harpsichord, usually in a wing-shaped or triangular case with one manual. The strings run at about a forty-five degree angle to the keyboard. It was a popular home instrument during the seventeenth and eighteenth centuries. The origin of the name is obscure, possibly deriving from its Italian inventor, Spinetti. Today the name is also applied to the early oblong-shaped pianoforte, or the modern miniature upright piano.

Cembalo, an abbreviation of *clavicembalo*, is the Italian and German name for the harpsichord; *clavecin* is its French name. A *claveciniste* is a harpsichord player, but it also refers to a French composer of the baroque period who wrote works for the clavecin (Couperin, Rameau, Daquin, Dandrieu, and others).

Clavier is the German generic name for stringed keyboard instruments, which include the harpsichord (virginal, spinet), clavichord, and fortepiano. Bach's Forty-eight Preludes and Fugues (*Das Wohltemperierte Clavier*), for instance, were intended for either the harpsichord or clavichord, depending on the player's preference or access. In Bach's time the term *clavier* also included the organ. In the nineteenth century the preferred German spelling became *Klavier*, and its meaning was restricted to the piano only.

The *clavicytherium* is an upright harpsichord, or vertical spinet. Today it is found only in museums.

RECOMMENDED READING

Harich-Schneider, Eta. *The Harpsichord: An Introduction to Technique, Style, and the Historical Sources*. St. Louis: Concordia, 1954.

James, Philip. *Early Keyboard Instruments from Their Beginnings to the Year 1820.* Chester Springs, Pa.: Dufour, 1930. Reprint: New York: Barnes & Noble, 1970.

Neupert, Hanns. *Harpsichord Manual: A Historical and Technical Discussion.* Kassel: Bärenreiter, 1968.

Russel, Raymond. *The Harpsichord and Clavichord*. London: Faber, 1973.

Winternitz, Emanuel. *Keyboard Instruments*. New York: Metropolitan Museum of Art, 1961.

Twentieth-Century Music: An Analysis and Appreciation

JUDITH LANG ZAIMONT

. . . in the long run the only human activities really worthwhile are the search for knowledge, and the creation of beauty. This is beyond argument; the only point of debate is which comes first.

—Arthur C. Clarke
Profiles of the Future

Is not beauty in music too often confused with something which lets the ears lie back in an easy chair?

—Charles Ives
"Postface" to *114 Songs*

THE COMPOSER

Without doubt, ours is a period of kaleidoscopic musical richness.

The spirit of scientific inquiry—an objective, general curiosity about the nature of things—characterizes our age and has prompted increasing performances of older music and a general growth of interest in music from all eras. Serious music performing groups vie with one another in directing the general listener's attention to their specific interests: the music of the Renaissance, the baroque, the classic or romantic eras, or that of our own time. As a consequence, the living composer has to struggle just to gather an audience; if his or her music then turns out to be difficult to assimilate on first hearing, he or she has only a small chance of success in communicating artistic substance, particularly if the audience's expectations have been formed mostly through exposure to music of the past.

Would we be better able to understand today's music if we weren't distracted by "historical" alternatives? Yes, if we greet the new music on its own terms, with understanding, and (to carry Coleridge's admonition beyond the realm of the theater) with a "willing suspension of disbelief." We should realize that the twentieth-century composer has been keeping pace with the tempo and temper of fluctuating times, via experiments and innovations that seem to have been, in hindsight, inevitable. It is the audiences who cling to the known in place of the new, who must be reassured that a given artwork has its place in the esthetic continuum.

What is it about the art of our time that seems to differentiate it so radically from that of the past?

Any art is best understood within its own frames of reference. The most easily distinguished factors affecting the progress of musical composition in our century are the political and social upheavals accompanying two global wars, and the growth of a constantly expanding communications network that promotes cross-fertilizations between Western music and the musics of Asia, Africa, Eastern Europe, and folk cultures throughout the world.

As a consequence of this cross-fertilization, composers have reevaluated the raw materials of their musical heritage (which might be described as a synthesis of melody, harmony, and simpler rhythmic motives) and have turned instead to exploring intricate rhythmic figures (hypnotically repeated and only slowly permuted) and melodic arabesques (of a freer, chantlike quality) borrowed from other cultures at the expense of harmony.

Sociopolitical upheavals have provoked an even more important alteration in outlook: our age has become, in Auden's phrase, "the age of anxiety," distinguished by the increased conviction on the part of most of us that the works of humankind are essentially impermanent. Never before has the creator felt so cut adrift from the art of the past; so decidedly, so overtly a composite tradition-breaker and history-maker. Indeed, since "our civilization is the first to have for its past, the past of the world, [since] our history is the first to be world history,"[1] the composer of our time has become obliged to juggle two burdens at once: to clarify his or her art as an outgrowth of the music of the past, and to sustain it as an art in evolution, responsive to the changing needs and requirements of modern times.

This is a tall order and one that most composers of the past felt no need to fill. They were much more likely to be commended by the public for demonstrating a conservative attitude than to be encouraged to innovate; the contexts of their times demanded it.

Our Western musical heritage, from the baroque through the romantic eras, may be described as a context, distinguished by [a] developing and characteristic kind of musical thinking [in which] every musical event has a "function" or a functional role [relating] it to what has come before and what will happen next. The basic psychological principle here is expectation; the basic musical technique is that of direction and motion. Out of this grow the characteristic ways in which musical lines will rise and fall and the ways in which simultaneous musical lines will relate to one another in harmonic patterns. The idea of expectation suggests the use of resolutions and non-resolution; of so-called dissonance and consonance; of intensity and relaxation; of cadence, accent, and articulation; of phrase and punctuation; of rhythm and dynamic; even of tempo and tone color.[2]

Historically, evolution by sudden jump was discouraged. Basic changes in raw materials, formats, and the composer's own orientation with respect to artistic materials were expected to take place gradually, over the space of several creative generations.

Not so in our century: the distinctive feature of twentieth-century music has been that change occurs at a dizzying pace. "More has happened in music in these few years than in any previous five-hundred-year period. . . . Every element of the musical language [has] had to be subjected to [deliberate] reappraisal and examination before it could be made part of the new art. . . ."[3] As a consequence, audience bewilderment has increased many times over. Being largely unaware of the separate steps that inspired most twentieth-century compositional innovations, listeners are naturally at a loss when confronting the end result.

Composers themselves have not let go of the past without a struggle. Although many alternatives to functional tonality were explored around the turn of the century, the upheavals of World War I prompted a step sideways rather than straight ahead, with a return to the materials, musical forms, and ideals of the eighteenth century (neoclassicism).

By contrast, after World War II artists consciously sought to cut their ties to a past now rendered horrific. To deny the past, through any and all means, became esthetically important, and the development of an objective, dispassionate, eminently rational music became the goal. Total conscious control of every musical element was the result: "integral" or "total" serialism, a compositional method in which composers were obliged to think objectively and rationally about every musical component, thus creating an entirely new music devoid of any vestige of tonality's "expectations" and/or the individual artist's "unconscious" inspirations.

Within the past two decades integral serialism's rationality has begun to be tempered by the reappearance of more subjective modes of expression. Complete control of musical materials is no longer the rule. Room has been made for the individual's voice to be heard again, within a more traditional context (neoromanticism); for the performer to become a partner in the creative process (aleatory music, the music of chance); to allude to music of the past or quote it directly, in either affectionate parody or pastiche (collage); to freely employ all twelve chromatic pitches in a nonrigorous manner, either in a tonal or nontonal framework; to create an expressive yet nonpersonal music using melodic and rhythmic materials (and philosophical ideal) borrowed from other countries and other cultures, including jazz or other popular music idioms of the West; to expand the sonic palette indefinitely by using electronic instruments, either alone or in conjunction with live performers; or to combine music with the other performing arts in the complex theatrical panoply termed a "mixed-media event."

Our time, then, is truly a period of kaleidoscopic musical richness: a stimulating, fertile era for composers of all persuasions.

THE LISTENER

But is it as stimulating a period for the listener? Perhaps it is not so much stimulating as bewildering.

When the listener says, fretfully, that the music of our time is too difficult, too alien, too complex to comprehend easily or all at once (or at all!), he or she is forgetting that one listens within the context of a specific acculturation. It's not just the new music of our own culture that may appear incomprehensible to the listener; music from other times and countries might seem equally impenetrable.

Although we like to think that our esthetic viewpoint is neutral and unbiased, in fact,

> contemporary musical ideas are still communicated in the context of a musical life whose structure, means, and institutions are largely derived from the late eighteenth and nineteenth centuries. . . . Some of our most fundamental ways of thinking about music and musical creations are also inheritances from the recent past. Indeed, our whole notion of "art" and artistic creation as a unique and separable human activity is a relatively modern Western idea, by no means universal in human experience. . . .[4]

Our cultural-historical framework, then, is quite specific, and operates not only as a mind-set for esthetic evaluation but also materially, in the continued conservation of musical institutions and implements which reached their full development between 1700 and 1900. These include the modern orchestra, opera, and chamber ensemble; the idea of a solo recital; the most common instruments; the bulk of the concert repertory for those instruments; the techniques for teaching music theory and performance through manipulating individual instruments; and the concept of the conservatory.

Once we understand the context from which we judge, we will no longer dismiss a piece on first hearing simply because it seems difficult or foreign. In truth it is too easy, and not strictly honest, to call a composition "beautiful" or "worthy" merely because it "lets the ears lie back in an easy chair." A surprising number of works originally damned as "monstrous" or "barbarous" *appear* to have matured over the years into distinguished masterworks.

Music, by its nature the most ephemeral and abstract of the arts, imposes its own framework for communication. In its "purest" form, music speaks to us through one sense only (hearing), unrolling steadily in time. Individual moments within a composition can never crystallize for prolonged examination (as with a painting or sculpture) but must be savored as they pass by. Without the buttress of a *visual* complement (as in ballet) or a *visual-linguistic* complement (as in film or opera), music must communicate fully through the narrow channels of sound and time alone.

Composers have long been aware of the limitations placed on them by the nature of their medium. As a result, the larger of the traditional musical forms are also the most highly redundant of all artworks. This must be. In order to sustain communication, involvement, and understanding with the listener, the music cooperates by stressing certain necessary aural landmarks via periodic repeats, variants, or echoes of previously heard material. It is no wonder, then, that at first hearing an extended through-composed piece of absolute music is the most difficult of all for even a cooperating listener to comprehend fully; if, in addition, its idiom is one which avoids the expected grammar and syntax of functional tonality, communication will be at a minimum.

Thus, it is not surprising to realize that opera, ballet, songs, choral works, and program music in general are the most popular of musical genres. With the program as a buttress, even a particularly abstruse musical configuration may be understood with relative ease. Programs may either unroll in time along with the music (as do song texts), or exist independently, in written or schematic form, for the purpose of being studied before the piece is played, as in the case of scenarios for tone poems.

These latter—the "program notes"—have changed since the last century to fit the more rational, highly constructed music of our time. Instead of merely providing a description of the series of events, works of art, or psychic struggles "depicted" in the music, the notes now usually contain information about the prescription according to which the piece has been written: its generative procedure or theoretic basis (for example, its specific tone row). The composer provides this information as an aid to listening, and the notes are a valuable, indispensible feature of concerts devoted solely to new music. Though they may occasionally seem complex and highly technical, they serve the same purpose as the scenario for *Ein Heldenleben* or the titles of Victor Hartmann's "pictures at an exhibition."

Aside from listening through a general cultural and esthetic filter, each of us hears through a personal filter established by the musical experiences of our youth. In our early years we heard and appreciated without intellectualizing; we thought that each piece was in perfect proportion, emerging whole from the composer's conscious. It may be quite different to return to these pieces in later years and view them critically. The music that once seemed so perfect may actually be flawed in detail or execution, according to a more mature understanding; yet it is difficult to consider these "old friends" as objectively as we consider music which has come to our attention more recently. Because we listen so uncritically when we're young, that is the best time for us to be introduced to newer idioms. If the new sounds can be accepted as natural then, we will be at least sympathetic to even more radical innovations as they are introduced.

However, we should remember that when we play or listen to music of the past we're dealing with works whose overall quality is remarkably high; we cut our musical teeth on Bach, Mozart, Beethoven, Chopin, and Debussy, not Buxtehude, Kalkbrenner, Türk, Moscheles, and Sinding. For music from our own century, however, the situation is different. Unless we choose to stay a strict sixty years behind the times, we must offer our ears and our cooperation equally to the music of all, at least on a first go-round. This is not just fair, but stimulating and esthetically gratifying as well.

COMPOSER AND LISTENER TOGETHER

It is true, though, that some composers don't go out of their way to make it easy for the listener. The same sophisticated technology that permits minute control over each musical element and shortens the time needed to develop and perfect every new idiom also permits the composer to operate free of technical limitation and to pursue continuous innovation as a goal in itself. Particularly in the last two-and-a-half decades, many composers have tunneled directly ahead (glancing back over their shoulders now and again at the dread specter of history catching up with them) on the premise that each new work should represent a "significant breakthrough." Rarely do these creators take the time to mine the veins of stylistic ores they have uncovered, nor do they permit their listeners time to linger over and savor the special qualities of each innovation, nor increase their understanding through repeated exposure to a particularly novel concept.

If, in truth, "the bond that connects all of twentieth-century music grows out of the fact that each composer and each piece has had to establish new and unique forms of expressive and intellectual communications"[5]; if, for example, "Stockhausen has knocked down his own house and built it up in a different way for every new work"[6]; if, in short, each composer becomes the sum total of a separate artistic movement, then listeners will have to learn to accept the situation, and draw up "scorecards" to keep track.

However, if composers recognize the inevitability of cultural lag and try to allow for it by slowing their flight to the future just a little, both listener and composer will benefit. Compromise on both sides is overdue:

> The time is past when music was written for a handful of aesthetes. Today vast crowds of people have come face to face with serious music and are waiting with eager impatience. Composers, take heed of this: if you repel these crowds they will turn away from you to. . . vulgar music. But if you can hold them you will win an audience such as the world has never before seen.[7]

This is as true for us today as it was for Prokofiev in 1937.

CHRONOLOGICAL SURVEY OF TWENTIETH-CENTURY STYLES

Before considering musical innovations in detail, it may be helpful to review briefly the various styles which have been formulated during this century. Only in the case of the first few styles will it be possible to categorize composers definitely; indeed, the trend so far has been toward eclecticism rather than compartmentalization.

For example, we might chart Stravinsky's growth in progressive terms, by style explored: juvenile works in an extended romantic vein with an infusion of impressionistic color consciousness, composed under the guidance of the great orchestrator Rimsky-Korsakov; the three ballets–*Firebird* (1910), *Petrouchka* (1911), and *Rite of Spring* (1913)–in which he added national flavorings to an impressionistic base at first, then gradually forged his personal, rhythmically vital, nonrigorous expressionism. After World War I he moved away from large canvases to works for smaller forces, written in a French-international vein incorporating a flirtation with jazz; some folk color is still present in *Les Noces* (1923), but more typical of this period is the lean, clean *l'Histoire du Soldat* (1918). Neoclassicism was the style of Stravinsky's middle years, always distinguished by his personal feeling for rhythms; a spare orchestral sound comprised of nonblending instrumental colors; astringent sonorities; and, in the area of form, a penchant for making transpositions by direct juxtaposition, without bridges. Perhaps the masterpiece of this period is the *Symphony of Psalms* (1930). In the mid-1950s Stravinsky adopted serial procedures, perhaps for their comforting frame of ordered rationality; *Agon* (1957) and *Threni* (1958) are two later works that are serial at least in part. Thus is it possible to think of Stravinsky's career as a counterpart to Picasso's, since both creators made it their business to keep abreast of every innovation in technique or esthetic philosophy, and to incorporate into their own vocabularies whatever might be of interest or relevance.

In the list below, I have attempted to place each composer in an appropriate context, based on the stylistic language he or she most commonly employed. One composer may appear in several categories. Readers may possibly disagree with certain of the categorizations, and are encouraged to do so.

(1) **Late Romanticism**: continuation of the Germanic romantic tradi-

tion. The music is often overblown, characterized by heavy emotionalism, huge orchestras, great symphonic lengths, and advances in harmony and orchestration.

Germany and Austria:	Anton Bruckner (1824–1896)
	Gustav Mahler (1860–1911)
	Hugo Wolf (1860–1903)
	Richard Strauss (1864–1949)
	Max Reger (1873–1916)
	Erich Korngold (1897–1957)
England:	Gustav Holst (1874–1934)
	Ralph Vaughan Williams (1872–1958)
Denmark:	Carl Nielsen (1865–1931)
Finland:	Jean Sibelius (1865–1957)
Russia:	Alexander Scriabin (1872–1915)
	Sergei Rachmaninoff (1873–1943)

(2) **Impressionism**: a style which attempts to capture a mood or evoke an atmosphere; the musical counterpart to symbolism in poetry and the paintings of Renoir, Monet, Pissarro, Dégas, and Cézanne. It still is a potent force today, particularly in the music of Olivier Messaien (1908–) and George Crumb (1929–).

France:	Claude Debussy (1862–1918)
	Maurice Ravel (1875–1937)
	Albert Roussel (1869–1937)
	Jacques Ibert (1890–1962)
	Germaine Tailleferre (1892–)
England:	Frederick Delius (1862–1934)
Italy:	Ottorino Respighi (1879–1936)
U.S.:	Charles Griffes (1884–1920)

(3) **Expressionism**: expressing the inner self, especially the subconscious. In the first part of the century this meant a jagged, uneasy music, achieved through using all twelve divisions of the octave impartially and denying a tonic in a nonrigorous fashion (atonality). After World War I, use of the twelve chromatic pitches was systematized: when placed in a prescribed order, they become the unique theme-scale (series) for each piece, which is then composed according to the contrapuntal rules governing imitative textures. Strict serial procedures may further be used to control musical materials other than pitch. In the last fifteen years rigorous control of all musical elements has been partially given up; the "new expressionism" concerns itself more with the end "sound" result than with the exact technical procedures used to generate a piece.

Atonalists

Germany and Austria:

- Arnold Schoenberg (1874–1951)
- Alban Berg (1885–1935)
- Anton Webern (1883–1945)
- Ernst Křenek (1900–)

Stricter Serialists

France: Pierre Boulez (1925–)
Germany: Karlheinz Stockhausen (1928–)
England: Humphrey Searle (1915–)
Italy: Luigi Dallapiccola (1904–1975)
U.S.: Wallingford Riegger (1885–1961)
Stefan Wolpe (1902–1972)
Ben Weber (1916–)
George Perle (1915–)
Milton Babbitt (1916–)
Ross Lee Finney (1906–)
George Rochberg (1918–) (now moving toward neoromantic style)

New Expressionists

Switzerland: Frank Martin (1890–1974)
Poland: Witold Lutoslawski (1913–)
Krzysztof Penderecki (1933–)
U.S.: Carl Ruggles (1876–1971)
Roger Sessions (1896–)
Hugo Weisgall (1912–)
Elliott Carter (1908–)
Miriam Gideon (1906–)
Leon Kirchner (1919–)
Ruth Crawford Seeger (1901–1953)

(4) **Objective movements**: two rigorously nonpersonal, unsentimental approaches.

"Urban" or "Machine" Music (music imitating machine sounds)
Switzerland: Arthur Honegger (1892–1955)
U.S.: George Antheil (1900–1959) (early works)

"Gebrauchsmusik" ("functional music," written for special occasions or a specific purpose)
Germany: Paul Hindemith (1895–1963)
Kurt Weill (1900–1950)

(5) **Neoclassicism**: a return to the ideals of the eighteenth century; a detached, objective style. French neo-classicists added a humorous, gently satiric note.

Russia/France:	Igor Stravinsky (1882–1971)
Germany:	Paul Hindemith (1895–1963)
France:	Erik Satie (1866–1925)
	Francis Poulenc (1899–1963)
	Darius Milhaud (1892–1974)
Russia:	Sergei Prokofiev (1891–1953)
	Dmitri Shostakovich (1906–1975)
U.S.:	Walter Piston (1894–1976)
	William Schuman (1910–)
	Peter Mennin (1923–)
	Louise Talma (1906–)

(6) **New Nationalism**: used scientific methods to research folk music, and stressed national color within the context of art music.

Russia:	Aram Khatchaturian (1903–1978)
England:	Ralph Vaughan Williams (1872–1958)
Hungary:	Béla Bartók (1881–1945)
	Zoltán Kodály (1882–1967)
Spain:	Manuel de Falla (1876–1949)
Czechoslovakia:	Leoš Janáček (1854–1928)
	Bohuslav Martinu (1890–1959)
Argentina:	Alberto Ginastera (1916–)
Brazil:	Heitor Villa-Lobos (1881–1959)
Mexico:	Carlos Chavez (1889–1978)
	Silvestre Revueltas (1899–1940)
Cuba:	Ernesto Lecuona (1896–)
U.S.:	Charles Ives (1874–1954)
	Douglas Moore (1893–1969)
	Howard Hanson (1896–)
	Roy Harris (1898–)
	Aaron Copland (1898–)
	Elie Siegmeister (1909–)

(7) **Extended Romanticism**: music which preserves and strengthens the nineteenth-century heritage of a fundamental lyric impulse by combining it with many twentieth-century chromatic, textural, and tone-color innovations. Basically tonal, avoiding trite harmonic progressions, this approach leans toward large-scale, programmatic works.

U.S.:	Alan Hovhaness (1911–)
	Samuel Barber (1910–)
	Gian-Carlo Menotti (1911–)
	Norman Dello Joio (1913–)
	Leonard Bernstein (1918–)
Australia:	Peggy Glanville-Hicks (1912–)
England:	Benjamin Britten (1913–1976)
Switzerland:	Ernst Bloch (1880–1959)

(8) **Tape Music**: electronically produced (synthesized) sounds: *musique concrète*; computer music. With the invention of the tape recorder in the late 1940s, a new means of expanding the sonic palette arrived. In 1948 Pierre Schaeffer established an electronic music studio in Paris, and in 1952 Otto Luening and Vladimir Ussachevsky began their experiments at Columbia University. This early music used pre-existing real sounds ("concrete" sounds) as raw material; they were taped and then altered by manipulating the tape in various ways or modifying it electronically.

A second kind of tape music used electronically generated tones for raw material. (Interest in electronic instruments goes back to the inventions of the Theremin [1924] and the Ondes Martinot [1928]. Both used two vacuum-tube oscillators to produce complex wave forms or "beat" notes.) In the electronic music labs of the '50s, pitches and timbres were created at the composer's discretion from sound-wave generators, and taped one by one.

In both concrete and electronic music the most violent contrasts and minute gradations of sound may be produced at the flick of a switch, resulting in an aural collage.

A significant step in the synthesis of sound occurred in 1955, when Harry Olson of RCA invented an "Electronic Music Synthesizer": an improved version of the machine was installed in the Columbia-Princeton Electronic Music Studio in the late '50s. In the RCA Synthesizer, as well as in Moog, Arp, Buchla, and other synthesizers, "every aspect of both pitched and nonpitched sound—including duration, quality of attack and decay (dying away), intensity, tone color and so forth—can be set out with precise definition, and any sound can be tested immediately and, if necessary, readjusted down to the finest possible gradations."[8] Control is usually accomplished by means of a keyboard or patchboard.

In *musique concrète*, the performer's role has been reduced to that of a "generator" of raw material; in synthesized and electronic music the performer is dispensed with entirely. Certain composers seem to be uncomfortable without human participation, and the most recent development has been an upsurge in pieces for tape and live performer. Among the most striking of these are Mario Davidovsky's *Synchronisms 1* through *6*, and the Variations for Flute and Electronic Sounds by Walter Carlos.

A further refinement in tape music has been provided by introducing the computer as a compositional tool. Now the entire musical environment can be built from scratch: not only may the timbres be constructed; not only may the sequence and juxtaposition of sounds (pitched and unpitched) be consciously controlled; but also the rules for proceeding from sound event to sound event. These must be broken down into their smallest components and fed into the computer via a detailed, comprehensive program. In addition, the aural result cannot be precisely determined until the computer's read-out is transformed into electromagnetic impulses on recording tape and played back through loudspeakers.

Thus, the computer may function either as a close approximation to a universal sound synthesizer or as a more active partner, the composer's agent. In the latter role, when properly programmed, the computer can make choices and decisions at any stage of the compositional process and to any degree desired. Interestingly enough, this leads to a kind of programming in which the machine makes similar "random" decisions to those made by a human performer in music of chance.

Nevertheless, "no matter how far-reaching the computer's participation in the composition, it remains the agent. The computer does not compose, it carries out instructions. Though its part in the process may increase significantly, the *computer as composer* must be considered a mirage."[9]

A partial list of composers active in this medium:

France: Pierre Boulez (1926–)
Italy: Luigi Nono (1924–)
Luciano Berio (1925–)
Germany: Karlheinz Stockhausen (1928–)
U.S.: Edgard Varèse (1885–1965)
Otto Luening (1900–)
Vladimir Ussachevsky (1911–)
Mario Davidovsky (1934–)
Lejaren Hiller (1924–)

(9) **Music of Chance (Aleatory Music)**: the performer is invited to participate in the creative process by making certain decisions at the moment of performance. Chance or aleatory music (from the Latin *alea*, "game of dice") leaves the performer free to exercise his best judgment in one or more areas, such as in the choice of dynamics, register, timbre, duration, etc. The freedom may be total or selective.

Morton Feldman: "Last Pieces," no. 1

In stochastic music the performer may elect to play only certain of the notes or sonorities offered; or to play phrases or sections of a piece in his own preferred order, using either all the given material or some of it in combination.

Directions for playing "Mobile":

Begin by playing any one of the outer, lettered squares; continue with any one of the connector squares; continue by returning to another lettered square, or the original one, if you wish, followed by another connector; and so on.

The order in which the given musical materials are played is mostly up to the performer. Thus, the overall form will vary from performance to performance. Other elements left to the performer's choice are tempo, dynamics, touch, etc.

The piece ends when everything on the page has been played at least once—unless a larger piece is preferred, in which everything will be played at least twice. Obviously, no two performances will be alike.

Sample performance scheme:

> N–two–N–three–I–three–U–three–E–three–B–one–A–one–G–three–G–one–D.

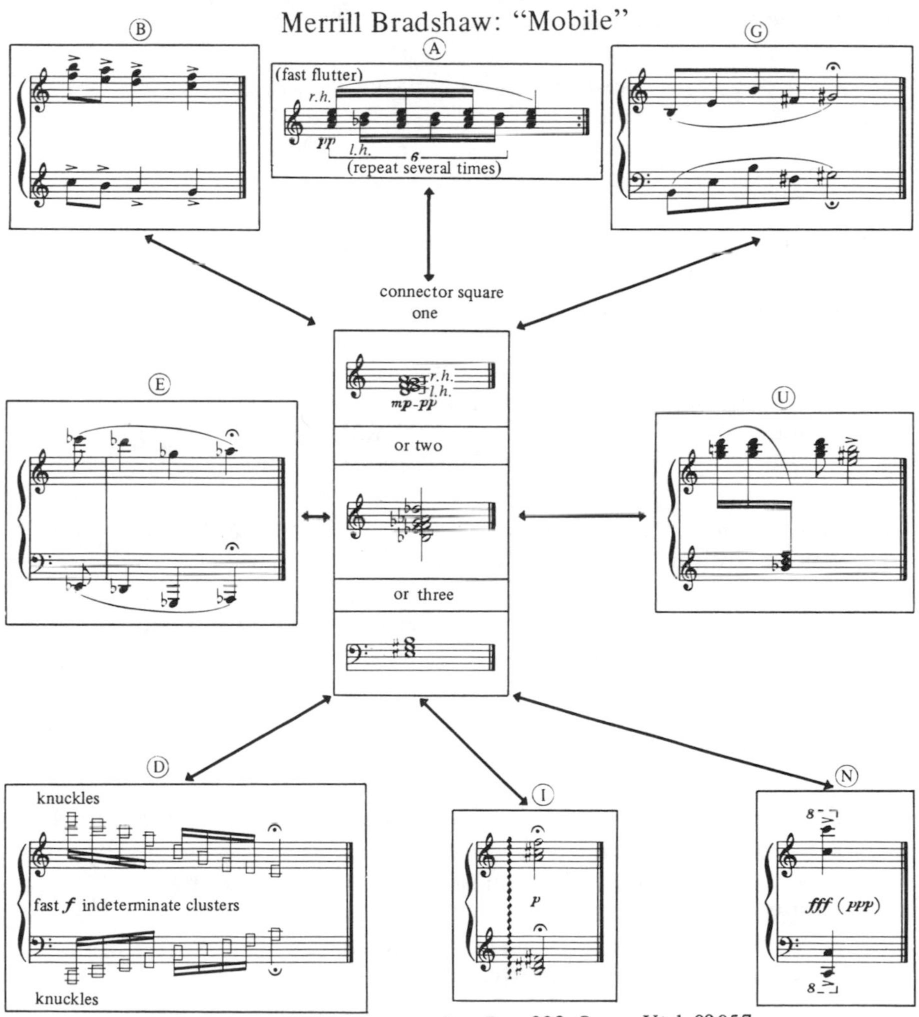

Improvisation on given materials (pitch, dynamics, articulations) may be offered by the composer. The given materials are usually boxed:

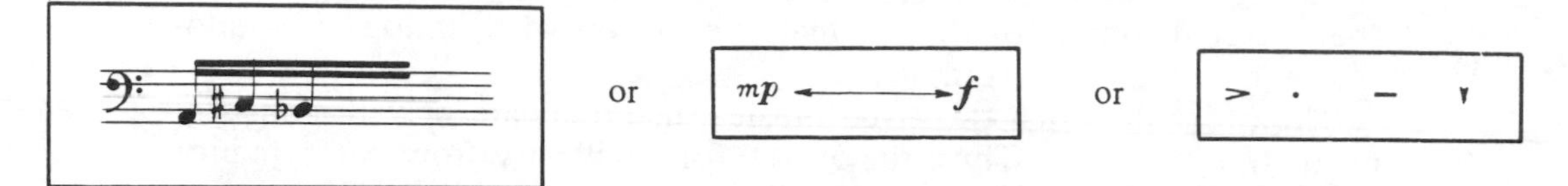

The listener may become the "performer" when composed sounds are purposefully trivial or absent. In John Cage's 4'33"(1954), a performer sits at a piano in silence (hence the title); the music comprises the random sounds which occur in the concert hall during the performance.

Indeed, all this music is linked through a common ideal: the desire to "destroy conventional musical continuity and liberate sound from the governance of memory, desire, and the rational mind."[10] To this end, the composer may choose to permit the content of the piece to be determined entirely randomly, perhaps by a roll of dice.

U.S.: Henry Cowell (1897–1965)
John Cage (1912–)
Lou Harrison (1917–)
Morton Feldman (1926–)

(10) **Individualists**

Harry Partch (1901–1974): investigated microtonality and built new instruments to perform his music.

Carl Orff (1895–): best known for stage works; the music features blocks of sound fashioned from percussive, repeated rhythms and simple diatonic harmonies.

Edgard Varèse (1885–1965): grandfather of electronic music and a man of vision. A pioneer in incorporating "noise" elements with pitch into the sonic palette.

George Gershwin (1898–1937): the American jazz-impressionist.

André Jolivet (1905–1974): noted for the subjective lyricism of his music, often built from scales of his own devising.

Olivier Messiaen (1908–): his is a personal, lyrical, expansive music that includes religious overtones and sounds from nature spread across vast canvases.

George Crumb (1929–): a specialist in highly programmatic music, he concocts beautiful, disturbing sound pictures from mere wisps of sound.

Steve Reich (1936–), Terry Riley (1935–), Philip Glass (1937–), Pauline Oliveros (1932–): using rhythmic and harmonic materials similar to those stressed by Carl Orff as well as an infusion of Eastern ideas on the meditative properties of music, these minimalists have contrived a hypnotic approach to music, still in its formative stages.

Steve Reich: *Piano Phase* for two pianos or two marimbas

Directions for performance of Piano Phase:

The number of repeats in each bar is not fixed, but a minimum of 16–24 per bar should be observed. The point throughout is not to count repeats but to listen to each bar until its two-voice relationship becomes clear to performer and listeners, then begin gradually to shift over to the pattern in the next bar.

The first performer starts at bar 1 and, after about six to twelve repeats, the second gradually fades in, in unison, at bar 2. After several seconds of unison the second player gradually increases the tempo very slightly and begins to move ahead of the first until he or she is one sixteenth note ahead, as shown at bar 3. The dotted lines indicate this gradual movement of the second performer and the consequent shift of phase relation between both performers. This process of gradual phase shifting and then holding the new stable relationship is continued.

NEW WAYS OF USING TRADITIONAL MUSICAL MATERIALS

When one looks into specific twentieth-century practices it soon becomes apparent that many are actually rooted in nineteenth-century developments. In the expanded timbral consciousness of Berlioz', Wagner's, and Mahler's orchestrations; in Schumann's preoccupation with syncopation; in the organic, compact and highly integrated forms devised by Brahms in his later years; and in a loosening tonal consciousness characteristic of the music of Wagner, Mussorgsky, Wolf, and Scriabin, we discover intimations of developments to come.

New ways of handling the traditional musical elements—rhythm, pitch, melody, tonality and harmony, texture or design, timbre and form—are also foreshadowed. In particular, "chromaticism; the extended and freer use of dissonance; the establishment of harmonic and melodic freedom; the use of harmonic, melodic, and structural ideas derived from folk music and early Western music; the concept of the structural interrelationships between all the parts of a musical composition; the discovery of the distant past and of non-Western music; the vast expansion of instrumental technique and color; the new freedom, complexity, and independence of rhythm, dynamics, and tone color—all these modern ideas have roots deep in the last century.[11] That composers have basically continued to explore the traditional elements, rather than turning from them, is a testament to the infinite potential inherent in these raw materials.

Two broad trends characterize the progress of music in our time: a desire to loosen the standardized supports of functional tonality and regularized rhythms to render them more plastic and more responsive, and a desire to make of music a more rational, less intuitive art by increasing the composer's conscious control over every aspect of every element.

RHYTHM

Rhythm, "the principle of organization that regulates the flow of music in time,"[12] animates and controls every aspect of a composition, placing each in correct proportion within the overall context by controlling duration.

In traditional terms, we talk of an "infinity" or "universe" of *pulses*, governed by the *rate of speed* at which they flow (tempo), and grouped according to a regularly recurring *accent pattern* (meter). Particular rhythms either reinforce the accent pattern of a meter

(*e.g.* $\frac{3}{4}$ 𝅗𝅥 ♩ | ♩. ♪ ♩ | ♫ ♩ ♩ |)

or run counter to it, for refreshment. Perhaps the greatest innovations in twentieth-century music have come in the domain of rhythm, which has become free from all restraint.

Nineteenth-century rhythmic refreshments were few in number and carefully regulated. Each movement usually preceded within a single meter, subject to "interference" via a) *syncopations*; b) *hemiolas*; c) *crossrhythms*, of the two against three variety, or more rarely, d) three against four.

Brahms: Intermezzo, op. 76 no. 6

Chopin: Fantasy-Impromptu, op. 66

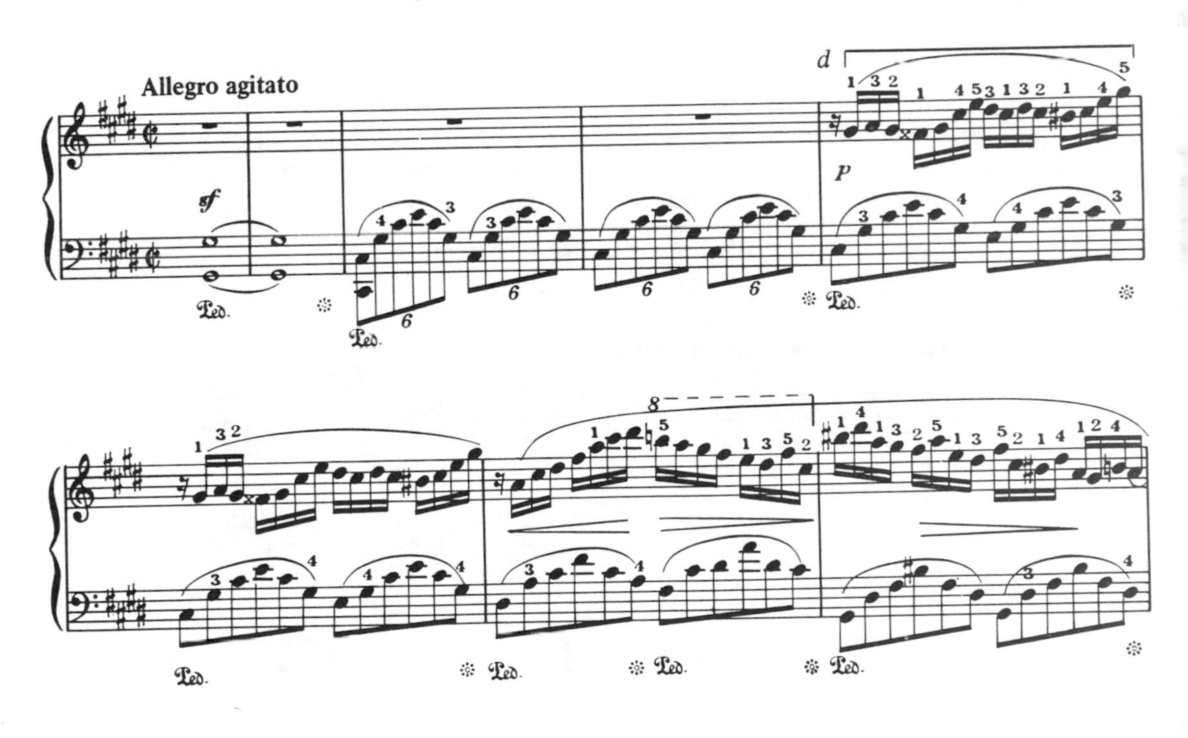

Scriabin: Sonata no. 5, op. 53

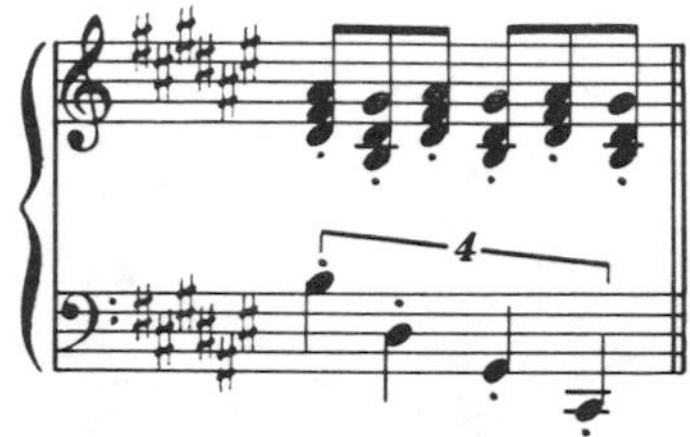

The rise of nationalist schools around the middle of the nineteenth century added the refreshment of accent patterns based on speech rhythms or national dances: Polish mazurkas and polonaises; Hungarian and Bohemian dance patterns (in the music of Liszt, Dvořák, Brahms, Smetana and others); the Norwegian influences in Grieg, etc. (Similarly in our century, much of Bartók's rhythmic verve derives from successful integration of Hungarian rhythms into a more complex rhythmic framework.) The Russians in particular loosened the straight-jacket of the inevitable downbeat by employing irregular or shifting meters.

Mussorgsky: *Pictures at an Exhibition*,
"Promenade" theme

This century has extended rhythmic refreshments in two directions, both of which were explored specifically to loosen the "tyranny of the bar line."

One trend returns to the freer rhythms of prose (or Eastern musics). Lines become more supple, less regularized; the bar line evolves into a visual device for the performer's convenience only, moving away from its former function as an orientation point for both performer and listener:

Strauss: *Till Eulenspiegel's Merry Pranks*

Music may be unbarred entirely (as in Feldman's "Last Pieces") or bar lines may be used merely to indicate the extent of thought groups, in the manner of recitative:

Judith Lang Zaimont: "April"
from *Calendar Collection*

The second trend has been to intensify the pulsed aspect of music, while at the same time remaining free from the closure of a regularly anticipated downbeat. Borrowing the nervous syncopations of jazz accomplishes this very well.

Barber: Sonata, op. 26
(fourth movement)

Multimetric writing becomes common, with meters changing in virtually every bar. Bars are grouped into phrases with great flexibility; phrases appear to grow beyond the confines of the bar (see below); and meters themselves become intricate, compounded in an additive sense from smaller rhythmic nuggets: $\frac{5}{4}=\frac{2+3}{4}$ $\frac{7}{8}=\frac{2+2+3}{8}$ $\frac{10}{4}=\frac{3+3+4}{4}$

Hugo Weisgall: *Sine Nomine*

Roy Harris: "Children at Play"
from *Little Suite*

An extension of the cross-rhythm is the *polyrhythm*, in which differing rhythms are superposed for long stretches. To unify the whole, *rhythmic ostinato* comes to the fore (particularly in the music of the neoclassicists). The modern *ostinato* (the Italian for "obstinate") is most effective when it is uneven with respect to the meter, or when several ostinatos of different lengths are used in combination. (Note left-hand ostinato in the previous and following examples.)

Hindemith: Sonata, no. 2
(first movement)

♩=c.108

Visually, one can identify certain styles, both personal and general, by their typical rhythmic configurations alone. Expressionist music—particularly totally controlled music—may be rapturous or spasmodic, but either way it tends to splinter the visual "beat" (usually a quarter note) into many tiny fragments of irregular length.

Milton Babbitt: "Partitions"

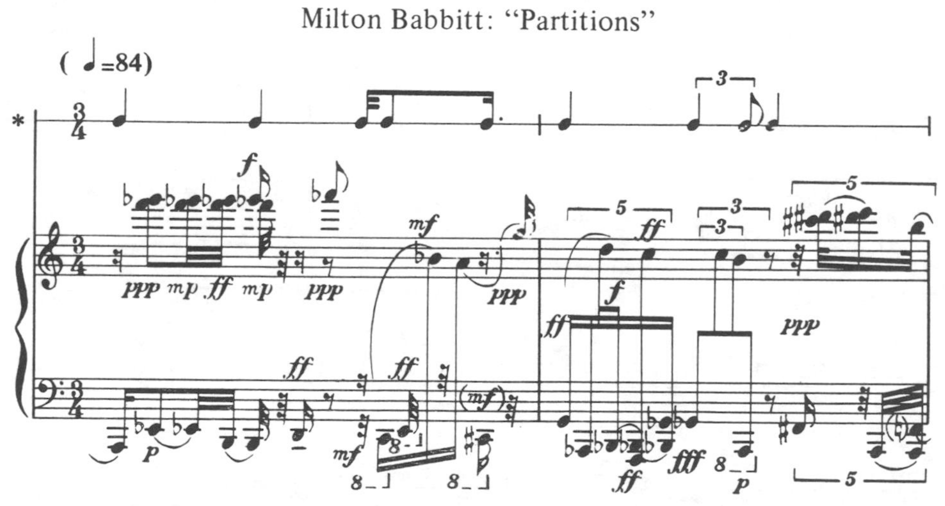

*The durational values on this line are intended solely to facilitate reading of the rhythmic aspects of the music by indicating those simpler subdivisions of the measure within the scope of which the less usual subdivisions occur.

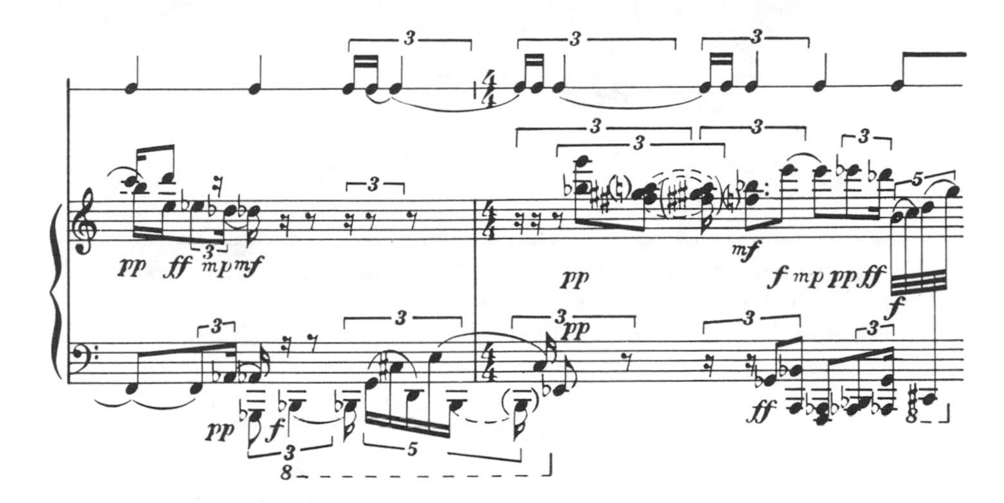

By contrast, neoclassic music usually builds its more intricate rhythms by "writing large" and increasing the tempo:

Peter Mennin: Toccata,
from *Five Easy Pieces*

PITCH

One way of viewing the increasing sophistication of pitch materials through the course of musical history is to consider the evolution of music in terms of a "progress" up the harmonic series.

*not in tune with tempered scale

This illustrates a *fundamental* pitch (𝅝) and its family of *overtones* or *harmonics* (●). Each component of the series is called a *partial*; partials are numbered according to their place in the series, with the fundamental as 1.

In ancient and primitive musics, pitch materials were consistent with partials 1, 2, 3, and 4, displayed in a monophonic context; this includes medieval organum. As the major and minor third became increasingly accepted (for example, in *fauxbourdon*), the triad (partials 4, 5, 6) emerged as a mainstay in the musical fabric. From the baroque through the early part of the romantic eras, the dominant seventh (partials 4, 5, 6, 7) was the prime chord of harmonic tension, containing as it does the strongest contrapuntal puller, the tritone, within the larger frame of a diminished triad (partials 5, 6, 7). The late nineteenth century saw the expansion of the dominant seventh to a dominant ninth chord (partials 4, 5, 6, 7, 9). Twentieth-century composers have gone beyond these lower partials to emphasize pitch materials drawn from the series' upper reaches.

Western music usually accepts the semitone as the smallest possible interval and divides the octave into twelve chromatic half steps. In our century, an infusion of Eastern music—which features many, more minute divisions of the octave—has given rise to a variety of artificially constructed musical systems devoted to *microtonality* (microtonal pitch materials lie beyond the seventeenth partial in the harmonic series):

> Theorists and composers argued that there were no important reasons why the octave could not be divided into smaller divisions than the semitone. Joseph Yasser, for instance, offered a nineteen-note scale consisting of twelve primary pitches (the tones of the chromatic scale) and seven microtonal auxiliaries; Busoni suggested a thirty-six note scale, with some pitches no more than a sixth of a tone apart; Harry Partch developed a forty-three tone scale; Alois Hába introduced new notational symbols for the quarter-tone scale.[13]

The Mexican composer Julian Carillo constructed a "chromatic harp" which uses 100 equidistant divisions of the octave. Many composers have followed Bartók's lead in his writing for strings, which routinely employs the quarter-tone as a heightened inflection. With the development of electronic instruments in the past thirty years, pitch discriminations of minute exactness are now possible and available for immediate use, obviating the need for specially constructed microtonal instruments.

Even when keeping strictly to the traditional twelve chromatic pitches, composers have aimed for a new flexibility in their ordering. We commonly think of a *scale* or *mode* as a succession of tones, usually separated by half or whole steps, arranged in ascending or descending order. Actually, it is the successive *pattern of intervals* that truly defines a scale, by specifying its pattern for construction. For example, the major mode,

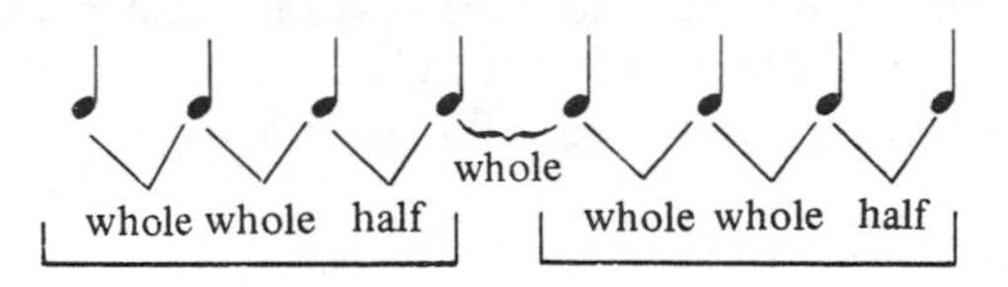

which may be considered as two identical *tetrachords* linked by a whole step. (The Dorian and Phrygian modes are also based on two identical tetrachords.)

In the twentieth century new scales or modes—both of the tetrachordal pattern and "through-composed"—have been consciously constructed.

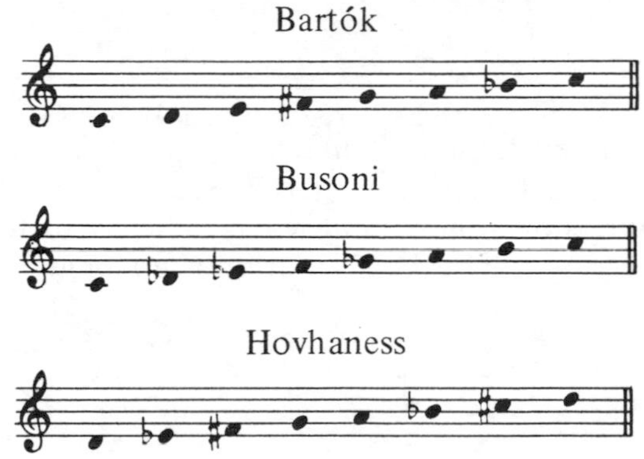

A scale need not contain seven pitches. The *pentatonic* (five-note) scale, a favorite of the impressionists, is found in Chinese, African, and Polynesian music, as well as in the music of American Indians, Celts, and Scots. In *La fille aux cheveux de lin* ("Girl with the Flaxen Hair"), Debussy uses a pentatonic scale to conjure a Scottish atmosphere, since this prelude was inspired by a poem by Robert Burns.

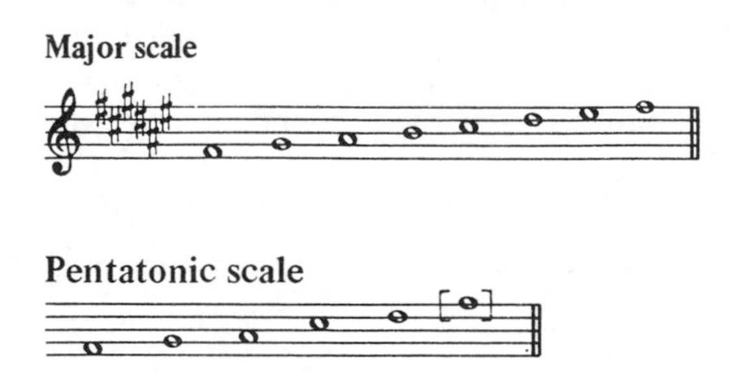

Debussy: *Nuages*

An interesting feature of the pentatonic scale is its "skeletal" nature: it lacks a leading tone. When spread over several octaves, it is seen to contain many potential tonic-dominant relations, each implying its own discrete scalar environment and equally persuasive:

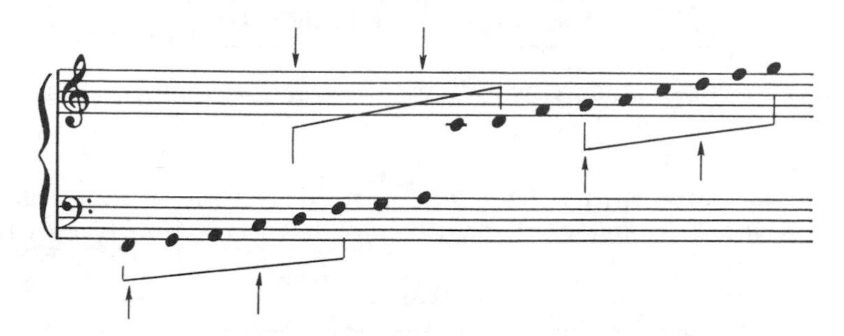

The *chromatic* scale is not really a scale, but rather a glossary of all possible pitches. When these are subdivided equally (according to a pattern implicit in the ordering of partials 7, 8, 9, 10, 11, of the harmonic series), two whole-tone scales result, each radically different from traditional scales because the "sol-do" relation is no longer present:

(The chromatic "collection" separated into the two whole-tone scales.)

The swimming, amorphous quality of whole-tone writing was much enjoyed by the impressionists and became a characteristic feature of their music. In *Voiles* ("Sails") from the first book of Preludes, Debussy uses a whole-tone environment almost exclusively. In addition, he often interpolates whole-tone passages within other pieces which are basically well-seated in major or minor, in order to maximize the contrast between the modes and highlight the suspended effect of the whole-tone sections:

Debussy: "Reflections in the Water,"
from *Images pour piano*, Book 1

Only two possible whole-tone scales exist. Within each, the sense of a particular tonic pitch can be achieved only by reiterating or otherwise highlighting a specific note; however, a vague dominant sensation may be produced through contrasting one whole-tone collection (in the role of dissonance) with the other (consonance).

MELODY

When we compare it to the vocally inspired melody of the nineteenth century, contemporary melody seems to have changed its character drastically. In shape, length, and construction it has become infinitely less rigid and less regularized, being now conceived instrumentally rather than vocally. It is true that in a few instances contemporary melody may be entirely athematic and unpredictable. Usually, however, the reasons for atypical configurations can be traced to strong influences from other musical elements on the melodic design:

(1) Melody may grow from a rhythmic impulse:

Bartók: *Mikrokosmos*, vol. 5 no. 122

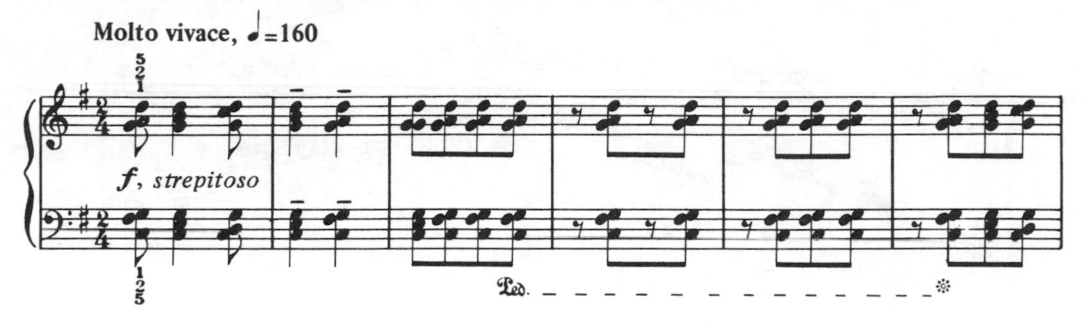

(2) Melody may come from some implication inherent in the pitch materials of the piece, such as a nontraditional scale, an ethnic influence, or a consciously controlled pitch environment, such as the ordering of the row in twelve-tone writing.

Ross Lee Finney: "Tired," *24 Piano Inventions*, no. 7

(3) Symmetry and exact repetition are avoided. There is less of a build-up or traditional arch in the contour. Repetitions, when they occur, are likely to be compressed variants of the original material; composers prefer to state a thing once rather than two or three times.

Jane Young: "I Won't Go,
Oh Yes You Will"

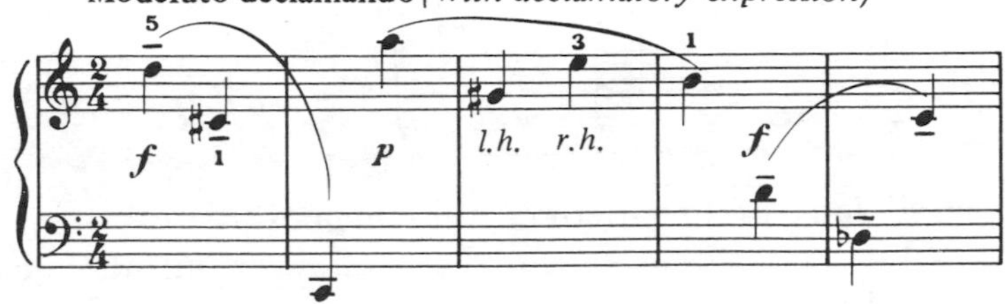

(4) Traditional punctuations are sidestepped: cadences are slurred over and the standard four-bar phrase is avoided, thus emphasizing the melody's asymmetric design (see Mennin's Toccata above).

(5) The melody may not grow from a harmonic framework at all, nor be supported by a background of regular rhythms and traditional harmonic progressions. "Individual tones are [liberated] from their former functions of upper neighbor, passing tone, appoggiatura, chord tones, etc."[14] This is absolutely the case in atonal expressionist music. The melody itself tends not to proceed in traditional scalewise motion or triadic leap, but instead moves disjunctly. One commonly encounters successive wide leaps in opposing directions, usually by an expressive or tensed interval: tritone, minor second, major seventh, major or minor ninth, etc.

(6) In length, the melodies may be either *discursive*—unfolding in long, convoluted arabesques of tones as in Samuel Barber's Adagio for Strings—or *epigrammatic*—either made from several short, self-contained convulsive bursts, or composed by continuously varying a single motivic cell. (This last is the very essence of Stravinsky's characteristic, additive melody: "the reiteration of similar melodic material in constant variation within a highly confined pitch field. One hears the same notes in ever new situations, the alternations being defined primarily by very subtle. . . rhythmic manipulations."[15])

Stravinsky: Allegro,
from "The Five Fingers"

The jagged look of twentieth-century melody derives from a technique called *octave displacement*. The following might conceivably be a melody of our time.

Actually, it is the theme from the second Kyrie of Bach's B-minor Mass subjected to octave displacement:

Bach: Kyrie, Mass in B minor

The procedure involves shifting selected tones (starred in the example) an octave above or below the register occupied by the body of the melody. The resultant contour is rich in expressive leaps and determinedly antivocal.

In the next example we can easily trace the steps by which Stravinsky constructed the lovely instrumental fugue subject in the second movement of *Symphony of Psalms*, which gains much of its expressive power from extensive use of octave displacement.

Raw material in rhythm:

As a single line, in one register:

Final version, with octave displacements:

Notice that voice leading in the first of these operates in traditional fashion; it is only in the final version that loose ends appear to be left dangling, due to octave displacement of selected pitches. At the same time, note that the final version is by far more striking and effective than either of the two intermediate ones.

The idea of doubling the melodic contour with a subsidiary line a fixed interval away goes back to the very beginning of Western polyphony. Parallel organum, used in the early middle ages, is an example of consonant melodic doubling.

In the twentieth century, consonant doubling is no longer the rule and melodies may be freely doubled at any dissonant interval:

Doubling at the interval of a seventh:

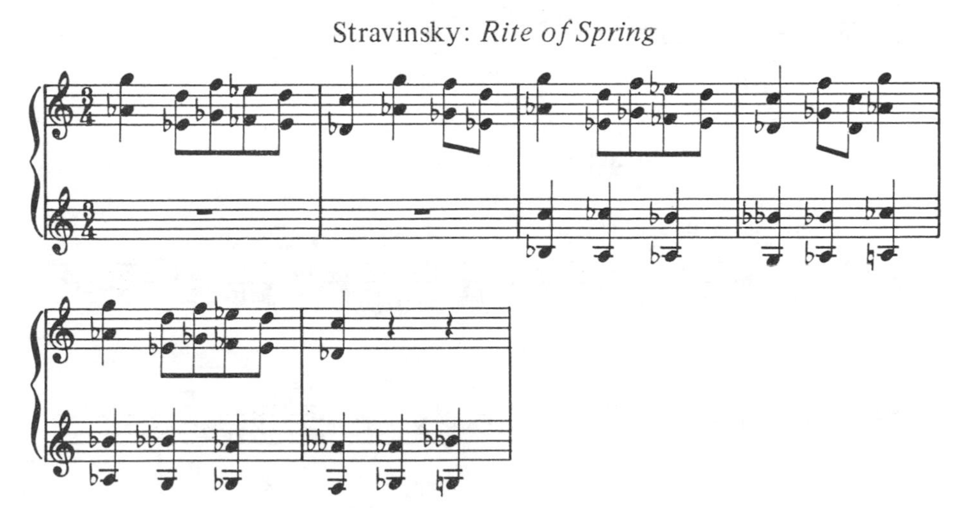

Indeed, organumlike sonorities or complete chords may be used in parallel with the melodic contour, as in Debussy's *La Cathédrale engloutie* ("The Sunken Cathedral") or in the following excerpts from *Pour le piano*:

Debussy: Sarabande
from *Pour le piano*

Debussy: Sarabande

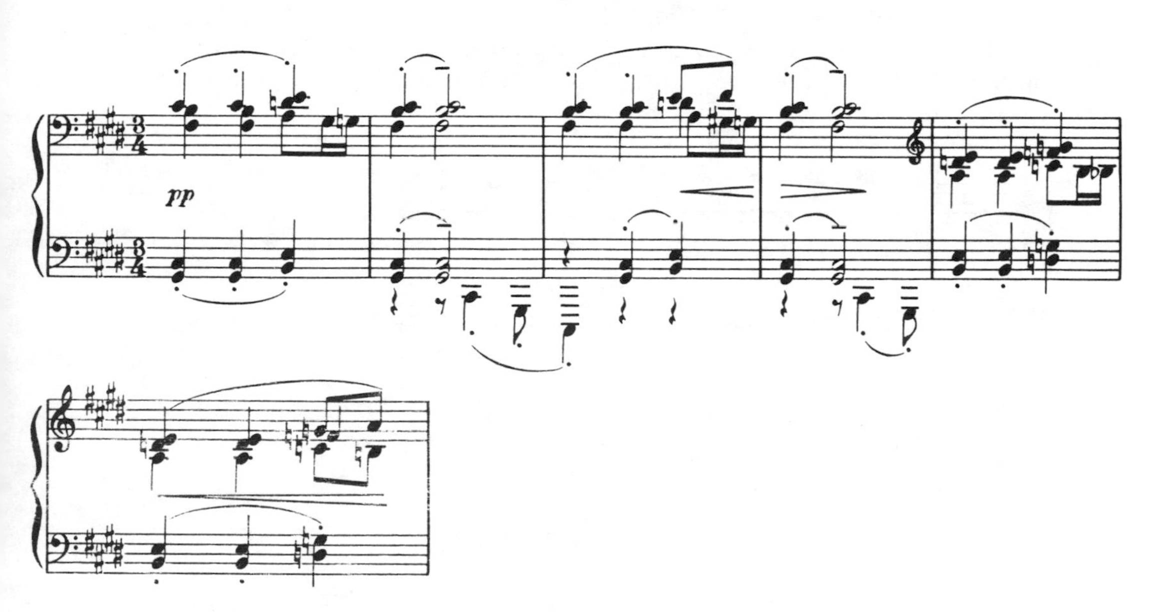

Stravinsky: *Rite of Spring*

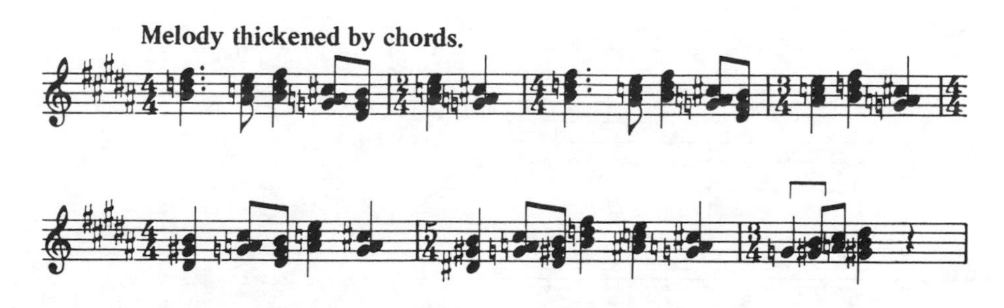

In fact, the musical contour—the overall shape and direction of the melodic line—has now assumed paramount importance, being accorded a significance greater than that warranted by merely summing up the totality of pitch content in a given passage. A precedent for the pre-eminence of contour over specific pitch content may be found in the venerable *glissando*, a gesture defined solely in terms of its precise extent and overall shape.

TONALITY AND HARMONY

Tonality, "the sense of relatedness to a central tone,"[18] —provides a center (the tonic) from which to judge relative consonance and dissonance. "Dissonance is the element that supplies dynamic tension, the forward impulsion that extends itself and comes to rest in consonance."[19] However, defining the active principle—dissonance—*absolutely* is virtually impossible.

From music's beginnings, our ears have progressed toward a greater and greater tolerance. For twentieth-century listeners, the distinction between what is consonant and what is dissonant has almost disappeared: we now term a sonority consonant simply because it seems less dissonant than its surroundings. The degree of a listener's musical sophistication directly influences perception in this matter. Other influences have to do with the sonority itself, with respect to the register in which it is placed, its duration, assigned dynamic level and articulation, timbre, and tempo.

Consider what happens to the perfect fourth (considered a definite dissonance in strict Palestrinian two-voice counterpoint) in the following two excerpts.[20]

In the first, the fourths are perceived as dissonant because the surrounding intervals (sixths) seem more stable. By contrast, in the second, the perfect fourths appear to be the only points of relative stability, since the rest of the intervals appear more tensed.

In *The Craft of Musical Composition*, Paul Hindemith systematized his perceptions of relative consonance and dissonance. The following table of intervals[21] illustrates his conclusions, arranged in order of increasing consonance.

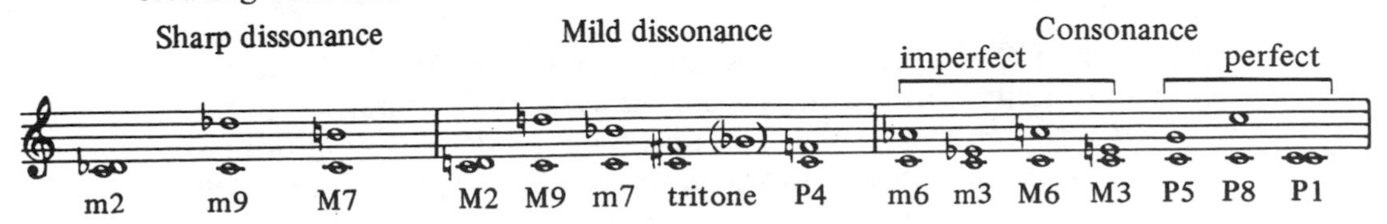

It is useful to compare this table with one's own perceptions. Although most of us will agree with the contents of the categories of sharp dissonance and consonance, the ordering of the middle group, mild dissonances, is open to question, particularly with regard to the tritone.

Once our perception has progressed to the point where at least certain of the mild dissonances are accepted as relatively stable, we must look beyond the pulling power of the traditional chords of tension—VII^{o7}, V^7, V^9, etc.—for fresher, more compelling alternatives. For many, the solution lies in displacing traditional dominant pivots with chords drawn from far afield, foreign to the chromatic domain of the home key. Prokofiev's hallmark is just this kind of displacement, using unexpected chords to replace chords of dominant function or in place of the VI as resolution of a truly *deceptive* cadence.

Prokofiev: *Peter and the Wolf*

Once composers took the first step of replacing the mainstays of traditional tonality with harmonic alternatives, the natural next step was to grant all twelve tones the freedom to circulate equally in orbit about a tonic pitch (or tonic sonority). In the following example, Bartók clearly establishes B–F-sharp as the locus around which all other pitches travel. The idea of major or minor no longer matters, and a key signature would only call for extra labor on the composer's part, since he would be obliged to cancel many of its accidentals in every measure. (Note how the idea of a *gesture* or *configuration* becomes paramount in measures 8 to 15; here, the shape and direction of the line matter more than individual pitches).

Bartók: Bagatelle, op. 6 no. 6

As an intermediate step between displaced harmonies a la Prokofiev and free chromaticism around a tonal center, *pandiatonic* harmony was introduced (around 1920) by the neoclassicists, notably Stravinsky. In reaction to the profligate chromaticism of both whole-tone and atonal idioms, the neoclassicists voluntarily restricted themselves to using only the pitches of a single key or mode–but according to *no* specific harmonic rules. Thus, triadic harmonies could be scrapped, if desired, without losing the sense of a single tonality governing over all.

Stravinsky: Andantino,
from "The Five Fingers"

American neoclassicism is distinguished by its penchant for pandiatonic and/or bitonal writing. (This is not surprising, in view of the fact that many of these composers studied with Nadia Boulanger of France, where they imbibed a Gallic sense of nicety in detail and overall proportion, as well as a predilection for "neat" sounds–all of which result in "civilized" scores.) Pandiatonic writing is not precisely equivalent to white-key music; the latter is a subcategory of the former, although a large one, since many composers purposefully chose C as tonic to emphasize their antichromatic stand.

In a parallel development, the triad was subjected to distortion by "fattening" it to a monstrous thickness. Third was piled upon third until "skyscraper" *polychords* were formed, essentially perceived as organumlike thickenings of the melodic line.

Stravinsky: *Petrouchka*

Coupling the idea of harmonic thickening with displaced harmony led to music which moved in broad, independent planes of sound:

William Schuman: *A Three-Score Set*
(second movement)

Pandiatonicism and polychords deal essentially with "disguised" triads. A more radical innovation was the decision to scrap the triad altogether and build sonorities based on intervals other than the third. Thus, we find the emergence of harmonic systems built on:

- the fifth (quintal harmony)

Gerhard Wuensch: "La Danse à Quinte"
from *Twelve Glimpses into Twentieth Century Idioms*

- the fourth (quartal harmony)

Gerhard Wuensch: "Four Square"
from *Twelve Glimpses into Twentieth Century Idioms*

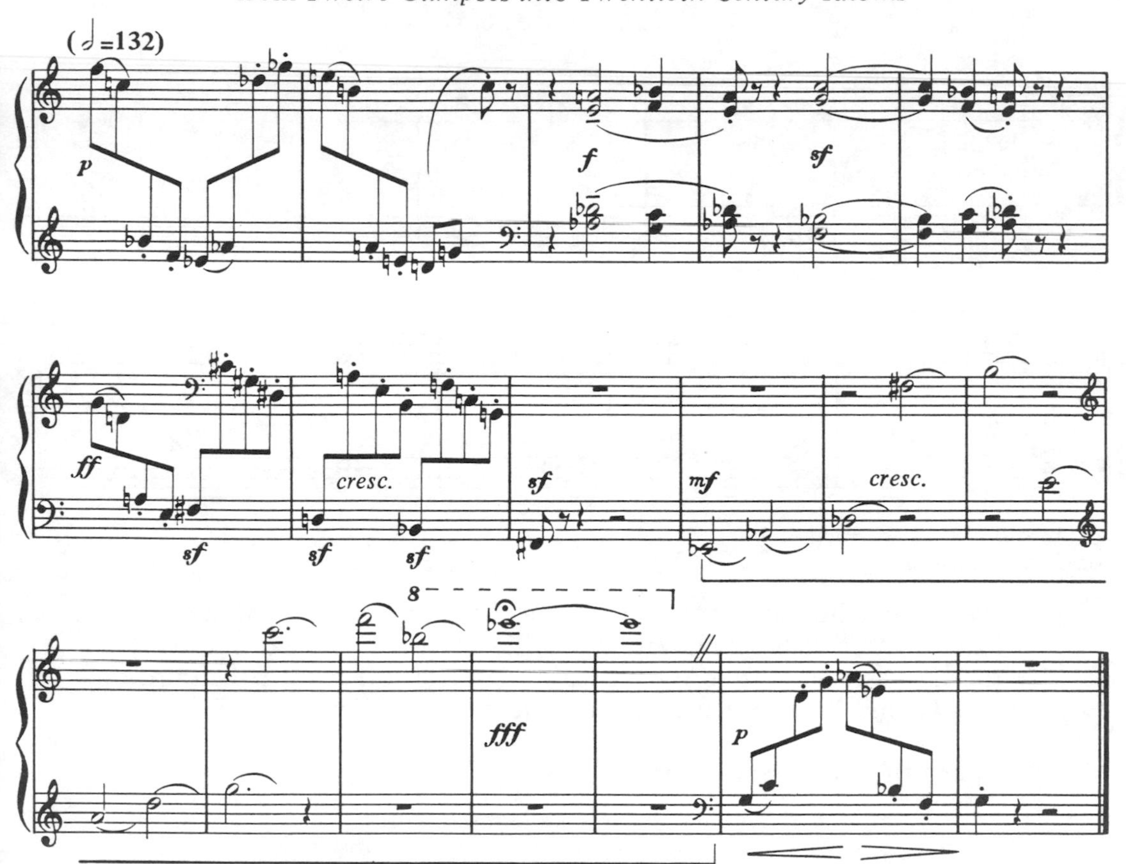

The striking beauty of Paul Hindemith's personal idiom derives from his use of quintal and quartal harmonies within a contrapuntal, tonal frame:

Hindemith: "A Swan"
from *Six Chansons*

- Seconds may be added to fourths, fifths, or triads, or in *clusters*. Clusters may be either relatively mild (as in the Bartók) or abrasively dissonant (as in the Doris Hays):

Bartók: *Mikrokosmos*, vol. 4 no. 107

Bartók: *Mikrokosmos*, vol. 6 no. 144

Doris Hays: "Sunday Nights"

TEXTURES, DESIGNS, AND PROCEDURES

In this century *linear* thinking has come to the fore, with its focus on the horizontal rather than the vertical plane.

An emphasis on line has led to the abandonment of a single key or a single central tone as a unifying factor over the course of an entire movement or piece. Now, two or more keys may be used simultaneously (in piano music, one for each hand) in a bitonal or polytonal design that derives its bite from clashing semitones:

Stravinsky: *Petrouchka*

Prokofiev: *Sarcasms*, no. 3

Bitonal or polytonal writing may or may not feature contrasting key signatures. Often in bitonal piano music, white keys are assigned to one hand and pitted against black keys in the other.

Each line in a texture need not be assigned an individual harmonic plane in order to achieve independence: the overall design may be merely a free, *dissonant counterpoint* (so called because the dissonances occur when the sharply directed lines coincide to "energize the movement and add to the propulsive power of the line"[22]). Hindemith's procedures are usually termed dissonant counterpoint, but the phrase may be equally descriptive of individual works by other composers:

Bartók: *Mikrokosmos*, vol. 3 no. 91

The idioms in which linear thinking is paramount are atonality and dodecaphonic (twelve-tone) writing.

A development of Arnold Schoenberg, atonality represents the next step beyond free chromaticism: all twelve chromatic pitches are defined as precisely equal, and any hint of a tonic is avoided by strictly forbidding any single tone to predominate. Naturally, all references of a traditional nature (any kind of chordal building-block, scale, etc.) are discarded along with the sense of tonality. Schoenberg's first true atonal composition is *Three Piano Pieces*, op. 11 of 1908.

Schoenberg: Three Piano Pieces, op. 11 no. 1

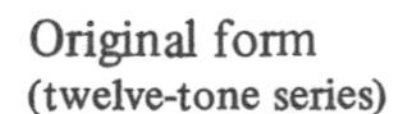

In truth, atonality is not in any sense a compositional method but rather a philosophic guide to the act of composing. Because new principles of organizing materials had to be developed for virtually every piece, each composer's atonal works are apt to be quite individualized.

Around 1915 Schoenberg began to feel that atonal music needed a definite organizing principle and compositional technique of its own, and he developed the concept of a *series*. A series or *tone row* is a particularized arrangement of pitches (usually all twelve chromatic ones) that becomes the theme-scale for a piece. The order in which the pitches are stated becomes all-important: by using the pitches in strict serial order only, any sense of a predominant tonic pitch is lost, and the *intervallic pattern* established by the original row (functioning as a template, in the manner of a traditional scale-pattern) enables the composer to transpose the series at will, by beginning it on any other of the remaining eleven pitches.

An entire composition may be constructed from the row in its original configuration (Webern's "*Kinderstück*", op. post.) either in the "home key" or with transpositions; or the row may be subjected to contrapuntal manipulations similar to those of traditional counterpoint. Pitch materials for *Twelve Easy Pieces* by Ernst Křenek:

Original form
(twelve-tone series)

Inverted form of the original
(obtained by changing ascending intervals to equivalent descending ones, and vice versa)

Retrograde form of the original
(obtained by proceeding from the last tone to the first)

Inverted form of the retrograde
(obtained by reading the inverted form backward)

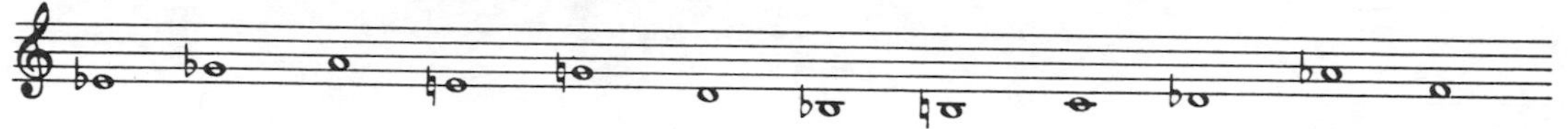

The *original* form of the row may be stated in reverse order (*retrograde*); *inverted* intervallically (note the symmetrical contours of the row and its inversion); and in *retrograde inversion*. The entire composition will thus consist of restatements of the series in any of its numerous guises, predetermining the entire pitch content of the piece—vertical as well as horizontal.
(Using only the retrograde and inverted forms of the row.)

Křenek: "Glass Figures,"
from *12 Short Piano Pieces*

Later, strict serial procedures were adapted by the integral serialists to control all other musical parameters, as well as pitch: dynamics, articulation, registral placement, rhythm, and timbre.

It is interesting to note that the system of ordering devised by those composers who rigorously sought to deny tonality is now being used to compose tonal music as well. Series of fewer than twelve pitches are often used; and one might construct a series of seven diatonic pitches (though not in scalar order), or something like the following, with strong tonal implications:

E C	A F	D A-flat B	G
I	IV⁶	VII° ⁷	"V"

TIMBRE AND FORM

"Form in new music can be examined from two points of view: first, there is *outer form*, which results from the sectional arrangement of musical idea, and second, there is *inner form*, which results from thematic and motivic connections." [23] Both outer and inner forms still rely on the basic architectural principles of repetition and contrast, but *compression, variation,* and *disguise* serve to veil structural outlines to such an extent that now we often perceive a single movement as an organic whole, and not as something composed of separate sections.

In particular, the twentieth-century sonata has been altered. It is frequently cast as a single movement whose outer design bears but a distant kinship to the classical architectural design of exposition–development–recapitulation (see Berg's Sonata, op. 1.).

The search for overall unification has produced an increasing number of both large and small works cast in *arch* or *mirror* form. In these, composers "permit the piece to unfold until the middle section has been reached, and then. . . have it reverse itself to the end: *i.e.*, ABCBA, ABACABA, etc." [24] Arch forms offer an excellent compromise between through-composition and the symmetrically balanced forms originally derived from various dances. Among the works using arch forms are Berg's *Lyric Suite*, Webern's *Six Pieces for Orchestra*, op. 6, Boulez' Piano Sonata no. 3, and Gregg Smith's *Magnificat*.

> The central formal problem facing the composer today, however, is not one of being able to create new outer arrangements, but rather either ways of achieving inner thematic unity, or even deciding whether inner thematic unity is any longer relevant in the music of today. In other words, it is a matter of how much control, and what specific types of control, the composer may justifiably use in creating a piece. [25]

Composers who favor maximally controlled music feel that deriving every element of the piece from relationships set forth in this initial series assures that the composition will be formally convincing–and consequently, they deny the role of intuition. On the other hand, composers of chance music feel that intuition–if it is "of the moment" and "all of a piece"–can go far toward eliminating the need to spell out structural relations in detail, in advance.

In both controlled and noncontrolled music, timbre has become an important form-building element. Instruments are being pushed to their registral and technical limits in the course of efforts to enlarge the sonic palette; at the same time, the "klang," or overall sound event of the moment, is fast becoming the new-music equivalent of the traditional theme or motive. In such diverse works as "The Game of Pairs" from Bartók's Concerto for Orchestra, Varèse's *Ionisation*, and Penderecki's *Threnody for the Victims of Hiroshima*, timbral contrasts largely determine sectional divisions, and are considerable factors in insuring the integrity and logical unity of the form overall.

INNOVATIONS IN PIANO TECHNIQUE AND NOTATION

In the last 125 years the role of composer has gradually grown distinct and separate from that of conductor, instrumentalist, singer, musicologist, acoustician, or any other music specialist. Such intense specialization within the field of a single performing art has proven to be a rather mixed blessing, mainly because of the increasing separation between the creator and re-creator, or performer.

However, isolating the role of "composer-specialist" has produced some remarkable advances and innovations in technique, because it has given the composer the luxury of enough time in which to examine the medium scientifically, detail by detail. Thus, every musical element can be broken down into its smallest component—its "molecule"—and subjected to experiment in order to determine the resultant sound effect of any change in its nature, however small. As a consequence, terms such as *pitch*, *duration*, and *loudness* became inexact for descriptive purposes when discussing an individual tone. A tone may now be specifically identified through noting its *frequency* (cycles per second, including any variations from the basic pitch produced by vibrato, tremolo, or microtonal inflection) and the length and dynamic character of each minute component: initial *attack*; main segment (*sustain*); tail (*decay*); and *cutoff*.

Naturally, such precise control over every aspect of every note meant that scores in traditional notation would grow increasingly detailed; and that one could look forward to the invention of new notational symbols to represent new effects.

Until the early 1950s, innovations in piano technique focused mainly on enlarging the instrument's timbral resources while increasing the independence of the hands at the keyboard. (Bitonality, for instance, may be considered an outgrowth of permitting each hand maximum autonomy by allotting each its own harmonic domain.)

In the rhythmic area we find the following techniques increasingly prevalent: an emphasis on intricate rhythms (Babbitt: "Partitions," p. 510, and Bartók: *Mikrokosmos*, p. 516); noncoordinating ostinatos; multimetric writing (Mennin: Prelude, p. 536) and Bartók: Bagatelle, p. 537); irregular meters (Mennin: Prelude, p. 536); greater use of polyrhythms (Babbit: "Partitions," p. 510); nonsymmetric phrase structures (Bartók: Bagatelle, p. 523); and frequent tempo changes (Bartók: Bagatelle, p. 537).

Bartók: *Mikrokosmos*, vol. 5 no. 133

Mennin: Prelude,
from *Five Piano Pieces*

Bartók: Bagatelle, op. 6 no. 12

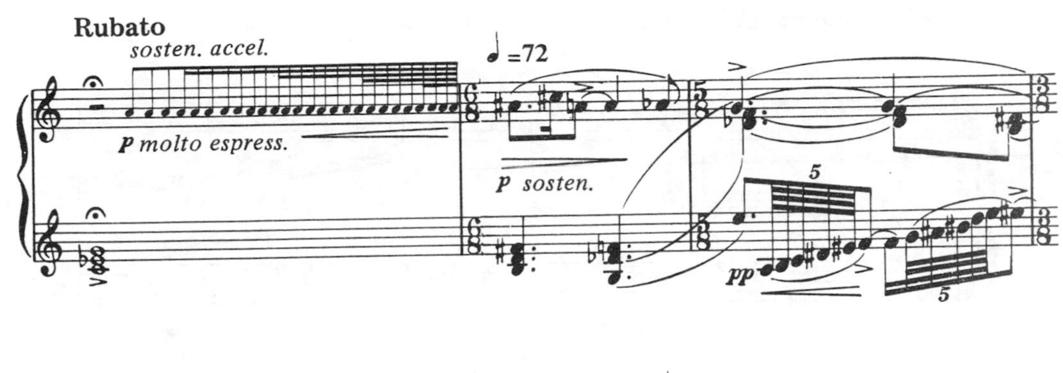

A single musical figure may be dispersed throughout the keyboard, and disparate textures succeed one another with great rapidity (Riley: *Five Little Movements*, p. 538). The hands no longer remain relatively stable in the center of the keyboard, but are often widely separated (Barber: Sonata, p. 539).

Dennis Riley: *Five Little Movements*, no. 2

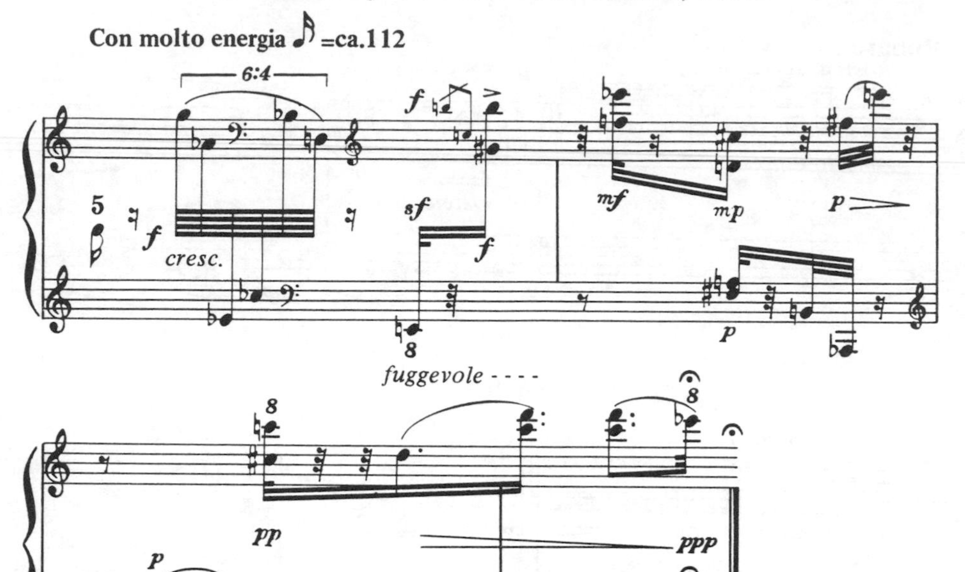

Webern: Piano piece, op. posth.

Barber: Sonata, op. 26
(fourth movement)

Doublings may be called for at unusual intervals. Chord spacings often lie outside traditional harmonic patterns and may be of the cluster type.

Schoenberg: *Six Little Piano Pieces*, op. 19 no. 6

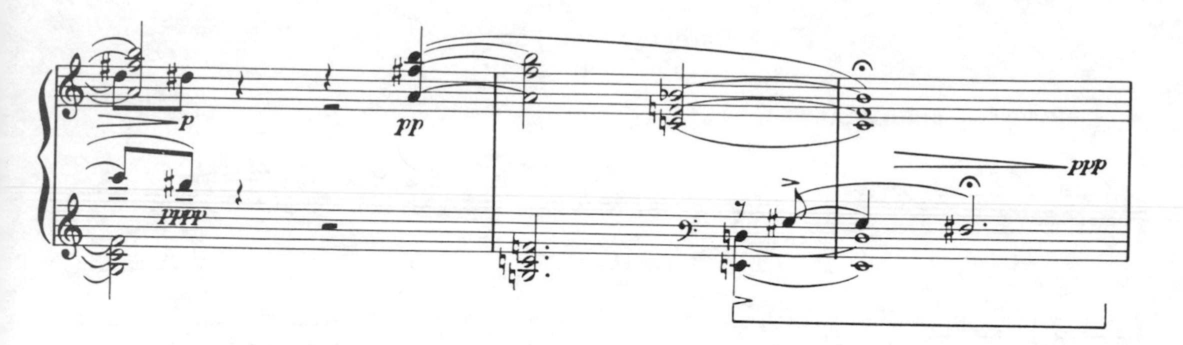

The whole musical fabric is likely to be discontinuous, demanding extreme agility on the performer's part in the negotiation of sudden registral shifts, awkward across-the-body cross-hand maneuvers and single-note exchanges, as well as expert control over a wide spectrum of variegated attacks and dynamics.

Webern: *Variations for Piano*, op. 27
(second movement)

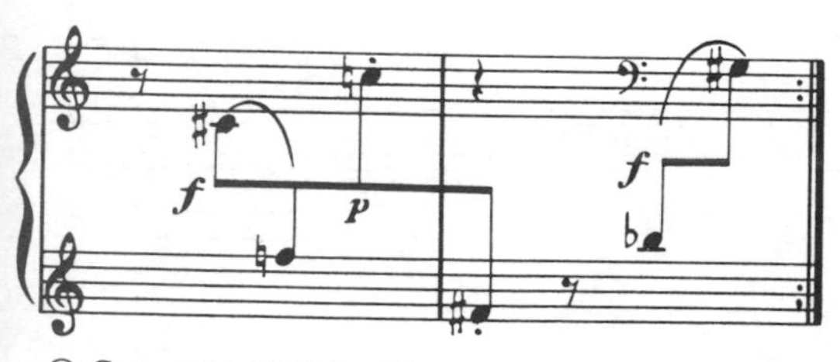

Attributes emphasized in nineteenth-century literature—seamless legato, singing tone, and expressive playing—are no longer of importance when tackling music written expressly for an instrument "with hammers." The percussive approach is stressed in the music of Cowell, Prokofiev, and Bartók. "Independent action of the fingers is often replaced by hammerlike strokes of the whole hand, molded into a specific pattern, often with the scope of an octave or more . . . . One hand will sometimes be called upon to play six- or seven-note chords, often percussively repeated. Octave passages and thirds do not glide, but are hammered out. . . . The peculiar technique is vital to the expression of the music, even in places where it is not vital simply to hitting the right notes." [26]

Prokofiev: Toccata, op. 11

Another common percussive device is the repeated pitch, "beaten out . . . with emphatic accent on each note, to set up a steady hammering sound." [27] Tone clusters, first used and named by Henry Cowell, add bite and vehemence.

Another innovation we owe to Cowell is that of playing directly on the piano strings, using the fingers or the whole hand to make them vibrate by plucking, stroking, strumming, or slapping. Cowell's "Aeolian Harp" is an excellent piece illustrating many of these performance techniques.

INNOVATIONS IN NOTATION

Most of the innovations in technique discovered or exploited since World War II have centered on expanding the timbral palette even further. Both totally controlled music and music of chance required the invention of new notational symbols and perfection of the old so that (1) every one of the composer's instructions could be indicated with minute exactness or that (2) it be made quite clear to the performer exactly which components were previously defined by the composer, and which left to the performer's discretion to improvise at the moment of performance.

Many composers insterested in total control turned to tape music. Here, since the taped result is at once the piece itself and the definitive performance, a score becomes superfluous, at least in its function as an instrument of communication to a performer. However, as more and more composers begin to write music for tape and live performers (which once again required a score), they were obliged to invent symbolic equivalents for electronic music sound events. Ironically, many of these notation symbols turned out to be strikingly similar to graphic notations already devised by composers of chance music.

Tone clusters became prominent features of the new music. Henry Cowell first used the term to mean a strongly dissonant group of neighboring pitches, which could be entirely chromatic (G–G-sharp–A–A-sharp–B); diatonic (F–G–A–B–C, D-flat–E-flat–G-flat–A-flat–B-flat, or A–B–C-sharp–D–E); or a mixture of both (C–D–E-flat–F-sharp–G–A-flat). In any case, they were precise clusters of a more or less narrow compass, meant to be played with the fingers, and perfectly capable of being notated in traditional fashion.

Clusters soon evolved beyond a narrow compass, becoming approximate rather than precise in pitch content, and began to be played with fists, flat of the hand, or forearm. A symbolic notation was developed for these clusters of wider compass, which has recently been refined:

(1) Precise clusters notated symbolically, in which the thick vertical line connecting a harmonic interval indicates that all chromatic tones within the interval are to be played:

all black keys

(2) Approximate clusters notated symbolically (all illustrations are eighth notes):

Either precise or approximate clusters may, in addition, be notated *proportionally*, that is, in a system where "all durations must be noted in spatial proportion to each other."[28] This is accomplished by precisely equating a note's horizontal placement on the page with the relative duration of its sound:

> If the durations are taken care of by horizontal distances, then there is no further need for durational symbols, such as the distinction in traditional notation between black and white noteheads, or flags, beams, dots, triplet numerals, and so on. All that are needed in proportionate notation are noteheads to indicate pitches and a single beam to show how long the pitches are to sound (beam=sound; no beam=silence)." [29]

Thus, precise clusters notated proportionally:

and approximate clusters notated proportionally:

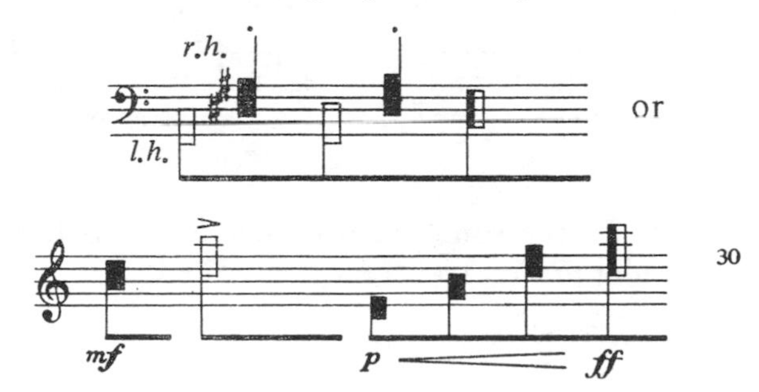

Also explored was the phenomenon of *sympathetic vibration*, in which keys are depressed silently (thus lifting the dampers), permitting the strings to vibrate in sympathy with overtones from other pitches actually sounded. Schoenberg adopted the diamond-shaped note head, usually used for string harmonics, for this effect.

The damper pedal has been brought to the fore as a timbral device. It may be used traditionally, in full and half pedals; to build several clusters into huge reverberant blocks of sound; to enhance attack effects:

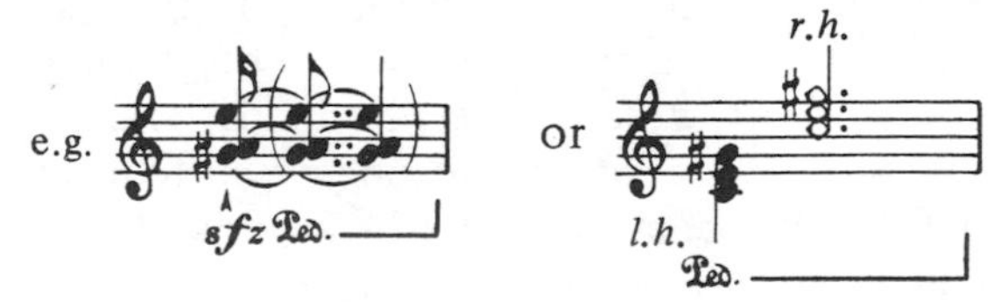

or all by itself, as a sound:

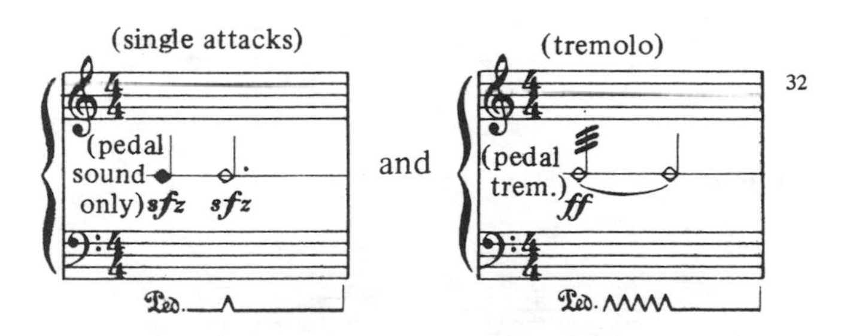

Huge expansion of the sonic palette became possible when composers began to consider *noise* as a sound component.

> John Cage's early experiments with the "prepared piano" paved the way for a wide range of unconventional usages. . . . Rubber threaded through the strings at harmonic nodes will give sounds of quiet, pale harmonic quality. Bolts or screws left free to move will produce buzzing tones, while those fixed firmly will make for dull, thudding percussive sounds with little or no "piano" tone. . . . Wire-wrapped bass strings can be scraped with knife blades. . . [or] the tone can be modified by pressing strips of plasticine over the strings and then playing the keyboard. . . . If metal rules are laid over the strings a percussive, clanging effect is obtained. With the sustaining pedal depressed, one can obtain magnificent cluster sounds by rapid glissandos over the strings or by striking several strings at once. . . . The use of a microphone inside the piano will greatly enhance these sound potentialities. [33]

"Nor is the pianist limited to the keyboard. He may be called upon to slam the lid down, strum the strings inside, even screech the piano stool across the floor ever so delicately; no noise possibilities are excluded if they can produce the desired effect." [34] These include slapping one's hands or fists on the music desk, the keyboard cover, or other parts of the instrument; and non-piano-involved participations by the performer, such as speaking, humming, shouting, singing, whistling, grunting, or other vocalizations.

Much use has been made of the piano's interior in both prepared and traditional setups. Indeed, individual strings are so often called for that the suggestion has been made to urge piano manufacturers to color the dampers black and white in the same pattern as the keyboard, to facilitate locating any given string. [35]

The strings may be excited to vibrate either by means of a plectrum or beater (such as a steel needle, a soft tympani stick, etc.), or directly by the player. Strumming and plucking–with the finger tip, nail, or knuckle–are commonly called for. In addition, when playing entirely inside the piano, the free hand may be called on to muffle or "stop" the string while the other hand actually sounds the pitch. As expected, extreme agility is required whenever it becomes necessary to maneuver from keyboard to strings and back again.

It is interesting to note that the new notation symbols, although originally devised to aid in the communication of specific effects, have themselves become the inspiration for further innovations.

Especially for music in which perceptible control over particular features is left to the performer, graphic rather than symbolic notation may prove a more perfect means of communicating the composer's intent. Picturing the intended result rather than giving detailed instructions on how to achieve that result may be the best and most economic way to communicate in certain idioms, particularly in situations calling for a sweeping but imprecise gesture.

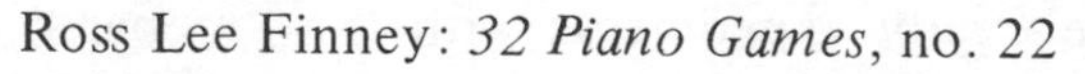

Ross Lee Finney: *32 Piano Games*, no. 22

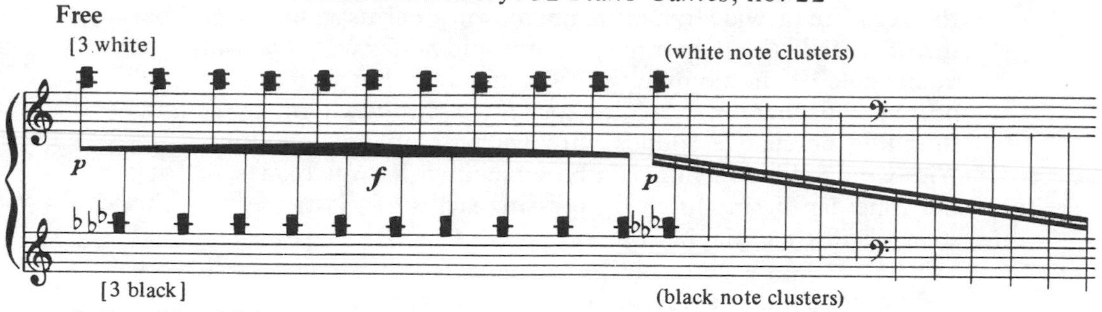

Ross Lee Finney: *32 Piano Games*, no. 28

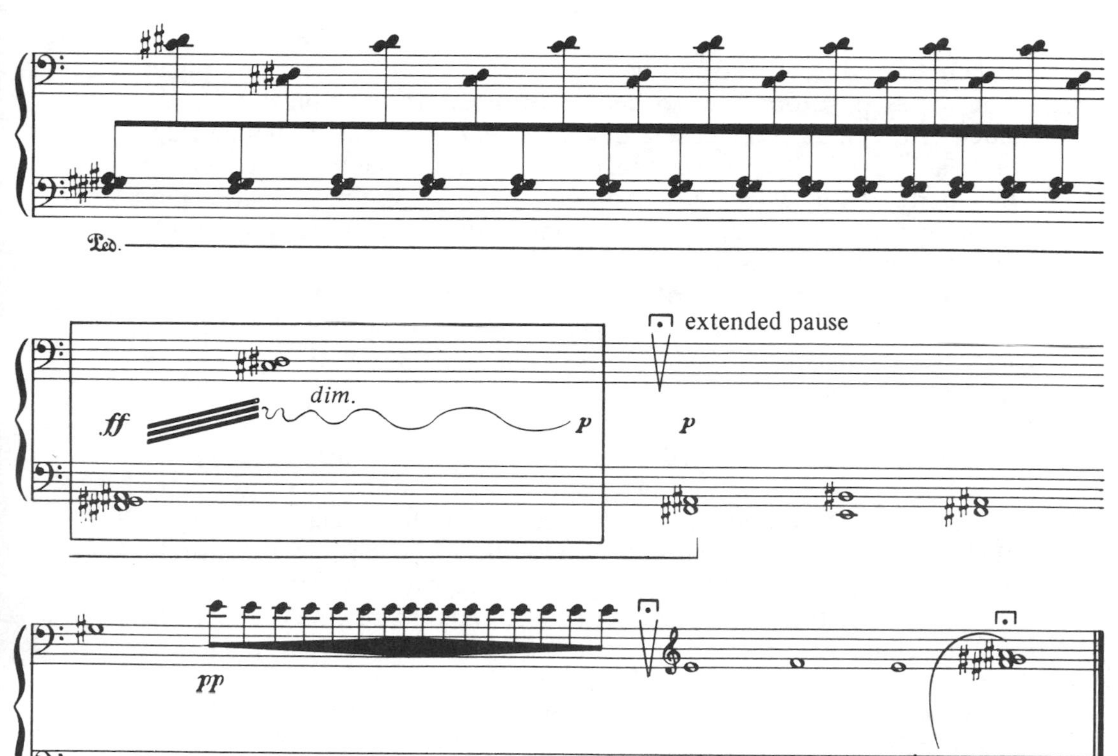

During the last seventy-five years we have seen music slowly evolve into dynamic sonic sculpture, taxing the composer's creative ingenuity and resourcefulness every step of the way. With the guidance of concerned and sympathetic teachers from this point on, we can look forward to a new generation of performers and listeners, equally sympathetic and resourceful, who will consider the new music in no way other than as a perfectly natural and congenial means of expression.

NOTES

1. Johann Huizinga, "A Definition of the Concept of History." In Raymond Klebansky and H.J. Paton, eds.: *Philosophy and History*. New York: Harper Torchbooks, 1963, 8.
2. Eric Salzman, *Twentieth-Century Music*, 4.
3. Reginald Smith Brindle, *The New Music*, 186; 6.
4. Salzman, op. cit., 2.
5. Ibid., 6.
6. Brindle, op. cit., 133.
7. Sergei Prokofiev, *Notebooks* (1937).
8. Salzman, op. cit., 156.
9. Gerald Strang, "Ethics and Esthetics of Computer Composition." In Harry B. Lincoln, ed., *The Computer and Music*. Ithaca: Cornell University Press, 1970, 41.
10. Brindle, op. cit., 126.
11. Salzman, op. cit., 3.
12. Joseph Machlis, *Introduction to Contemporary Music*, 40.
13. Donald Chittum, "Music Here and Now," Part 2: "The Pitch Materials of New Music," 30.
14. Alice Canaday, *Contemporary Music and the Pianist*, 10.
15. Robert P. Morgan, "Towards a More Inclusive Musical Literacy," Part I, 11.
16. Cited in Marion Bauer, *Twentieth-Century Music*, 191.
17. Ibid.
18. Machlis, op. cit., 32.
19. Machlis, op. cit., 23.
20. Cited in Welton Marquis, *Twentieth-Century Music Idioms*, 48.
21. Adapted from Marquis, op. cit., 49.
22. Machlis, op. cit., 52.
23. Chittum, op.cit., Part1: "Gesture and Organization in New Music," 23.
24. Ibid., 23, 46.
25. Ibid., 46.
26. Susan Calvin, "Modern Revolution in Piano Writing," 42.
27. Ibid., 41.
28. Kurt Stone, "New Notation for New Music," Part 2, 56.
29. Ibid.
30. Cited in ibid., 58.
31. Quoted from "International Conference on New Music Notation Report," 96.
32. Quoted from ibid., 94–95.
33. Brindle, op. cit., 160–61.
34. Calvin, op. cit., 42.
35. "International Conference on New Musical Notation Report," 96–97.

BIBLIOGRAPHY

Bauer, Marion. *Twentieth-Century Music: How It Developed, How to Listen to It* (rev. ed.). New York: G.P. Putnam's Sons, 1947.

Brindle, Reginald Smith. *The New Music: The Avant-Garde Since 1945*. London: Oxford University Press, 1975.

Cage, John (compiler and arranger). *Notations*. New York: Something Else Press, 1969.

Calvin, Susan. "The Modern Revolution in Piano Writing." *The American Music Teacher*. April-May 1969.

Canaday, Alice. *Contemporary Music and the Pianist: A Guidebook of Resources and Materials*. Alfred Publishing Co., Inc. 1974.

Chittum, Donald. "Music Here and Now." *The American Music Teacher*. Part 1: "Gesture and Organization," September-October 1971, 23, 46; Part 2: "The Pitch Materials of New Music," January 1972, 30, 35; Part 3: "Improvisation, Chance, Indeterminacy," February-March 1972, 30, 37, 40; Part 4: "Serial Music and Total Organization," April-May 1972, 34–35; Part 5: "Tape Music and Multimedia," June-July 1972, 28–29.

Contemporary Music and Audiences. Canadian Music Council, 1969.

Copland, Aaron. *The New Music 1900–1960* (rev. ed.). New York: W.W. Norton, 1968.

Crowder, Louis L. "Piano Music of the Twentieth Century." *An Anthology of Piano Music:* Volume 4: "The Twentieth Century," Denes Agay, ed. New York: Yorktown Music Press, 1971.

Hindemith, Paul. *A Composer's World: Horizons and Limitations* (Charles Eliot Norton Lectures 1949–1950). Garden City: Anchor Books/Doubleday, 1961.

——. *The Craft of Musical Composition*, rev. ed. New York: Associated Music Publishers, 1945.

"International Conference on New Musical Notation Report." *Interface: Journal of New Music Research*, November 1975.

Lincoln, Harry B., ed. *The Computer and Music*. Ithaca: Cornell University Press, 1970.

Machlis, Joseph. *Introduction to Contemporary Music*. New York: W.W. Norton, 1961.

Marquis, Welton. *Twentieth Century Music Idioms*. Englewood Cliffs, New Jersey: Prentice-Hall, 1964.

Morgan, Robert P. "Towards a More Inclusive Musical Literacy: Notes on Easy Twentieth Century Piano Music" (Parts 1 and 2). *Musical Newsletter*, January 1971; April 1971.

Myers, Rollo H. *Twentieth-Century Music* (2nd ed.). London: Calder and Boyars, 1968.

Peyser, Joan. *The New Music: The Sense Behind the Sound*. New York: Delacorte Press, 1971.

Read, Gardner. *Music Notation: A Manual of Modern Practice*. Boston: Allyn and Bacon, 1964.

Salzman, Eric. *Twentieth-Century Music: An Introduction*. Englewood Cliffs, New Jersey: Prentice-Hall, 1967.

Stone, Kurt. "New Notation for New Music" (Parts 1 and 2). *Music Educators Journal*, October 1976; November 1976.

Wilder, Robert D. *Twentieth-Century Music*. Wm. C. Brown Company, 1969.

What Is Jazz?

STUART ISACOFF

When Bartolommeo Cristofori invented the pianoforte in 1709, the event ushered in a new musical and social era. Earlier, musical performances were often buried in the inner sanctums of aristocratic parlors, or restricted and controlled by High Church decree. In 1449, for instance, the king of Scotland declared that minstrels were to live "decently" or leave the country: any minstrel found performing would have his ears cut off; if caught a second time, he would be hanged. Of course, official attitudes were not always so severe, but it was not until the mass production of pianofortes in the late eighteenth century that instrumental music became the commoner's plaything.

The distinction between popular (frivolous) and classical (important) music remains even today, however. "Serious musicians" are usually thought to be free from contagion by popular tastes, despite a growing recognition that such categories are silly and artificial. A case in point is the early attitude toward jazz, a kind of music which, according to John Philip Sousa, "makes you want to bite your grandmother." But the spontaneity and drive which characterize jazz are as much the experience of Bach, Beethoven, and Mozart as that of Thelonious Monk, Bud Powell, and Duke Ellington. Throughout history the greatest masters have also been consummate improvisors, and many gems of our musical repertoire are simply notated versions of superb improvisations. Although jazz, as a synthesis of African, American, and European traditions, falls within certain distinctive stylistic boundaries, its basic elements are the same as those which form the backbone of all musical craft.

Thus, the teacher may use jazz materials to instruct the student in all of the traditional concepts—harmony, rhythm, voice leading, dynamics—while employing a format which is appealingly contemporary, and which holds great interest for most students. There is a rich and varied repertory of jazz materials written with intelligence, wit, and feeling. It is, therefore, well worthwhile for piano teachers to investigate the characteristics of jazz style. The task is not a difficult one. From its primitive beginnings to contemporary sophisticated works there are common threads which bind and clarify this art and make it accessible.

JAZZ RHYTHM

The heart of jazz is its distinctive rhythm, a combination of African and European elements, reflecting two different musical approaches. In both idioms notes and note groups are accented through such common, orthodox devices as:

However, the differences between the African and European concepts of rhythm are more pronounced than the similarities.

European rhythmic elements are organized to reinforce a strong metrical scheme, a repeating pattern of accents that usually appear in groups of two, three, or four beats. Hence, the music flows out of a constant tension and relaxation effected against a metrical background. This feature strongly characterizes and dominates the musical life of the West; as C.P.E. Bach wrote, "each meter carries a kind of compulsion within itself."

African rhythm, on the other hand, is additive: one rhythm added to another, no bar lines, and no sense of meter. This is derived from the rhythm and stress of tribal language; it evolved and developed through the use of "talking drums," a tool of communication. The three elements of speech in West African languages—rhythm, intonation (or pitch inflection) and accent—become translated to percussion music, and African melody clearly reflects African spoken languages.

SYNCOPATION

Since African rhythm is free of metrical boundaries, one of the most noted features of early jazz, syncopation, finds its origins not in an African contribution to jazz music, but in European composition and performance practice since the fifteenth century. How did syncopation develop as a major expressive and stylistic device among early ragtime and jazz musicians? By tracing the strands of European and African influences (and the social context in which they merged), a clear answer presents itself, one which sheds light on the whole history of jazz.

The earliest writings on syncopation are by the fourteenth-century theorists Philippe de Vitry and Johannes de Muris. The original concept was one of breaking up a series of rhythmic values by changing the placement of a large-value note to situate it between two shorter ones. Thus, the figure,

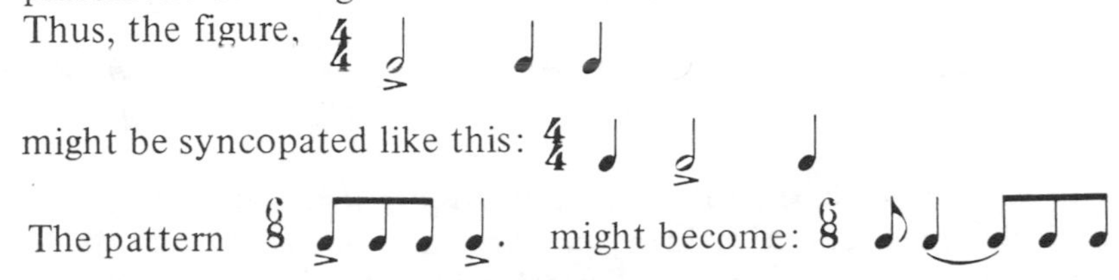

might be syncopated like this:

The pattern might become:

In the classical period, syncopation was used extensively to create rhythmic and melodic tension. A conflict is created between the accents implied by the bar line and those found in the melody: a sort of war over where the strong beat belongs.

accents implied by bar line:

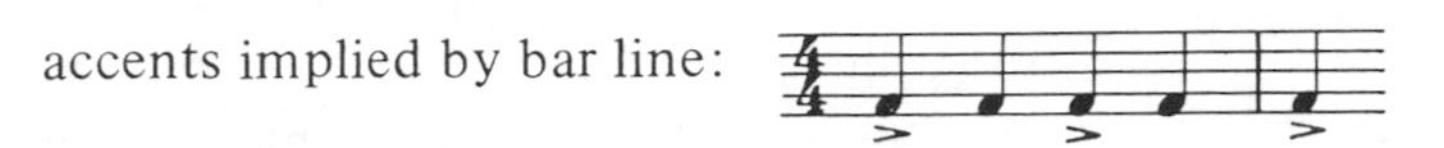

accents of syncopated phrase:

This tension, however, is short-term, and finds release quickly in a reestablishment of the expected order.

Beethoven: Bagatelle, op. 126

Syncopation in African music is actually not syncopation at all, according to its Western theoretical meaning. Of course there is a good deal of rhythmic polyphony, with overlapping downbeats giving Western ears an impression of shifting meters and syncopated patterns. For the African musician, however, each line is a musical entity in itself, not an off-beat complement to the line being played with it. Observe, for instance, the overall effect brought into play by the concurrent rendition of these three independent rhythmic patterns:

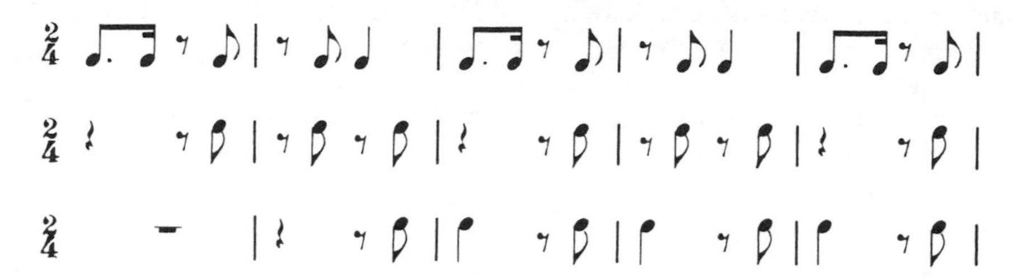

This music is simply an exciting, instinctively constructed pastiche of numerous individual repetitive ideas performed simultaneously, much like the collective improvisation of a Dixieland band.

African slaves brought this musical conception to the United States in their work songs, dances, and rituals. Music played an important social role; it was used in healing, marriage, hunting, and other occasions. In some African cultures, litigants in civil suits sang their cases before the chief and village. These songs of complaint may very well have been the wellsprings of the blues.

In America, the dominant culture of European immigrants had a tremendous influence on the shape of black music. The Africans' rhythmic polyphony became molded within metrical boundaries. Independent lines took on the appearance of syncopated phrases, with one difference: the repetitive aspect of African musical lines was retained. Whereas European syncopation was used to create momentary suspensions of normal pulse and displacement of metric accents, African lines became "ragging" patterns, "boogie" basses, etc., constant and ever-present.

These repetitive bass patterns were employed by jazz pioneers like Jimmy Yancy:

The Europeans had other musical devices which lent themselves to this synthesis of traditions called jazz. The "jazz feel," for example, in which note values are spontaneously lengthened and shortened during performance, has its equivalent in the baroque convention known as *notes inégales* (literally "unequal notes"), the altering of the relative time values of certain pairs of notes, especially those moving in step-wise progression. The exact degree of unequalness was at the performer's discretion and eludes precise notation. An approximate illustration could be given by the following options:

played (any of the following versions):

In modern jazz, eighth notes and dotted eighths followed by a six-teenth are played with a triplet feeling: ♫ or ♫. = ♩♪

The character of early jazz, especially ragtime, also relies heavily on certain time-honored patterns of Western rhythm known as the *scotch snap* and the *hornpipe*,

which the slaves must have heard in the white man's fiddle music and folk songs. The works of baroque and classical masters also abound with these formulas.

Mozart: Serenadc no. 6, K. 239
(*Serenata Notturna*)

Handel: *Water Music*

Beethoven's Piano Sonata, op. 111, contains some surprisingly syncopated variations on the hornpipe pattern:

The right-hand syncopation Beethoven uses in the second measure is very close to the augmented hornpipe rhythm—Charleston syncopation—used in jazz as a left-hand accompanying device:

Ragtime is a natural habitat for both the hornpipe and the scotch snap.

Turpin: "A Ragtime Nightmare"

Lamb: "Ragtime Nightingale"

The hornpipe is also evident in the boogie-woogie figures shown earlier as well as in the blues "shuffle":

in the "easy" swing style of the '30s and early '40s:

Butterfield: "Salt Butter"

in the relaxed and detached "cool jazz" approach of Dave Brubeck and others in the '50s:

Isacoff: "One for Dave"

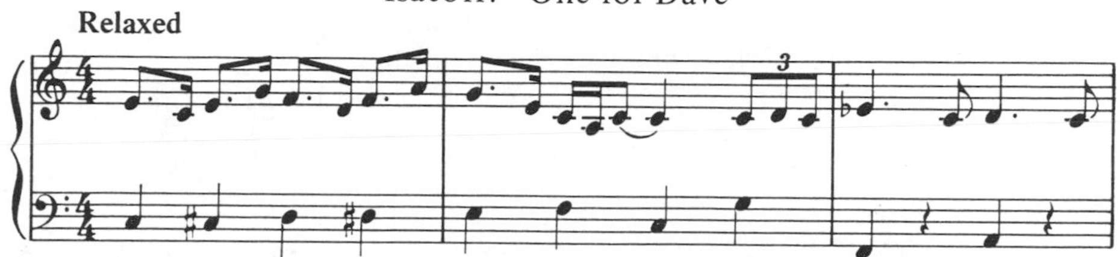

and even jazz-rock musicians have used the hornpipe by simply placing it, in augmented form, after the downbeat of a measure:

Of course, in actual performance, none of these examples will reflect the precise hornpipe rhythm. The easygoing, loose quality of true jazz defies exact notation; there is always a harking back to the African influence, to that fluid rhythmic freedom unhampered by meter and bar line. In the course of a performance (which in jazz is nearly synonymous with improvisation) the jazz musician is likely to vary the degree of syncopation from measure to measure, causing something like rhythmic vertigo or *notes inégales* gone wild. He may, for example, vary figures from 3 to

play quintuplets; set up a disparity, a kind of metrical divergence between the left and right hands, such as

Isacoff: "Out-of-Phase"

This technique also has a European classical equivalent, although a milder one: the *melodic rubato*, which C.P.E. Bach described as follows:

> When the execution is such that one hand seems to play against the bar and the other strictly with it, it may be said that the performer is doing everything that can be required of him. It is only rarely that all parts are struck simultaneously. As soon as the upper part begins slavishly to follow the bar, the essence of the rubato is lost, for then all other parts must be played in time.

One might say that some aspects of jazz rhythm are a cubist version of classical rubato.

Recent developments in jazz involve other manipulations of accent and meter. These include:

Accent shifts:

Meter changes:

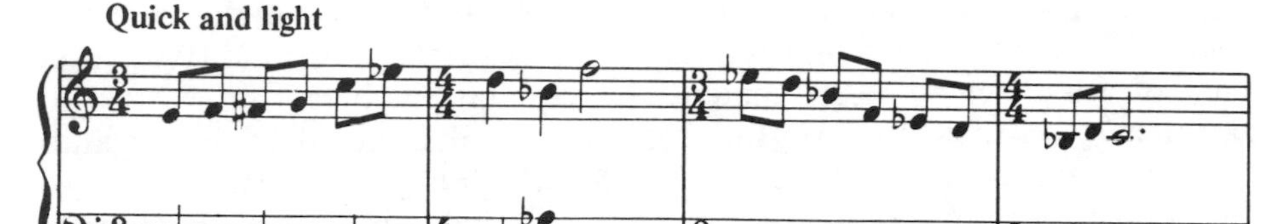

Conversion of meters (most frequently from three beat units to four, or vice versa). Observe, for instance, how the following repetitive rhythm pattern in $\frac{3}{4}$ acquires an excitingly new profile through its placement into $\frac{4}{4}$:

All the foregoing rhythmic devices can be traced to a combination of African and European roots.

JAZZ MELODY

In all but the most recent phases of jazz style, melody is based on the chordal structure which underlies the original tune used for improvisation. Even in so-called jazz tunes, there is always a clear connection between the melody and the harmonies which support it, so that the melody appears to spring from the harmonies rather than the other way around. Several approaches are used to create these melodies, including scales and modes, chordal and passing tones, upper and lower neighbors, sequences, and embellishments.

The so-called blue notes, those notes which add a bluesy sound to jazz melodies, are non-European in origin.

One might speculate that, just as the Afro-Americans created rhythmic formulas which consistently resided outside the normal metrical pulse, so might they have created a melodic counterpart which suspends the distinctions between major and minor tonalities, between perfect and diminished intervals. In practice, the effects of these blue notes are achieved by contrasting them with the ordinary major scale. Just as the rhythmic fluctuations and syncopations found in jazz playing must periodically return to a metric home base, so must the blue notes be used with discrimination: when used too often in a short span of time, they become monotonous and boring.

How were these blue notes selected? Gunther Schuller suspects that they result from two tetrachords:

These tone sequences are found in abundance in African music. Here is one song excerpt in which major and minor thirds, as well as perfect and diminished fifths, are interchanged:

The form in which the "blues scale" is often presented,

is actually a pentatonic scale in inversion:

The one factor which, more than any other, accounts for the ambiguity in the quality of the intervals used in jazz melody, is clearly the indifference the Afro-American musician must have felt toward the rigid major scale. The languages from which Africans derived their musical concepts often have as many as nine different pitch levels affecting the semantic and grammatic structures of their sentences. After years of living with these subtle pitch distinctions, it could not have been easy or desirable for Africans to remold their musical world into a European diatonic framework.

Traditional: "Amazing Grace"

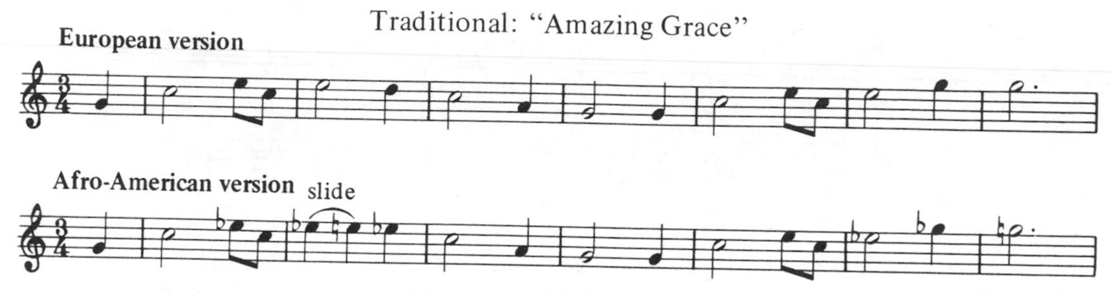

Somewhat related to blue notes in effect, but traditionally European, is the device of embellishment, an important melodic factor in jazz playing. This can take the form of a simple grace note (a half step below the main note), or melodic variations on certain note sequences, as in the following example:

In the 1950s, jazz melody gained added sophistication through the gifted practitioners of the bebop trend (Charlie Parker, Dizzie Gillespie, and others). Chord tones and blue notes were integrated with such elements of European musical tradition as passing tones, upper and lower neighbors, and the rich chromaticism of late nineteenth- and early twentieth-century music.

Powell: "Strictly Confidential"

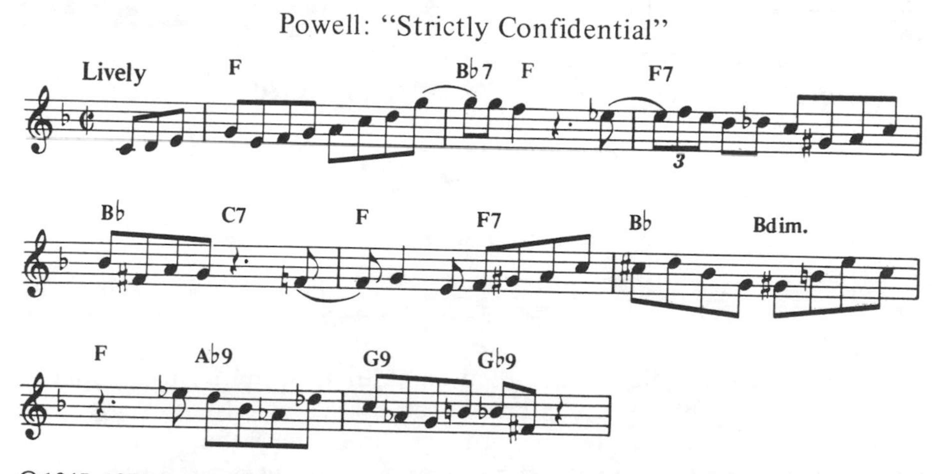

Contemporary jazz figurations sometimes employ *real sequence* which often creates a polytonal flavor.

JAZZ HARMONY

Harmonization in jazz is based heavily on the sound of the dominant seventh chord and often employs a good deal of parallel motion:

In fact, the progression V-I is often accomplished by a simple half-step descent in the upper voices, making use of the harmonically ambiguous augmented fourth or diminished fifth (tritone), with its dominant sound:

A combination of nonscale tones such as blue notes and the influence of modern European harmonies of Debussy and others have produced a jazz chord vocabulary which includes ninths, elevenths, and thirteenths in their unaltered, augmented, and diminished forms; as well as quartal harmonies and other dense chords of almost tone-cluster quality.

Gerald Martin: "Patterns"

Note that the C13 becomes a G♭7 (♯9) when a G-flat is placed in the bass, and a G♭13 becomes a C7 (♯9) when a C is placed in the bass.

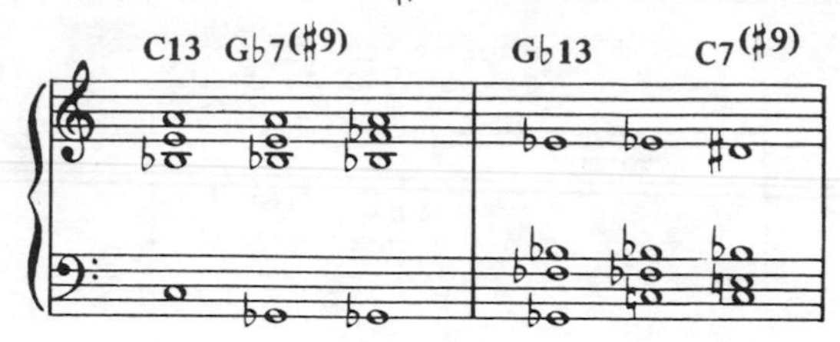

Because of this tritone relationship, any circle-of-fifths progression may be executed as a series of parallel, chromatically descending voices as in the example below.

Chords in jazz are often used in unexpected ways. Sometimes, for example, a dominant chord may be freely exchanged with one whose root is a tritone away (as in the previous example). At other times a chord will be played in which the root tone is left out; these voicings sometimes make use of the sound created by placing notes a minor second away from each other. In fact, the minor second is one of the most important intervals in modern jazz harmony.

chords with root missing (note minor seconds):

Isacoff: "Justice"

other chords with minor seconds:

Monk: "Off Minor"

Whenever possible, successive chord tones (whether altered or not) should follow the voice-leading rules of classical European harmony. A mark of good jazz writing and playing is the smooth and logical manipulation of voices from one chord to the next.

Gmajor Fmajor B♭major Dmajor

Am9 D7(♭5 ♭9) Gm9 C13(♭9) F7(♯11) B♭maj9 A13(♭9) D6/9

II V II V V I V I

These qualities of harmonization, integrated with attractive spontaneity of melody and rhythm, are well illustrated by the following excerpt:

Powell: "I'll Keep Loving You"

Slowly

Jazz is a genuinely American musical expression deeply influenced by African folk traditions and European classical elements. Its various forms and stylistic manifestations–including ragtime, blues, swing, bebop, modern jazz–are a fertile ground on which rhythmic flair, technical dexterity, and improvisational skill can grow. Playing jazz can offer the student an opportunity, rare in the traditional teaching process, to alter the concept of a piece with each performance. In summary, one might answer the question posed in the title of this section by paraphrasing the famous saying about chess: "As a game it is science, as science it is a game." What is jazz? As entertainment it is a musical education, as musical education it is entertainment, which has intrigued and delighted people of the twentieth century the world over.

RECOMMENDED READING

Brandel, Rose. *The Music of Central Africa*. The Hague: Martinus Nijhoff, 1961.
Dankworth, Avril. *Jazz: An Introduction to its Musical Basis*. London: Oxford University Press, 1968.
Schuller, Gunther. *Early Jazz: Its Roots and Musical Development*. New York: Oxford University Press, 1968.
Southern, Eileen. *The Music of Black Americans*. New York: W.W. Norton, 1971.
Stearns, Marshall. *The Story of Jazz*. New York: New American Library, 1958.
Tirro, Frank. *Jazz–A History*. New York: W.W. Norton, 1977.

Jazz and the Piano Teacher

DENES AGAY

Introducing the piano student to the pleasures of jazz requires, first of all, a degree of sympathy and identification with the idiom on the teacher's part. To teach jazz and to impart the joy and vitality of this American musical expression to the student, one should be familiar with its musical essence (see "What Is Jazz," p.549) and, most important, should not harbor any esthetic or pedagogic reservations about it. Once these preconditions are present, the teacher is well advised to outline a plan of preparatory steps whereby the characteristic elements of jazz can be introduced gradually and, as much as possible, on the simplest levels.

One must keep in mind that good jazz playing is not just the result of assiduous study; rather, it depends on an instinctive, improvisatory application of certain creative impulses in the fields of rhythm, melody, and harmony, projected with the right kind of digital facility. Its ultimate refinement and excellence cannot be taught. However, those students (and there are many of them) who like jazz and want to study it can be given the proper start and be guided, at least part of the way, to a point where their individual capabilities and motivations can take over.

The heart of jazz is improvisation, an extemporaneous molding and shaping of the underlying musical elements. Its idiomatic profile is given not so much by what is played but by how it is played. In the mainstream of music literature, styles—classic, romantic, impressionist, etc.—were created by the master composers of various periods and embodied in their works. In jazz, styles have been established by outstanding individual performers. Jazz, however, does have certain traits which are common to all its variants. The introduction of these common characteristics should be the first step in any teaching plan.

One such basic trait is a steady, strong metric pulse, a pronounced beat underlying and supporting the entire structure of musical manipulations. This pulse should be felt and implied even under long-held notes and chords. In the beginning, and even later on, light tapping of the beat units with the right foot (heel on the floor) will help to maintain and emphasize the metric momentum. There is a wide choice of suitable appealing materials among the many well-known folk songs, play tunes, children's songs, and spirituals. The following tentative plan may furnish some ideas as to how these traditional melodies can lead the early grade student on a progressive exploration of the jazz idiom. It should be remembered that each of the following examples illustrates only one sample of many possible variants. At every step of the way the student should be encouraged to make up individual versions of the same tune. Naturally, only those patterns and variants should be used which are consistent with the student's grade level and native skill.

• Select a well-known melody. Play it "straight" at first with a pronounced beat. Tap the beat units with your foot, or with the left hand on the piano.

"London Bridge"

• Provide the melody with a simple bass. There are several kinds of bass patterns which will fit a melody. Play this one, at first without the melody, with a good beat, then add the tune in the right hand.

• Arrange the melody notes into a syncopated pattern. Play it at first with the right hand only (tapping the beat), then add the bass (which is the same as in the preceding examples).

• Try this more interesting variant of the melody, with some changes in the bass, too. The hornpipe pattern ( ) occurs very often in jazz.

• Melody in thirds with a "walking bass":

• Another version, with the simplest ostinato boogie pattern in the bass:

• For a more modern harmonization of the melody, try this step-by-step sequence of diatonic seventh chords:

• Keeping the same chord progression in the left hand, the melody may be varied in many ways. Play this version and also invent one or two others.

• From ragtime to modern jazz, a commonly used accompaniment pattern is the familiar "oom-pah" formula, variously called "swing bass" or "stride bass." (The middle voice in the right hand is optional.)

• The innumerable variation possibilities inherent in a good tune can take the jazz player as far afield as imagination and ingenuity allows. The following "ballad" version varies all elements of the theme and retains only the form (phrasing) structure. (Slight alterations of the melody's rhythm pattern are possible:

At this point teacher and student should select a few other simple tunes which lend themselves to these treatments. Make at least one or two jazz versions on each song. The many suitable ones include "Aunt Rhody," "Merrily We Roll Along," "When the Saints Come Marchin' In," "Three Blind Mice," "This Old Man," "Jingle Bells," "Turkey in the Straw," "Row, Row Your Boat," "The Drunken Sailor," "Ol' Time Religion," "Skip to My Lou," "Li'l Liza Jane," "Frère Jacques," etc.

In an imaginative jazz arrangement the repetitions of the main theme usually occur in varied forms:

Quite often variety is provided by the addition of *breaks* (*riffs*), improvisatory fillers on phrase-ending long notes:

"There's No Hidin' Place"

Fats Waller: "Sneakin' Home"

Interesting melodic variety can be achieved by the addition of grace notes, blue notes, and various other embellishments:

"Skip to My Lou"

Although purists may disagree, Dixieland, ragtime, blues, boogie, swing, bebop, and rock can all be considered jazz styles, as far as the piano student is concerned. All these popular genres emerged on the American musical scene one by one from about the turn of the century to the present. For the purposes of early-grade jazz study, blues and boogie are especially suitable idioms because of their easily identifiable elements and their appealingly full sound even at the simplest grade levels.

The prototype of blues is a harmonic sequence of twelve measures, divided into three phrases, with a freely improvised, expressive melody line:

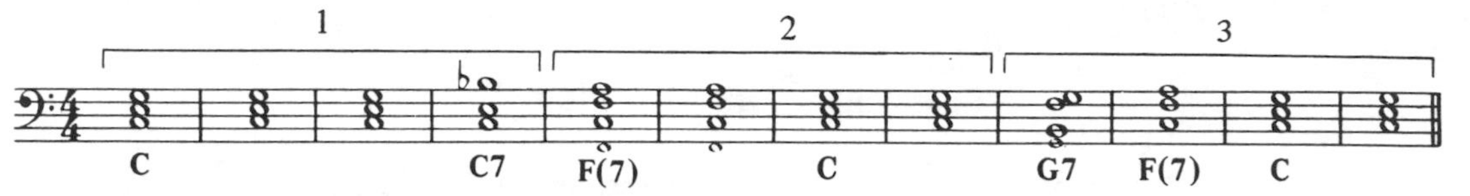

This sequence is not rigid, of course; harmonic shifts and chord enrichments (seventh chords instead of triads, for instance) occur very often:

Traditional Blues Melody

Boogie-woogie, as developed in the '20s and '30s, was originally built on the harmonic scheme of the blues. Its mood and tempo, however, became quite different: more joyful and more propulsive. The essence of boogie is an ever-recurring bass pattern, a usually lively "basso ostinato" providing a solid rhythmic background for a strongly punctuated right-hand melody. The following two excerpts illustrate combinations of blues harmonies and boogie bass patterns:

"The Lonesome Road"

Gerald Martin: "Good Night Boogie"

Below is a progressive listing of other bass figures in the boogie vein. Each pattern should be practiced in a I-IV-V-I (tonic-subdominant-dominant-tonic) chord sequence, repeating once each measure. Also, each sequence should be transposed to one or two other suitable keys, in which the shifting patterns lie easily under the hands. (All patterns can also be played .)

a
b
c
d
e
f
g
h
i
j
k
l
m

As the student's technical and musical capabilities progress, other, somewhat more demanding styles can be introduced to further stimulate creative thinking and introduce more recent and current idioms. Bebop was formulated in the 1940s by solo improvisations of a few outstanding instrumentalists (Dizzie Gillespie, Charlie Parker, and others). Its characteristics are a lively beat, complex rhythms, and a driving, restless melody line, often sung to nonsense syllables. For instance:

Given the proper preparations and having acquired a measure of improvisatory skill and bravado, the student may want to undertake converting some well-known tunes into bebop and modern jazz vignettes. Using the familiar "London Bridge" as a melodic springboard, this version jumps quite a distance:

Rock and roll has been dominating the field of popular music since the mid-1950s. Pianists should be aware that this is not as keyboard oriented a genre as most other jazz styles. Its most conspicuous traits are the placing of accents on the second and fourth beats of a measure, instead of the normally accented first and third beats, and a pronounced eight-to-the-bar pulse. Also characteristic is the frequently modal flavor of melodies and harmonies. Some of the simplest rock-bass patterns are these:

The following example is a rock version of "London Bridge." Try other bass patterns and select other tunes appropriate for such treatment.

Good jazz playing requires a considerable degree of creative contribution from the player. Even a most meticulously notated jazz piece or arrangement will sound stiff, artificial, and anemic if played note by note as written, without an imaginative input from the performer. Delivery must be easygoing, relaxed, and individualized at all times. The advancing student should increasingly be left to his or her own devices in jazz explorations. The selection of tunes to be arranged, the style and treatment the theme should receive, and the details of execution should gradually become the student's creative domain, under the teacher's guidance and constructive supervision. There are now many fine publications available which furnish interesting and instructive jazz repertories; some of them also supply varying amounts of theoretical and pedagogical information. Jazz can be a pleasurable and useful phase of piano education and it certainly merits the teacher's earnest and sympathetic attention.

RECOMMENDED SELECTIONS

JAZZ SOLOS, JAZZ DUETS (Recital Notebooks Nos. 9 and 10) Agay (Yorktown)
THE JOY OF JAZZ, THE JOY OF BOOGIE AND BLUES, THE JOY OF RAGTIME Agay (Yorktown)
S. SCHWARTZ JAZZ LIBRARY (11 vols.) (Hansen)
JAZZ FOR PIANO Konowitz and others (Lee Roberts-Schirmer)
JAZZ, BLUES, RAGTIME PIANO STYLES Matt Dennis (Mel Bay)
ROCK WITH JAZZ, 5 vols. Stecher, Horowitz, Gordon (Schirmer)
JAZZ AND BLUES, 6 vols. Kraehenbuehl (Summy-Birchard)
HOW TO PLAY BLUES PIANO Kriss (Acorn)
MORE REAL COOL PIANO Agay (Presser)
ROCK ME EASY Olson (Carl Fischer)
AN ADVENTURE IN JAZZ Noona-Glover; AN ADVENTURE IN RAGTIME Hinson-Glover (Belwin)
BLUES FOR FUN Sheftel (Douglas)
JAZZ—AND ALL THAT 2 vols. Clarke (Myklas)
FROM RAG TO JAZZ Isacoff (Consolidated)
JUNIOR JAZZ Gordon; FACES OF JAZZ Smith (Marks)
JAZZETTES Berkowitz (Frank)
FOUR DANCE IMPRESSIONS Agay (Presser)
REFLECTIONS IN MODERN JAZZ Waldron (Fox)
JAZZ SAMPLER McPartland, Brubeck and others (Marks)
RHYTHM FACTORY 135 rhythmic patterns Metis (Marks)
ROCK MODES AND MOODS Metis (Marks)
POP/ROCK SKETCHES One piano, four hands Metic (Marks)
THE RAGTIME CURRENT Bolcom, Morath and others (Marks)
THE JAZZ PIANIST (3 books) Mehegan (Fox)
STYLES FOR THE JAZZ PIANIST (3 books) Mehegan (Fox)
POPULAR AND JAZZ PIANO COURSE (3 vols.) Stormen (Progress)

The Piano Teacher and Popular Music

DENES AGAY

The pedagogic challenge inherent in the title of this section has been present since the dawn of piano instruction. This writer's first involvement with the problem occurred at the age of five—not as a teacher, of course, but as a student. Being a musically precocious child, by that age I could play by ear the melodies and pieces I heard and liked: folk songs, popular tunes, and pleasing fragments from the piano-teaching repertory to which I had been exposed through my older brother's practicing. When shortly after my fifth birthday it was decided that I should begin formal piano lessons, my mother took me to our small town's only teacher, Aunt Kornelia; and after proper introductions, my proud mother coaxed me to perform for the dear old lady. Without hesitation, I plunged into *The Merry Widow* waltz. After my closing chord the teacher drew my mother into a corner of the studio for a whispered conference, then came over to me, put a benign hand on my shoulder and said, "This is nice, son, but we'll have to stop this kind of playing now that you will begin to learn how to really play the piano."

Although I have not forgotten the scene and the statement, it has never been entirely clear for me whether the somewhat cryptic condemnation referred to the type of music I played or to the way I played it. Probably it referred to both and, needless to say, it considerably dampened whatever enthusiasm I may have had for piano tutoring. I did attend my lessons, practicing the given curriculum dutifully, if somewhat reluctantly, but the fun of playing the tunes I liked, in my own way, was largely gone.

In fact, the little pieces and exercises Aunt Kornelia assigned were the well-known, musically dull staples so popular in the piano primers of that day, which—while they did fit it into a somewhat staid and anemic pedagogical scheme—were, as pure music, hardly superior to *The Merry Widow* waltz. All this I discovered, of course, only much later in life, after having had the opportunity to analyze and draw conclusions for myself.

THE IMPORTANCE OF A WIDE-SPECTRUM REPERTORY

Piano study should not alienate and abruptly tear the young student away from everyday musical experiences and diversions. It should not lift the child into a kind of pedagogical ivory tower where only carefully prescribed, pedigreed music is played and heard, and where the prevailing sounds of the world around us are all but filtered out. On the contrary, the repertory of piano study should present the widest possible musical spectrum, incorporating not only the literature of piano, past and present, but also well chosen samplers of other appealing, lighter musical idioms the student is exposed to in everyday life, provided that these selections are esthetically acceptable and can be made to serve a useful purpose within the teaching plan.

The question of whether popular music has a place in the student's repertory is answered affirmatively here—but with some important qualifications. This is a personal view, of course, but it can be supported by historical precedent, pedagogical consideration, and sound psychological reasons. Certain popular dance forms have always been a part of the teaching repertory. In the eighteenth century the minuet, gavotte and polonaise, in the nineteenth century the waltz, polka, and mazurka, to mention a few, were standard teaching fare; so there could hardly be a valid reason, in principle at least, why the dance forms and rhythms of our time should be excluded.

Important teaching books of the past, going back as far as two centuries and more, can well illustrate the imaginative and uninhibited manner in which the student's needs for a well rounded, up-to-date repertory were met. For instance, the *Little Notebook for Anna Magdalena Bach*, which dates from 1725, contains, in addition to Bach's two partitas, many light, melodic keyboard dances by unknown writers and also numerous vocal pieces of both religious and secular nature. One of these, in the latter category, praises the pleasures of pipe-smoking.

An even better example is the delightful and meticulously organized *Little Music Book* Leopold Mozart gave his son, Wolfgang, on the boy's seventh birthday (1763). There are more than one hundred pieces in this collection, grouped into twenty-five suites. A great variety of selections here—dances, songs, and character pieces—are all in a light, popular vein, in the so-called gallant style. Telemann is represented by numerous little dances, but most of the other selections are either anonymous or were written by composers who are all but forgotten today. One of these obscure writers merits special attention within the context of this discourse. He is Sperontes, pseudonym for J.S. Scholze, a gifted and enterprising German musician who collected about one hundred popular keyboard pieces of his time, commissioned a poet (what we would call a lyricist) to set words to them, and published the result in two volumes of Odes. These collections became phenomenally popular, inspiring many imitators throughout the eighteenth century. There are numerous vocal selections, written in the manner of Sperontes, in the Mozart *Notebook*. The collection is strictly "contemporary"; none of the pieces included was more than thirty years old at the time of compilation. It is also interesting to note that the period's almost insatiable demand for minuets was well catered to by the inclusion of thirty-two such dance pieces. We can easily guess the motive for this: Leopold Mozart, an erudite musician and educator, knew that Wolfgang was not only a prodigy and a genius, but also a normal seven-year-old student, whose attention and interest had to be held and stimulated with astutely assembled popular teaching pieces; hence the dozens of minuets and the overall light vein of the collection.

THE CLASSICS' USE OF POPULAR THEMES

There was another route by which the popular melodies of the eighteenth and nineteenth centuries found their way into the literature of piano study: the variation form. Nearly all keyboard composers of those periods, including the great masters, utilized popular tunes, arias, and little dance pieces as themes of such works. It is true that the real value of these variations lies in the craft and ingenuity with which simple ditties are transformed into larger, many-faceted, often imposing musical structures. The fact remains, however, that the source of inspiration was a popular melody, which was chosen by the composer not only because it contained the germ of possible development into a larger form, but also because it was popular; the people wanted to play it and to hear it. It almost automatically held a promise of wide appeal for the entire work.

The great pedagogues of the past, beginning with Clementi, Hummel, Dussek, Czerny and continuing with a long succession of important nineteenth-century teacher-composers, made frequent use of musical materials with wide popular appeal. Their piano methods and teaching books contain a profusion of study pieces based on folk songs, operatic themes, and other popular melodies of varied description. All this is not meant to imply that such selections had unquestioned musical value or pedagogic validity in every instance, but only to point out that these notable musicians and teachers had no esthetic qualms about arranging, transcribing, or paraphrasing popular melodies of their time whenever they felt that these themes could be put to good didactic use.

"SALON" REPERTORY

The purists of today are inclined to view this with a condescending smile and ascribe it to a naive aberration of taste, which, they feel, left its stamp on a considerable body of nineteenth-century piano music of the so-called "salon" variety. There was, to be sure, a prodigious amount of music written for the pianist of those days, and for a good reason. The piano in the parlor being the only medium of home entertainment (there was no radio, television, or phonograph a hundred years ago), the demand for all kinds of piano music was great and unceasing. Inevitably the quality of the output was uneven, a good portion of it mediocre or worse. However, it should be remembered that this vast repertory of piano music contained—had to contain—everything the musical public wanted to hear and play. In the absence of mechanical or electronic reproduction media, most musical enjoyment and entertainment originated through live performance at the piano. As a result, nearly all music, weighty and light, was available in keyboard versions. Solo or duet arrangements of symphonies, string quartets, orchestral overtures, and operatic excerpts, intermingled with a prodigious conglomeration of piano solos from Chopin, Mendelssohn, and Schumann to "The Maiden's Prayer," "The Dying Poet," and "The Ben-Hur Chariot Race," were staple items of the Victorian piano bench. Under these circumstances the piano student's craving for light popular fare was not too difficult to satisfy. Clearly, the piano teacher did not run a great risk of being censured by assigning a student a "Home Sweet Home," *La Donna è Mobile*, or "Oh! Susannah" if these strains could often be heard in august concert halls—if in more pretentious versions—played by the great virtuosos of the day.

"SERIOUS" VS. "POPULAR"

This cozy nineteenth-century coexistence of serious and popular music in the study repertory was not too long-lived. In a few decades, certainly by the 1920s, the dichotomy of the two categories became increasingly more pronounced, and the concommitant problems for the teacher more acute. The reasons for this were numerous: the advent of phonograph, radio, and later, television, made the piano in the parlor nearly obsolete as the focal point of family entertainment. The pushing of a button or turn of a knob instantly produced music. Through these media, songs could become popular overnight, fizzle out in a few months and be replaced constantly by new ones. The life cycle of popular music became accelerated, in sharp contrast to the solid durability of the classical repertory.

Other important shifts took place within music and pedagogy itself: changing attitudes toward musical styles and idioms, including an especially critical stance toward the peripheral output of the romantic era; increased emphasis on stylistic authenticity in performance and editions and a trend, continuing to the present, to teach only from the original text (*Urtext*) and to limit the course of study to pieces written expressly for the piano. From this evolved a curriculum of sturdier musical content, but also one which, we are beginning to realize, had tendencies to become overly restrictive and pedantic. Teaching pieces based on familiar themes became questionable not only because they were popular music, but also because they were "arrangements," not originally written for the keyboard.

It would take more space than is available here to list all the sound arguments as to why arrangements, per se, should not, and indeed, cannot, be entirely excluded from the repertory, especially during the early years of instruction. Suffice it to say that a rigid attitude of banning all keyboard adaptations is not only lacking in valid esthetic and pedagogic justifications, but also would deprive the student of many valuable, appealing, and useful teaching pieces at a time (in the early grades) when the original keyboard literature does not offer an adequate variety and certainly not an abundance of materials. (see "Arrangements: To Teach or Not To Teach Them," p. 587)

POPULAR MUSIC AS STUDY MATERIAL

To what extent and in what manner may popular music arranged for piano serve the purposes of study? Many important considerations should be kept in mind. First, we must realize that popular and dance music is much more youth-oriented today than it ever was in the past. Until the years following World War I, young people in their late teens and twenties were the pacesetters and taste-makers. In the 1930s, the midteen "bobbysoxers" were the dominant group to be catered to, and two or three decades later the screaming fans surrounding Elvis Presley and the Beatles were to a large extent even younger. This gradual lowering of the age bracket has had a substantial influence on the style and character of popular music.

In the past it was the melody—easy to grasp, ingratiating—that was the essential element. Today, especially in rock and roll, a strong, steady, visceral beat is the dominant factor and a melody, more often than not, is only a utilitarian chant through which the message of the lyrics is communicated. These lyrics, incidentally, now often go beyond the customary variations on the "I love you" theme: they express many other adolescent sentiments, aspirations, social comments, and a rebellious impatience with the growing-up process. In other words, the pop tunes of today are not only musical entertainment, but also a social phenomenon, which makes the task of integrating them into the piano student's course of study a difficult and delicate one.

Another purely musical problem is that rock and roll, by and large, is not pianistic. Its essence and main attraction, that infectious rhythmic vitality, is best conveyed by various instrumental groups (guitar, bass, brass, synthesizer, etc.) but is all but lost, or at least considerably paled, in a solo keyboard version. Numerous other popular idioms are eminently pianistic: ragtime and boogie are *par excellence* piano music, and folk songs naturally lend themselves to a well-sounding pianistic treatment even on the earliest grade levels. These categories offer a potentially large reservoir of materials, which, with a properly constructive and sympathetic attitude on the teacher's part, may go a long way toward satisfying the student's thirst for up-to-date music. In addition, there is an ever-increasing literature of attractive, pedagogically sound contemporary pieces written in popular styles specifically for study purposes.

All this will help but cannot solve all the problems. The world of popular music is in a constant state of flux, with trends, fashions, and styles appearing and disappearing, with new melodies reaching the top of the popularity charts and others fading away in rapid succession. It can be anticipated that a good portion of the student body will always be fascinated by this steady parade of hits and will express a desire to play and to learn whatever is the newest and latest.

TEACHERS' ATTITUDES

Reactions to such requests should be guided by the student's age, ability, and background; inevitably, the teacher's taste, preferences, and pedagogic principles will also play a decisive role. On one end of the spectrum we have the teacher who refuses to have anything to do with the "popular stuff" and will say, in effect, "I have a good method, an interesting curriculum, and the student who wants to play something else can find another teacher." A highly principled attitude, perhaps, but also, I believe, a narrow, dogmatic one which may scare off a potentially good student, without an effort having been made to guide him or her on to broader musical understanding. The other extreme is the teacher who, to prevent a possible dropout or, for a variety of other reasons, uncritically yields to all requests, thereby diluting the repertory with an assortment of inferior and useless popular items.

Between these two widely divergent attitudes are numerous middle-ground stands. One involves occasionally yielding to the student's request to add a pop tune or two to the regular study materials, mainly to appease, perhaps to help the student over a certain adolescent phase, in the hope that the student eventually will come through this stage of rag, boogie, and rock and return to the fold, to the study of classics, to "good" music. Some teachers will include popular music only after the study and practice of other materials. Still another widely held view is that popular songs should not be assigned as part of the lesson, but a student who wants to play them should be encouraged to do so independently, as a kind of off-the-record social activity. Playing these tunes by ear and improvising on them may also be approved, but only on the student's own time and not under a structured teaching plan.

These approaches, while displaying a degree of understanding and flexibility in handling the problem, also share an unmistakably aloof, negative stance toward popular music. It is placed in a distinct, separate category, apart from the "regular" teaching fare, and marked, at least by implication, as something automatically inferior and lacking in educational substance. A growing number of educators feel, as does this writer, that a more constructive plan is desirable and possible, without sacrificing sound musical and teaching principles.

It is of primary importance that a teacher not be entirely isolated from the popular music scene. An open mind and an inquisitive ear are recommended if one is to be aware of what is going on along the Tin Pan Alley marketplace. Periodic surveys can be made to ascertain what, if any, items show enough quality, or at least enough redeeming features, for inclusion in the regular repertory. True, a large portion of the pop field is a musical wasteland, but a sufficiently patient and sympathetic scrutiny will often reveal gratifying melodic and harmonic surprises. Songs, pieces of sufficient interest which will not degrade the study course and will please the student, can serve a useful teaching purpose: promote technique, make the study of theory (harmony, form) more palatable, and inspire creativity through improvisation, arranging and composition.

In general terms, the most important factor is the teacher's attitude; he or she should be alert as to the availability of suitable melodies and pieces, and inventive enough to adopt such materials, if necessary, to the individual student's needs, so that the pieces correspond to the grade level of other lesson assignments. It is imperative that the playing of such popular pieces not mean the abandonment of the sound principles of technique; the correct position of hands, fingers, wrist, and arm applies here too, and any relaxation of these standards may lead to sloppy and harmful playing habits.

ADAPTATIONS FOR STUDY

If the regular piano-vocal edition of a song is not the right version for a student, as often happens, the desired changes may be marked on the copy by the teacher. Should substantial alterations seem necessary, a new, neatly notated copy can be prepared. (All popular songs, with the exception of genuine folk tunes, are protected by copyright; multiplication and sale are prohibited by law.) Songs on the top of popularity charts are often available in simplified versions, and these too can be modified to suit specific needs. Gradually, with the proper direction, the student should be able to make these changes and prepare the copies. On the earliest grade levels a melody may be divided between the hands, with an occasional harmonic interval providing accompaniment in the left hand; or the teacher may want to participate by playing a few supportive notes in the bass. Some tunes lend themselves to being played on all-black keys ("Amazing Grace" and "Old Mac Donald," for instance) and can then be shifted a half step higher to practice transposition.

Some songs, especially the folk-based ones, may often be harmonized just by the tonic, subdominant, and dominant chords ("Love Somebody," "Michael, Row the Boat Ashore," "When the Saints Come Marching In," and others):

I IV V7 I

The same chords in proper sequence will also furnish the harmonic underpinning for the classic twelve-bar blues pattern. (See "Jazz and the Piano Teacher," p. 563)

These chord sequences should always be practiced in various keys, with constant encouragement for playing by ear and improvisation. In songs presenting a more extended harmonic vocabulary, chords may be similarly simplified so they lie easily under the hands, without wide jumps and constant lateral motion. The harmonic functions and chord names should at all times be clear to the pupil.

TEACHING THEORY AND TECHNIQUE

Since the texture of popular music is predominantly homophonic (melody with accompaniment), it is eminently suitable for the study of harmony, or more specifically, for developing familiarity with chord functions and sequences through keyboard experience. This can equip the student for preparing arrangements; that is, for providing melodies with fitting harmonies in suitable patterns of pianistic accompaniment. In this area, as in the field of ear training and improvisation, popular music offers built-in educational opportunities. The classical or "serious" repertory must be performed always as written, without deviation from the printed note picture. No such restriction inhibits the playing of popular songs; on the contrary, a good tune, whether played from notes or by ear, can be the springboard for the player's creative manipulations: improvisation, variation, arranging, all of which should be encouraged by the teacher.

The basic form elements of music, especially the phrase, can be well illustrated with popular songs, because of their melodic simplicity. Analysis of their phrasing patterns can further lead to the understanding of binary and ternary forms, which are indeed the most common frameworks in which popular songs are written.

A dance tune usually must be played in strict time and with rhythmic precision. These are disciplines which, once learned, can serve the student in the performance of the entire repertory. On the other hand, the typical romantic rubato, a freely flowing melody in the treble, against the regular beat of the bass, is also the heart of a nice, soulful blues improvisation.

The various aspects of technique and formulas of execution embodied in the teaching literature of the eighteenth and nineteenth centuries also apply to the performance of popular music. Cantabile touch is the right one to project the melody of a love theme or ballad; forearm rotation and relaxed wrist action are necessary to play the steadily moving, fluent bass patterns of boogie and blues; solid chords, repeated and broken chords—usually in triplets—provide the harmonic and rhythmic support of rock music; firm finger action will achieve rhythmic precision; the conventional ragtime accompaniment, octave basses leaping to middle-range chords, can make a fine placement study; and good jazz playing requires technical competence in all its phases and aspects.

"I often include popular music in the lessons, but I have no specific, separate formula for teaching it: I don't treat it as something different," a respected teacher wrote to me recently. This statement goes to the heart of the matter. Properly selected favorite songs of the day, with a little interest and imagination on the teacher's part, can be integrated into the standard teaching repertory and may well serve specific teaching needs. The key element in this endeavor is the teacher's attitude, the way he or she views, evaluates, selects, and utilizes this material. To that end the following suggestions might be considered:

- Listen to, rather than ignore, the teenager's music.
- Make the student aware that you are interested in his world of entertainment; establish a warm rapport in discussing frankly, openly, and on a mature level, new songs, new recordings, new trends; whether you agree or disagree, you will gain esteem and affection.
- Evaluate and select teaching pieces with an open mind; discard the inhibiting notion that music is divided into two distinct, separate categories: serious and popular. Judge all music as being good, bad, or mediocre, regardless of whether it is played in a concert hall or on the hit parade. Have an understanding of all idioms and a love for all kinds of good music, from baroque to jazz and rock.
- Through a continuing process of discussing and analyzing popular music, guide the student, gently and systematically, toward more discriminating levels of musical perception and taste. With this attitude, music educators ultimately may even influence and improve the quality of songs mass-produced to please the adolescent generation.

RECOMMENDED SELECTIONS

See also "Jazz and the Piano Teacher," p. 563)

Broadway Classics, vols. A-B-C, arr. Agay (Warner).
Broadway Classics as Duets, vols. A-B-C, arr. Agay (Warner).
Broadway Showcase of Famous Melodies, vols. A-B-C, arr. Agay (Warner).
Lots of Pops–and Technic Too, 3 vols., Glover, (Belwin).
Something Light, 3 vols., Olson (Carl Fischer).
Sixty-two Easy Popular Piano Pieces, arr. Brimhall (Hansen).
Popular Choice: 53 Pieces, (MCA).
Sounds of Today, 3 vols., (Warner).
Hundred Giant Hits, arr. Lane (Big 3).
The Wonderful World of Richard Rodgers arr. Glover (Chappell).
Guidelines to Improvisation–Quick Steps to Pop Piano 3 vols., Kahn (Warner).

Arrangements: To Teach or Not to Teach Them

DENES AGAY

The piano teacher can hardly avoid being confronted with this problem, for which, it may be stated at the outset, there is no simple, unequivocal answer. There certainly is no dearth of views and utterances, pro and con, on the subject, some of them valid, others too opinionated and biased. On the one hand our age of authenticity, with its insistence on textural and interpretative purity, either outrightly condemns the didactic use of arrangements, or views it with utmost suspicion. Opposing this stance are those who, in the name of practical considerations and plain musical common sense, urge a more relaxed and tolerant attitude. How should a teacher decide? What should be the guiding principles?

Perhaps it is best first to clarify the terms involved. *Arrangement* is usually defined as an adaptation of a piece of music for a medium other than the one for which it was originally written, without any alterations in its musical substance (a piano arrangement of a vocal or string composition, for instance). *Transcription* is considered by most as synonymous with arrangement, with perhaps just a hint of more adaptive leeway. A *paraphrase* is a free adaptation of a piece, usually for a solo instrument, in which the musical ideas of the original serve as a springboard for the adapter's inventive manipulations and elaborations, and as such is quite close to the *variation* form. (Liszt's paraphrases of operatic arias, for instance).

The dichotomy between *arrangement* and *original composition* as two distinct categories of music was not always as pronounced as it is today. We tend to forget or overlook the long and venerable history of arrangements and arrangers, beginning with the profusion of anonymous lute adaptations of vocal pieces in the sixteenth century and continuing with Bach, Mozart, Beethoven, Brahms, Liszt, and an illustrious succession of other masters who frequently, and without esthetic qualms, arranged, rearranged, transcribed, and paraphrased their own and other composers' themes and pieces. Obviously, the reorganization or translation of certain musical ideas into new media did satisfy their artistic credo, regardless of whether the basic material they adapted was of their own or someone else's invention.

When and for what reasons did these attitudes change? Why did arranging, for centuries a respected creative activity, become an esthetically suspect act of musical rethinking? The proliferation of clumsy, inept, and tasteless adaptations certainly contributed to the change of climate, but by far the strongest factor has been the prevailing and often obsessive present-day concern for authenticity in texts and performing manners. A violin piece arranged for piano, or vice versa, becomes automatically condemned on the grounds that it distorts the composer's original intentions, the well-known arranging practices of Bach, Mozart, et al. notwithstanding.

A few years ago, in an article written for the *Musical Times* of London, Hans Keller, noted British critic, diagnosed quite admirably the reasons for this stiff antiarrangement attitude: "We do indeed show an overriding need for authenticity, so much, so unthinkingly so that it looks a little like a collective compulsion, an obsessional neurosis. I recently played some old records of Bronislav Huberman to a composer friend, an ex-violinist whom I knew to be interested in unconventional, unstreamlined interpretations. He was delighted as long as he heard original violin pieces. But when I proposed to play him one of Huberman's Chopin arrangements (in which, to my mind, he shows more understanding of Chopin's structures than many a Chopin specialist at the keyboard), he was horrified. . . . He was unwilling to give Huberman the benefit of that minimum of *a priori* confidence which is a great artist's due. . . . Strictly speaking, our authenticity cult is really a midcentury affair: even in the late '30s when Huberman might play these Chopin arrangements as encores, nobody, even musicologists, noticed anything amiss. It is, I think, the progressive artistic insecurity of our age that has gradually turned our search for authenticity into a compulsion: the less you know instinctively what's good, both in creation and in interpretation, the more frantically you depend on extraneous, historical, scientific evidence."

THE IMPORTANCE OF UNBIASED JUDGMENT

The above analysis is sound and clear, and worth remembering. We can resist extraneous pedantic pressures and can avoid being influenced by rigid, preconceived attitudes only if we are able and confident to judge on our own what is good and what is inferior in music, regardless of the music's origin. The question of whether or not, or to what extent, arranged materials should be used can then be decided the way it should be: with an open mind, guided by taste and the student's individual needs.

What the student needs is a teaching repertory of quality and variety. Unquestionably, original pieces by masters of all periods must form the core of such repertory; and the more advanced the student becomes, the more restricted he or she should be to the original keyboard repertory. This, however, does not mean that arrangements, especially during the early years of instruction, should, or indeed can, be entirely excluded. The literature of elementary, original keyboard pieces is rather sparse and the use of adaptations during the first year or two of instruction is nearly inevitable. But even on the intermediate levels, the total exclusion of arrangements could hardly be justified by any sound esthetic or pedagogic standards. Such an inflexible attitude would deprive the student of numerous categories of attractive, enjoyable, and useful pieces at a time—during the early years of study—when the original keyboard literature does not furnish an abundance of materials.

An intelligently maintained middle-road attitude seems to be the soundest approach to this problem. Both extremes should be avoided. It is wrong to dilute and degrade the student's repertory with indiscriminately selected, inferior arrangements, but equally wrong is a stiff, unyielding exclusion of all adaptations.

At a national convention of piano teachers a couple of years ago, I was expounding my views on these matters at a seminar, and was challenged with a strong dissenting opinion by one teacher in the audience. "I teach only original piano music," she declared; "there is plenty of it and I would not touch an arrangement with a ten-foot pole." To prove her point she immediately produced a handsome printed program of her last student recital. Even a cursory examination of this program yielded some interesting clues to the basic weakness and vulnerability of such an unyielding doctrine. To begin with, there were at least three items on the program, which, strictly speaking, could not be classified as original piano music: a German dance by Haydn, often anthologized, which is a piano version of a minuet movement from one of his symphonies; a rondo from one of Mozart's Viennese Sonatinas, which the master originally wrote for three wind instruments, and a contradanse in E-flat by Beethoven, originally conceived for orchestra and later also used in a more elaborate piano version as part of an extended variation. I pointed out these facts to the teacher, but had no opportunity to pursue the matter further. It would have been most interesting to find out whether or not the revelation about the original status of these works caused their banishment from her repertory. More important, the same program contained numerous pieces of notorious mediocrity, which proved conclusively that the lofty banner of "original piano music only" was just a convenient camouflage for questionable taste and insecurity of judgment. One can draw an obvious conclusion from this episode. The fact that a piece was originally composed for the keyboard does by no means guarantee its quality and didactic usefulness. Similarly, however, the concept of "arrangement" should not get an automatic imprimatur unless and until it has been examined, to quote Hans Keller again, to ascertain "what has been arranged, what the purpose of the re-creative act is, and how the job has been done."

WHAT, WHY AND HOW TO ARRANGE

Let us deal with these criteria one by one. What type of music, adapted for the piano, merits inclusion in the student's repertory? Generally speaking, any kind of appealing material–vocal or instrumental, old or new–which has some inherent musical quality. If someone finds *musical quality* hard to define, perhaps we can construe the requirement simply as music which has something pleasing and interesting to say; music which conveys its composer's inventiveness and skill. In any case, it should be of the type, in style and texture, which lends itself to a well-sounding pianistic treatment in the adapter's chosen grade level, from the earliest to the most advanced. The wonderful world of folk music admirably meets these requirements on all counts, but there is a profusion of suitable materials in other areas too: music written for the voice, for other instruments, for orchestra, the theater, and carefully chosen items from the constantly changing catalog of popular music. There is one category of arrangements which should be approached with extra scrutiny: the simplified versions of works originally written for the piano. It does not make much sense, pedagogically or otherwise, to assign to the student a simplified arrangement of a piece which, in the not too distant future, he or she may be able to play as originally written. On the other hand, if an unpromising, early-grade student expresses an irresistible urge to play Chopin's "Military Polonaise" or Liszt's *Liebestraum*, (to mention only two typical examples of very popular but technically very demanding works), which most likely will never be accessible to him in the original, the teacher may decide in favor of letting him play a competent adaptation. Each case should be decided according to its specific circumstances: the work in question; the student's grade, caliber, and overall potential; and numerous other possible considerations of personality and background.

The purpose of arranging music for piano is, or should be, to infuse variety and diversity into the teaching repertory, especially on the early grade levels, and to give the student an opportunity to reproduce on the piano frequently heard music to which he is attracted. In brief, the role of arrangements is to supplement the repertory of original keyboard music, not to replace it.

After examining the criteria of what is proper and suitable material for piano adaptations, and what the purpose of such arrangements should be, there remains the most important aspect of scrutiny: the evaluation of the arrangement itself, the critical appraisal of how the job of adaptation has been done. Here a piano teacher cannot compromise, but must apply the highest standards. Only a good arrangement is acceptable, regardless of the merit of the underlying musical idea.

An arrangement is good if in a pianistic setting it preserves and possibly enhances the musical substance of the original. The mood and character must remain intact. Melody, basic harmonic functions, and rhythmic patterns should not be altered, but rather "translated" to the language of the piano, with only the smallest, musically negligible changes, made inevitable by the anatomy of the hands and the topography of the keyboard. At its best, the arrangement should reflect not only the adapter's high professional competence, taste, and pianistic instincts, but also a creative involvement and gift of invention. With all these attributes present, an arrangement can approach, indeed attain, the status of an original creation. Bartók's piano adaptations of Hungarian, Slovakian, and Rumanian folk tunes are outstanding examples in this category. Of course, we cannot expect or insist on such creative excellence in every instance, but we can regard these miniatures as ideal models to guide our standards of judgment. (See "The Piano Teacher and Popular Music," p. 577).

CHART OF FREQUENTLY-USED CHORDS

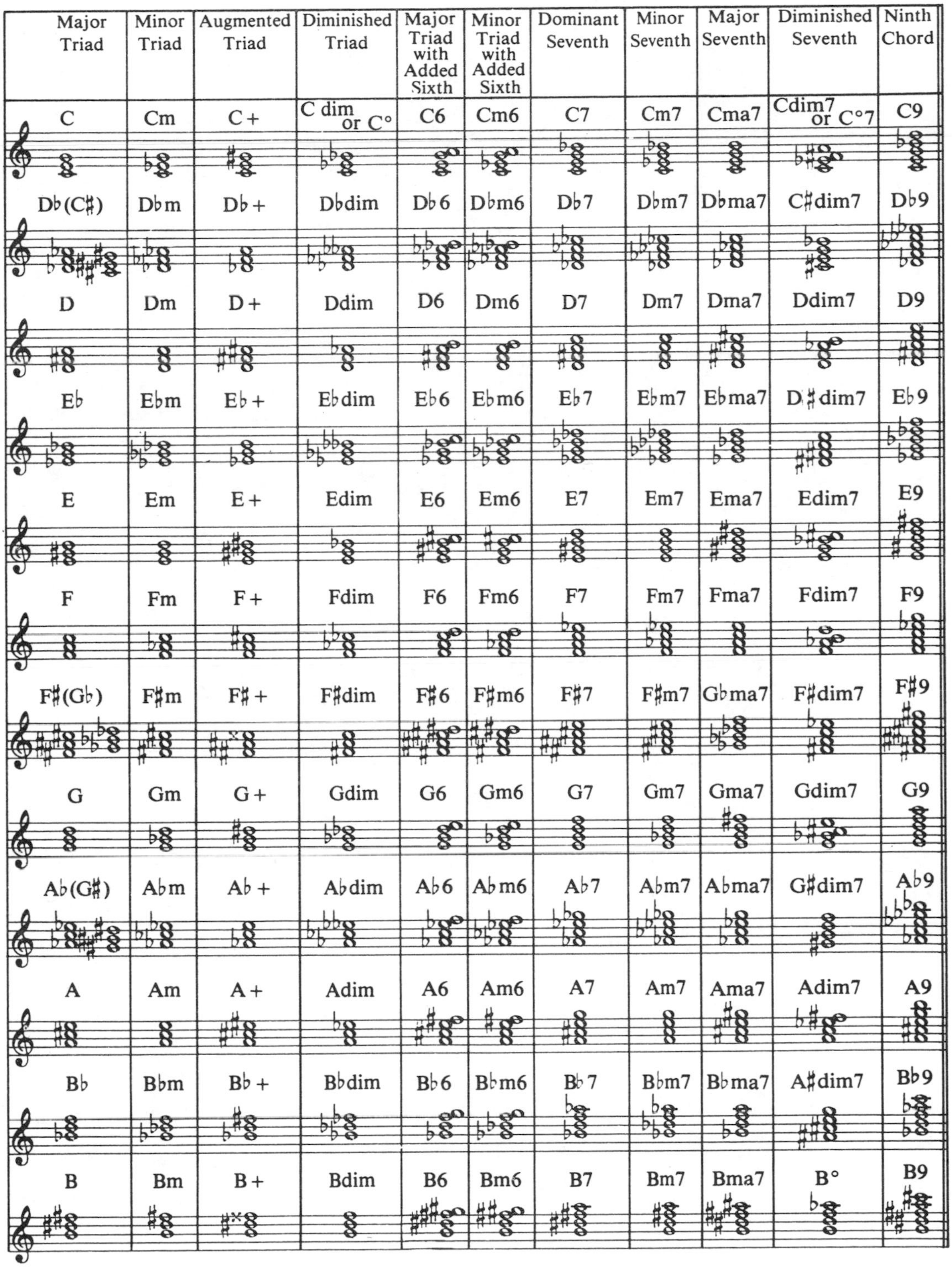

Major Triad	Minor Triad	Augmented Triad	Diminished Triad	Major Triad with Added Sixth	Minor Triad with Added Sixth	Dominant Seventh	Minor Seventh	Major Seventh	Diminished Seventh	Ninth Chord
C	Cm	C+	C dim or C°	C6	Cm6	C7	Cm7	Cma7	Cdim7 or C°7	C9
D♭(C♯)	D♭m	D♭+	D♭dim	D♭6	D♭m6	D♭7	D♭m7	D♭ma7	C♯dim7	D♭9
D	Dm	D+	Ddim	D6	Dm6	D7	Dm7	Dma7	Ddim7	D9
E♭	E♭m	E♭+	E♭dim	E♭6	E♭m6	E♭7	E♭m7	E♭ma7	D♯dim7	E♭9
E	Em	E+	Edim	E6	Em6	E7	Em7	Ema7	Edim7	E9
F	Fm	F+	Fdim	F6	Fm6	F7	Fm7	Fma7	Fdim7	F9
F♯(G♭)	F♯m	F♯+	F♯dim	F♯6	F♯m6	F♯7	F♯m7	G♭ma7	F♯dim7	F♯9
G	Gm	G+	Gdim	G6	Gm6	G7	Gm7	Gma7	Gdim7	G9
A♭(G♯)	A♭m	A♭+	A♭dim	A♭6	A♭m6	A♭7	A♭m7	A♭ma7	G♯dim7	A♭9
A	Am	A+	Adim	A6	Am6	A7	Am7	Ama7	Adim7	A9
B♭	B♭m	B♭+	B♭dim	B♭6	B♭m6	B♭7	B♭m7	B♭ma7	A♯dim7	B♭9
B	Bm	B+	Bdim	B6	Bm6	B7	Bm7	Bma7	B°	B9

SIX

ASPECTS OF PEDAGOGY

The Training of the Piano Teacher

HAZEL GHAZARIAN SKAGGS

In general, the training of a teacher should provide a thorough knowledge of music, competence as a pianist, and the skills and personality necessary for teaching.

COURSES OF STUDY

A survey of catalogs shows that colleges, including universities and music schools, attempt to fulfill the above criteria through three or four categories:

- Performance
  - Applied music (private piano study, generally two half-hour lessons a week)
  - Recital class
  - Recital in the senior year
  - The requirement of such courses as sight reading, ensemble, or piano accompaniment
  - Public performance in ensemble groups may also be required
- General Musicianship
  - Sight singing
  - Ear training
  - Harmony
  - Keyboard harmony
  - Counterpoint
  - Theory—form and analysis
  - Composition

History of music
Literature of the piano

- General Education
  English
  Humanities
  Physical, biological, social, and behavioral sciences (psychology)
  Language
- Pedagogy (not available at all colleges)
  Pedagogy—generally from two to four credits during the entire four-year program—includes methods of piano teaching with a survey of materials, possibly teaching demonstrations, and in some instances the opportunity to teach a few students every week.
  Psychology courses, such as general psychology, child development, and adolescent psychology may be considered here as well as under general education.

Upon completion of a four-year program with course work from all three categories, and possibly two to four required credits in pedagogy, one qualifies for the bachelor of music degree. Advanced degrees concentrate on such specialized fields as education, performance, and composition.

If the undergraduate program offers no pedagogy courses, it is advisable to enroll in one of the many summer workshops offered to teachers. Many of these provide college credit and may be of additional value even if one's college does have a good pedagogy program.

SELECTING A SCHOOL

In selecting a college or conservatory, the chief concern should be the study program offered and the caliber of teachers on the faculty. The schools' catalogs provide the most pertinent information. Some schools, particularly universities, demand more academic studies than others. A diploma program, on the other hand, will include the least number of liberal arts courses.

If the student plans to live away from home, he or she should make sure there will be adequate practicing facilities; financial aid and placement opportunities may also be important considerations, and a visit to the school's campus ought to be included in the final decision-making.

MUSIC COLLEGE ADMISSION REQUIREMENTS

The student applying for admission into a music degree program must not only be a high school graduate but must also show sufficient talent and promise in his or her chosen area of study; in some instances the student may be accepted on a tentative basis. Those students majoring in piano usually must pass a proficiency test similar to the following example, to be performed from memory:

- All major and minor scales and arpeggios
- A composition by Bach, possibly as easy as a two-part invention or as difficult as a prelude and fugue from the *Well-Tempered Clavier*
- A difficult sonata (or sonata movement) by Haydn, Mozart, or Beethoven
- A nineteenth-century composition and/or a twentieth-century one

CHOOSING PRIVATE OR COLLEGE STUDY

Some students may prefer to study privately rather than enroll at a school; the advantage is that the student can select his or her own teachers, own time, and own pace of advancement. Furthermore, practicing will not be jeopardized by a rigid schedule of classes and examinations.

No specific training is mandatory for the private piano teacher, as opposed to preparing for a career in school music education. If several busy, successful teachers in the same area were interviewed, it would certainly develop that all had vastly different backgrounds. One teacher might have been trained privately; another partly privately but including courses at a conservatory; another may have a diploma from a first-rate music school plus advanced private study; and another may have earned both a bachelor's and a master's degree in music. With such diversity of background among successful teachers, the young pianist may find it difficult to decide how to prepare for his career as teacher. However, since a college degree has become essential in qualifying for many career positions today, it is probably advisable to choose accredited college training rather than private study. Perhaps a combination of the two—four years in college, followed by several years of private study—may provide the best of two possible worlds. The three-year diploma course offered by some conservatories may also allow more freedom in practicing and curriculum choice.

The pianist who wants to teach on a school faculty, however, no longer has the freedom to study only privately. He *must* go to college, for a bachelor's degree is required, and eventually a master's and a doctorate are usually expected. On a school faculty one of his commitments may well be to perform periodically for the faculty and student body on campus, so his or her training as a performing pianist will have to be rigorous and complete. (This does not mean that a private teacher need not or does not have equally superior qualifications as a pianist.)

CONTINUING STUDIES

For the established teacher continuing his studies either to maintain or improve skills, there are many options. More and more colleges and master teachers are offering pedagogy workshops during the summer vacation. *Clavier* magazine (1418 Lake Street, Evanston, Illinois 60204) publishes an annual directory of summer workshops in its March issue, followed by a supplement in a later issue. These workshops may be on such topics as pedagogy and materials, group piano, class piano, group teaching for the very young, or principles of the Maier technique. They may last only a few days or several weeks. The teacher may select one for both study and relaxation on a campus where one can also have comfortable living accommodations.

Those teachers who continue practicing and performing often arrange for private study with a master teacher on a semimonthly or even less frequent basis. Some teachers continue to work toward advanced degrees. Others rely solely on teachers' magazines, conventions, and meeting programs for new materials, methods, and ideas.

PERSONAL QUALIFICATIONS

In addition to having the necessary credentials to teach, it is important that teachers cultivate desirable personality traits and conduct their business in a stable and ethical way. Whether or not piano teachers must be concert pianists as well as teachers is a matter of personal preference. Average full-time teachers with a myriad of adult responsibilities are unlikely to have the time and energy for their own practicing. Essentially, they need not necessarily be up to concert performance, but they should be able to sight-read well enough to hold the respect of their students.

SCHOOL CATALOGS

The following school catalogs were used in the preparation of this section:

(1) Brandon University, Brandon, Manitoba, Canada 1976–1977
(2) Elizabethtown College, Elizabethtown, Pennsylvania 17022, 1973–1975
(3) Fredonia State University College, Fredonia, New York 14063, 1975–1977
(4) Indiana University, Bloomington, Indiana 47401, 1976–1977
(5) Kansas State University, Manhattan, Kansas 66506, 1976
(6) Madison University, Harrisonburg, Virginia 22801, 1976–1977
(7) Manhattan School of Music, New York, New York 10027, 1976
(8) Peabody Conservatory of Music, Baltimore, Maryland 21202, 1976–1977
(9) Sherwood Music School, Chicago, Illinois 60605, 1975–1977
(10) Stanford University, Stanford, California 94305, 1975–1976

RECOMMENDED READING

Egbert, Marion S. *Career Opportunities in Music*. Chicago: American Music Conference, 1966.

Laster, Harold M. "You Too Should be an Admission Counselor." *The American Music Teacher* May–June 1978.

Ward, John Owen. *Careers in Music*. New York: H.Z. Walck, 1968.

Four-Way Piano Teaching: Criticism, Demonstration, Analysis, Inspiration

WALTER ROBERT

CRITICISM

The usual piano lesson consists of a more or less finished performance of a prepared piece "executed" by the pupil, and by more or less detailed criticism of the performance by the teacher. This may range from a vague (I call it low-frequency) comment, "Very nice, but practice it some more, it could be still better," to the ultrasensory "Already too loud!" pronounced by the hypersensitive maestro right after, if not before, the first chord is struck by the student.

Very often, the student's performance is a fractured rendition, punctuated by the student with pithy remarks such as "oops" and "wait" and concluded, not with a bang, but with the whimper, "At home I played it perfect." If the teacher allows these lecture recitals and spoken program notes to become established performance practices, the pupil may never be able to perform without stoppages.

Frequently, however, it is not the student who stops the piece midway, but the teacher who breaks in with a criticism. I do not mean to say that the teacher must listen in mute suffering until the last blow has been struck against the composer, but that he or she should not interrupt a student every other measure to make corrections. If the first few measures show that a working session is in order, then phrases, harmonies, and even notes should be scrutinized thoroughly. On the other hand, if the performance is reasonably adequate, then I believe the

Reprinted from *Clavier*, January 1971. Used by permission of the Instrumentalist Company.

teacher should listen and make specific recommendations later.

While the student should be told both the good and the bad features of the lesson, the teacher should not indulge in generalities such as "pretty good, but still a little rough in places." Remarks like "It does not have enough profile," "Your playing lacks depth," "It should sound more brilliant" do not help the student, unless the teacher also makes it clear that the *siciliano* rhythm that did not have "profile" was played not, as it should be, like "Amsterdam, Rotterdam," but more like "Liverpool, Manchester," that "depth" requires arm weight, emphasis on the bass, and richer pedal, while brilliance cannot be achieved with the pulse-feeling in $\frac{4}{4}$ instead of $\frac{2}{4}$.

General criticism might be noted by the teacher in writing, at the head of the composition, in addition to the oral discussion. For detailed criticism, a system of symbols understood by the student is the neatest and clearest method for marking up a page of music. The marks should be carefully written and placed, not scrawled across a page. Circle the wrong note or notes; indicate pedals by one of the prevailing methods; use breath marks or carefully drawn slurs for phrasing. Abbreviations can be used: *Rh* for rhythm, *T* for technique, *fing.* for fingering, *art.* for articulation, ∽ for *rubato*, ⟶ for *accelerando*, ⟵ for *ritardando*, and others you and your students agree upon. An *X* at the area in question and the proper symbol or abbreviation placed in the margin makes the exact meaning clear.

The teacher must bear in mind that sooner or later it is time to stop criticizing. There are almost always psychological reasons and other considerations that force the teacher to be satisfied, at least temporarily, with the plateau that the student has reached at a given point.

Teaching by criticism was developed almost to a ritual by the violin pedagogue Carl Flesch. His students played from an unmarked copy while he sat at a distance and marked up a second copy. This copy was used for detailed discussion with musical illustrations. The markings were erased for the next lesson.

A successful teacher of my acquaintance writes her criticisms into the student's notebook while the pupil plays. This saves time and gives the student a ready reference manual for the week's practice. It is a sure stopper for "You did not tell me this" or "Last time you said. . . ." It also is a great help to the parent.

Another useful tool is the tape recorder. I use it to record my criticisms, illustrations, and the student's attempts at imitation. Occasionally I will put the entire lesson on tape although usually I do not turn the machine on until after the initial play-through. The student marks up the score while listening to the tape at home.

A student's progress can be measured through periodic tapings of lessons, and I sometimes keep these tapes for my own records, but I do not allow the student to retain the tape longer than a few days.

DEMONSTRATION

Teaching by example probably is the approach with the longest tradition. According to available sources, the *bel canto* singing teachers of the eighteenth century taught exclusively by demonstration, and much of the piano teaching of the nineteenth century was done in this way.

In those days, the teacher was often the only model available. Our ancestors were lucky if they could hear two different interpretations of Beethoven's "Appassionata" Sonata in a decade. We can hear recorded and live versions almost at will.

The most effective way of teaching by demonstration is, of course, repeated performance of sections of a composition to set up a model for the student to follow; the purpose may be to show a more musical and expressive interpretation of a phrase, or to illustrate the motions required for the desired effect.

Many teachers use artists' recordings for demonstrating. Most advanced students strive to hear a recording of a piece they have just been assigned.

In either case there are drawbacks. If incapable of performance of that piece, the teacher may not have the aural acuity to perceive the salient features of the recording to point them out to the student. And it is doubtful that the student really hears what is recorded; also, it has been my experience that students often hear what they want to hear. A student will give a pedal concert with keyboard accompaniment because "that's how Rubinstein plays it."

For these reasons the type of teaching that was commonly practiced in the nineteenth century, especially the authoritarian infallibility of the master who demonstrated and expected the student to imitate unquestioningly, is not for our time.

For the beginner, the teacher will play almost everything assigned. As the student advances and becomes more self-sufficient, it will not be necessary for the teacher to perform everything concert fashion. But the teacher must have the potential to perform the work decently if given the proper time to learn it.

No piece of music should be assigned that the teacher has not played at least slowly, without pedal, note by note, preferably also single hand and with conscious attention to rhythm, harmony (accidentals!), and fingering.

There are many "standard" mistakes that I get at every extended examination period or contest:

> C instead of C-sharp in Bach's first Invention, measure 11, last eighth note.
>
> D instead of D-sharp in Haydn's Sonata in D major, first movement, fourth measure of the development section, last eighth note.

Eighth-note motion instead of sixteenths at the opening of the middle section of Beethoven's "*Für Elise*."

D instead of D-flat in Beethoven's Sonata, op. 2 no. 1, in the thirteenth, eleventh, and ninth measures before the end of the first movement.

In Brahms' Intermezzo, op. 117 no. 2, E-flat instead of E-double flat on the third beat of measure 35.

The octave C-C instead of A-A in Brahms' G-minor Rhapsody, measure 2, last beat.

A wide selection of wrong notes in Mozart's D-minor Fantasy, starting with G instead of G-sharp on the last sixteenth note of measure 23.

When I witness this type of involuntary note-slaughter, I am sure that it is seldom accidental, and that it is the teacher, not the student, who is guilty.

ANALYSIS

Students very often are unable to distinguish between melody and accompaniment, especially in compositions of the romantic period, where the melody is often embedded in the accompaniment texture. First point of analysis: isolate the melody. Second point of analysis: establish the direction and shape of the melody; in other words, its underlying dynamic curve. The accompaniment may include neighbor notes, passing tones, grace notes, or what not, which can be sources of misreading and note mistakes.

Students should know in what key they are playing, not just at the beginning, but in the middle of a piece. Merely pointing out a wrong note does not help a student know why he or she misread the score. To insure insight and transfer of learning, you must analyze the harmonic content and explain to the student why the wrong note was wrong.

Some rhythms need to be broken down (analyzed) by counting out loud each of their component shortest values, or better, by making sure that the student "feels" the flow of the music.

Analyze the technical difficulties of a passage by

(1) subdividing the passage into its recurrent component parts, thereby explicating its harmonic basis;
(2) establishing a fingering principle;
(3) analyzing the most appropriate motions to achieve the desired result.

Especially in this last phase, analysis is sorely needed and rarely forthcoming. How often do we not find a student coming in after a week of conscientious practice, hitting a wrong note time and again, not because it was misread, but because of an awkward manual approach, perhaps combined with a poor fingering.

All this analyzing, I believe, should be done in a manner that avoids theorizing, academese, and five-syllable terms. In fact, scarcely any talking is necessary. The melody should be played without accompaniment; then the accompaniment without the melody; wherever possible the accompaniment may be blocked, nonharmonic tones omitted; this will lead to insight into the chord progressions, resolutions, and cadences. This is truly a case where learning by doing is the exciting thing. Rhythms must be felt, not mathematically calculated; counting aloud, clapping, finding words that fit the note values are much more efficacious than lectures on iambic, anapestic, or asymmetrical groupings of notes. The same practical approach should be used for the breaking down of passages into components, finding fingerings and purposeful motions. Terminology is the business of the theory teacher. Just as orchestras hate talkative conductors, piano pupils resent lecturing piano teachers. The student and the teacher should interact making music, not talking about it.

INSPIRATION

The fourth method of teaching is by inspiration. By this I mean that the piano teacher assumes the role of the orchestra conductor and treats the student as a one-person symphony. This is achieved by counting aloud, singing or playing along with the student, leading on by gestures or by whatever means, on the spur of the moment.

This method is more exciting for teacher and student than any other. It presupposes certain conditions *sine qua non*. First of all, the student must be able to play the piece correctly up to tempo and with enough ease to be able to follow the teacher's signals; he or she must be responsive and willing to respond. The teacher must have imagination, inner hearing, and the reasonable assurance of a right vision of the composer's intentions to be Pygmalion and breathe life into his Galatea. He or she must be enough of an extrovert and possess enough personal magnetism to make signals unmistakably clear and convincing, even coercive.

Moderation and restraint in the use of this method are necessary to preserve the teacher's voice as well as to prevent the student from turning into an automaton executing the orders of a once-a-week Frankenstein.

SUMMARY

An experienced teacher will immediately and almost instinctively feel which approach—criticism, demonstration, analysis, or inspiration—is the most appropriate in working with a student, and have the empathy to use one or the other, or a combination, in a given learning situation. He or she will plan lessons so that different approaches are used within the lesson and in the sequence of contacts with the student.

All four ways should be used—none is the only valid one—and all have their limitations. The teacher must beware of narrowing the teaching approach to only one of the four. Personality will probably make a teacher more effective in one or two, rather than equally in all four. We should all reexamine our teaching routines and not permit ourselves to fall into the rut of teaching only by criticism, or only by demonstration, or only by analysis, or only by inspiration.

What Are the Elements of a Good Piano Lesson?

MAY L. ETTS

The answer to this question will depend on a number of factors. Who is taking the lesson? A seven-year-old, an adult beginner, or a teen-ager who has studied for four or five years? Is the lesson private or group? A half-hour or an hour? In any case one must realize that a good lesson plan should cover not only a single session, but the whole term, for each student.

First of all, the teacher must establish a warm rapport with, and gain the confidence of, the pupil, whether a beginner or a transfer student. Psychologists have found that a student who apparently had no aptitude for a given subject when studying with one teacher suddenly took an interest in that subject when transferred to another instructor.

The time that the student spends with the teacher is very short, whether a half-hour for a beginner or an hour for a more advanced student, whether in a group or alone. To reap the most from every precious moment, the teacher should prepare the lesson in advance, know what each pupil has accomplished and what is to be taught, and be ready for the difficulties in playing each piece, study or technical drill, rather than coming upon them unexpectedly.

It is important that the pupil learn how to practice. From the new assignment, take a difficult measure or passage. Have the student play it slowly, each hand alone, to the first beat of the next measure. (This is to avoid a pause at the end of the measure, or accenting the last note of the measure.) Practice to avoid faults that occur frequently in stu-

Reprinted from *Keyboard Consultant*, Spring 1973. Used by permission.

dent performances: are the rhythmic values correct? Is the pupil able to clap the rhythm and count the values? Are the notes correct? What about fingering? After playing hands alone slowly and correctly, play faster. Next, play hands together, slowly, then faster. Whatever the problem–rhythmic, technical, accuracy, reading for self-study, or sight reading–it should be worked out at the lesson, as it is expected to be practiced at home. This helps establish good study habits.

Pieces for self-study, easy enough for the student to be able to play well within one week without help from the teacher, are very important. Later, several pages may be assigned, but only one heard at the lesson. Unless a student is able to play self-study material easily, sight reading will be a problem. Sight reading, of course, is a most important part of the lesson. The material assigned must be easy and contain only those elements with which the student is familiar. One can "sight read" a daily newspaper in a familiar language, but not in an unknown foreign language.

Technique, touch, and tone studies should be presented. The hand position usually requires much attention, and technique, touch, and tone suffer when the hand falls on a collapsed fifth finger, when the thumb hangs, or when joints "break." Simple "tickling" of the keys with the fingertips is a helpful first step. Some pertinent technical drills may be played at the beginning of each lesson as warmups and then integrated with problems in the studies and pieces. This procedure, while very valuable, actually requires little time.

Theory, ear training, and keyboard harmony, as well as some creative work, are other important elements of a good lesson, and should not be omitted. Decide what the student should cover during the season and assign something for each lesson, possibly varying from week to week, including assignments of written work. Analysis is helpful. Students may identify or write scales, chords, intervals, phrases, and cadences which are contained in their pieces or study material.

Review is also very important. Through review the student develops ease, style, and finesse. Only through thoughtful repetition may a well-prepared piece be brought to exhibit fine polish, greater musical contrasts, more musically shaped phrases, cleaner pedaling, more secure memorization.

Repertory must not be forgotten; not only memorization of new pieces, but maintaining a group of pieces in a state of readiness to play at any time. It is a mistake for a student to feel that once a piece is memorized it is "finished," dropped forever and forgotten. How can a teacher hear memorized pieces in the short period of a lesson? Some weeks hear a complete piece or two, other weeks hear sections. Ask to hear the last page or even the last line, the section after the double bar, or the beginning of the G-major section, and so on. This keeps the student prepared. Repertory classes and studio recitals are valuable, save time, provide great incentives, and give the necessary experience of playing for an audience. At such classes, having students constructively criticize each other fosters alert observation. Students should be encouraged to play at church, school, community events, and at home.

Ensemble playing is one of the greatest aids for developing rhythm, precision, fluent reading, and enhancing musical pleasure. It has tremendous value in developing coordination, cooperation, and listening, and it helps to eliminate self-centered attitudes. The student may learn a part alone, and when ready to play together, a partner may come in at the end of the lesson, or vice versa. If a duet is being learned, the students may practice at each other's homes; for two-piano works, special rehearsal periods may be assigned. Whatever the problems may be, the interest, enthusiasm, and resultant stimulation of work in general make any effort more than worthwhile.

Rote Playing and Rote Teaching

DENES AGAY

Learning by rote means learning by imitation and retention. It enables the student to memorize and reproduce certain aural impressions and kinetic keyboard patterns without having to read or in any way refer to a written score. The teacher demonstrates; the student repeats by imitating the specific motions to produce the desired sound. A good many pianistic dexterities, especially in the fields of technique and sight reading, are attained by this method of learning, often without the player's being aware of it. Rote learning aids in mastering scales, chords, arpeggios, harmonic progressions, and cadences; it also helps tone production and keyboard touches (legato, staccato, portamento, etc.). Fluent sight reading is also promoted by the instinctive application of motion patterns assimilated by a repetitive (rote) practice.

Despite its many practical applications, rote playing and teaching is considered a somewhat controversial subject in some pedagogical circles. Those opposed to it feel that rote playing on the elementary level may inhibit and hinder learning to play by reading notes, and gives the student an artificial sense of accomplishment. This simply is not so, if the teacher knows when and how rote teaching should take place. True, if rote playing is overdone or indiscriminitely taught, the student's mechanical keyboard experiences may get ahead of the theoretical capacity to read and understand music. In other words, what the student can play by rote may overshadow in sound and overall effectiveness the material he or she can play by reading notes. This should not be allowed to happen and, indeed, does not happen if rote teaching is carefully planned to proceed parallel to and in preparation for the teaching of pertinent theoretical concepts.

Playing carefully selected rote pieces holds important advantages for the student, whether young or adult, during elementary studies. Playing without the printed score focuses all mental attention and physical responses on the tactile problems at hand, without the necessity for eye involvement to follow the score and without the analytical-mental process of interpreting printed notes and translating them into kinetic responses. Another advantage of rote teaching is that it can be tailored to the individual student's needs and capacities. Emphasis can be given to strengthening weaknesses while at the same time giving the student confidence. There is now a wide choice of attractive rote pieces available in print. These pieces can be learned without much effort as they lend themselves to imitative learning and to easy aural and tactile retention. Rote teaching has sound pedagogical justification. It can materially contribute to the general advancement and learning pleasure of students, especially those, regardless of age, who for various reasons progress at a slower than average pace, and who may need more time and special considerations in acquiring necessary skills.

THE FIRST KEYBOARD CONTACTS

This section is meant to give teachers some ideas and furnish concrete examples whereby the beginning student can be introduced to the piano and be guided in the first keyboard explorations through little pieces and exercises learned by rote.

Even the very first lesson presents opportunities for taking advantage of the usefulness of rote procedures. The topography of the keyboard, the arrangement of black-key groups, the location and direction of high and low notes, can easily be taught through the first little pieces the student can play by rote. It is important that these first playing experiences involve a wide range up and down the keyboard so that the student can immediately gather aural and tactile impressions of the entire instrument.

In the beginning the student does not have to know the letter names of the keys or the notes on the staff. Rote playing is based on imitation and memorization. The pupil is shown, by logical steps, what to do, and repeats what is shown. Nor does the student have to count. The short phrases, especially when supplied with words, strongly indicate meter and rhythm. Even when counting is introduced, it is advisable that at first, the student chant the words while playing, then turn to counting.

Here are some examples for initial keyboard explorations. Many others can be created by the imaginative teacher to suit individual needs.

"Bells Are Ringing"

Bells are ring - ing ting - a - ling,
Bells are ring - ing ding - dong.

"Up and Down"
r.h.
l.h.
This way up, This way down. This way down, This way up.
"High and Low"
High, low, high; Low, high, low, High, high, low.
"Mountain Climb"
Climb - ing up moun - tains we're climb - ing up high.
Com - ing down to the ground and say good - bye.
"Black Key Frolic"
r.h.
l.h.
r.h.
l.h.
r.h.
l.h.
r.h.
r.h.
l.h.

"Black and White"

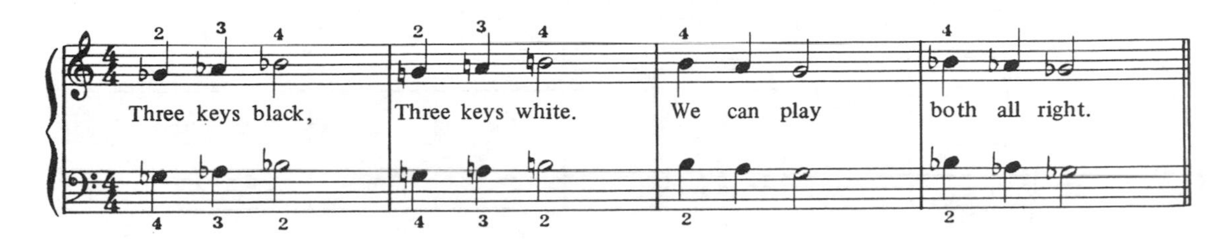

Playing *legato* is a rather difficult discipline for beginning pianists, and usually requires time and practice. The weight of the hand or arm, securely supported by the fingertips, must be transferred gradually from one key to another for a smooth continuity of sound. At first this is best accomplished by the three middle fingers because of their approximately equal length and anatomical structure. The following example should be played both in G-flat and in G, at first by each hand separately, then by both together.

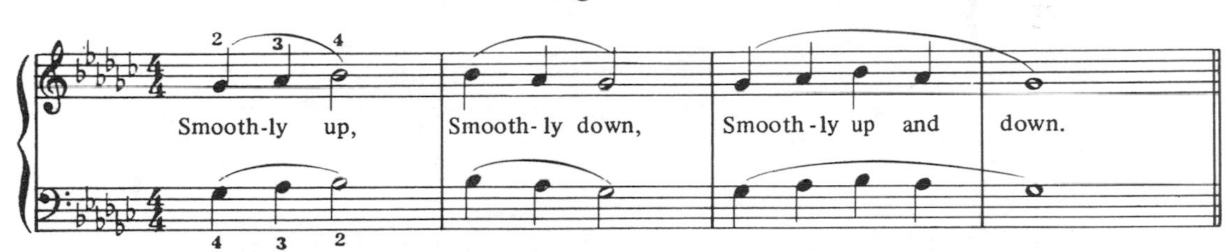

At this point "Mountain Climb" may be repeated so that the three-note groups are played strictly legato.

"Staccato Piece"

"Little Scherzo"

Pieces involving all five fingers should be introduced early.

"What a Day!"

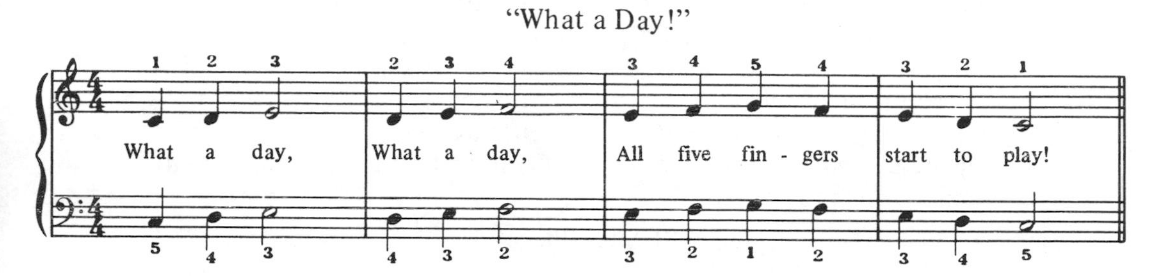

The above piece can also be taught by playing all quarter notes *staccato*. Transpose into several other keys. The next piece—"Play Tune"—is in a shifting five-finger position.

The three-measure phrases should be played legato. The piece can also serve as a staccato étude: quarter notes played *staccato*, half notes *tenuto*. Transposition into G major may also be useful.

Agay: "Play Tune"

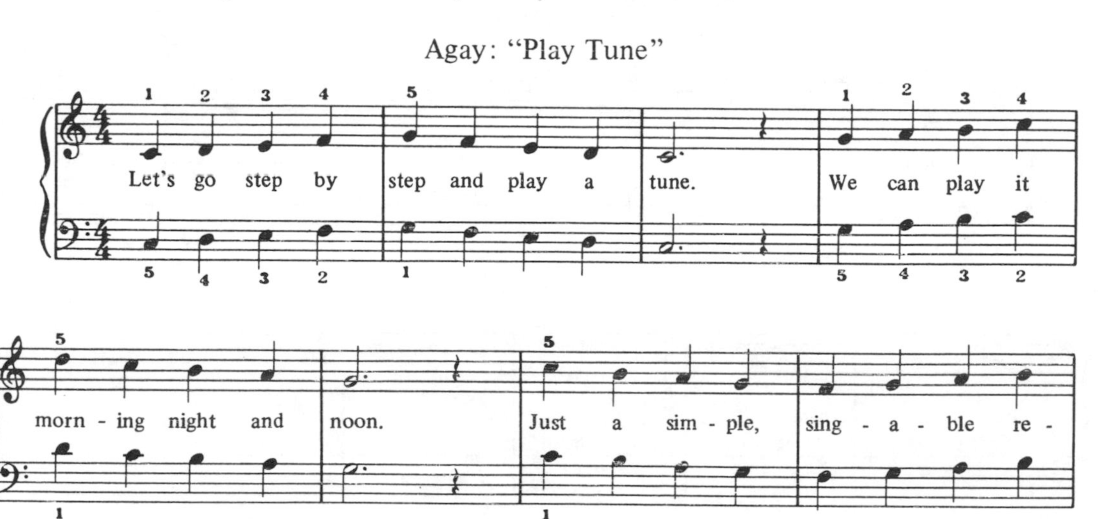

The last six measures
may be repeated.

When learning the notes' letter names, the student's first task can be playing and naming all white keys successively from the bottom of the keyboard (A) to the top, using the third finger first with the right hand, then with the left.

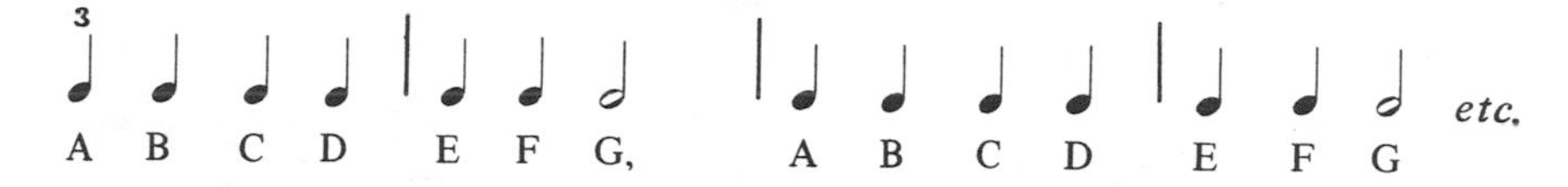

Three "A-B-C Songs"

Arpeggios and *arpeggio*-like figures are especially suitable and showy vehicles for over-the-keyboard travels. The following piece is built on the twelve-bar harmonic sequence of the blues: I-IV-I-V-I. The legato arches should be played smoothly.

"The Glider"

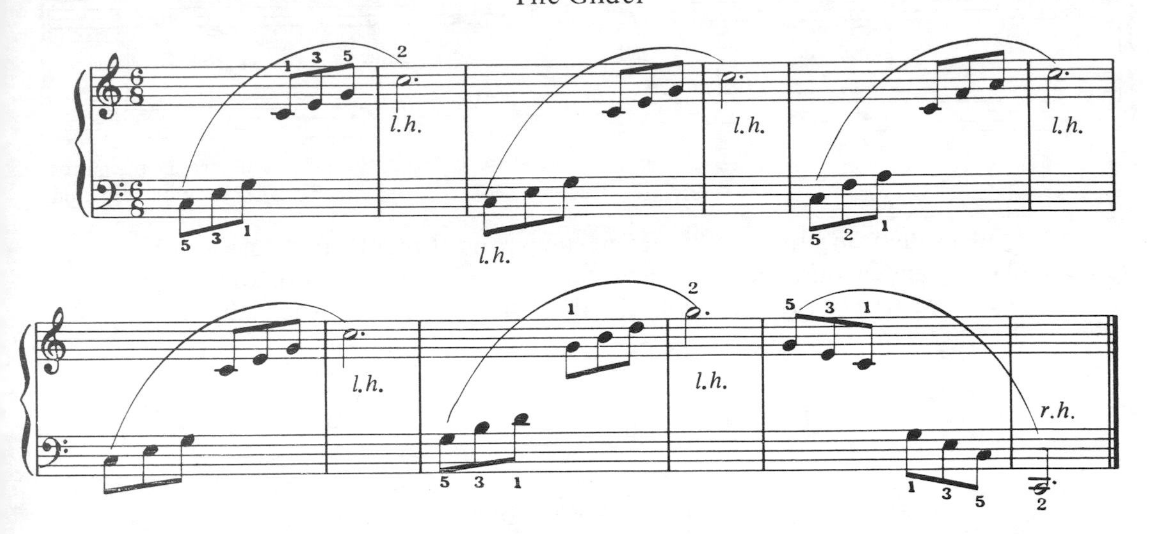

By playing the next piece and singing the words, the student can get an idea of how the black keys derive from the white ones, and gain familiarity with the half-step interval. (At first, play one hand at a time.)

"Sharps and Flats"

The following two pieces offer an opportunity for playing on various dynamic levels, as well as double notes and chords.

"The First Serenade"
Moderato
"From Olden Times"
Andante
f (repeat p)
rit.
"Scale Melody"
r.h.
l.h.

All the pieces presented so far were meant only to provide guidelines and examples of how technical and theoretical concepts can be introduced and learned through rote playing. The teacher's files should contain an ample number of appropriate selections, a varied repertory of attractive rote pieces, illustrating practically all aspects of elementary keyboard skills and theoretical matters, ready to be given to the student progressively from the very beginning. In addition, the teacher must be alert and creative enough to adapt materials or compose new ones to fit the student's individual needs. It is extremely important that the selected rote materials should be interesting, well written, and suitable for the intended teaching purpose. Also, they must be constructed in a manner that features *repetitive patterns* of melody, rhythm, and harmony so that they can be easily imitated and memorized. It often helps if the piece has a descriptive title, which promotes understanding, identification with the music, and more effective performance.

Ostinato bass patterns of all sorts are especially suitable features of rote pieces. The repeated patterns in the left hand are very easy to remember, so all attention can be focused on the right-hand part.

"Moody Dance"

"Skip to My Lou" Boogie

The following steps in teaching rote material are suggested:

- The teacher plays the piece through from beginning to end, to give the pupil an idea of what it is and how it should sound.
- The teacher plays the piece again, slower this time, breaking it down into sections and pointing out repetitive or other important features. Questions can be asked to make sure that the student has a grasp of the particulars. (Can you hum the melody? Is it repeated? Where? Is it repeated exactly or is there any change? Can you clap this rhythm? How many times does this rhythm appear?)
- The pupil begins to play the piece, imitating the teacher's demonstration phrase by phrase, section by section. Once individual sections are memorized, they are gradually connected.

The next two selections (which can also serve as little recital pieces) contain many of the constructional elements and keyboard features which were dealt with individually in previous examples. They can also furnish the teacher an opportunity to analyze and test the step-by-step teaching procedure outlined above.

"Keyboard Frolic"

Agay: "Moonlit Pagoda"

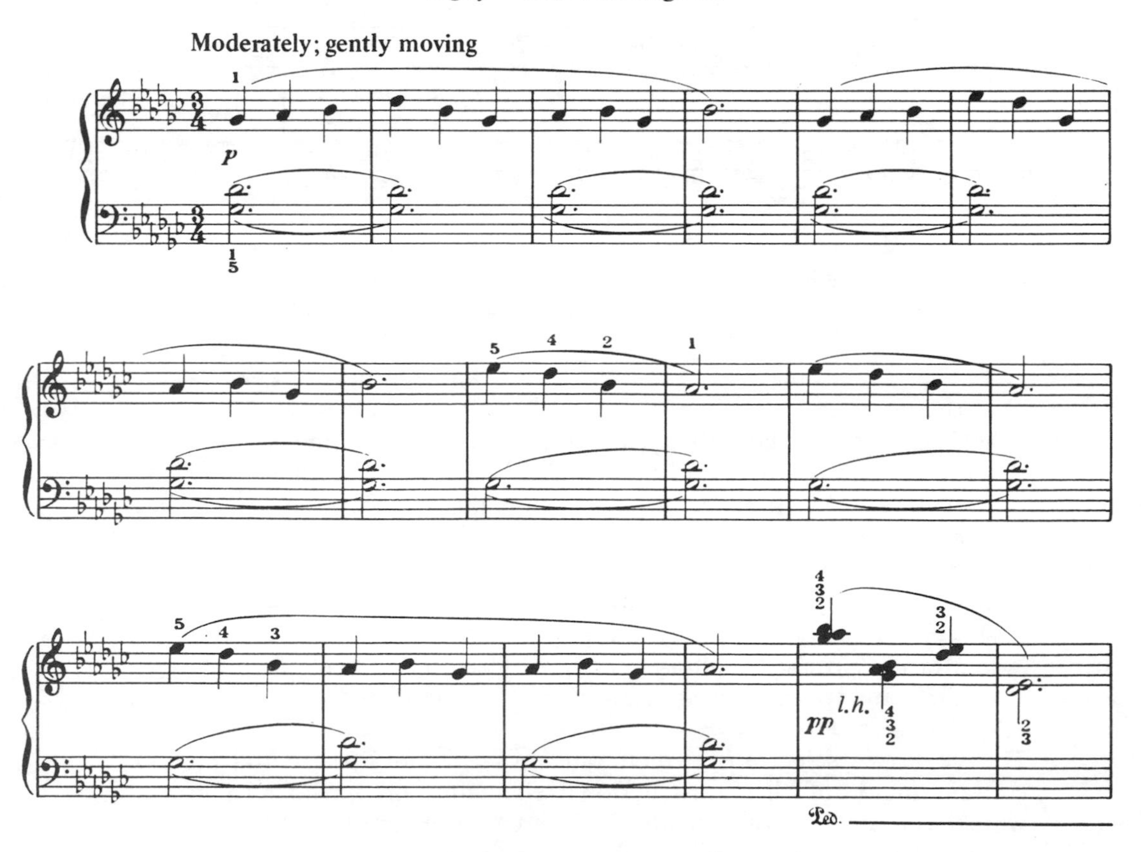

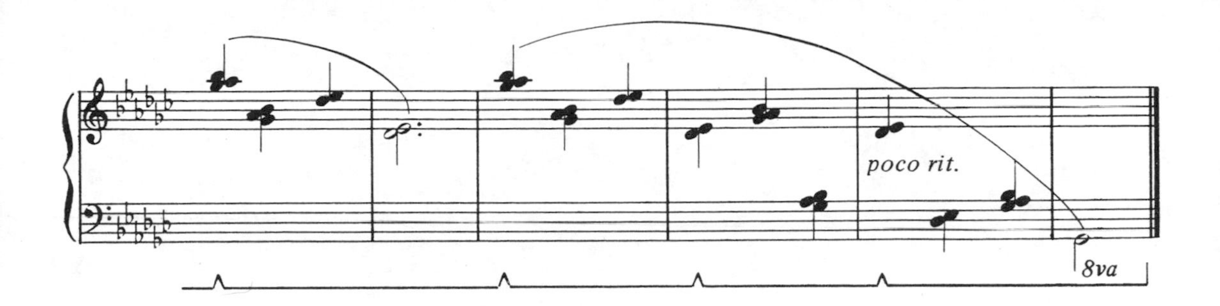

In summary it should be emphasized that rote playing can be an important pedagogical tool in teaching many keyboard skills and musical concepts. If guided properly and with judicious restraint, it can also be an unfailing confidence booster and a source of incentive for all budding pianists.

RECOMMENDED READING

Agay, Denes. *The Joy of First-Year Piano*. New York: Yorktown Music Press, 1972.

Cornfield, Edith. "Teaching by Rote." *Clavier* September 1969.

Diller, Angela. *Rote Teaching–What It Is and How To Do It*. New York: G. Schirmer, 1953.

Last, Joan. *Keyboard Games for the Very Young Pianist*. London: Oxford University Press, 1972.

Maier, Guy and Helen Corzilius. *Playing the Piano: A Course of Rote Training for Beginners*. New York: J. Fischer and Bro., 1929.

The Tape Recorder: An Indispensable Teaching Aid

YLDA NOVIK

Only a few years ago, tape recorders were rarely found in the studio of the private piano teacher. He or she would enviously eye the university or conservatory colleague who could schedule access to a machine for recording students' performances. Now that inexpensive tape recorders are available, many private teachers consider them as necessary a part of their teaching equipment as pianos and blackboards.

I confess that initially the sole use of my first tape recorder was to record the annual student recital and then play each child's performance back so he or she could listen in awe and wonderment. Also, what greater joy for the proud parents than to resavor little Vladimir's performance for yet another time? That limited use resulted from my absolute terror of operating all things electrical, from vacuum cleaners to televisions, until they had been in our house for weeks, by which time I was certain that they were thoroughly domesticated and would not bite when touched. My scientist husband coped with the beast for me at recitals.

At last, when he bought a new model for me, which he said "anyone could operate," it was placed next to the piano for daily teaching purposes. And how the uses seemed to increase as time went on!

USE AT REPERTORY CLASSES

My students became very performance oriented as a result of partici-

---

Revised by the author from an article originally published in *The American Music Teacher*, June–July 1968. Used by permission.

pation in my repertory classes. Fortunately, they have outlets for performance via the large number of recitals sponsored by local music teachers' organizations. Therefore, the first and most obvious use for our tape recorder was in preparation for these performances. As we all know, it is invaluable to hear ourselves as a means of discovering obvious mistakes and rough spots. Furthermore, the tape preserves the playing so that colleagues and coaches can comment on errors that our subjectivity might blur or gloss over. Also the psychological factor of knowing the "ear" was listening makes the taped performance one in which student's play with greater concentration than if they were only playing for their good friend, the teacher.

Once the piece is taped, we work in one or a combination of several possible ways. Sometimes we play back the entire piece without commentary, then discuss it as a whole after it is concluded. At other times, the student is asked to stop the tape when something is displeasing, and rework it, there and then. Still another approach is for me to stop the tape and make the comments. Often we tape a small stubborn fragment, in order to polish phrasing, dynamics, or technical evenness, playing it over numerous times until we are both pleased. Then the entire composition is taped once more, with the two versions played back in succession, so the pupil can hear the improvement.

Occasionally, an argumentative student will dispute having played out of time, or having hit a wrong note. He or she has to play for "the truth machine" and then must accept what he or she hears. "Hearing is believing" is our motto.

PREPARATION FOR CONCERTS

Then there is the student who comes to a series of lessons unprepared or misprepared. I say, "We're going to play back your performance of this piece right now so that you will have to listen to it and suffer as I do every week." This never fails to put an end to a slump, and progress resumes. The adage of being one's own best critic most certainly applies to all musicians, as well as piano pupils—if they are given an opportunity for self-criticism.

In addition to being performance oriented, my students are also "contest happy," and participate in two large national student-level competitions which utilized taped performances. The Baldwin keyboard achievement awards are judged from reel tapes, sent in to state, then divisional, and finally national levels. It is open to students in grades 7 through 9, or roughly twelve through fourteen years of age. I have been very much impressed by watching my contenders taping and retaping and polishing their pieces to the utmost level of their abilities. The growth in each and every participant continues into a vastly improved quality of work thereafter, regardless of what stage of the contest has been reached.

The Young Chopin Competition held in Buffalo for students under seventeen has its preliminary round submitted on reel tape and serves as a good example. The finalists are selected from their tapes, then compete in person. Again, as in the Baldwin, it has been thrilling to see my students strive for that almost unattainable level of absolute perfection. I turn my piano and tape recorder over to these contestants on weekend hours when no lessons are scheduled and they work entirely on their own at the tapes. Generally, I am at my desk in another part of the house, marveling at their maturity, determination, and endless patience, as they spend hours on any given piece.

TAPED LESSONS

And now, the most important use of the tape recorder: taping every lesson. With the advent of the inexpensive, easy-to-use cassette recorder (even the really cheap ones are adequate), all of my students are required to have their own affordable versions of these remarkably convenient machines. The student comes in for a lesson with a cassette tape, puts it in my cassette recorder, and the entire lesson is recorded from start to finish. (This is also a convenient half-hour timekeeper.) This tape, needless to say, played once or twice at home during the ensuing week, serves to remind students of all the things which were said and done at the lesson. They say that it is like taking me home with them for an extra lesson or two each week. I should add that this does not create an overdependent situation because there comes a time when we stop taping. This is only when I am certain that practice habits are well established, and in all cases there is no decline in the quality of lesson preparation.

Since not every student can afford to buy recordings of the pieces being learned—and many of the easy ones are not recorded—students borrow another cassette on which I record for them the music they are studying so they may become familiar with it. Of course, there are two definite schools of thought about listening to music on which one is working. Since I believe in utilizing every possible means to familiarize oneself with the compositions—such as thematic and harmonic analysis—I am ardently in the buy-the-records-and-learn camp. But I say with great emphasis, "Do not copy the performer's style. Use the record only as a means of becoming better acquainted with the music. Remain objective."

Another fallout of the taped lesson occurs when a student comes for a lesson but has forgotten to bring the music. Once upon a time this meant that the student might use my music for the lesson, but had no satisfactory way of annotating the lesson comments because I preferred not to have markings on my copies. Now I can lend a cassette, and tape the lesson as usual.

Occasionally, I have students who live so far away that they are able to study only once a month. Midway between lessons they mail me a tape of their playing so that I may comment on their progress and make any corrections. This process is not as impossible as it appears to be, since I now own not one, but several tape recorders of each type (reel and cassette). I make my remarks into a second tape recorder, phrase by phrase, as the lesson tape is being played on the first tape recorder and simultaneously being recorded on the second. Both tapes are mailed back to the long-distance student, giving essentially all the benefits of an in-person lesson. Twin tape recorders are also put to use for making copies of any contest or recital tapes which students want duplicated. It is really a good idea to have multiple copies of precious tapes as a form of insurance should anything happen to the originals.

Take-home tapes are also an excellent means of drilling the student in ear training. For example: I make up simple four- or eight-measure tunes which are to be played at home by ear, first in the original key and then transposed to all twelve keys. For the next step, the students add chords and improvise different styles of accompaniments.

Each new student who comes to me is given instructions to tape each piece he learned, when we both feel it is polished. Actually I don't check on this consistently, but I try to impress upon the student the fact that he or she can have a life-long music diary, something to chuckle about years later while listening again to those fruits of the early years of study.

Yet another facet of the tape recorder's versatility is in concerto and two-piano work. In each case I tape the other piano part so that the student can use it at home to become familiar with the ensemble. Such a short-cut and time-saver on rehearsals! I must confess that, as half of a two-piano team, I have inveigled my partner into taping his part. Thus in our busy lives we require a minimum of rehearsals, inasmuch as he was only the flick of a switch away.

There are undoubtedly many other uses of the tape recorder for teaching and playing music that have not occurred to me but are obvious to my colleagues. As I utilize this indispensable teaching aid more and more, I can only regret the years that I did not use it to full advantage.

The Teacher-Student Relationship: Some Common-Sense Suggestions

HAZEL GHAZARIAN SKAGGS

To insure the best possible learning climate and relationship between themselves and their students, piano teachers may be guided by the following common-sense rules:

(1) Show your students that you care about them. The teacher is a friend to each student, but not a pal. Gatherings such as rehearsals, recital parties, and concerts may provide further opportunities to affirm your interest in the student as a person.
(2) It is best to establish your authority at the first meeting and retain it at all times so that your students respond with friendly respect.
(3) Recognize individual differences. For instance, challenging material may motivate one child but frustrate another. A recital may be exciting for an outgoing child and devastating to a shy one.
(4) Reinforce good behavior. Inappropriate behavior, unheeded, may disappear. The child who constantly cries and receives comfort because of it will be encouraged to continue crying. Also, clowning will continue with an appreciative audience, but usually will disappear when unobserved.
(5) Encourage students; don't be negative. Rather than say "You forgot to make the crescendo here," comment: "This section is well done, and when you make the crescendo here, it will be even better." A sense of achievement, not failure, provides motivation for continued learning.
(6) Work toward improving the student's self-esteem. There is,

however, the danger that overpraise may lead to the student's considering an artistic career when his or her talents are not solid and broad enough to meet the demands of a life goal.

(7) In working with groups, do not resort to anger to maintain discipline. A display of anger is a waste of time and energy; it is debilitating and it diminishes your dignity and authority.

(8) In helping students, use common sense rather than psychoanalytical methods. Unless trained as a psychologist, the teacher can do more damage than good. If, in your opinion, a student's behavior is highly inappropriate, it is best to relate your observations, *not* your conclusions, to the student's parents.

(9) Furnish the studio so that it is a pleasant and cheerful place, reflecting your outlook, taste, and personality.

(10) Remember, the lesson time is for the student. Do not overdo talking or demonstrating at the piano.

Parental Involvement

DENES AGAY

The ideal parents, from the teacher's point of view, are those who display a constructive interest in the child's study and progress without being overzealous or meddlesome about it. Some degree of parental involvement, then, is entirely normal, even desirable. Parents who are totally indifferent or disinterested will not help the child's progress; on the contrary, they will create a musically dull and sterile home atmosphere, which may stifle the child's initiative. It is extremely important for the teacher to realize this and not to regard every parental inquiry and request as unreasonable or unnecessary interference.

It may happen, of course, that parental attention becomes exaggerated and disruptive. To cope with this is often a delicate problem requiring not only professional competence but a great deal of tact and diplomacy. Obviously it would be impossible to suggest remedies that would apply in every situation, except one ancient common-sense rule: head off trouble before it starts. The teacher should realize that most problems can be avoided and friction averted by certain preventive measures taken at the very beginning of the instruction.

The first and most important step is to establish and maintain a relationship with the parents which is open, friendly and relaxed— a relationship which is based on cooperation and mutual understanding. The parent's goodwill and willingness to cooperate, however, may not be enough; it helps more if they know *how* to cooperate, how to handle certain problems which are likely to occur between lessons, and, in general, how to maintain and stimulate the child's interest.

For this reason it is advisable to have an informative talk with the parents when lessons begin. During this talk the teacher may outline methods and planned curriculum and discuss the solutions to certain problems with which the parents may easily become involved: the age-old problem of practicing, for instance.

How much is the child supposed to practice? What time of day is the best? Should an unwilling child be coaxed to practice? These and numerous other related questions should be discussed so that the parents are equipped to form a sound opinion about them from the beginning. This will prevent later complications and misunderstandings.

It should be pointed out to the parents that children usually make very good progress under a set routine, and there is nothing wrong in keeping them in line and reminding them of their daily duties, whatever these may be: homework, taking a bath, or practicing the piano. At the same time it should be remembered that the practice period should not interfere with the youngster's rightful recreational activities. Furthermore, practicing should never be imposed as a matter of punishment. Parents should express pleasure and not be stingy with praise for work well done; also an occasional request to play a certain piece will no doubt be appreciated and act as a booster. In general, the rule should be motivation and incentive, not coercion.

In another area, parents should be urged to be flexible and understanding in their attitude toward different musical styles. For instance, if the child enjoys playing contemporary music, parents should not be critical, even if they happen not to be attracted toward the modern sound. Popular songs should not be frowned upon, either; they may provide the student with the necessary "shot in the arm" to maintain interest or overcome certain lags in the daily practice habit, so that eventually the student can proceed to study material of a higher caliber.

These, of course, are just a small sampling of the topics which may be discussed. The teacher can prepare a long list of other pertinent items and, naturally, the parents, too, should be encouraged to ask questions and express thoughts about the entire subject area. It is important to remember that the proper spirit of the meeting is not one of teacher's lecturing parents but of a friendly discussion during which ideas are exchanged. The teacher may prefer to have the meeting with a group of parents instead of just one or two. These meetings may be held at regular intervals, such as at the beginning and the end of the school year, or as the need arises.

Despite all careful preliminary briefings, complications may still arise. Some parents may turn out to be "difficult," all precautionary measures notwithstanding. For these cases we would like to offer the teacher the following suggestions:

- Be cool and calm; do not, under any cirsumstances, lose your temper.
- Examine, as carefully and as objectively as you can, the child's entire curriculum and review the progress made.

- If you feel that there is no objective reason for any complaint or dissatisfaction, bring this (as tactfully as you can) to the parents' attention. This does not mean that you have to be stiff and unyielding in every respect. Slight adjustments and harmless excursions can be made within the student's repertory to please parents.
- Should parental attitude become hopelessly unreasonable so that you have no choice but to discontinue the child's instruction, bow out with dignity and, if possible, without traces of ill-feeling.

We earnestly feel, though, that the giving up of a student because of parental difficulties should be an extremely rare occurrence. In most cases it can be avoided by know-how, patience, and tact. It should be kept constantly in mind that music lessons are a three-way effort by teacher, student, and parents. If the parents are made aware that their attitude and cooperation play an essential part in this joint effort, their involvement will rarely be the kind which could lead to serious complications.

RECOMMENDED READING

Wills, Vera G. and Ande Manners. *A Parent's Guide to Music Lessons*. New York: Harper & Row, 1967.

SEVEN

PRACTICAL CONSIDERATIONS

The Business of Teaching

HAZEL GHAZARIAN SKAGGS

The teacher with a private studio, unlike the member of a school faculty, is self-employed and obliged to operate the studio as a business. Net income is derived from the total amount received from the sale of services, minus those expenditures necessary to provide those services.

FEES*

The price the teacher sets on the services—piano lessons—is as crucial as the price the merchant sets on wares. Therefore, it is important that lesson fees be determined after careful consideration of such factors as:

(1) What has the teacher to offer? What is an objective evaluation of the training, education, performance skills, personality, experience, etc.?
(2) How much of a need is there for these services in the community? What is the competition?
(3) What are the incomes and attitudes of the parents in that area? What can parents afford and what are they willing to pay?
(4) What will the expenses be? What is the percentage of cost in every dollar earned? An elaborate studio with expensive equipment and high upkeep may make it necessary to charge more for lessons. A large uneconomical car for the itinerant teacher may drastically reduce earnings.

*Since all figures in this chapter were surveyed in 1977-78, an upward adjustment is reasonable.

(5) Where will the studio be located? In renting or purchasing property for a studio, the teacher must realize that if the cost of the studio is disproportionate with total earnings, the net income will be inadequate. Also, the studio must be accessible to the kinds of students desired. (Youngsters will not be found in a retirement community). A studio in an area that is safe for children to walk or for parents to drive (some drivers don't like to stop on highways or back-out on busy streets, etc.) will be an asset in attracting students.

The choice of fee may well make the difference between success or failure. Let us examine a case history to illustrate this point. Two concert pianists of equal training and skill move to a suburban area. Pianist A knows her worth and without further investigation decides to set her fee at $25 a lesson. She rationalizes that $25 is only half what she has been paying her master teacher. Pianist B feels that although as a performing pianist with more than the required academic credentials to teach and with some teaching experience she merits $25 a lesson, she wonders whether or not that fee fits the needs of the community she has chosen to work in.

Her investigations reveal that the community suffers no shortage of teachers; rather, there is a plethora of them. City teachers make the one-hour trip to suburbia to give lessons at the students' homes; young untrained college students continually advertise for students; established teachers are generally busy; and a few outstanding musicians have few or no students. Rates range from $2 to $15 an hour. The popular fee is about $6 a half-hour for an experienced reputable teacher. A fee of $10 to $15 for a forty-five minute to one-hour lesson is more readily subscribed to if the teacher goes to the home. Also, parents are more inclined to pay the higher studio fees when their children are advanced rather than beginners. Some career-minded students travel to the nearest city for lessons with master teachers.

On the basis of these facts pianist B decides to charge $8 for forty-five minutes in her studio. If the $8 fee proves to be unpopular, she can, as a last resort, give half-hour lessons. She allocates only one room in her home for teaching and uses the single grand piano she already owns; she makes no further investments either in furnishings or a second piano. Fortunately her studio is conveniently located within walking distance of schools on a traffic-free street, and easily accessible by car.

Eight months later, in June, pianist B has twenty students to present in a year-end recital while pianist A, although she has tried to get students, has none. As time passes pianist B begins to have more applicants than she can accept. She now makes lessons available only by the year, with tuition paid in nine equal installments; her fee is increased; a second piano is purchased and gradually she begins to furnish the studio and a waiting room. The overpriced pianist A remains unemployed.

In determining a fee the teacher must consider that music study is generally considered a luxury and not a necessity like food, clothing, heating, etc. Even the income of the only teacher available in a community will be tempered by what parents are able and willing to spend on an extra cultural advantage for their children.

WHERE TO TEACH

In some areas, a majority of parents wish to have their children's lessons at their own homes. A service charge may be made for this type of teaching. Because lessons at the students' home are popular, a new teacher may begin as an itinerant and later, when better known, change to studio teaching, either entirely or in part.

There are many teachers who prefer traveling for a number of reasons: freedom from confinement in their own homes, lack of interference in their family life, and elimination of the expense of furnishing, equipping, and maintaining a studio. In sum, the average teacher who wishes to earn as much as possible may find traveling more profitable.

Of course, the tremendous advantage of lessons in the student's home is that it eliminates the problem of student transportation. Some parents with infants or without cars find it difficult to consider studio lessons. Other parents prefer home lessons for their personal convenience and comfort. But there are some serious disadvantages in these lessons for both teacher and student.

(1) Very few homes are without such distractions as the arrival of visitors, phone calls, pets, younger siblings.
(2) The student doesn't have the opportunity to be exposed to the musical environment that a studio provides: grand pianos, music bulletin boards, other students.
(3) The home teacher's own music library and store of new materials are not accessible. Also lacking may be the advantages of a second piano, tape recorder or record player.
(4) The teacher is a guest in the student's living room, whereas in the studio he or she enjoys the comfort of being at home.
(5) The teacher loses time traveling, and may become detained by talkative parents, traffic conditions, bad weather, or automobile problems.

AUGMENTING INCOME

All too often the piano teacher's net income will not leave a sufficient amount to be spent on pension plans, hospitalization, disability insurance, and unemployment protection. The piano teacher may well have to forfeit these benefits in order to enjoy self-employment and the opportunity to do the kind of work that is preferred.

Some of the ways in which the teacher may augment income are the following:

(1) Teaching preschoolers or adults in the morning.
(2) Teaching adults later in the evening or at evening adult schools.
(3) Encouraging students to take longer lessons.
(4) Eliminating makeup day lessons and using the time to enroll extra students.
(5) Adding class theory lessons to regular schedule.
(6) Offering introductory piano, private or class, in the summer on a six-week basis to children who have never studied before.
(7) Charging more for intermediate and advanced levels; for example, $10 for beginner, $12 for intermediate, $15 for advanced.
(8) Shortening a longer-than-average term schedule, such as 38 or 40 weeks, and keeping the same tuition, thus providing a few weeks paid vacation.
(9) Charging for the initial interview by considering it a special first lesson.
(10) Adding extra fees for registration, recital tickets, use of the studio music library, etc.
(11) Remembering to include a periodic cost-of-living increase.
(12) Receiving commissions from piano stores for leads and recommendations.

Too often teachers permit the cancelled unpaid-for lesson to deplete their incomes. There must be an understanding that regardless of how many lessons the student attends, the parent pays for the total number for which the student is enrolled. Missed lessons are generally made up by the teacher. Some teachers prefer not to make up these lessons. A variety of ways in which individual teachers handle the missed lesson problem can be found in the brochures listed on p. 647.

NEW STUDENT

When the parent calls to inquire about lessons, the teacher may want to obtain the following information:

Who referred the parent to the teacher
Who referred the student to the teacher
Student's age
Student's school grade
Previous study experience
When the parent and child can come for an interview

A few teachers do not like to give their fee schedules over the telephone. If so, they take the risk of wasting their and the parent's time on an interview. No matter how much the parent may desire the lesson, if the price is not right for the family, the child cannot be enrolled in the studio.

INTERVIEW

Generally there is no fee for the initial interview, since its primary purpose is to establish good will and rapport between teacher, parent, and pupil. For many teachers it is the only scheduled time that is ever set aside to meet with the parent. The interview also provides the opportunity for clarification of studio rules and assurance that the best possible program of study is being offered the child.

Some teachers use the interview for evaluating the student's personality and aptitude. In instances where teachers are selective in accepting students, it is a time for declining those applicants who do not meet the required studio standards. An interview may begin with the teacher's asking the student such questions as: What school do you attend? Do you belong to any clubs? When is your birthday? What is your favorite subject? Did you ever study dancing? As the student begins to feel more at ease with the teacher, the teacher may invite the student to play.

If a beginner, the prospective student may want to play a song picked out by ear or a piece learned by rote. He or she may be able to read music. What the beginner is able to do at the keyboard and how quickly he or she learns what the teacher demonstrates, may well determine the course of study. In the case of the child with no keyboard skills, responses in a series of tests such as matching tones, playing by ear, and learning by rote a piece with one and two hands will provide the clues to what course of study may be suitable.

TRANSFER STUDENTS

In the matter of transfer students, the wise teacher will try to assess not only the student's performance and the information the child gives on past study, but to find out what the prospective student's learning speed is at various levels. This may be accomplished by practicing some new lines of music.

Regardless of what the teacher's conclusions are in respect to the child's proper placement, if the child has not been away from the piano for too long a period of time, the kindest procedure is to make the course of study seem continuous rather than a step backward. One way of achieving this is to assign material on a variety of levels.

If the parent is changing teachers out of dissatisfaction, the new teacher must bear in mind that any learning situation is dependent upon the interaction between the teacher and student. Therefore the student's inadequacies are not necessarily the previous teacher's fault. Interest in the program of study with other teachers may be shown, but it is best not to pass judgment on any of it. Time can better be spent planning the future than rejecting the past.

STUDENT FILE

For the teacher who wants a detailed file on the student, the interview is the time to acquire the necessary information. The file may include the following:

Name, address and phone number
Referred by
Parent's names
Birthday
School grade
Beginner or transfer student
If transfer student:
  Length of previous study
  Materials used
  Reason for changing teachers
Instruments played
Other activities: clubs, dancing, sports, etc.
Favorite school subject
Favorite music
Number of children in family; position among them
What day or days student is free for piano lessons
How much time student plans to devote to piano
Occupation (if student is adult)

HOW TO ATTRACT NEW STUDENTS

For the teacher just beginning a career, a variety of approaches may be used to attract students. The following steps may also be considered by the established teacher, although most new students will be from the recommendation of those already enrolled.

(1) Giving a small musicale expressly to encourage the audience to recommend the teacher to others or consider lessons for themselves.
(2) Leaving business cards at the local music store and with public school music teachers.
(3) Introducing oneself as a teacher to neighboring teachers who may wish to give students they have no time for.
(4) Joining local music teachers' groups (their directories are often mailed to parents)
(5) Attending club, community, and church gatherings to meet as many parents as possible, or adults who may want to study.
(6) Advertising under classified music instruction in the local newspaper.
(7) Performing in public as often as possible.

GUIDES FOR BUSINESS PROCEDURES

From a random survey of brochures of successful studios, the charts below were compiled to serve as guides for setting up new studios or improving business procedures of existing ones.*

Tuition and Missed Lessons

From a studio in the rural Midwest:

Private half-hour lessons: $4 per lesson.

Each ten-week term payable in advance.

No deductions for missed lessons.

Lessons are rescheduled only if advance notice has been given, and then only for illness.

From a studio in the suburban East:

Private lesson: $12 an hour.

All lessons paid monthly in advance.

No charge for five recital classes which all students are required to attend.

No lesson makeups. Any lessons missed will be considered made up by the recital classes.

From a studio in an Eastern town:

Tuition fee: $52 for each term (three terms, twelve weeks each); nine private half-hour lessons each term; three one-hour groups in each term.

Student responsibility and lesson attendance: "Since a student contracts the teacher's time when he enrolls, he is expected to be present for his lesson period, including the monthly group lesson. The lesson period assigned each pupil becomes his personal and financial responsibility for the entire term. That time is saved for him and is of no value to anyone else. No allowance or deductions for missed or cancelled lessons except in cases of extended illness. Under no circumstances need a professional teacher consider forgetfulness, lack of preparation, school or social conflicts a valid excuse."

(Note: the above teacher gives three private lessons and one group session each month.)

From a studio in a Southwestern town:

Rates: "My piano instruction is divided into two terms which parallel the fall and spring terms of the school year. The charge for the fall term (four months) for one child is $72 and for the spring term (five months) is $90. This fee may be paid in $18 installments at the beginning of each month. If more than one child from the same family is enrolled, the charge is $60 and $75 per child, to be paid in $15 installments."

Missed lessons: "Makeup lessons will not be given for a missed class lesson. Generally, makeup lessons for missed semiprivate

*The teachers from whose brochures quotations are made are Sylvia Atherton Daniels, California; Doris C. Downey, Virginia; Cheryl Hennecy, Florida; Arnetta Jones, New York; Maud Salter, Illinois; Marian J. Stickels, Michigan; Mary Tryer, Texas; Adele Velo, New Jersey; and Bernard J. Wickenheiser, Pennsylvania.

lessons will not be given, but certain exceptions can be made at my discretion. In the case of a missed lesson a new assignment will be given by phone."

Other Fees

"Elementary-level books and sight-reading materials may be rented. The usual fee is 50¢ per book. Notebook sheets of special material and popular arrangements are 15¢ each; all others as marked, including tax."

Purchasing Music

"I will provide necessary music for each child and bill parents for music at end of the month."

"Music materials are supplied at cost plus 10 percent of original cost to cover sales tax and postage."

Holidays

"Lessons which fall on school holidays will be held as usual, unless prior arrangements have been made."

Sample calendar:

Music teacher's convention: October 20–21. No lessons on those dates.

Thanksgiving Day: November 27. Makeup lessons on Friday, November 28; please schedule if desired.

Two-week Christmas holiday beginning December 22. Lessons resume on January 5.

One-week Easter holiday, April 18–April 25.

May 31: Memorial Day. Lessons if desired.

"Holidays and vacations will be announced as the season progresses."

Summer Study

"Arrangements may be made for summer lessons as convenient."

"Summer music study is a must to assure a maximum rate of progress. . . . The summer term consists of six weeks and includes five private and one group lesson."

Incentives

"Most Progress" award: Student's name and year inscribed on an achievement plaque which hangs permanently in the studio.

Cash prizes: for best composition entries.

Certificates and pins: composition and audition participants.

Parents may visit lesson every two months.

"As an incentive for good lesson attendance, twelve consecutive lessons of attendance earn one free lesson (no makeups on free lessons). As further incentive for good attendance there will be a

$1 charge for lessons cancelled less than seven days in advance. Conversely, a $1 credit will be given for lessons cancelled by the teacher less than seven days in advance. Prizes will be awarded at the Christmas party for the best yearly attendance."

BROCHURES

Whether a simple leaflet or a more elaborate multipage print, brochures can be effective promotional tools. The following sample is one possibility:

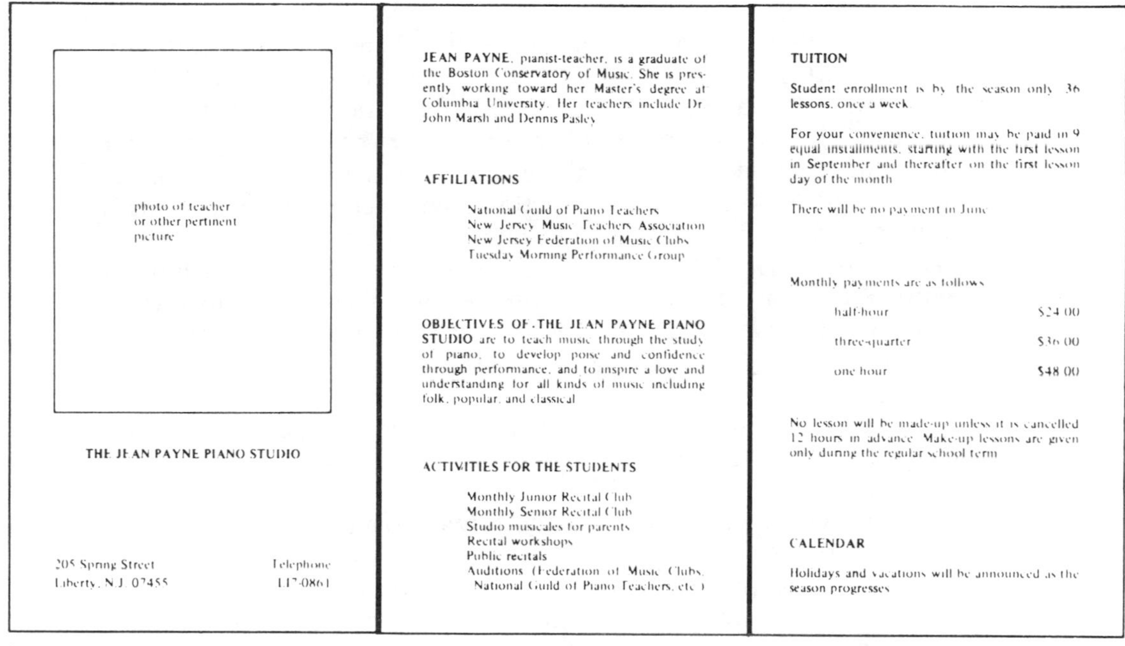

photo of teacher
or other pertinent
picture

THE JEAN PAYNE PIANO STUDIO

205 Spring Street
Liberty, N.J. 07455

Telephone
LI7-0861

Page 1

JEAN PAYNE, pianist-teacher, is a graduate of the Boston Conservatory of Music. She is presently working toward her Master's degree at Columbia University. Her teachers include Dr. John Marsh and Dennis Pasley.

AFFILIATIONS

National Guild of Piano Teachers
New Jersey Music Teachers Association
New Jersey Federation of Music Clubs
Tuesday Morning Performance Group

OBJECTIVES OF THE JEAN PAYNE PIANO STUDIO are to teach music through the study of piano, to develop poise and confidence through performance, and to inspire a love and understanding for all kinds of music including folk, popular, and classical.

ACTIVITIES FOR THE STUDENTS

Monthly Junior Recital Club
Monthly Senior Recital Club
Studio musicales for parents
Recital workshops
Public recitals
Auditions (Federation of Music Clubs, National Guild of Piano Teachers, etc.)

Page 2

TUITION

Student enrollment is by the season only. 36 lessons, once a week.

For your convenience, tuition may be paid in 9 equal installments, starting with the first lesson in September and thereafter on the first lesson day of the month.

There will be no payment in June.

Monthly payments are as follows:

half-hour	$24.00
three-quarter	$36.00
one hour	$48.00

No lesson will be made-up unless it is cancelled 12 hours in advance. Make-up lessons are given only during the regular school term.

CALENDAR

Holidays and vacations will be announced as the season progresses.

Page 3

Generally brochures do not make any reference to delinquency in payments. Teachers take care of unpaid bills in much the same way that a doctor or a dentist might: sending statements, and if unheeded a telephone call, to arrive at some understanding as to when the amount can be paid.

RECORD KEEPING

The piano teacher today has no choice but to keep accurate records for the purpose of reporting taxable income (or the lack of income) to the Internal Revenue Service. Income records are derived from:

(1.) Duplicate receipt books which are used for all cash tuition payments.
(2.) Deposit entries in the checkbook (or savings account) when tuition payments are made by check.
(3.) Cash entries when checks are cashed instead of deposited.

The income from both the cash receipt, cash entries, and check or saving deposits must equal the payments made by students as totaled from their individual accounts. Student records may be kept in a single book, allowing a page for each student, or on bookkeeping file cards, a single file card for each student.

It is of the utmost importance to keep track of all pertinent expenses by filing receipts the teacher retains from cash payments (or checkbook entries) for various expenditures necessary for the operation of the business. Cancelled checks with bills serve as a record of these expenditures and must be retained should an Internal Revenue Service audit require their proof.

There is no doubt as to what income is, but there is some uncertainty as to which expenditures are legal deductions in terms of tax regulations. Also, because of changes in the law, these deductions are not the same every year. The teacher had best keep an account of all expenses. Later it can be determined which are allowable as deductions and which are not. A careful reading of the instructions that accompany tax forms is helpful. Any doubtful points may be clarified by a phone call or visit to the IRS office. J.K. Lasser's *Your Income Tax* (Simon and Schuster) may provide further assistance. Those who prefer not to prepare their tax returns still have to prepare for their accountants or lawyers all the figures necessary for reporting an accurate statement of net income (or loss).

The expenses that are usually deductible from gross income, and need to be recorded and accounted for, are:

(1) Rental of studio and all additional expense for the maintenance of that studio.

(2) Home studios: after determining the percentage of the home used for teaching (if two rooms of a six-room house are used, the percentage is 33-1/3), deduct only that percentage of expenses in the following costs:

- [a] Utilities (gas, electricity, heating oil, telephone, etc.).
- [b] Insurance, mortgage interest, taxes and depreciation (if home-owner), cost of cleaning, gardening, snow removal, etc.
- [c] Renovation of studio rooms.

(3) Depreciation of piano or pianos, equipment (tape recorders, typewriter, adding machine), furnishings such as draperies, chairs, and filing cabinets. Suggested life of piano may be from ten to twenty years; record player, five years; carpeting, ten years.

(4) Traveling expenses if lessons are at students' homes. This includes a pro-rated depreciation of the car, determined by the proportion of business use.

(5) General expenses

- [a] Piano tuning and repair
- [b] Stationery supplies and postage
- [c] Music and books to be used at studio
- [d] Advertising: newspaper and magazine ads, cards, signs, etc.

[e] Awards
[f] Recitals (includes programs, tuning, hall rental, refreshments, flowers, etc.)
[g] Tapes, records, professional magazines
[h] State taxes
[i] Dues to professional organizations
[j] Fees for workshops, conventions, (travel and living expenses included), college courses, and private lessons when for the maintenance of professional skills
[k] Fees paid to accountant or lawyer for such services as preparation of income-tax forms

Additional forms that may help the teacher in setting up a simple bookkeeping and billing system are below.

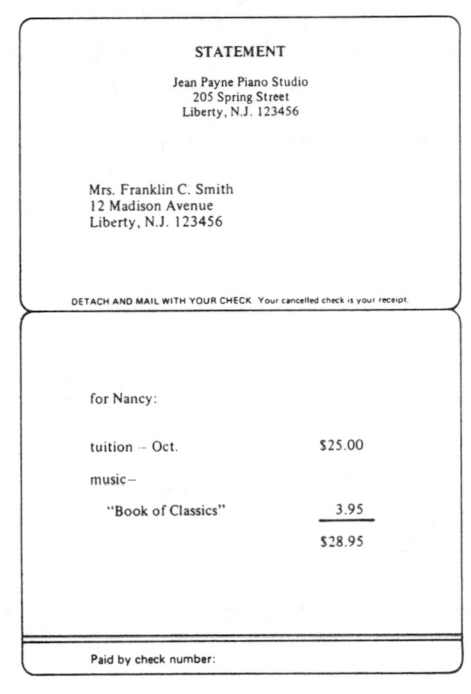

STATEMENT

Jean Payne Piano Studio
205 Spring Street
Liberty, N.J. 123456

Mrs. Franklin C. Smith
12 Madison Avenue
Liberty, N.J. 123456

DETACH AND MAIL WITH YOUR CHECK. Your cancelled check is your receipt.

for Nancy:

tuition – Oct.	$25.00
music–	
"Book of Classics"	3.95
	$28.95

Paid by check number:

All kinds of other adaptable forms are available at stationery stores.

Record of Expenses

	stationery supplies	postage	recording expenses	mus. books for studio	awards	recital expenses	professional club dues	magazines	studio rent	electricity	phone	furnishings	misc.
9/3 R.H. Stationery	6.51												
9/7 Lawson's Music				3.20									
9/10 Post Office		13.00											
9/14 R.H. Stationery	5.49												
9/21 Lawson's Music				1.75									
9/30 Donald Clark									150.00				
10/1 Jason's Radio (tape)			6.20										
10/1 Lane's Dept. Store												14.53	
10/1 Post Office		.65											
10/5 Lawson's Music					7.80								
	12.00	13.65	6.20	4.95	7.80				150.00			14.53	

DISABILITY AND RETIREMENT

In case of disability or approaching retirement, the teacher should be in touch with the local Social Security office as soon as possible. Regardless of age or health, it is wise to obtain periodically a statement of earnings. Such a request should be sent to: Social Security Administration, P.O. Box 57, Baltimore, Maryland 21203. For information regarding disability coverage, write to the Department of Health, Education and Welfare, Social Security Adminstration, Bureau of Disability Insurance, Baltimore, Maryland 21241.

Self-employed piano teachers are eligible to establish a retirement plan under the Keogh Act. This law enables them to set aside each year a portion of their earnings (up to 15 percent of adjusted gross income) for a retirement fund. The tax on this yearly sum will be deferred until retirement, when, presumably, income and tax bracket will be lower.

Information concerning the Keogh Plan may be secured from the IRS, savings banks, mutual funds, and stock and insurance brokers.

The business methods a teacher chooses will depend on his or her needs, personality, and understanding of financial matters. In any case it is sound policy to maintain orderly files and preserve records on all income, expenses, and relevant activities.

RECOMMENDED READING

Benner, Lora. "Let's Talk Business." *Clavier* March–April 1964.

——. "Schedules, Rates, Income." *The Benner Handbook for Piano Teaching.* Schenectady, N.Y.: Benner Publishers, 1975.

Boutilier, Mary. "Black Ink and Red." *Clavier* January1967.

Errico, Josephine M. "The Vanishing Make-up Lesson." *Clavier* November 1967.

Lasser, J.K. *Your Income Tax.* New York: Simon and Schuster, revised annually.

O'Bryne, John C. "Tax Savings." *Clavier* February 1968.

Ott, Pat Bernard. "How to Obtain a Waiting List." *Clavier* November 1966.

Schamen, Alvin. "Easy Bookkeeping for the Piano Teacher." *The Piano Teacher* November–December 1961.

Skaggs, Hazel Ghazarian. "Is Summer Study Necessary?" *Clavier* March–April 1965.

Stone, Marion. "This Business of Teaching Music." *Clavier* February 1968.

The Piano: Construction and Care

HAZEL GHAZARIAN SKAGGS

HISTORY

The first piano was made in about 1710 by the Italian instrument maker Bartolommeo Cristofori. This instrument was very much like a harpsichord except that its strings were not plucked, but hit by a hammer. Because of this difference, the softness and loudness of each note could now be controlled by the player. Therefore it was named *piano-forte* using the two Italian words that mean "soft" and "loud."

In Germany, where the clavichord was popular, the piano mechanism was encased into the oblong form of that instrument rather than the harpsichord. It was in this shape that the Germans introduced the piano to the English. For some time only square pianos were made, but in the latter part of the eighteenth century the harpsichord-shaped piano reappeared. The square piano, however, continued to exist until about 1900.

Meanwhile, changes were also taking place in the piano mechanism. The escapement action greatly facilitated the repetition of notes, and the invention of the damper pedal provided the means to a more resonant, finely calibrated sound. In 1800 the first upright piano, with the harp dropping below the keyboard, was patented. Later, in 1821, the invention of the double escapement by Erard in Paris still further improved the repetition action.

The Americans were not idle either. In 1843 they were responsible for the first iron frame cast in one piece for a grand piano. By mid-nineteenth century the use of cross-stringing, invented in 1830, became common. This made possible the use of longer strings and gave the piano still further richness of tone.

THE PIANO TODAY

Today the piano keyboard consists of eighty-eight notes—seven-and-a-third octaves—a substantial growth from the first piano, whose range was about four and a half octaves. The mechanism of the piano is constantly being improved upon, while size, style, and shape undergo slight alterations to meet the needs of a changing society. The piano as we know it today may be purchased in the following models:

Spinet	36 to 38 inches high
Console	40 to 42 inches high
Upright (Studio)	46 to 52 inches high
Baby Grand	about 5 feet long
Parlor Grand	about 6 to 7 feet long
Concert Grand	9 feet long

A glance inside the piano will reveal that the very lowest bass notes (about six to eight) consist of one thick string (copper wire wound about a steel string); then the notes have two strings, not as thick but still with copper wiring wound about a steel string; and finally about two octaves above the lowest bass note, each note has three steel strings.

Notes on the keyboard may be identified by *octave registers,* generally used by musicians, or by *key numbers,* popular with piano tuners and technicians.

OCTAVE REGISTERS

Below "Middle C"

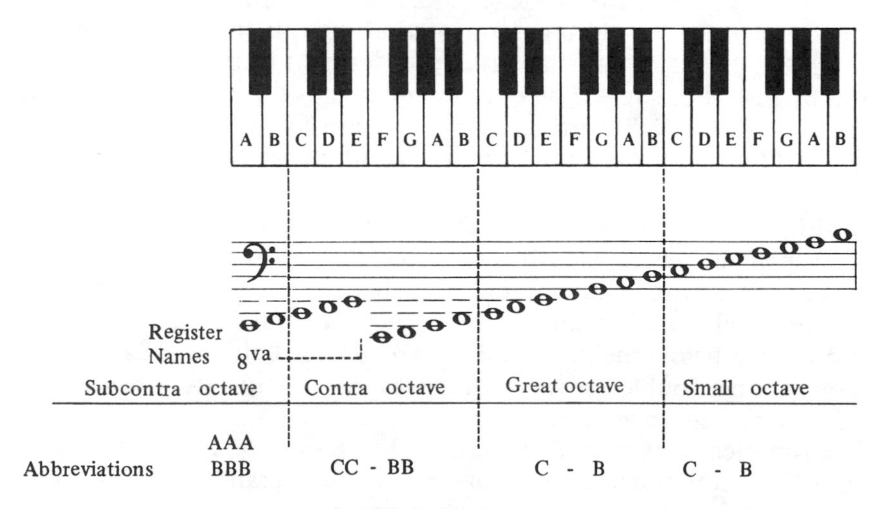

(The lowest note is Subcontra A; abbreviated: AAA)

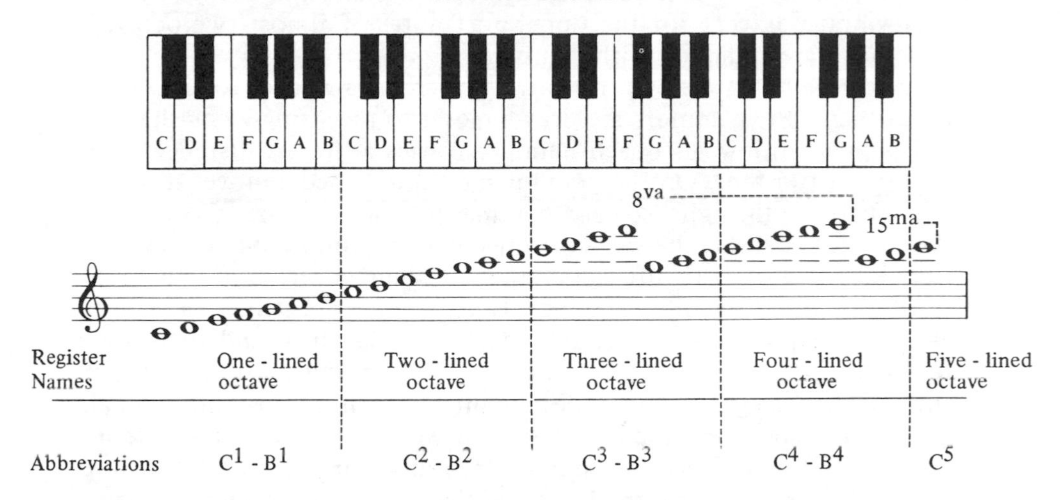

KEY NUMBERS

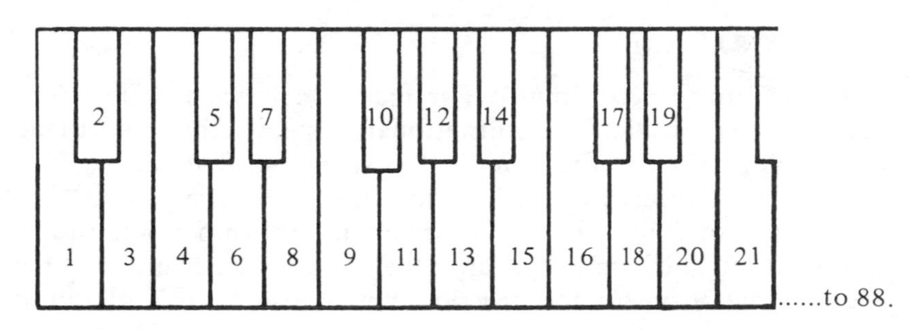

The grand piano action is made up of the *key*, the assembly of levers called the *wippen*, the *hammer*, and the *damper*.

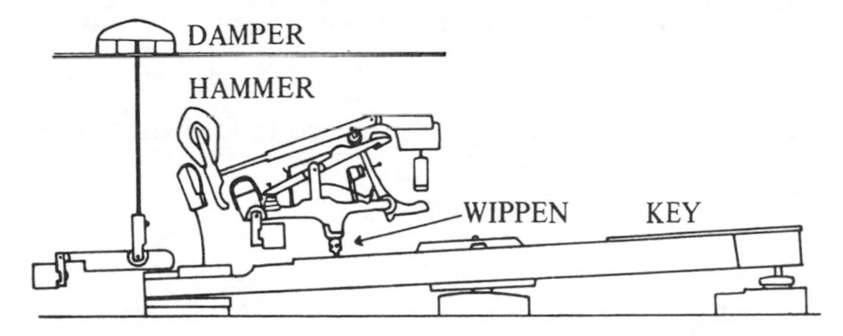

PEDALS

There are generally three pedals on the piano. The damper pedal, located at the right, is the most frequently used. When it is pressed down, all the dampers are lifted up away from the strings so that the strings are free to vibrate. When the damper pedal is released to its "up" position, the dampers return to rest on the strings and the strings can no longer vibrate. Except for the uppermost notes of almost two octaves, all the notes are equipped with dampers.

The soft pedal, located at the left, helps create a weaker tone. On the vertical piano the hammers are drawn closer to the string when the soft pedal is pressed down, so each hammer travels a shorter distance, thus creating a softer tone. On the grand piano the soft pedal moves the keyboard a little to the right, so each hammer hits one less string.

The middle pedal is the *sostenuto* pedal, often found only on a grand piano. Its function is to lift the damper or dampers from a single note or group of notes so only the single tone or tones are sustained. This is done by first playing the note or notes to be sustained and then pressing down the sostenuto pedal. The use of this pedal is so limited that pianos other than grands are seldom equipped with the sostenuto pedal. Sometimes, usually on smaller pianos, the middle pedal is not a sostenuto pedal. Its function is either purely decorative, or it can be a muffling device to lower a felt strip the length of the keyboard between the hammers and strings for a softer sound.

PIANO CARE

Piano tuning, according to The Piano Technicians Guild, Inc., a professional organization of international scope, is "the task of readjusting the pitch of each of the piano's 230 strings so that they will correctly harmonize with each other." It does not include any other work. The care of a piano, however, entails much more than periodic tuning. Since temperature and humidity vary, the state of the piano is altered with each change. Constructed of wood, metal, leather, and felt, all of which react differently to climatic and environmental changes, the piano begins to go out of tune and out of regulation from the moment it is left on its own. Except for a major concert pianist, full-time service is not feasible, but piano teachers may maintain their pianos at a high level of efficiency by following the schedule of good care given below.*

Tuning	
keeping the piano up to A-440 pitch (A above middle C–#49 in the piano tuner's system of identification–vibrates at 440 cycles per second)	two to four times a year
Action regulation	
the adjustment of all mechanical parts between finger and string	every three to five years; more if piano is heavily used or owner requires fine results

*Porter, Thomas. "A Pianist's Guide to Effective Piano Maintenance." *Clavier*, May–June 1966.

Voicing hammers are softened or hardened to obtain the desired tone quality	every two years if piano is used six hours or more a day
Hammers replaced hammer shanks	every six years; twelve to fifteen years
Keyboard felt and key tops replaced	twelve to fifteen years
Rebuilding may include all of the above plus restringing, repair of soundboard (even replacement), replacing wrest-pin plank, regilding the plate, repairing or replacing the bridges	piano may not need rebuilding for thirty years if given proper care

The teacher may recommend to students and parents the dos and don'ts of piano care listed below.

What To Do for Your Piano

- Keep the temperature and humidity constant in the room where you have placed your piano (excessive dryness and excessive humidity are harmful.)
- Clean the keys with a slightly damp cloth. For stubborn marks, run the cloth over a cake of soap, then rub the spot lengthwise. Dry with a soft cloth.
- Close the piano when doing housework.
- Replace a loose ivory immediately.
- Select your piano technician with care and follow his or her advice.

What Not To Do to Your Piano

- Don't place piano in a very damp room.
- Don't place vertical pianos directly against a wall; leave a few inches so that the sound is not cut off.
- Don't place piano near a heating source, drafts, or cooling units.
- Don't place such objects as vases, pictures, and trinkets on your piano; they will cause annoying vibrations.
- Don't place any containers with water on the piano. Should the water spill, wetness can cause serious damage.
- Don't use oil on any part of the piano.
- Don't try to remove dust from inside your piano. This is a task for a piano technician.
- Don't demoth your piano at any time without consulting your piano technician. On your own you may do more damage than good, including damage to yourself.
- Don't close a piano that has ivory keys. Without light the ivory

may become yellowed.

- Don't move your piano yourself; employ professional piano movers.

In general, the best advice to piano owners is to use the instrument regularly, for a played piano stays in better condition than an idle one.

BUYING A USED PIANO

In a 1975 article in *Music Journal*, Nada Mangialetti recommended the following guidelines for buying a used piano*:

- Look on the metal plate or the tuning block for the serial number. A dealer or piano technician can look up this number and tell you exactly when the piano was made, and whether parts are still available for it. Avoid pianos made before 1900 unless you want a museum piece, not a functional instrument. Pianos made during wartime or depression years are more likely to have had money-saving corners cut.
- Look inside the piano: each key in the treble section should cause a hammer to strike three strings at once. (Some 64-note pianos have two strings per key.) The bass section should have two strings per key; the extreme bass section, only one string per key.
- Check for rust on the tuning pins. This may affect how well the piano will hold a tuning.
- Play *each* key individually. As soon as your finger releases a key, the damper inside the piano should fall back on the strings and stop them from sounding. The keys should not stick.
- Beware of pianos that are badly out of tune. *Restoring them to proper tuning is not always a simple matter.* Even a few detectable bad notes may be a sign of other, unseen troubles.
- Press down the right-hand damper pedal (sometimes incorrectly called the loud pedal). This should raise all the dampers at once, allowing all the strings to sound indefinitely as you strike each key. The pedal shouldn't squeak or stick.
- Press down on the left-hand soft pedal. On grand pianos, this should move the keyboard sideways, so that each hammer strikes only two strings, instead of three. On vertical pianos, it should move the hammers closer to the strings, so the striking force is less. Neither the pedal, hammers, nor keyboard should stick or rattle.
- A minor crack in the sound board usually does not affect the tone quality very much; but a crack in the metal plate means the piano is ready to be junked.
- Used grands are more often in better condition than used verticals. They are generally made better to start with, and are usually treated better.

*Reprinted from *Music Journal*, 1975. Used by permission.

- Who owns the piano now? A serious student or musician who probably cared for it properly? A school, church, or family with young children who may have neglected or misused it? Was it used by inexperienced students for learning purposes? Or by advanced musicians for occasional concerts? Is it just a decorative showpiece that has been sitting in someone's fancy living room for years without regular tunings? You can tell a lot about the piano by looking at the owners and their home.

RECOMMENDED READING

Bie, Oscar. *A History of the Pianoforte and Pianoforte Players.* New York: Da Capo Press, 1966.

Cooper, Martin, ed. *Music and Musicians.* New York: Hawthorn Books, 1958.

Mohn, Norman Carroll. "Your Friend the Piano Tuner." *The Piano Teacher* July–August 1963.

———. "Wanted: A Good Used Piano." *The Piano Teacher* January–February 1965.

———. "Voicing." *The Piano Teacher* September–October 1965.

Porter, Thomas. "A Pianist's Guide to Effective Piano Maintenance." *Clavier* May–June 1966.

———. "The Grand Piano Action." *Clavier* May–June 1967.

Sargent, George. "Temperament." *Clavier* May–June 1968.

Sumner, William Leslie. *The Pianoforte.* (rev. ed.) New York: St. Martin's, 1966.

Wills, Vera G. and Ande Manners. *A Parent's Guide to Music Lessons.* New York: Harper & Row, 1967.

The New Copyright Law: A Primer for Music Teachers

DENES AGAY

What is copyright?
"The exclusive right to the publication, production, or sale of the rights to a literary, dramatic, musical, or artistic work. . . granted by law for a definite period of years to an author, composer, distributor, etc." (Webster's).
How can one tell if a work is copyrighted?
All copyrighted works bear a copyright notice: the date of copyright, the name of the owner together with the word *copyright* and/or the symbol ©. (For instance: © Copyright 1939 by John Smith, or just © 1939 by John Smith). Any work published without copyright notice automatically becomes public domain.
How long does the law protect a copyrighted work?
Under the old law, which was replaced in 1976, the term of copyright was twenty-eight years, with possible renewal for an additional twenty-eight years. However during the legislative process leading to the new law, all copyrights from September 19, 1906 which had been renewed but which otherwise would have expired (on September 19, 1962) were extended, so that they did not fall into public domain. To be safe, a music educator should assume that any publication which bears a copyright notice of 1906 or later is protected.

According to the new law, works created after January 1, 1978 are protected for the life of the composer (author) plus fifty years. Copyrights in effect on that date, if renewed, will continue for seventy-five years from the date the copyright was originally secured. For instance, a work copyrighted in 1910 and renewed will be protected until 1985.

Is it permissible to copy, by hand or by machine, a copyrighted work?
In general, it is not; to do so would be breaking the law and tantamount to stealing property. However, there are certain special circumstances under which teachers may copy a work or part of it without securing permission. For instance, quotations and partial reproductions for the purposes of teaching, research, or criticism are permissible under the time-honored doctrine of "fair use." In determining whether use made of a work in a particular case is fair or not, the law lists the following essential factors to be considered:

- the purpose and character of the use (educational or commercial?)
- the amount and substantiality of the portion used (how much is being copied?)
- the effect on the potential market of the work, or on its value (is the owner, through this copying, denied a just financial return on the work?)

The new law further elaborates on fair use and stipulates the following instances in which music educators, without permission, may:

- make a copy of a lost piece in an emergency, if it is replaced with a purchased printed copy in due course
- for academic purposes in class study, make one copy per student of an excerpt which does not amount to a performable unit (such as a section or movement) and which in no case amounts to more than ten per cent of the whole work

Expressly prohibited are the following:

- copying to avoid purchase
- copying music for any kind of performance (note emergency exception above)
- copying without including the copyright notice
- copying to create compilations and anthologies
- reproducing material designed to be consumable, such as workbooks, standardized tests, and answer sheets
- charging students beyond the actual cost involved in making copies as permitted above

Can a copyrighted work be recorded?
The copyright owner has the exclusive right to reproduce the copyrighted work on phonograph records. There are, however, exceptions which permit music educators to

- make a single recording of a student performance for evaluation and rehearsal purposes, or for preservation in the school's or teacher's archives
- make a single copy of a sound recording or tape of copyrighted music for the purpose of aural exercises and examinations

Once records of a nondramatic musical work have been distributed to the public in the United States under the authority of the copyright owner, any other person may obtain a compulsory license to record the work by complying with certain procedures and by the payment of the royalty provided by the law. It must be borne in mind that the *first* recording of a work and its distribution in recorded form requires the consent of the copyright owner.

Is it permissible to arrange a copyrighted work?

Making arrangements of a piece of music is an exclusive right of the copyright owner, but under the fair use clause the following, with specified limitations, are conceived to be reasonable exceptions:

- printed copies which have been purchased may be edited or simplified provided the fundamental character of the work is not distorted, or the lyrics, if any, altered, or lyrics added if none exist
- the compulsory license for recording includes the privilege of making a musical arrangement of a work to the extent necessary to conform it to the style or manner of interpretation of the performance involved, but the arrangement shall not change the basic melody or fundamental character of the work. Quite obviously, this privilege is not meant to extend to so-called serious compositions.

Anyone wishing to arrange a copyrighted work must (with the exceptions noted above) obtain permission from the copyright owner. In order to simplify this process, various teachers' and publishers' organizations prepared a standard form for the request and granting of permission. Such copies may be obtained, free of charge, by writing to any of the following organizations:

National Music Publishers Association, Inc. (NMPA)
110 East 59th Street
New York, New York 10022

Music Publishers Association of the United States (MPA)
130 West 57th Street
New York, New York 10019

Music Educators National Conference (MENC)
1902 Association Drive
Reston, Virginia 22091

Music Teachers National Association (MTNA)
2209 Carew Tower
Cincinnati, Ohio 45202

National Association of Schools of Music
11250 Roger Bacon Dr., suite 5
Reston, Va. 22090

Is it permissible to copy a work which is permanently out of print?
Permission of the copyright owner is necessary. Standard forms requesting such permission may be obtained, free of charge, from the organizations listed above.
What about copyrighted editions of masterworks, originally created long before the enactment of any copyright laws; do they have the same protection?
The copyright pertains to the editorial marks (tempo, dynamics, phrasing, pedal, etc.) and the explanatory texts. The basic work, as originally notated by the composer, is public domain. The same is valid for copyrighted arrangements and adaptations. Copyright protects only the changes and alterations from the original; the composer's original conception is public domain.

In general, caution and scrutiny are recommended in this area. The law does not require specification in the copyright notice as to what elements of the work are in fact protected by copyright; only occasionally do we find a specific notice such as: This arrangement © copyright 1979 by Lyra Music Co.
What are the penalties for infringement?
Copyright infringement is more serious than a parking violation and needs to be viewed with concern. A music educator found making illegal copies or otherwise infringing may face very substantial penalties, especially if willful infringement for commercial advantage and private financial gain is proved.

The law specifies certain alleviating circumstances. If the court finds that the infringer "was not aware and had no reason to believe that his or her acts constitute an infringement" the fine may be reduced to a minimum of $100. Also, the court is further instructed "to remit statutory damages in any case where an infringer believed and had reasonable ground for believing that his or her use of the copyrighted work was a fair use—if the infringer was. . . an employee or agent of a nonprofit educational institution, library or archives acting within the scope of his or her employment. . . "

This should in no way be construed by teachers as all the protection they need for anything they do. As always, ignorance of the law is no excuse. Music educators need to understand fair use and make the most of the privileges it grants, but they must also abide by its very definite limitations. Where any doubt exists as to the permissibility of the usage, it is advisable to contact the copyright owner for clarification.
Where can one get general information on copyrights, registration procedures, etc.?
The copyright law of the United States is administered by the Copyright Office. This office registers claims to a copyright, it catalogs all registrations, and issues certificates of registration, but it does not "grant" or "issue" copyrights. Statutory copyright protection is afforded by federal law when certain requirements are met. It is secured by the claimant by following a prescribed registration procedure. All mail to the Copyright Office should be addressed to:

Register of Copyrights
Library of Congress
Washington, D.C. 20559

Can a copyrighted work be performed anywhere, anytime?
Although performance use is one of the copyright owner's exclusive rights, the special needs of music educators and others are recognized in the limitations on these rights and are specified in the law. Music educators should take special notice of the very limited nature of these exemptions. The following are *not* infringements:

- Performance of any copyrighted work by instructors or pupils in the course of face-to-face teaching activities of a nonprofit educational institution, in a classroom (or similar place devoted to teaching).
- Performance of a nondramatic literary or musical work at a school concert if there is no purpose of direct or indirect commercial advantage, no fee or compensation paid to the performers, promoters, or organizers, and no admission charge; if there is an admission charge, all of the proceeds must be used only for educational or charitable purposes. The performance may not take place if the copyright owner objects in writing seven days before the event.
- Performance of a nondramatic literary or musical work on closed-circuit television to other classrooms or to disabled students for teaching purposes, only if the transmission is part of the systematic instructional activities of a nonprofit educational institution, and only if the performance is directly related to and of material assistance to the teaching content of the program.
- Performance of nondramatic literary or musical works or of dramatic-musical works of a religious nature, in the course of services at places of worship or at religious assembly.

Complete information concerning licensing of performances of copyrighted (nondramatic) musical works may be obtained free from any of the three performing rights organizations:

American Society of Composers, Authors and Publishers (ASCAP)
One Lincoln Plaza
New York, New York 10023

Broadcast Music, Inc. (BMI)
40 West 57th Street
New York, New York 10019

SESAC, Inc.
10 Columbus Circle
New York, New York 10019

Performance of a dramatic-musical work—an opera, ballet, musical comedy, etc.—is customarily licensed by the copyright owner of the performing right, usually the publisher or licensing agent.

Teachers' Organizations

HAZEL GHAZARIAN SKAGGS

PURPOSE AND BENEFITS

Music teachers' organizations provide their members with a variety of opportunities not otherwise available. This is particularly true for those who teach in isolation in their private studios. Geographical location, membership size and members' needs will to a large extent determine the organization's objectives. Generally, teachers' groups will offer most of the following benefits:

- Exchange of ideas with colleagues
- Lectures and workshops to introduce new ideas, reinforce old ones, and improve teaching standards
- Opportunities for teachers to perform for each other at meetings or give public recitals
- Music programs by visiting artists
- Suggestions for uniform business methods
- Certification plans for teachers*
- Group insurance plans
- Incentives for students: auditions, recitals, and contests
- Scholarship and welfare funds

*Music Teachers National Association, Inc. has an active certification plan to promote recognition of music teaching as a profession. One of the objectives of certification is to "motivate the teacher to obtain and maintain professional growth through guidelines for study, performance, leadership, and professional activities."

- Publications (journals, magazines, etc.)
- Exhibits: teaching materials, textbooks, audio-visual aids, electronic labs, pianos, studio equipment, etc.
- Conferences and conventions (national organizations schedule state, regional, and national meetings to exchange ideas with teachers from all parts of the country)
- Rapport with such local groups as the public school, music store, community concert program, etc.; on the national level, sponsorship of special projects (Music in Our Schools Week, etc.), cooperation with professional organizations, government agencies, music industry, etc.
- Fellowship—special events such as dinners, parties, and group attendance at concerts

The fringe benefits of membership in a music organization are many. The well-established teacher with an excess of students may refer students to a member teacher. Enduring friendships may be formed, and meeting with one another may result in such professional ties as performing together, collaborating on publications, or even operating a school.

PIANO TEACHERS' ORGANIZATIONS

There are some organizations which are exclusively devoted to piano teachers. With the exception of the National Guild of Piano Teachers, they are locally based, but membership may be of regional or national scope. Three such organizations are the New England Pianoforte Music Teachers' Association (Boston), the Piano Teachers Congress of New York, Inc., (New York City), and the Texas Group Piano Association (Denton). There are also some piano associations that represent the students (or descendants) of a single master teacher. In this category are The Leschetizky Association, Inc. and The Alton Jones Associates, Inc. Both are based in New York City, but membership rolls are international.

Since local organizations have no office addresses, information on becoming a member can best be attained through personal contact such as through a local music store or fellow teachers, watching local papers or music magazines for notices of meetings and special events, or making inquiries from national organizations.

NATIONAL ORGANIZATIONS

Following is a list of the foremost national music teachers' organizations with pertinent information regarding each. A letter to any of these will bring a prompt reply regarding membership.

Music Educators National Conference
1902 Association Drive
Reston, Virginia 22091

Membership
64,000; music teachers at all institutional levels, from preschool through college and university. Student members are college and university students enrolled in music education.

Purpose
"Advancement of music education is the principal objective of MENC. MENC aims to provide leadership in professional growth for the music educator; a national voice for music education; a clearing house for school music activities and interests; correlation between music education in the United States and other parts of the world." (from MENC fact sheet, July 1976)

Publications
Music Educators Journal, nine times yearly
Journal of Research in Music Education, quarterly
Music Power, newsletter, quarterly
Materials on music education, including filmstrips

Conferences
State, regional, national (biennial in even-numbered years)

Principal Projects
Although most activities are of primary interest to educators in public school music, there are also programs in piano pedagogy.

Music Teachers National Association
408 Carew Tower
Cincinnati, Ohio 45202

Membership
15,000; faculty members of music schools and private music teachers, concert artists, and student members.

Purpose
". . . to raise consistently the level of musical performance, understanding, and teaching in America." (from MTNA's membership invitation)

Publications
American Music Teacher, six times a year
Books including Kenneth Drake's *The Sonatas of Beethoven* and, from the MTNA Resource Series, *Keyboard Bibliography*

Conventions
Local, state, regional and national (annual)

Principal Projects
MTNA Scholarship Foundation, Certification, Group insurance, Student activities (auditions, contests in performance and composition, and performance opportunities).

National Federation of Music Clubs
Suite 1936
310 South Michigan Ave.
Chicago, Illinois 60604

Membership
500,000; in 5,000 junior, student, and senior organizations.

Purpose
Dedicated to finding and fostering young musical talent, championing American music, and sponsoring a variety of projects that advance the cultural life in America

Publications
Music Clubs Magazine, five times yearly
Junior Keynotes, four times yearly
Many guides, pamphlets, and bulletins

Conventions
State and national (biennial)

Principal projects
Auditions, nonprofessional composers' contests, awards, study grants, scholarships and sponsorship of National Music Week (first full week of May each year), Crusade for Strings, annual "Hands Across the Sea" broadcast in observance of United Nations Day, annual February Parade of American Music, and Music in Hospitals

National Guild of Piano Teachers
American College of Musicians
Box 1807
Austin, Texas 78767

Membership
85,000; teachers and students (about 9,000 teachers). Approximately 75,000 students participate in various yearly events, principally adjudicated auditions.

Purpose
To provide students concrete and appropriate incentives so that every student in the auditions "becomes a winner of an award commensurate with his attainment."

Publications
Piano Guild Notes, bimonthly
The Guild Syllabus

Principal Projects
National Piano Playing Auditions, Annual Composition Test, National Music Scholarship Fund, Van Cliburn Competition ($10, 000 award), International Piano Recording Competition

PIANO PERIODICALS

In addition to the official magazines of national teachers' organizations, there are some periodicals that teachers of piano will find helpful and interesting.

Clavier, 1418 Lake Street, Evanston, Illinois 60204. A magazine for teachers of piano and organ, nine times a year.
Contemporary Keyboard, Keyboard Players International, Box 907, Saratoga, California 95070. Deals mainly with jazz, popular, and contemporary (electronic) music. Issued bimonthly.
Keyboard Arts: A Journal for Keyboard Teachers, 741 Alexandria Road, Princeton, New Jersey 08540. Three times a year. (Published by National Keyboard Arts Associates.)
Music Journal, 370 Lexington Avenue, New York, New York 10017. A journal for music educators, performers, dealers, and music lovers; ten times a year, plus summer and winter annuals.
The Piano Quarterly, P.O. Box 815, Wilmington, Vermont 05363. January, April, July, and October.

Organizations which may be of further interest to teachers are:

American Association for Music Therapy
Leo Shatin, President
Education Building
35 West 4th Street
New York, New York 10003
Membership: 350

American Liszt Society
Fernando Laires, President
Department of Music, University of Florida
Gainesville, Florida 32611
Membership: 100 plus

American Matthay Association
Donald Hageman
834 Riverview Terrace
Dayton, Ohio 45407
Membership: 160

International Bach Society
Rosalyn Tureck, Director
165 West 57th Street
New York, New York 10019
Membership: 150

Leschetizky Association
Genia Robinor, President
105 West 72nd Street
New York, New York 10023
Membership: 400

The above list was obtained from The National Music Council, 250 West 57th Street, Suite 626, New York, New York 10019. All organizations described and listed in this chapter are members of The National Music Council, which is comprised of representatives from these organizations and others of national scope and activity.

Appendix I: The Master Teachers and Their Pupils

DENES AGAY

	pupil of:	*teacher of:*
Eugène d'Albert (1864–1932)	Franz Liszt	Wilhelm Backhaus
C.P.E. Bach (1714–1788)	Johann Sebastian Bach	J.C. Bach Jan Dussek
Ludwig van Beethoven (1770–1827)	Christian Neefe	Karl Czerny Ferdinand Ries
Felix Blumenfeld (1863–1931)	Nikolai Rimsky-Korsakov Anton Rubinstein	Vladimir Horowitz
Ferruccio Busoni (1866–1924)	Wilhelm Mayer	Rudolf Ganz Percy Grainger Joseph Lhevinne Selim Palmgren Egon Petri
Teresa Carreno (1858–1917)	Louis Gottschalk Anton Rubinstein	Edward MacDowell Egon Petri
Frédéric Chopin (1810–1849)	Friedrich Kalkbrenner	Karl Mikuli
Muzio Clementi (1752–1832)	Carpani Santarelli	Johann Cramer John Field Johann Hummel Friedrich Kalkbrenner Ignaz Moscheles

	pupil of:	*teacher of:*
Alfred Cortot (1877–1962)	Louis Diemer	Gina Bachauer
Karl Czerny (1791–1857)	Ludwig van Beethoven	Joseph Dachs Theodor Kullak Theodor Leschetizky
Joseph Dachs (1825–1896)	Karl Czerny	Vladimir de Pachmann
Edward Dannreuther (1844–1905)	Ignaz Moscheles	James Friskin
Louis Diemer (1843–1919)	Antoine Marmontel	Alfredo Casella Alfred Cortot Robert Casadesus Emil Frey
Anna Essipoff (1851–1914)	Theodor Leschetizky	Alexander Borovsky Sergei Prokofiev
John Field (1782–1837)	Muzio Clementi	Maria Szymanowska Alexander Villoing
Leopold Godowsky (1870–1938)	Camille Saint-Saëns	Clarence Adler David Guion Harold Henry Mana-Zucca Walter Rummel
Louis Gottschalk (1829–1907)	Camille Saint-Saëns	Teresa Carreno
Vladimir Horowitz (1904–)	Felix Blumenfeld	Byron Janis Ivan Davis
Johann Hummel (1778–1837)	Muzio Clementi Joseph Haydn W. A. Mozart	Adolph Henselt Ferdinand Hiller Sigismond Thalberg
Friedrich Kalkbrenner (1785–1849)	Muzio Clementi	Frédéric Chopin George Mathias Camille Saint-Saëns Sigismond Thalberg
Wanda Landowska (1877–1959)	Moritz Moszkowski	Alice Ehlers Ralph Kirkpatrick
Theodor Leschetizky (1830–1915)	Karl Czerny	Fanny Bloomfield Alexander Brailovsky Anna Essipoff Ignaz Friedman Ossip Gabrilovitch Mark Hambourg Ignace Paderewski Wassily Safonov Artur Schnabel Isabella Vengerova Arthur Schnabel

	pupil of:	*teacher of:*
Rosina Lhevinne (1880–1976)	Wassily Safonov	John Browning Van Cliburn Mischa Dichter
Franz Liszt (1811–1886)	Karl Czerny Antonio Salieri	Eugène d'Albert Hans von Bülow Moritz Moszkowski Moriz Rosenthal Emil Sauer Alexander Siloti Constantin von Sternberg Carl Tausig Stephan Thoman
Guy Maier (1892–1956)	Artur Schnabel	Leonard Pennario
Antoine Marmontel (1816–1896)	Pierre Zimmermann	Charles V. Alkan Isaac Albeniz Georges Bizet Claude Debussy Louis Diemer Vincent d'Indy Marguerite Long Edward MacDowell
Georges Mathias (1826–1910)	Friedrich Kalkbrenner	Isidor Philipp Stepane Pugno
Tobias Matthay (1858–1945)	George Alexander Macfarren	Clifford Curzon Myra Hess Ray Lev Irene Scharrer
Karl Mikuli (1821–1897)	Frédéric Chopin	Moriz Rosenthal
Ignaz Moscheles (1794–1870)	Muzio Clementi	Edward Dannreuther Edvard Grieg Rafael Joseffy William Mason Felix Mendelssohn
Moritz Moszkowski (1854–1925)	Theodor Kullak	Gustave Becker Josef Hofmann Wanda Landowska Joaquin Turina
Ignace Paderewski (1860–1941)	Theodor Leschetizky	Harold Bauer Ernest Schelling Sigismond Stojowski

	pupil of:	*teacher of:*
Isidor Philipp (1863–1958)	Georges Mathias Camille Saint-Saëns	Maurice Dumesnil Guiomar Novaes Beveridge Webster
Sergei Rachmaninoff (1873–1943)	Nicolai Zverev	Gina Bachauer
Moriz Rosenthal (1862–1946)	Franz Liszt Karl Mikuli	Robert Goldsand
Anton Rubinstein (1829–1884)	Alexander Villoing	Felix Blumenfeld Teresa Carreno Arthur Friedheim Ossip Gabrilovitch Josef Hofmann Alberto Jonas
Nicholas Rubinstein (1835–1881)	Alexander Villoing	Emil Sauer Alexander Siloti
Wassily Safonov (1852–1918)	Theodor Leschetizky	Wictor Labunski Joseph Lhevinne Rosina Lhevinne Nicolas Medtner Alexander Scriabin
Camille Saint-Saëns (1835–1921)	Friedrich Kalkbrenner	Louis Gottschalk Isidor Philipp Leopold Godowsky
Olga Samaroff (1882–1948)	Ernest Hutcheson Constantin Sternberg	William Kapell Eugene List Rosalyn Tureck
Artur Schnabel (1882–1951)	Theodor Leschetizky	Victor Babin Clifford Curzon Leonard Fleisher Boris Goldovsky Guy Maier
Clara Schumann (1819–1896)	Friedrich Wieck	Natalie Janotha Mathilde Verne
Alexander Siloti (1863–1945)	Franz Liszt	Serge Rachmaninoff
Sigismond Stojowski (1869–1946)	Ignace Paderewski	Oscar Levant Mischa Levitzki Arthur Loesser Guiomar Novaes
Carl Tausig (1841–1871)	Franz Liszt	Rafael Joseffy

Stephan Thomán (1862–1940)	Franz Liszt	Béla Bartók Ernö Dohnányi Fritz Reiner
Isabella Vengerova (1877–1956)	Theodor Leschetizky	Samuel Barber Leonard Bernstein Lucas Foss
Mathilde Verne (1865–1936)	Clara Schumann	Harold Samuel (Cutner) Solomon

Appendix II: The Keyboard Composers: A Selected Chronological List

DENES AGAY

Byrd, William – English (1543–1623)
Gabrieli, Giovanni – Italian (1557–1612)
Sweelinck, Jan Pieterszoon – Dutch (1562–1621)
Gibbons, Orlando – English (1583–1625)
Frescobaldi, Girolamo – Italian (1583–1643)
Chambonnières, Jacques Champion – French (1602–1672)
Froberger, Johann Jakob – German (1616–1667)
d'Anglebert, Jean Henri – French (1628–1691)
Lully, Jean-Baptiste – French (1632–1687)
Buxtehude, Dietrich – Danish-German (1637–1707)
Blow, John – English (1649–1708)
Pachelbel, Johann – German (1653–1706)
Purcell, Henry – English (1659–1695)
Kuhnau, Johann – German (1660–1732)
Fischer, Johann Kaspar Ferdinand – German (1665–1746)
Couperin, François – French (1668–1733)
Telemann, Georg Philipp – German (1681–1767)
Dandrieu, Jean François – French (1682–1738)
Rameau, Jean Philippe – French (1683–1764)
Handel, George Frideric – German (1685–1759)
Bach, Johann Sebastian – German (1685–1750)
Scarlatti, Domenico – Italian (1685–1757)
Zipoli, Domenico – Italian (1688–1726)
Muffat, Gottlieb – German (1690–1770)
Daquin, Louis-Claude – French (1694–1772)

Seixas, Carlos de – Portuguese (1704–1742)
Martini, Giovanni Battista – Italian (1706–1784)
Pergolesi, Giovanni – Italian (1710-1736)
Bach, Wilhelm Friedemann – German (1710-1784)
Bach, Carl Philipp Emanuel – German (1714–1788)
Benda, Jiri Antonin – Czech (1722–1795)
Soler, Antonio – Spanish (1729–1783)
Haydn, Franz Joseph – Austrian (1732–1809)
Bach, Johann Christian – German (1735–1782)
Hässler, Johann Wilhelm – German (1747–1822)
Cimarosa, Domenico – Italian (1749–1801)
Clementi, Muzio – Italian (1752–1832)
Mozart, Wolfgang Amadeus – Austrian (1756–1791)
Türk, Daniel Gottlob – German (1756–1813)
Dussek, Jan Ladislav – Czech (1760–1812)
Beethoven, Ludwig van – German (1770–1827)
Cramer, Johann Baptist – German (1771–1858)
Hummel, Johann Nepomuk – German (1778–1837)
Diabelli, Antonio – Italian-Austrian (1781–1858)
Field, John – Irish (1782–1837)
Weber, Carl Maria von – German (1786–1826)
Kuhlau, Friedrich – German-Scandinavian (1786–1832)
Czerny, Karl – Austrian (1791–1857)
Schubert, Franz – Austrian (1797–1828)
Glinka, Mikhail Ivanovich – Russian (1804–1857)
Burgmüller, Friedrich – German (1806–1874)
Mendelssohn, Felix – German (1809–1847)
Chopin, Frédéric – Polish (1810–1849)
Schumann, Robert – German (1810–1856)
Liszt, Franz – Hungarian (1811–1886)
Alkan, Charles-Henri – French (1813–1888)
Henselt, Adolph von – German (1814–1889)
Volkmann, Robert – German (1815–1883)
Gade, Niels Vilhelm – Danish (1817–1890)
Kullak, Theodor – German (1818–1882)
Köhler, Louis – German (1820–1886)
Gurlitt, Cornelius – German (1820–1901)
Raff, Joachim – German (1822–1882)
Franck, César – French (1822–1890)
Smetana, Bedřich – Czech (1824–1884)
Reinecke, Carl – German (1824–1910)
Gottschalk, Louis Moreau – American (1829–1869)
Brahms, Johannes – German (1833–1897)
Saint-Saëns, Camille – French (1835–1921)
Mussorgsky, Modest Petrovich – Russian (1839–1881)
Tchaikovsky, Peter Ilyich – Russian (1840–1893)
Dvořák, Antonin – Czech (1841–1904)
Grieg, Edvard – Norwegian (1843–1907)

Fauré, Gabriel – French (1845–1924)
Moszkowsky, Moritz – Polish-German (1854–1925)
Sinding, Christian – Norwegian (1856–1941)
Albéniz, Isaac – Spanish (1860–1909)
Arensky, Anton – Russian (1861–1906)
MacDowell, Edward – American (1861–1908)
Debussy, Claude – French (1862–1918)
Gretchaninoff, Alexander – Russian (1864–1956)
Nielsen, Carl – Danish (1865–1931)
Sibelius, Jean – Finnish (1865-1957)
Busoni, Ferruccio – Italian-German (1866–1924)
Rebikoff, Vladimir Ivanovich – Russian (1866–1920)
Satie, Erik – French (1866–1925)
Granados, Enrique – Spanish (1867–1916)
Novak, Vitezslav – Czech (1870–1949)
Scriabin, Alexander – Russian (1872–1915)
Reger, Max – German (1873–1916)
Rachmaninoff, Sergei – Russian (1873–1943)
Ives, Charles – American (1874–1954)
Schoenberg, Arnold – Austrian (1874–1951)
Ravel, Maurice – French (1875–1937)
Falla, Manuel de – Spanish (1876–1946)
Dohnányi, Ernö – Hungarian (1877–1960)
Palmgren, Selim – Finnish (1878–1951)
Scott, Cyril – English (1879–1970)
Bartók, Béla – Hungarian (1881–1945)
Szymanowsky, Karol – Polish (1882–1937)
Turina, Joaquin – Spanish (1882–1949)
Stravinsky, Igor – Russian (1882–1971)
Kodály, Zoltán – Hungarian (1882–1967)
Webern, Anton – Austrian (1883–1945)
Casella, Alfredo – Italian (1883–1947)
Villa-Lobos, Heitor – Brazilian (1887–1959)
Toch, Ernst – Austrian (1887–1964)
Ibert, Jacques – French (1890–1962)
Martin, Frank – Swiss (1890–1974)
Prokofiev, Sergei – Russian (1891–1953)
Milhaud, Darius – French (1892–1974)
Piston, Walter – American (1894–1976)
Hindemith, Paul – German (1895–1963)
Cowell, Henry – American (1897–1965)
Tansman, Alexandre – Polish-French (1897–)
Gershwin, George – American (1898–1937)
Harris, Roy – American (1898–)
Poulenc, Francis – French (1899–1963)
Tcherepnin, Alexander – Russian (1899–1977)
Antheil, George – American (1900–1959)
Copland, Aaron – American (1900–)

Křenek, Ernst – Austrian (1900–   )
Khatchaturian, Aram – Russian (1903–1978)
Kabalevsky, Dmitri – Russian (1904–   )
Shostakovich, Dmitri – Russian (1906–1975)
Creston, Paul – American (1906–   )
Barber, Samuel – American (1910–   )
Lutoslawski, Witold – Polish (1913–   )
Dello Joio, Norman – American (1913–   )
Ginastera, Alberto – Argentine (1916–   )

General Bibliography

GENERAL HISTORY, STYLE, PERFORMANCE PRACTICES

Apel, Willi. *Masters of the Keyboard: A Brief Survey of Pianoforte Music*. Cambridge, Mass.: Harvard University Press, 1947.

Bie, Oscar. *A History of the Pianoforte and Pianoforte Players* (1899). New York: Da Capo Press, 1966.

Dart, Thurston. *The Interpretation of Music*. New York: Hutchinson University Library, 1954; New York: Harper and Row, 1963 (paperback).

Dorian, Frederick. *The History of Music in Performance*. New York: W.W. Norton, 1943.

Gillespie, John. *Five Centuries of Keyboard Music*. Belmont, Calif.: Wadsworth Publishing Co., Inc., 1965. New York: Dover, 1972 (paperback).

Kirby, Frank E. *A Short History of Keyboard Music*. New York: Free Press, 1966.

Lang, Paul H. *Music in Western Civilization*. New York: W.W. Norton, 1941.

Newman, William S. *The Sonata in the Baroque Era* (rev. ed.). (*History of the Sonata Idea*, vol. I). Chapel Hill: University of North Carolina Press, 1966. New York: W.W. Norton, 1972 (paperback).

——. *The Sonata in the Classic Era*. (*History of the Sonata Idea*, vol. II). Chapel Hill: University of North Carolina Press, 1963. New York: W.W. Norton, 1972 (paperback).

——. *The Sonata Since Beethoven*. (*History of the Sonata Idea*, vol. III). Chapel Hill: University of North Carolina Press, 1969. New York: W.W. Norton, 1972 (paperback).

Schoenberg, Harold C. *The Lives of the Great Composers*. New York: W.W. Norton, 1970.

Ulrich, Homer, and Paul Pisk. *A History of Music and Musical Style*. New York: Harcourt, Brace, Jovanovich, 1963.

PIANISTS

Chasins, Abram. *Speaking of Pianists*. New York: Knopf, 1962.
Loesser, Arthur. *Men, Women, and Pianos*. New York: Simon and Schuster, 1954.
Schoenberg, Harold C. *The Great Pianists*. New York: Simon and Schuster, 1963.

PIANO PEDAGOGY

Bastien, James. *How To Teach Piano Successfully*. Park Ridge, Ill.: General Words and Music Co., 1973.
Benner, Lora M. *The Blue Book: A Practical Manual of Piano Teaching*. Schenectady, N.Y.: Benner Publishers, 1969.
——. *The Gold Book: Piano Materials and Teaching Methods*. Schenectady, N.Y.: Benner Publishers, 1970.
Bolton, Hetty. *On Teaching the Piano*. London: Novello, 1954.
Ching, James. *Piano Playing: A Practical Method*. London: Bosworth, 1946.
Diller, Angela. *The Splendor of Music*. New York: G. Schirmer, 1957.
Edwards, Ruth. *The Compleat Music Teacher*. Los Altos, Calif.: Geron-X, Inc.1970.
Everhart, Powell. *The Pianist's Art: A Comprehensive Manual on Piano Playing for the Student and Teacher*. Atlanta, Ga.: Author, 1958.
Gát, József. *The Technique of Piano Playing*. London: Collet's Holdings, Ltd., 1965.
Kochevitsky, George A. *The Art of Piano Playing: A Scientific Approach*. Evanston, Ill.: Summy-Birchard Co., 1967.
Last, Joan. *The Young Pianist*. London: Oxford University Press, 1954.
Newman, William S. *The Pianist's Problems* (3rd ed.). New York: Harper & Row, 1974.
Seroff, Victor. *Common Sense in Piano Study*. New York: Funk & Wagnalls, 1970.
Slenczynska, Ruth. *Music at Your Fingertips* (rev. ed.). New York: Cornerstone Library, 1968.
Whiteside, Abbey. *Indispensibles of Piano Playing* (2nd. ed.). New York: Scribner, 1961.

MUSIC FOR THE KEYBOARD

Butler, Stanley. *Guide to the Best in Contemporary Piano Music: An Annotated List of Graded Solo Piano Music Published Since 1950*. Metuchen, N.J.: Scarecrow Press, 1973.
Chang, Frederic Ming, and Albert Faurot. *Team Piano Repertoire: Manual of Music for Multiple Players and One or More Pianos*. Metuchen, N.J.: Scarecrow Press, 1976.
Hinson, Maurice. *Guide to the Pianist's Repertoire*. Bloomington, Ind.: Indiana University Press, 1973.
Hodges, Sister Mabelle L. *Representative Teaching Materials for Piano Since 1900*. Chicago: De Paul University Press, 1970.
Hutcheson, Ernest, and Rudolph Ganz. *The Literature of the Piano*. New York: Knopf, 1964.
Kern, Alice, and Helen Titus. *The Teacher's Guidebook to Piano Literature*. Ann Arbor, Mich.: J.W. Edwards Publisher, Inc., 1964.
Lubin, Ernest. *The Piano Duet*. New York: Grossman Publishers, 1970.

HARMONY

Frackenpohl, Arthur. *Harmonization at the Piano* (3rd ed.). Dubuque, Iowa: William C. Brown, Co., 1977.

Goetschius, Percy. *The Materials Used in Musical Composition: A System of Harmony*. New York: G. Schirmer, 1913.

Harder, Paul O. *Harmonic Materials in Tonal Music* (2 vols.). Boston: Allyn and Bacon, Inc., 1968.

Lloyd, Ruth and Norman. *Creative Keyboard Musicianship: Fundamentals of Music and Keyboard Harmony Through Improvisation*. New York: Dodd, Mead, 1975.

Ottman, Robert. *Elementary Harmony* (2nd ed.). Englewood Cliffs, N.J.: Prentice-Hall, Inc. 1970.

Piston, Walter. *Harmony* (3rd ed.). New York: W.W. Norton, 1962.

FORM AND STRUCTURE

Benjamin, Thomas, Michael Horvit, and Robert Nelson. *Music for Analysis*. Boston: Houghton Mifflin, 1978.

Fontaine, Paul. *Basic Formal Structures in Music*. New York: Appleton-Century-Crofts, 1967.

Lemacher, Heinrich and Hermann Schroeder. *Musical Form*. English edition revised and translated by Robert Kolben. Cologne: Musikverlage Hans Gerig (MCA Music), 1967.

Schoenberg, Arnold. *Models for Beginners in Composition*. New York: G. Schirmer, 1943.

Stein, Leon. *Structure and Style*. Evanston, Ill.: Summy-Birchard Co., 1962.

COUNTERPOINT

Jeppesen, Knud. *Counterpoint*. Englewood Cliffs, N.J.: Prentice-Hall, Inc., 1960.

Piston, Walter. *Counterpoint: Eighteenth- and Nineteenth-Century Styles*. New York: W.W. Norton, 1947.

Salzer, Felix, and Carl Schacter. *Counterpoint in Composition: The Study of Voice Leading*. New York: McGraw-Hill, 1969.

Searle, Humphrey. *Twentieth-Century Counterpoint*. London: Ernest Benn, Ltd., 1954.

EAR TRAINING

Horacek, Leo, and Gerald Lefkoff. *Programmed Ear Training* (4 vols.). New York: Harcourt, Brace, Jovanovich, 1970.

Lawton, Annie. *Foundations of Practical Ear Training* (2 vols.). London: Oxford University Press, 1933.

Thomson, William Ennis, and Richard P. Delone. *Introduction to Ear Training*. Belmont, Calif.: Wadsworth Publishing Co., 1967.

ORCHESTRATION AND CONDUCTING

Kennan, Kent. *The Technique of Orchestration* (2nd ed.). Englewood Cliffs, N.J.: Prentice-Hall, 1970.

Piston, Walter. *Orchestration*. New York: W.W. Norton, 1955.

Rudolf, Max. *The Grammar of Conducting*. New York: G. Schirmer, 1950.

UNDERSTANDING AND ENJOYING MUSIC

Bernstein, Leonard. *The Joy of Music*. New York: Simon and Schuster, 1959.

Brofsky, Howard and Jeanne Shapiro Bamberger. *The Art of Listening: Developing*

Musical Perception. New York: Harper & Row, 1969.
Copland, Aaron. *What to Listen for in Music* (rev. ed.). New York: McGraw-Hill, 1957.
Einstein, Alfred. *Greatness in Music*. New York: Oxford University Press, 1941.
Hoffer, Charles R. *The Understanding of Music*. Belmont, Calif.: Wadsworth Publishing Company, Inc., 1967.
Machlis, Joseph. *The Enjoyment of Music* (3rd ed.). New York: W.W. Norton, 1970.
Newman, William S. *Understanding Music* (2nd ed.). New York: Harper & Row, 1961.
Wink, Richard and Lois G. Williams. *Invitation to Listening: An Introduction to Music*. Boston: Houghton Mifflin, 1972.

AMERICAN MUSIC

Agay, Denes. *Best Loved Songs of the American People*. Garden City, N.Y.: Doubleday, 1975.
Chase, Gilbert. *America's Music* (rev. 2nd ed.). New York: McGraw-Hill, 1966.
Hitchcock, H. Wiley. *Music in the United States: A Historical Introduction*. Englewood Cliffs, N.J.: Prentice-Hall, 1969.
Lomax, John A., and Alan Lomax. *Folk Song U.S.A.* New York: Duell, Sloan and Pearce, 1947.
Machlis, Joseph. *American Composers of Our Time*. New York: Thomas Y. Crowell, 1963.
Southern, Eileen. *The Music of Black Americans*. New York: W.W. Norton, 1971.

MUSIC DICTIONARIES AND ENCYCLOPEDIAS

Apel, Willi, and Ralph T. Daniel. *The Harvard Brief Dictionary of Music*. Cambridge, Mass.: Harvard University Press, 1960.
Baker's Biographical Dictionary of Musicians (5th ed., revised by Nicolas Slonimsky). New York: G. Schirmer, 1958. 1965 Supplement by Nicolas Slonimsky.
Barlow, Harold, and Sam Morgenstern. *A Dictionary of Musical Themes*. New York: Crown, 1948.
Grove's Dictionary of Music and Musicians, 10 vols. (5th ed., edited by Eric Blom). New York: St. Martin's Press, 1960.
Thompson, Oscar, ed. *The International Cyclopedia of Music and Musicians* (9th ed., edited by Robert Sabin). New York: Dodd, Mead, 1964.
Westrup, J.A., and F.L. Harrison. *The New College Encyclopedia of Music*. New York: W.W. Norton, 1960.

MAGAZINES AND PERIODICALS

Clavier: A Magazine for Pianists and Organists. 1418 Lake Street, Evanston, Illinois 60204.
Keyboard Arts. National Keyboard Arts Associates, 741 Alexander Road, Princeton, New Jersey 08540.
Piano Guild Notes. Official Publication of the National Guild of Piano Teachers. P.O. Box 1807, Austin, Texas 78767.
The American Music Teacher. Official Journal of the Music Teachers National Association. 408 Carew Tower, Cincinnati, Ohio 45202.
The Piano Quarterly. Box 815, Wilmington, Vermont 05363.
The Robert Dumm Piano Review. 144 Fleetwood Terrace, Silver Springs, Maryland 20910.

Contributors' Bylines

Joseph Banowetz, pianist, pedagogue, and writer, has been performing extensively in the United States, Europe, the Soviet Union, Mexico, and Canada. An authority on the music of Liszt, he has edited and recorded numerous works of the romantic master. A professor of piano at North Texas State University, his articles appear regularly in leading periodicals.

William and Louise Cheadle, acclaimed duopianists, are both graduates of Juilliard and recipients of numerous grants and awards. Following their successful debut in New York's Alice Tully Hall in 1975, they have been performing extensively. Currently both are on the faculty of Westminster Choir School in Princeton, New Jersey, where William is professor of piano and Louise is director of the conservatory division.

John H. Diercks received his musical training at Oberlin and the University of Rochester (Eastman School of Music), with composition and piano as his principal areas of concentration. His works, distributed by twenty publishers, have been performed throughout the world. As a performer, he has concertized extensively. Since 1962 he has written reviews for the *Roanoke* (Virginia) *Times-World* as well as for national journals. At Hollins College, where he is Professor of Music and Chairman of the Department, Dr. Diercks teaches theory, composition, piano, and pedagogy.

May L. Etts, teacher and lecturer on pedagogy, was a pupil and assistant of Guy Maier. She is president of the Brooklyn Music Teachers

Guild; past president of the Piano Teachers Congress of New York and the Associated Music Teachers League; an examiner adjudicator of numerous teachers' organizations; editor of highly regarded teaching publications.

Rosetta Goodkind is presently on the faculty of the Manhattan School of Music and New York University. She was on the faculty of the precollege division at the Juilliard School from 1941 to 1969. A recipient of the Mason and Hamlin Teacher Award (1969), she is a frequent jury panelist and adjudicator at piano competitions and auditions. Presently co-chairman of the New York State Music Teachers Association, District I.

Maurice Hinson, professor of church music at the Southern Baptist Theological Seminary, is an authority on piano literature and pedagogy. He is the author of the massive source book *Guide to the Pianist's Repertoire* and of many magazine articles and reviews.

Stuart Isacoff, teacher, editor, and arranger, holds an M.A. in composition from Brooklyn College, where he received a Rockefeller Foundation Grant for research in American music. He is the author-editor of numerous piano textbooks and collections. Currently he is on the jazz faculty of William Paterson State College in Wayne, New Jersey.

Ylda Novik, a highly successful and inspired teacher, died at the height of her career in early 1976. She was contributing critic of the *Washington Star*, piano editor of *The American Music Teacher* (1968–1972), author of many magazine articles, and a faculty member of George Washington University and Montgomery College in Maryland.

Sylvia Rabinof, a pupil of Simon Barere and Rudolf Serkin, has concertized extensively all over the world, frequently with her violinist husband, the late Benno Rabinof. She is on the faculty of the Juilliard School and Brevard Music Center in North Carolina. She is the author of the textbook *Musicianship Through Improvisation*.

Walter Robert, pedagogue and author, was born in Italy and studied in Vienna, where he received the Bösendorfer prize as the best graduate of the State Academy of Music (1931). An acclaimed teacher, clinician, and adjudicator, he recently retired as professor of piano at the Indiana University School of Music. He is on the board of advisors of *Clavier* magazine.

Hadassah Sahr is currently on the teaching staff of Teachers College (Columbia University) and the Manhattan School of Music Summer School. She has presented lectures, recitals, and master classes in many sections of the country and is a contributor to *The Piano Quarterly*.

Hazel Ghazarian Skaggs, group piano specialist, composer, psychologist, and author, is a graduate of the New England Conservatory of Music. She holds a B.A. and M.A. in psychology from Fairleigh Dickinson University. She is national chairperson and judge for the National Composition Test (NGPT), president of The Piano Teachers Congress of

New York, member of the editorial board of *Leisure Today*, and director of Music Counseling Services.

Anita Louise Steele is currently head of the music therapy program at The Cleveland Music School Settlement. She is on the executive committee of the National Association for Music Therapy and an associate editor of the *Journal of Music Therapy*. She is the author of numerous articles on behavioral research and on teaching the handicapped.

Judith Lang Zaimont, a recipient of twenty-six awards for her compositions, studied at Columbia University, Queens College, and Juilliard. She is a Woodrow Wilson fellow, a MacDowell Colony fellow, and a Debussy fellow of the Alliance Française. Active as composer and performer, she has taught at Adelphi University, Queens College, and New York City Community College.

Index